Methodological and Technological Advances in Death Investigations

Methodological and Technological Advances in Death Investigations

Application and Case Studies

Edited by

Ann H. Ross
North Carolina State University,
Department of Biological Sciences, Raleigh, NC

Jason H. Byrd
University of Florida College of Medicine,
William R. Maples Center for Forensic Medicine,
Gainesville, FL, United States

ELSEVIER

ACADEMIC PRESS
An imprint of Elsevier

Academic Press is an imprint of Elsevier
125 London Wall, London EC2Y 5AS, United Kingdom
525 B Street, Suite 1650, San Diego, CA 92101, United States
50 Hampshire Street, 5th Floor, Cambridge, MA 02139, United States
The Boulevard, Langford Lane, Kidlington, Oxford OX5 1GB, United Kingdom

Notices

Knowledge and best practice in this field are constantly changing. As new research and experience broaden our understanding, changes in research methods, professional practices, or medical treatment may become necessary.

Practitioners and researchers must always rely on their own experience and knowledge in evaluating and using any information, methods, compounds, or experiments described herein. In using such information or methods they should be mindful of their own safety and the safety of others, including parties for whom they have a professional responsibility.

To the fullest extent of the law, neither the Publisher nor the authors, contributors, or editors, assume any liability for any injury and/or damage to persons or property as a matter of products liability, negligence or otherwise, or from any use or operation of any methods, products, instructions, or ideas contained in the material herein.

ISBN: 978-0-12-819394-5

For information on all Academic Press publications visit our website at https://www.elsevier.com/books-and-journals

Publisher: Stacy Masucci
Acquisitions Editor: Elizabeth Brown
Editorial Project Manager: Tracy Tufaga
Production Project Manager: Gomathi Sugumar
Cover Designer: Mark Rogers

Typeset by TNQ Technologies

Contents

List of contributors

Saskia Ammer
University of Coimbra, Coimbra, Portugal

Derek T. Anderson
Department of Electrical Engineering and Computer Science, University of Missouri, Columbia, MO, United States

Eric Bartelink
California State University, Chico, Chico, CA, United States

Jason H. Byrd
University of Florida College of Medicine, Gainesville, FL, United States

AnnMarie Clark
Maples Center for Forensic Medicine, University of Florida, Gainesville, FL, United States

Luke Cunningham
Raleigh/Wake City-County Bureau of Identification, Raleigh, NC, United States

Tim Gallagher
District 1 Office of the Medical Examiner, Pensacola, FL, United States

Mike Galloway
Raleigh/Wake City-County Bureau of Identification, Raleigh, NC, United States

Kim Gin
Sacramento County Coroner, Retired Kim Gin Professional Solutions, LLC - Owner/CEO, Fairhope, AL, United States

Christine Glenn
Raleigh/Wake City-County Bureau of Identification, Raleigh, NC, United States

Amanda R. Hale
Department of Biological Sciences, North Carolina State University, Raleigh, NC, United States; SNA International for the Defense POW/MIA Accounting Agency, Joint Base Pearl Harbor-Hickam, Oahu, HI, United States

Stephanie Hartley
SNA International Contractor Supporting the DPAA Mission, Alexandria, VA, United States

Oscar Ibáñez
Panacea Cooperative Research S. Coop., Ponferrada, Spain; Andalusian Research Institute in Data Science and Computational Intelligence, University of Granada, Granada, Spain; Faculty of Computer Science, CITIC, University of A Coruña, A Coruña, Spain

Stacey Johnson
Raleigh/Wake City-County Bureau of Identification, Raleigh, NC, United States

Jan Seaman Kelly
Diplomate of the American Board of Forensic Document Examiners (ABFDE), Las Vegas, NV, United States; Questioned Document Section in the American Academy of Forensic Sciences, Las Vegas, NV, United States

Robyn Kramer
University of Otago, Dunedin, New Zealand

Rubén Martos
Panacea Cooperative Research S. Coop., Ponferrada, Spain; Department of Physical Anthropology, University of Granada, Granada, Spain

Pablo Mesejo
Panacea Cooperative Research S. Coop., Ponferrada, Spain; Department of Computer Science and Artificial Intelligence and Research Centre for Information and Communications Technologies of the University of Granada, Granada, Spain

Bryce Murray
Department of Electrical Engineering and Computer Science, University of Missouri, Columbia, MO, United States

Andy Parker
Raleigh/Wake City-County Bureau of Identification, Raleigh, NC, United States

Nicholas V. Passalacqua
Western Carolina University, Cullowhee, NC, United States

Marin A. Pilloud
Department of Anthropology, University of Nevada, Reno, NV, United States

Sharon L. Plotkin
General Section in the American Academy of Forensic Sciences, Miami, FL, United States

Gene Robinson
Gene Robinson Consulting, Wimberley, TX, United States

Ann H. Ross
Department of Biological Sciences, North Carolina State University, Raleigh, NC, United States

Haley Russo
Cook County Office of the Medical Examiner, Chicago, IL, United States

Lerah Sutton
University of Florida Maples Center for Forensic Medicine, Gainesville, FL, United States

Sarah Voeller
North Carolina State University, CCSI, International Association for Identification, Raleigh, NC, United States; Cambridge Regional College, Cambridge, England, United Kingdom

Daniel J. Wescott
Texas State University, Department of Anthropology, Forensic Anthropology Center at Texas State, San Marcos, TX, United States

Preface

The premise for this volume, *Methodological and Technological Advances in Death Investigations*, was to encompass a broad range of forensic science disciplines. Our aim was to bring together these diverse disciplines as medicolegal death investigations are inherently multidisciplinary in nature. Furthermore, we sought to highlight recent advances within various forensic science disciplines.

Regarding crime scene investigations, Chapter 1 by Kelly and Plotkin delves into how these investigations evolved in response to the 2009 National Academy of Sciences report. In Chapter 2, Parker and colleagues provide a comprehensive guide on the latest techniques for lifting and processing latent prints from various surfaces. Watson and Wescott, in Chapter 6, present an innovative method of using unmanned aerial systems for locating clandestine burials in large remote areas. Chapter 7, authored by Voeller, introduces a method for reassociating skeletal elements in a commingled mass grave scenario using Geographic Information System (GIS) mapping methods. Sutton and Gallagher, in Chapter 4, explore the complexities of establishing the postmortem interval, highlighting the persistent challenges despite extensive research in this area.

New approaches in forensic anthropology are addressed in Ammer and coworker's chapter on using stable isotopes to establish provenance (e.g., geolocation) of unidentified human remains along the southern border of the United States and its use in identifying border crosser deaths. In Chapter 12, Hale and colleagues address the challenges of adult age estimation using bone mineral density as a viable option to overcome the shortfalls of traditional age estimation methods that rely on macroscopic bone degeneration. Chapter 3 by Martos and colleagues highlights the application of computer science such as AI to issues in forensic anthropology.

Standards for identification in mass fatality incidents are presented in Chapter 10 by Gin and Chapter 11 by Byrd and Ross. Chapter 5 by Clark, Hartley, and Byrd outlines methods for differentiating human and nonhuman skeletal remains especially useful in settings of human and nonhuman commingling. In Chapter 8, Ross and Passalacqua present protocols for a multidisciplinary approach to investigating and identifying unidentified human remains that include medicolegal experts such as medical examiners and forensic anthropologists, law enforcement, and IGG to resolve these complicated cases.

The chapters within this volume collectively demonstrate the multifaceted nature of medicolegal death investigations, showcasing the interconnections between various forensic science disciplines.

CHAPTER

1 Crime scene investigations response to the NAS report of 2009

Sharon L. Plotkin[1] and Jan Seaman Kelly[2,3]

[1]*General Section in the American Academy of Forensic Sciences, Miami, FL, United States;* [2]*Diplomate of the American Board of Forensic Document Examiners (ABFDE), Las Vegas, NV, United States;* [3]*Questioned Document Section in the American Academy of Forensic Sciences, Las Vegas, NV, United States*

1. Introduction

Sources of bias are well known in science, and a large amount of effort has been devoted to understanding and mitigating them. The goal is to make scientific investigations as objective as possible, so the results do not depend on the investigator. Additionally, science seeks to publish its discoveries, findings, and conclusions so that they are subjected to independent peer review; this enables others to study biases that may exist in the investigative method or attempt to replicate unexpected results.

The premium that science places on precision, objectivity, critical thinking, careful observation and practice, repeatability, uncertainty management, and peer review enables the reliable collection, measurement, and interpretation of clues in order to produce knowledge.

The 1993 Daubert v. Merrell Dow Pharmaceuticals Inc., 509 US. 579 specified a forensic discipline must satisfy the following five factors in order for expert testimony to be admitted: (1) whether the theory or technique in question can be and has been tested; (2) whether it has been subjected to peer review and publication; (3) its known or potential error rate; (4) the existence and maintenance of standards controlling its operation; and (5) whether it has attracted widespread acceptance within a relevant scientific community. Daubert opened the door for the law to create a framework of how forensic science can be a reliable source in answering questions of the court. The impact of Daubert was significant as it initiated research, proficiency testing, published standards for all facets of a forensic discipline, and the acceptance of the forensic science by the scientific community. Prior to 2009, forensic science and the law were separate entities with each following their own paradigms.

The Science, State, Justice, Commerce, and Related Agencies Appropriations Act of 2006 became law in November 2005. Under this statute, the NAS was authorized by Congress to conduct a study on forensic science. Outcomes reported from this study indicated that "while a great deal of analysis exists of the requirements in

Methodological and Technological Advances in Death Investigations. https://doi.org/10.1016/B978-0-12-819394-5.00010-9

the discipline of DNA, there exists little to no analysis of the remaining needs of the community outside of the area of DNA" (NAS, 2009). As a result, funds were provided to the NAS to create an independent Forensic Science Committee. This committee comprised members of the forensics community representing operational crime laboratories, medical examiners, and coroners; legal experts; and other relevant scientists.

In February 2009, the NAS issued their report (*Strengthening Forensic Science in the United States: A Path Forward*) in response to growing concerns from the legal system and the public regarding the effectiveness and scientific foundation of the forensic disciplines being applied by law enforcement agencies and crime laboratories. While the forensic science practitioner community disagreed with many of the findings of the report, there was general consensus that additional research, funding, and standards were in order (Ballou, 2019).

"The focus here is not on the reliability or validity of particular forensic techniques but rather on quality control systems for laboratories."[1] To achieve qualitative control systems that are consistent throughout the United States, the report listed 13 recommendations.

1. Establishing the National Institute of Forensic Science (NIFS)
2. Establishing standard terminology for reports and testifying
3. Addressing issues of accuracy, reliability, and validity in the disciplines
4. Separating public forensic laboratories from law enforcement agencies administration or control
5. Researching sources of human bias in forensic science
6. Developing tools for advancing measurement, validation, reliability, information sharing, proficiency testing and to establish protocols for examinations, methods, and practices
7. Require mandatory accreditation of all forensic laboratories and certification for all forensic science practitioners
8. Laboratories should establish routine quality assurance procedures
9. Establish a national code of ethics with a mechanism for enforcement
10. Support higher education in the form of forensic graduate programs, to include scholarships and fellowships
11. Improve the medico-legal death investigation system
12. Support AFIS interoperability through the development of standards
13. Support the use of forensic science in homeland security

The 2009 NAS Report critiqued instrument-based and examiner-based forensic science disciplines and found the fundamental requirements of reproducibility, reliability, and accuracy in results were not met in the examiner-based disciplines. Unlike DNA, footwear or tool mark evidence identification/elimination is based on the expert's training and experience to determine the significance of individual

---

[1] NAS Report at 6.

characteristics. In forensic document examination, the range of variation in the combination of characteristics in a handwritten text is the basis for a conclusion. The committee was concerned the significance of the characteristics has not been researched to determine the reliability of methods used in pattern/impression disciplines.

Historically, the two greatest inhibitors of forensic science have been the lack of adequate funding and a uniform quality control system. The NAS recommendations include an adequately funded federal program to provide the financial support for forensic disciplines and the medical examiner system. The necessity of adequate federal funding and a uniform quality control system cannot be overemphasized as the majority of law enforcement forensic operations are state and local agencies with limited budgets. The consequence of underfunding state and local agencies can lead to inadequate crime scene collections or forensic examinations resulting in unsolved cases and wrongful convictions (Garrett, 2020). The lack of comprehensive quality control measures impacts court testimony as the admission of flawed or misleading evidence can lead to an erroneous conviction (NAS, 2009).

The 10th anniversary of the NAS Report revealed progress toward the improvement of forensic science. The Department of Justice, with the National Institute of Science and Technology ("NIST"), established the National Commission on Forensic Science (2015 through 2017). The Organization of Scientific Area Committees ("OSAC") was established for development of standards in the forensic disciplines. NIST funding to conduct research on the accuracy, reliability, and validity of existing forensic methods and to develop new methods continues through grants awarded to forensic practitioners and research scientists. The National Institute of Justice (NIJ) funded Human Factors working groups (Ballou, 2019).

The Honorable Judge Harry T. Edwards acknowledged on the 10th anniversary of the 2009 NAS Report that progress had occurred, but added more progress was needed. The failure to establish "a strong, independent, strategic, coherent, and well-funded federal program [with a culture that is strongly rooted in science] to support and oversee the forensic science disciplines" has not been established (Edwards, 2019). Such a program would ensure forensic testimony provided to jurors is science-based through research and testing, adherence to task-specific standards, and uniform quality control procedures.

The independence of forensic laboratories is listed as the fourth recommendation, which is a strong indicator of the importance in separating forensics from law enforcement agencies. The Houston Forensic Science Center (HFSC) in Houston, Texas, adopted a management-oriented approach as a corporation and is the only independent forensic agency in the United States. Revising processes through standards, blind testing, and a stringent quality control system has been HFSC's foundation for success (Garrett). Even though separation of forensics from law enforcement may well be the most difficult recommendation to complete, it is anticipated that separation of forensic laboratories from law enforcement agencies will be the norm.

The impact of the 2009 NAS Report has and will continue to be far-reaching. The linchpin for future progress in implementing and supporting all 13 recommendations is federal funding. The federal government's commitment to adequate funding will result in comprehensive forensic standards and uniformity in quality control procedures to ensure continuity in forensic evidence recovery, examination, reporting, and testimony throughout the United States and reduce or eliminate wrongful convictions.

According to the NAS Report, various disciplines in forensic science provided important evidence that has contributed to the successful prosecution and conviction of criminals as well as to the exoneration of innocent people. For the past 2 decades, advances in forensic science disciplines have been able to demonstrate that some of these disciplines have greater potential in assisting law enforcement in identifying criminals. Many crimes that may have gone unsolved are now being solved because forensic science is helping to identify offenders. Those advances, however, also reveal that, in some cases, vital information and courtroom testimony may be based on faulty forensic science analyses and may contribute to wrongful convictions of innocent people led by inaccurate expert testimony and the admittance of flawed or misleading evidence. Consideration must be made that if we are to respond to the success of forensic science that the potential danger of giving unfounded weight to evidence and testimony, which resulted from imperfect testing and analysis must be recognized (NAS, 2009).

Ensuring continued improvements will assist law enforcement officials while involved in investigations to identify offenders with higher reliability. This will pave the way to reduce the occurrence of wrongful convictions (NAS, 2009).

2. Crime scene investigations

The NAS report also states that there exists a disparity among forensic science operations at all agencies and jurisdictional levels and agencies due to funding, access to analytical instrumentation, the availability of skilled, trained personnel, certification, accreditation, as well as oversight. The quality of forensic practice in most disciplines differs greatly due to the absence of adequate training, continuing education, rigorous mandatory certification and accreditation programs, and adherence to vigorous performance standards. It is because of this variation in qualifications in hiring crime scene personnel as well as the requirements once hired that brings us to the point of crime scene personnel. These shortfalls continue to be a viable threat to the quality and credibility of forensic science practice (NAS, 2009).

As we examine the role of crime scene investigators, the NAS report articulated that this personnel is responsible for searching and collecting evidence at the scene and preservation and securing evidence in packaging that prevents manipulation, alteration, and/or destruction with its purpose of being submitted to labs for analysis (NAS, 2009).

Dr. Saferstein was a chief forensic scientist who retired in 1991 from the New Jersey State Police (NJSP) and then worked at the NJSP Forensic Science Bureau for 21 years. He was a leading national expert and author in the field of forensic science and was a highly recognized and a sought-after consultant, contributing to many high-profile cases throughout the country (https://news.aafs.org/section-news/richard-saferstein-phd-retired-fellow-of-the-criminalistics-section-july-2017). In a conversation with Dr. Richard Saferstein, he commented that in many of the private cases, he testified in as an expert that it has been the handling the evidence that had been the most contested point in trial testimony (Fig. 1.1).

Dr. Richard Saferstein headed the crime laboratory of the New Jersey State Police, which is one of the largest forensic laboratories in the United States.

FIGURE 1.1

Richard Saferstein.

Courtesy of Teresa 'Lilly' White, PhD.

Dr. Saferstein served as an expert witness over 2000 times in nearly 150 federal and state courts involving a variety of forensic issues. Dr. Saferstein authored numerous papers notable textbooks in criminalistics and forensic science (https://www.blogtalkradio.com/behindtheyellowtape/2011/10/15/forensic-science-discussion-w-richard-saferstein).

Evidence must be recognized as possessing the ability to link an individual to a crime scene along with a possibility of their involvement with the crime. Equally as important is the ability of physical evidence to exonerate or exclude suspects from suspicion if physical evidence collected at a crime scene is found to be different from standard/reference samples collected from that suspect. The purpose of physical evidence recognition is so that it can be collected and analyzed. If untrained crime scene personnel respond to scenes and lack the training to accomplish this important role, then critical evidence may be overlooked (Saferstein, 2012).

In understanding the importance of physical evidence, Dr. Bruce Hyma (chief medical examiner Miami Dade Medical Examiner's Office-deceased) stated that the body rarely solved the case. It is the evidence that is located on the crime scene that does (Fig. 1.2).

Dr. Bruce Hyma, the longtime director of the Miami-Dade Medical Examiner's Office and a renown figure in the forensic pathology community, was appointed the Chief Medical examiner in 2001 (https://alumniassociation.mayo.edu/obituaries/bruce-a-hyma-m-d-path-1987/).

However, the background, training, and experience of crime scene personnel can affect the outcome of such evidence. If the evidence is not collected and preserved in such a way to prevent any alteration, manipulation, or destruction from occurring, then the science performed thereafter cannot be true.

If evidence and laboratory tests are improperly handled and/or analyzed, incorrect outcomes result in a false sense of significance. Bias, incompetence, or a lack of internal controls for the evidence introduced into labs can very likely result in juries being misled leading to wrongful convictions or exoneration. The possible outcome of this injustice could result in juries losing confidence in the dependability of testimony and valid evidence might be discounted whereby innocent persons might be convicted or guilty individuals acquitted (NAS, 2009).

The NAS report also reported the importance of the CSI Effect and how this impacted the views of those laypersons (i.e., television viewers) outside the forensic disciplines. Media attention has focused on what is being called the "CSI Effect," named for popular television shows that are focused on police forensic evidence investigation. The CSI Effect refers to the real-life consequences of exposure to Hollywood's version of the presentation of law, order, and science (Fig. 1.3).

The CSI Effect was first articulated by Maricopa County (Arizona) District Attorney Andrew Thomas. Thomas complained that juries had become less likely to convict because CSI had improperly heightened their evidentiary expectations of the prosecution and, in turn, was causing an epidemic of wrongful acquittals (https://oxfordre.com/criminology/display/10.1093/acrefore/9780190264079.001.0001/acrefore-9780190264079-e-40).

FIGURE 1.2

Bruce Hyma.

Courtesy of the Miami Dade Medical Examiner Department.

According to one 2006 weekly Nielsen rating.

- 30 million people watched *CSI* on one night.
- 70 million watched at least one of the three *CSI* shows.
- 40 million watched two other forensic dramas, *Without a Trace* and *Cold Case.*
- Those ratings translated into this fact: five of the top 10 television programs that week were about scientific evidence in criminal cases. Together, they amassed more than 100 million viewers (https://nij.ojp.gov/topics/articles/csi-effect-does-it-really-exist).
  Jurists and directors of crime laboratories articulate that jurors have every case that will contain forensic evidence will be conclusive. The fictional characters portrayed in these television show present an unrealistic representation of the daily operations of crime scene investigators and the capabilities of crime laboratories (NAS, 2009).

FIGURE 1.3

CSI Effect.

Courtesy of Andi R. Plotkin.

A study by Schweitzer and Saks found that compared to those who do not watch CSI, CSI viewers were "more critical of the forensic evidence presented at the trial, finding it less believable. Viewers of these forensic science shows stated more confidence in their verdicts than did nonviewers." (Jurimetrics, Vol. 47, p. 357, Spring 2007).

Prosecutors and defense attorneys have reported jurors questioning them in the courtroom, citing "reasonable doubt" and refusing to convict because they believed that other evidence was available and not adequately examined (NAS, 2009).

According to the CSI shows, cases are solved in an hour, highly technical analyses are completed within minutes, and the capabilities of the lab and instrumentation are often exaggerated, misrepresented, misleading, and fabricated. In courtroom scenes, forensic examiners state with certainty their findings or a match (between evidence and suspect), along with a demonstration of the stated technique used to determine the result. These television programs suggest that convictions are quick with no mistakes being made (NAS, 2009).

So, what does this all mean and how can we as a forensic discipline overcome these challenges?

- Crime scene investigations begin at a local, state, or federal level with investigators responding to the crime scene. Important standard operating procedures must be in place to guide all personnel in the collection and preservation of evidence.

- If investigators do not recognize and adhere to rigorous standards in the collection and preservation of evidence on crime scenes, then the science conducted thereafter cannot be true help and accurate.
- Crime scene investigators must be able to apply scientific methods, techniques, skill, and knowledge in the application of the law and the recognition of the complexities involved with the examining physical evidence at crime scenes.
- Identifying and setting industry standards is critical for guaranteeing that the professionals responsible for the investigation of the crime scene are skilled and trained to approach the identification, collection, and analysis of physical evidence in a similar fashion.
- Certification from the International Association for Identification in the areas of crime scene investigations, analyst, and reconstruction should be implemented to ensure that current industry standards and procedures are being addressed and complied with (Fig. 1.4).

The International Association for Identification (IAI), which holds the distinction of being the largest forensic association in the world, is focused on the physical forensic science disciplines. Within the field of crime scene investigation, individuals may be certified in one of four designations.

- Certified Senior Crime Scene Analyst
- Certified Crime Scene Reconstructionist
- Certified Crime Scene Investigator
- Certified Crime Scene Analyst

In the end, we must ensure that we who are involved in the forensics sciences remain true to its purpose: to provide continuous improvements in forensic science practices to reduce the number of wrongful convictions. To ensure the integrity of the sciences remains intact, we must be willing to undertake compliance with nationally recognized policies, accreditation, certifications, and adherence to rigorous standards in pursuit of the truth.

International Association for Identification

FIGURE 1.4

International Association for Identification.

Source: https://www.crimesceneinvestigatoredu.org/csi-certification/.

3. OSAC response to the NAS report

Contributor: Steven Johnson, Past President, the IAI Chair, OSAC FSSB.

In response to the NAS report, the American Academy of Forensic Sciences (AAFS) was approached by the National Institute of Standards and Technology (NIST) in late 2013 to consider a collaborative enterprise that would unify the existing forensic Scientific Working Groups (SWGs) and be dedicated to the establishment of forensic standards across a broad spectrum of disciplines. Other forensic associations, having been made aware of the NIST/AAFS collaboration, asked to have a seat at the table. In January of 2014, representatives from the National Association of Medical Examiners (NAME), Society of Forensic Toxicologists (SOFT), Association of Firearms and Toolmark Examiners (AFTE), American Society of Crime Laboratory Directors (ASCLD), and the International Association of Identification (IAI) joined AAFS at a meeting with NIST in Gaithersburg, MD to discuss this enterprise and establish a "path forward." What resulted was the creation of the OSAC for the Forensic Sciences, a group of over 550 dedicated professionals representing the interests of over 15,000 forensic science practitioners and their respective disciplines.

In early January 2014, I was the first Vice President of the IAI and was asked by then President, Lesley Hammer, to represent the IAI's interests on the newly created OSAC. As a part of this enterprise, OSAC established a leadership group identified as the Forensic Science Standards Board (FSSB) and placed representatives from each of the aforementioned forensics associations, six research representatives, three resource committee chairs, and a NIST Ex-Officio member. These 20 individuals represented a broad cross-section of forensic experience and provided exceptional direction at the earliest stages of OSAC's genesis. The mission of OSAC is "*(s)trengthening the nation's use of forensic science by facilitating the development of technically sound standards and guidelines and encouraging their use throughout the forensic science community.*"[2] It is important to note that OSAC is ***not*** a standards development organization (SDO). The role of OSAC is to create draft standards. There are several SDOs available to the organizations dedicated to drafting and implementing standards. Among them are the International Organization for Standardization (ISO), American Society for Testing and Materials (ASTM), American Dental Association (ADA) and, most recently, the AAFS Academy Standards Board (ASB). These SDOs review standards, provide expert input, allow for public comment, and issue approved standards for implementation. These SDOs are critical to getting the developed standards to the community with consensus buy-in. The OSAC enterprise has a related but different approach.

First, a little history. OSAC was initially created with a hierarchy that had the FSSB at the top providing strategic guidance and final approval for drafted standards

[2] NIST OSAC website: https://www.nist.gov/topics/organization-scientific-area-committees-forensic-science.

and guidelines for publication on an OSAC Registry.[3] The organization is governed by a Charter and Bylaws[4] and provided further direction with Terms of Reference[5] for each element of the OSAC hierarchy. The hierarchy included Scientific Area Committees (SACs) that further represented 23 (and later 25) forensic discipline subcommittees. The FSSB, SACs, and subcommittees may also create Task Groups (TGs) that can assist with the standards creation process. These SACs and subcommittees were affiliated based on the forensic functionality and linkage between disciplines. In the chart below, you can see the original OSAC organizational structure[6] (Fig. 1.5).

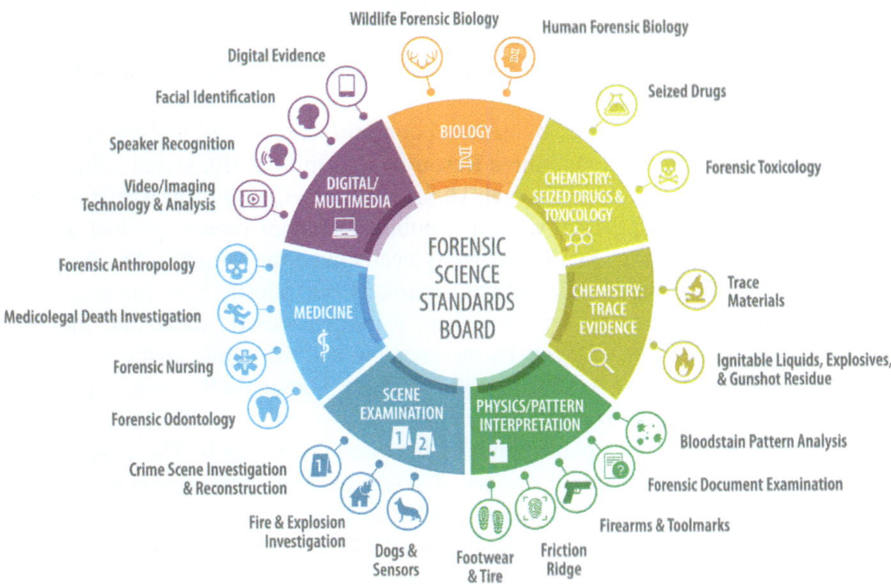

FIGURE 1.5

OSAC organizational structure.

Reprinted with permission from the Organization of Scientific Area Committees (OSAC) for Forensic Science.

[3] NIST OSAC website: https://www.nist.gov/topics/organization-scientific-area-committees-forensic-science/osac-registry.

[4] NIST OSAC website: https://www.nist.gov/topics/organization-scientific-area-committees-forensic-science/charter-bylaws-and-terms-reference.

[5] NIST OSAC website: https://www.nist.gov/topics/organization-scientific-area-committees-forensic-science/charter-bylaws-and-terms-reference.

[6] NIST OSAC website: https://www.nist.gov/topics/organization-scientific-area-committees-forensic-science/osac-organizational-structure.

3.1 OSAC organizational structure

OSAC members and affiliates make up a multi-level organization consisting of.

- A Forensic Science Standards Board (FSSB)
- Seven Scientific Area Committees (SACs)
- 22 discipline-specific subcommittees (SCs)
- FSSB Resource Task Groups
- Following our core principles of **balance**, **consensus**, **harmonization,** and **openness**, these experts work together to facilitate the development of scientifically sound standards and guidelines for the forensic science community.

Additionally, the OSAC Program Office (OPO) consists of NIST staff who provide operational support to the organization.

https://www.nist.gov/organization-scientific-area-committees-forensic-science/osac-organizational-structure.

Draft standards were created by each subcommittee, reviewed and approved by the respective SAC, forwarded to three Resource Committees (RCs) and a Statistics TG representing interests from a Legal, Human Factors, Quality Infrastructure and Metrology perspective and finally, after a public comment period, pushed up the chain to the FSSB for final adjudication and placement on the Registry. The Registry originally listed standards and guidelines separately but, shortly after the establishment of OSAC, all documents for the registry were considered "standards" moving forward. Additionally, OSAC keeps its membership and the public aware of the enterprise's progress with the publication of a monthly Standards Bulletin,[7] quarterly newsletter[8], and an annual report.[9]

OSAC was, in essence, a plane being built as we were flying it. There were a lot of lessons learned during the first 4 years of existence, and, in the summer of 2017, NIST sent out a Request for Information (RFI) to solicit input from the public on what form OSAC should take in the future. NIST's original intent was to get OSAC started and find another home to manage and fund the enterprise after an indeterminate period (five to 10 years). After reviewing dozens of suggestions, NIST agreed to continue the management of the OSAC enterprise for the foreseeable future but recognized the need for improvement and restructuring of the enterprise to improve efficiencies and speed up the standards creativity process.

OSAC is currently made up of over 550 forensic practitioners, academics, statisticians/metrologists, researchers, human factors scientists, the legal community, and quality assurance experts to serve on subcommittees in a more collaborative

[7] NIST OSAC website: https://www.nist.gov/topics/organization-scientific-area-committees-forensic-science/osac-standards-bulletin.

[8] NIST OSAC website: https://www.nist.gov/topics/organization-scientific-area-committees-forensic-science/osac-newsletter.

[9] NIST OSAC website: https://www.nist.gov/topics/organization-scientific-area-committees-forensic-science/news-communications/annual-report.

effort. With the proposed changes coming out of the RFI review, none of the current members would be asked to step down. Their participation, it is hoped, would be impacted in a positive way. Rather than having the Legal, Human Factors, Quality Infrastructure RCs, and Statistics TG review the proposed standards at the end of the process, members of those groups were embedded in the subcommittees to be a part of process from the beginning. All these members will remain affiliated as TGs moving forward. SACs would be restructured, and subcommittees would be consolidated or expanded. Additionally, the role of the FSSB as a final arbiter of the standards will be eliminated and allow the SACs and public comment to complete the process ahead of submission to an authorized SDO. Included in this process will be Standards Technical Review Boards (STRBs) that will determine viability of those standards that must meet the criteria for said technical appropriateness. Ultimately, all these standard documents created by the OSAC subcommittees and placed on the registry of approved (and now proposed) standards must be vetted through one of many approved SDOs. Once the SDO approves a standard, it can be made available through that organization to forensic science service providers and practitioners. In addition to the creation of standard, guideline, and best practice documents, OSAC created a forensic lexicon[10] with over 4000 terms, including OSAC Preferred Terms that should be considered during document development. These terms will be managed with edits, additions, and removals to be considered on a continuous basis. Finally, OSAC invites organization subcommittees and TGs to propose Technical Publication[11] that likely fall outside the definition of a standard or guideline.

Membership on OSAC is voluntary and limited to two, 3-year terms. These terms were staggered at the inception of OSAC, and, as we entered our fifth year of existence in October of 2018, approximately one-third of the OSAC membership must be replaced with new experts. Mindful of this, OSAC maintains a database of affiliate members (who can and do assist with the current standards development effort) and a pool of applicants from which to draw for openings across the OSAC spectrum. OSAC 2.0, as it is currently being socialized, will roll out effective October 1, 2020. There will be some changes to the structure, but the overall mission of OSAC will remain the same; providing professional and scientifically grounded standards to ensure the improvement of best practices in the forensic science community.

[10] NIST OSAC website: https://www.nist.gov/topics/organization-scientific-area-committees-forensic-science/osac-lexicon.

[11] NIST OSAC website: https://www.nist.gov/topics/organization-scientific-area-committees-forensic-science/osac-lexicon.

4. Forensic document examination and other forensic disciplines

Jan Seaman Kelly—Forensic Document Examiner since 1987. Diplomate of the American Board of Forensic Document Examiners (ABFDE) and a Fellow of the Questioned Document Section in the AAFS.

The 2009 NAS Report committee expressed concern when addressing specific disciplines. Handwriting examinations may be of some value, and the committee recognized the limited research to quantify the reliability and reproducibility of examination methods used by trained forensic document examiners. For shoeprint and tire tracks and toolmarks/firearms examinations, the committee was concerned over the limited amount of research focused on the number of characteristics required for an identification. The committee also commented on the lack of standard terminology in shoeprint/tire track case reports. The committee addressed specific issues in each of the pattern/impression disciplines; however, the criticisms focused on the lack of research to determine if the results of examiner-dependent examinations are reliable, accurate, and valid.

Although there has been only limited research to quantify the reliability and replicability of the practices used by trained document examiners, the committee agrees that there may be some value in handwriting analysis. Analysis of inks and paper, being based on well-understood chemistry, presumably rests on a firmer scientific foundation. However, the committee did not receive input on these fairly specialized methods and cannot offer a definitive view regarding the soundness of these methods or of their execution in practice (NAS, 2009).

Forensic document examination standards were published through ASTM between 1993 and 2012. In 2013, SWGDOC assumed the role as publisher of the standards in 2013. The published standards that do not involve instrument-based examinations are: The Scope of Work of a Forensic Document Examination, Minimum Training Requirements for Forensic Document Examination, Terminology Relating to the Examination of Forensic Document Examination, Examination of Handwritten Items, and Terminology for Expressing Conclusions of Forensic Document Examiners. The current 21 standards and future standards will undergo the revision and vetting process in the OSAC. The final version of the standard will be submitted to the SDO, the ASB, for publication.

Forensic document examiners have participated in academic research and proficiency testing since 1993. The comments in the 2009 NAS Report provided direction that further academic research should focus on the reliability and validity of the methodology.

The future of forensic document examination will be standardization in methodologies, reports, and testimony. A college degree focused on science will be the minimum education requirement for forensic document examiner applicants. The completion of a standardized 2-year training program by all trainees, and certification of all document examiners through a recognized forensic document examination certification body will be required. Practitioners will continue to partner with academia to research and validate examination methodologies, proficiency testing of forensic document examiners, and standards will be published by the ASB.

Forensic document examiners have participated in academic research and proficiency testing since 1994. Committee comments in the 2009 NAS Report provided direction that further academic research should focus on the reliability and validity of methodologies. The Human Factors Working Group for Handwriting publication, Forensic Handwriting Examination and Human Factors: *The Report of the Expert Working Group for Human Factors in Handwriting Examination* was released in 2020.

SWGTREAD is the scientific working group for footwear and tire impression examiners. One of several ongoing research projects include A Quantitative Assessment of Shoeprint Accidental Patterns with Implications Regarding Similarity, Frequency and Chance Association of Features (SWGTREAD). This research addressed the NAS committee's concern for the lack of data on the variability of class or individual characteristics or about the validity or reliability of the method.

The footwear and tire impression discipline have 17 SWGTREAD standards. These standards are progressing through the OSAC process. ANSI/ASB Best Practice Recommendation 021, and, ASB Technical Report 097, Terminology Used for Forensic Footwear and Tire Evidence, First Edition, 2019 are three documents published and posted on SWGTREAD.

The Scientific Working Group for Friction Ridge Analysis, Study and Technology (SWGFAST) published the latent print and 10 print standards and other relevant documents on its website. There are 18 standards, a Guideline for the Articulation of the Decision-Making Process for the Individualization in Friction Ridge Examination, and a Model Policy for Friction Ridge Examiner Professional Conduct (Latent and Tenprint) SWGFAST, 2019.

In 2012, the Human Factors Working Group for Latent Prints published *Latent Print Examination and Human Factors: Improving the Practice Through a Systems Approach.*

The important thing to remember about the NAS report is that they are recommendations. They are guidelines that all labs should follow; however, well-funded and proactive labs were already doing most of their recommendations. Accredited labs conduct research, are proficiency tested in each discipline, have criminalist certifications, and participate in studies. These guidelines are very good for the science; however, funding is pivotal to the success of small and large laboratories incorporating the basic guidelines.

The consensus of practitioners in the examiner-based forensic disciplines is the conclusion scale that will be revised with the removal of the definitive conclusion of identification. In the future, the conclusion scale will most likely range from a limited (qualified) identification to a definitive elimination.

Providing funding to support the needs of forensic science laboratories and practitioners, the future will include:

Research to establish the reliability and validity of methods in all forensic disciplines and academic proficiency testing will be commonplace.

Practitioners will continue to partner with academia to research and validate examination methodologies, proficiency testing of forensic document examiners, and standards will be published by an SDO such as the ASB.

A 4-year degree or higher in science will be required to enter the forensic science field.

The completion of a standardized training program for all trainees is required.

Certification will be required of every forensic scientist.

Forensic laboratories will be independent and not part of a law enforcement agency.

5. Crime laboratories response to the NAS report

Contributor: **Jorge Bello**—unit manager, Broward Sheriff's Office Crime Laboratory, Association of Firearms and Tool Mark Examiners.

The field of forensic science was taken aback by the initial news that the NAS report was extremely critical of forensics in general. Crime laboratories were eagerly awaiting the actual report to be released to see what the future would hold for them and what the path forward was going to be. Needless to say, once the report was released a collective sigh of relief could be felt from labs all over the United States. The criticisms found within the report were not necessarily aimed at forensic science but at funding for research and at oversight of laboratories. The other issues which were criticized by many labs were already in the process of addressing, which included certification for examiners and accreditation for laboratories.

Many of the issues brought about are outside of the control of crime labs. For example, oversight of the labs is out of control of the laboratories. Several crime laboratories have requested to be independent of police departments, but this approval must typically come from some lower level of government like county commissions or mayors' offices, and these locals do not want to be seen as removing services from their constituents. Additionally, in many cases, there are treatises, which would need to be rewritten as some counties have contract in place with municipalities which state that they will provide forensic services to constituents. So, as you can see, the matter of making labs independent is not a simple matter of just saying the lab is independent.

Another area in which forensic laboratories struggle is in requiring certification across the board for all examiners. One of the many reasons is that all forensic disciplines have different organizations, which offer certification for those specific disciplines. If you were to require just one certification the American Board of Criminalistics (ABC) certification program, which is held by the AAFS is likely the most complete program. However, even with this complete program, there are downsides. The testing for the ABC certification does not include practical examinations, which means that examiners are tested on their knowledge of forensics but not whether they are physically capable of performing the examinations themselves. A second pitfall is that there are no specific subject area exams for the comparative sciences like Firearms or Latent examination. That means that a latent print examiner certified by the ABC may have answered about 10 questions on latent prints, and they now hold a certification, which seems to give them more credibility. What many laboratories have opted to do is to offer financial compensation for examiners who seek certifications pertaining to the disciplines in which they practice. This allows examiners the option to seek the most appropriate certification offered either by the ABC, the International Association for Identification (IAI), or the Association of Firearm and Toolmark Examiners (AFTE) maintenance of these certifications is an additional problem where funding is critically needed. For example, there are approximately 165 certified examiners in AFTE, the remaining 1500 or so members were polled to see why they were not certified and of those who responded the most common response was that they would be unable to keep up with recertification which occurs every 5 years due to their agencies' inability to send them to training (https://afte.org).

There are several areas where progress has been made in leaps and bounds. One of these areas is certainly that of funding for research. The National Institute of Justice provided several grants, which practitioners and academics alike used in order to research the foundations of forensic science as well as researching the technologies implemented and new technologies. Thanks to these grants, many new technologies have been implemented in all areas of forensic science. Many sciences including latent print examination and firearm and tool mark examination are also getting closer to applying statistical certainties to their conclusions thanks to these research funds.

The NAS Report encouraged laboratories to seek accreditation, and today, it is very rare to find a laboratory, which is not accredited. Accreditation essentially means that you agree to follow the standards that are set forth by a third-party institution. These standards are intended to guide laboratories to perform the highest quality of work with regards not only to the examinations being performed but also to the quality of testimony given and the ethical practices the laboratories follow. Most laboratories have gone even further allowing their examiners to become assessors for these accrediting bodies, so that they may in turn go out to asses other laboratories to determine whether they are following the standards they agreed to follow.

Another task which the NAS report said was critical for crime laboratories was standardization. Standardization, not only through accreditation, but for reporting of results and casework as well. In order to accomplish this task, the NAS report suggested greater oversight at the federal level over crime laboratories. With all of this in mind, the National Institute of Standards and Technology now administers the OSAC for Forensic Science. The OSAC was created not as a standard creating organization but as an attempt to unify organizations under one umbrella, and this way recommendations for definitions and terminology would be coming from one location. The OSAC subcommittees have already published several lists of definitions and terms to be used by crime laboratories; some of the subcommittees have even published standards for how examinations are to be conducted and how reports should be worded. The standardization of exams and reporting is key to the forensic sciences as it will allow anyone who reads reports from any agency anywhere in the United States to understand what the reports mean and how those conclusions were reached.

6. Conclusion

Forensic science is by no means perfect; however, in great part, due to the NAS Report, large strides have been made in making forensic science a more reliable field. The necessity for forensic science to be almost infallible has brought about ideas such as accreditation, certification, and verification, and in combination with new technology, forensic science has truly come much closer to this seemingly impossible task.

References

Ballou, S. (January 2019). The NAS report ten years of response. *JFS, 64*(Issue 1), 6–9.

Edwards, H. T. (2019). *Tenth anniversary of the landmark report on forensic evidence*. https://www.innocenceproject.org/judge-edwards-nas-statement.

Garrett, B. (2020). The costs and benefits of forensics. *Houston Law Review, 57*, 594–616, 593.

National Academy of Sciences. (2009). *Strengthening forensic science in the United States: A path forward*.

Saferstein, R. (2012). *From crime scene to crime lab*. Upper Saddle, NJ: Pearson.

The CSI Effect. (2007). Popular fiction about forensic science affects public expectations about real forensic science. *Jurimetrics, 47*, 357.

Further reading

Certification Options for Crime Scene Investigators. https://www.crimesceneinvestigatoredu.org/csi-certification.

Human Factors Handwriting Working Group. (2020). *The report of the expert working group for human factors in handwriting examination*. https://forensicstats.org/blog/2020/02/27/nist-releases-new-report-on-human-factors-role-in-handwriting-evaluation.

Innocence Project Staff. Ten years later: The lasting impact of the 2009 NAS report https://www.innocenceproject.org/lasting-impact-of-2009-nas-report/.

Merlino, M., Freeman, T., & Dahir, V. (2010). *Validity, reliability, accuracy, and bias in signature identification*. National Institute of Justice Grant.

Merlino, M. (2015). *Cognitive human factors and forensic document examiner methods and procedures*. National Institute of Justice.

NIST OSAC. https://www.nist.gov/topics/organization-scientific-area-committees-forensic-science.

Richard Saferstein. https://news.aafs.org/section-news/richard-saferstein-phd-retired-fellow-of-the-criminalistics-section-july-2017.

Scientific Working Group for Friction Ridge Analysis, Study and Technology. http://clpex.com/swgfast/.

Scientific Working Group for Footwear and Tire. https://treadforensics.com/.

Scientific Working Group for Forensic Document Examiners. https://www.swgdoc.org/index.php/standards/published-standards.

Taylor, M. K., Kaye, D. H., Busey, T., Gische, M., LaPorte, G., Aitken, C., et al. (2012). *Latent print examination and human factors: Improving the practice through a systems approach.* https://www.nist.gov/publications/latent-print-examination-and-human-factors-improving-practice-through-systems-approach.

The Association of Firearm and Toolmark Examiners (n.d.). https://afte.org.

The 'CSI Effect': Does it ieally exist? https://nij.ojp.gov/topics/articles/csi-effect-does-it-really-exist.

CHAPTER

Techniques for processing porous and nonporous surfaces for latent friction ridge impressions

2

Andy Parker, Luke Cunningham, Stacey Johnson, Christine Glenn, Mike Galloway
Raleigh/Wake City-County Bureau of Identification, Raleigh, NC, United States

1. Introduction

The development, enhancement, and analysis of friction ridge deposits left at crime scenes have been used for over a century in forensic investigations. The collection of friction ridge skin patterns from a crime scene aids in the identification of persons of interest or suspects in a case. Prior to discussing the various techniques that can be used to develop this type of forensic evidence, it is important to understand the factors and general limitations involved in friction ridge skin deposit patterns.

Friction ridge skin is located on fingers, palms, and the soles of the feet. As such, there is the potential for a person to leave an impression of their unique friction ridge patterns any time contact occurs between their friction ridge skin and an external surface. If the impression is left in a foreign substance such as blood, grease, paint, or another contaminant found at the scene, then the impression maybe visible prior to any enhancement techniques. These prints are referred to as patent prints. Often times, the details of patent prints can be enhanced to improve the quality and clarity of the print, which will be discussed throughout this chapter.

If contact occurs between the friction ridge skin and an object at a crime scene, but no impression is apparent or visible to the naked eye, a latent print may be developed. The impression of the friction ridge skin patterns left under these circumstances would be the result of deposits from the surface of the skin onto the surface of the object. These deposits are composed of water, fatty acids, amino acids, and triglycerides. Simply stated, the oil and water produced naturally within a human body are secreted through the skin and can be present in different quantities on the friction ridge skin. Naturally, the absence or abundance of these secretions on the friction ridge skin will be a significant factor in an impression being present on the surface it comes in contact with.

As latent impressions are composed of soluble elements, the type of surface they are deposited on will be a factor in the technique used to enhance the detail of the impression. If the deposits are left on a porous surface, such as paper or an untreated wood, the deposits, over time, will likely be absorbed into the surface. Conversely, if the deposits are made on a nonporous surface, such as glass or plastic, the deposits may remain on the surface for a longer period of time (Table 2.1).

Methodological and Technological Advances in Death Investigations. https://doi.org/10.1016/B978-0-12-819394-5.00007-9

Table 2.1 Latent fingerprint processing guide per substrate.

Surface:	Adhesive (Seq.)	Investigative blood reagents	Blood enhancement reagents	Nonporous	Nonporous wet (Seq.)	Porous (Seq.)	Porous wet
	Crystal violet	Bluestar	Leuco crystal violet	Cyanoacrylate fuming	Small particle reagent	Iodine	Oil Red O
	Adhesive-side powder	Lumiscence	Acid yellow	Dye stains	Sudan Black	DFO	Physical developer
			Amido black (aqueous/methanol)	Crystal violet		1,2 Indanedione	Silver nitrate
			Ninhydrin			Ninhydrin	
			Phloxine			Physical developer	
						Silver nitrate	

Many of the chemicals and reagents used in latent development can be harmful or carcinogenetic. Proper safety precautions should be used based on the manufacture's safety guidelines or from the Safety Data Sheet (SDS/MSDS) accompanying the chemicals.

Different processing techniques have been developed and should be utilized depending on the deposited surface. Consideration should also be given as to the contrast of the developed friction ridge detail and the surface it is on. The table provided should be used as a reference and an outline for the techniques contained within this chapter (Table 2.2).

Table 2.2 Latent fingerprint processing guide per deposit.

Triglycerides/Amino Acids/Proteins	Sebaceous oils	Eccrine deposits	Water	Skin cells
Cyanoacrylate fuming	Cyanoacrylate fuming	Silver nitrate	Cyanoacrylate fuming	Crystal violet
DFO	Oil Red O	DFO		
1,2 Indanedione	Physical developer	1,2-Indanedione		
Ninhydrin	Crystal violet	Ninhydrin		
	Iodine Small particle reagent	Silver nitrate		

2. Nonporous substrates

2.1 Cyanoacrylate ester (Fig. 2.1)

FIGURE 2.1

Cyanoacrylate ester.

Cyanoacrylate (CA) fuming is used to develop latent prints on nonporous and semiporous items. The fuming reacts or polymerizes with the moisture and the sebaceous oils with the latent print deposits and appears as white to almost translucent (Gardner, 2005).

Proper cooling of a sample relative to the environment resulted in several changes that increased visualization. Decreasing the temperature 5–20F to the ambient environment caused more CA to condense on the fingerprint, allowing greater resolution. The cooling of the object changed the physical form of the polyethyl-CA product, making the print more opaque improving contrast. The resulting polyethylcyanoacrylate had more surface area, which provided for more opportunity for color uptake. The greater the opacity caused by the cooling allows more of the fluorescent emission to be reflected from the layers near the surface of the sample (Steele et al., 2012).

Latent prints developed at high humidity are not only more visible immediately because of the light scattering of the fibrous deposit, but the greater surface area will also absorb much more dye during enhancement procedures (Kent, 2013).

Cyanoacrylate fuming hindered the subsequent enhancement of blood marks by the water formulation of protein stains. The methanol enhancement formulation may damage some substrates and be detrimental to blood presumptive and confirmatory tests. The use of vacuum CA fuming may be a suitable option when both latent and blood marks are present because vacuum CA creates a thinner and lighter layer of polycyanoacrylate across the substrate (Mutter et al., 2018).

Fingerprints subjected to harsh conditions including heat, low humidity, or UV light often produce poorly developed results after CA fuming due to lack of moisture deposits. The use of 10% w/v methylamine as a pretreatment strategy to rehydrate the fingerprint prior to CA fuming can increase the development (Montgomery et al., 2012).

Relative humidity does not have an effect on the development of fingerprints when in evidence storage; therefore, there is not a need to require controlled humidity conditions in custody storage rooms (Schwarz & Hermanowski, 2012).

After the items have been fumed and the fingerprint is fixated by the CA, there are multiple processes that can be done to the latent print to enhance the development including powders and dye stains. Dye stains are used to dye the CA developed latent prints to produce a comparable fingerprint. These prints can be viewed under an alternate light source (ALS) and documented with a camera using a yellow/orange/red filter depending on the wavelength the dye stains fluoresce. The dye stains often fluoresce in a yellow/orange/red color. The dye stains discussed in this section will include: Ardrox, Basic Yellow, MBD, RAY, Red-Yellow, Rhodamine 6G, thenoyl europium chelate (TEC), and White Star; these dye stains are commercially available as premixed solutions (Table 2.3).

Table 2.3 Dye stain chart[a].

	DYE stain	ALS wavelength	Filter color
POROUS	1,2-Indanedione	Begin 515 nm	Orange
	DFO	495–550 nm Maximum: 514 nm	Orange Orange/red
NONPOROUS	Ardrox	UV light: 280–360 nm Forensic light: 435–480 nm	Yellow Yellow

Table 2.3 Dye stain chart[a].—*cont'd*

	DYE stain	ALS wavelength	Filter color
	Basic yellow 40	UV light: 365 nm	Yellow/ orange
		Forensic light: 415–485 nm	Yellow/ orange
	MBD	415–505 nm 415–470 nm	Orange Yellow
	RAY	450–550 nm	Orange/ red
	(Rhodamine 6G, Ardrox, Basic yellow mixture)		
	Red-yellow	400–490 nm	Orange
	(Basic Red & Basic yellow mixture)		
	Rhodamine 6G	495–540 nm	Orange
	White–Star	UV light: 280–365 nm	Orange
		Forensic light: 400–490 nm	Orange

[a] *This chart is to be used for guidance; please use your discretion when examining evidence.*

There are several methods of CA fuming treatments including a liquid glue (Cyanowand, Cyanoshot, heat acceleration) or commercial "Gel-pack."

Cyanowand is a commercially available butane-powered heat tool and self-igniting. The wand is portable and handheld. The heat is generated from butane and heats the CA cartridges and in return emits the super glue vapor to fixate the latent prints (Austin Police Department Forensic Science Bureau, 2019a). The cyanowand is designed for well-ventilated areas including outdoor scenes and vehicles (Raleigh/Wake City-County Bureau of Identification, a).

Cyanoshot is a commercially available two-part superglue process that is self-heating. The activator cannister is placed into the jar of activator solution, and the glue is emptied onto the metal top of the activator cannister. Cyanoshot is designed for efficient processing of the interior of vehicles (Raleigh/Wake City-County Bureau of Identification, b).

The heat acceleration method uses a fuming chamber, a water container, and liquid CA. The CA is heated in the chamber to emit the super glue vapor; the vapor polymerizes with latent print residues. Evidence items are placed in the chamber between 5 and 20 min (depending on the size of the chamber, the humidity, and the amount of items that are present in the chamber), before items are removed and examined. The CA chamber is best used for smaller items of evidence including burglary tools, firearms, and knives (Austin Police Department Forensic Science Bureau, 2019b).

Gel-Packs are commercially available and use a fuming chamber, a water container, and CA in a gel form (gelatin). The gelatin is heated in the chamber to emit the super glue vapor; the vapor polymerizes with the latent print residues. Evidence items are placed in the chamber between 30 and 60 min (depending on the size of the chamber, the humidity, and the amount of items that are present in the chamber). The Gel Packs take longer to heat and, therefore, have a longer evidence processing time than the liquid form of CA (Austin Police Department Forensic Science Bureau, 2019c).

Precautions and incompatibilities

Items that contain moisture.

Items submitted for Biology examination.

Light-colored surfaces which present little contrast.

CA fuming will work best if the chamber has between 70% and 80% relative humidity.

CA fuming is best when the items are lightly fumed.

Fingerprints can be over/under developed (Chesapeake Bay Division International Association of Identification, 2017a).

Heat acceleration/gel pack

- Small plastic items should be hung from a cross support.
- Allow ½ inch between items and the walls of the chamber.
- In larger chambers, spot processing can be avoided with a fan.
- Openings of a firearm should be covered prior to fuming.
- CA fuming may impair blood print enhancement techniques.

Cyanowands/cyanoshot

- Use exhaust fan or respiratory protection when using these methods in an occupied room.
- Avoid dropping or a hard blow to the wand as the ceramic burner may be damaged.
- Only refill with butane.
- Do not store in sunlight or where want is exposed to excessive heat for long periods of time.
- Do not store near heaters or furnaces.

Materials and chemicals

Heat acceleration

- Fuming chamber with water container
- Heater with aluminum dish
- CA
- Warm to hot water

Gel pack

- Fuming chamber with water container
- CA in a gelatin and sealed in an aluminum package

- Warm to hot water

Cyanowand

- Fuming chamber or enclosed area to seal in fumes
- Fuming want with butane fuel cylinder
- CA fuming cartridges
- Warm to hot water

Cyanoshot

- Fuming chamber or enclosed arear to seal in fumes
- Activator cannister
- Activator solution
- CA

Processing procedure
Heat acceleration/gel packs

- Place item(s) into the enclosed fuming chamber
- Add glue (either liquid CA in an aluminum dish, gel-pack, cartridge)
  - For liquid CA allow 10 drops of glue per five square feet of space
- Add humidity source (warm water)
- Fume
  - Time will vary on size of chamber, the amount of humidity present, and the amount of items processed in the chamber
  - A five square foot chamber will take from 5 to 20 min to process
- Monitor often for development
- After fuming, allow the chamber for 10 min to vent
  - Do not open the door of the chamber to vent
- Evaluate development under an oblique light source
- If necessary, the fuming process can be repeated

Cyanowand

- Fill the fuming wand fuel cylinder
  - Ensure the want is OFF and cool
  - Hold the want downward so the refill nozzle will be in the upward position
  - Press the nozzle of the butane fuel cylinder downward
  - When full, the butane fuel will vent through the refill valve
  - Examine the fuel (clear liquid) through the gas level window
- Start the fuming wand
  - Place a fuming cartridge on the hot air tip
  - Set control lever to #3 (midway)
  - Slide the switch to the ON position
  - Hold the ignition button for a period of 3 seconds and slowly release
  - A red glow should be visible when looking into the view window
  - Repeat the last two steps if the want has not ignited

- Use the fume wand
  - A dense stream of CA vapors will begin to emerge within a minute
  - Hold the fuming wand 6–9 inches from the targeted area
  - Slowly sweep the vapor stream over the surface
    - Do not hold wand too close or too long over an area
    - Do not hold wand too far away or too short over an area
  - The fuming process can be repeated
- Remove the CA cartridge
  - Turn the wand in the OFF position
  - Place the extraction tool over the cartridge
  - Remove the cartridge by slowly pulling the cartridge away from the wand
  - Place the cartridge on a surface capable of withstanding heat and allow to cool

Cyanoshot

- Place the activator cannister side down
- Place into the activator solution
- Empty the glue onto the metal top of the activator caniste

Collection/documentation

The latent evidence should then be photographed utilizing proper photography techniques for documenting latent evidence.

Additional processing treatments such as dye stains and powders can be used after the fuming process that may provide better contrast or visibility.

Shelf-life and disposal

Heat acceleration

Small bottles of liquid CA can be stored at room temperature and large bottles of liquid CA can be stored in the refrigerator. There is an indefinite shelf-life for liquid CA.

Gel pack

Opened gel packs must be secured in a zip lock plastic bag. Both opened and unopened gel packs should be stored in a refrigerator. Opened gel packs are good for 6 months and unopened gel packs are indefinite.

Cyanowand

Fuming wands and fuel should be stored in a cool area, and fuming cartridges should be stored in a container until ready to use. There is an indefinite shelf-life for CA fuming cartridges if kept from the heat. Equipment life for fuming wands.

Cyanoshot

The activator canister and the jar of activator solution should be stored in a cool area. The activator canister and the jar of activator solution are to be disposed after each use.

Disposal

Wrap CA (solid, cartridges) in paper after they have cooled and discard in appropriate waste receptable.

2.2 Ardrox (Fig. 2.2)

FIGURE 2.2

Ardrox.

Ardrox is used to dye CA-developed latent prints on various colored surfaces. These prints can be viewed under an ALS and documented with a camera and yellow filter. This method is effective on nonporous surfaces and has a yellow fluorescence (Raleigh/Wake City-County Bureau of Identification, c).

The dye stain RAY may be used on a surface after Ardrox treatment (Chesapeake Bay Division International Association of Identification, 2019b).

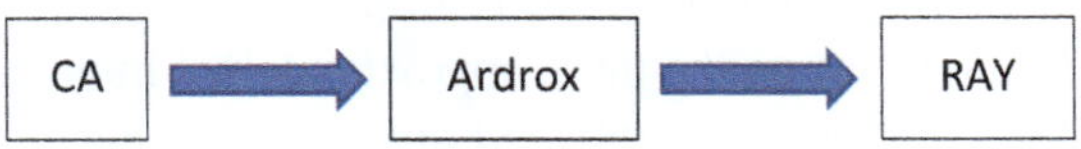

Precautions and incompatibilities

Do not mix the working solution using a magnetic stirrer.

Surfaces that absorb too much of the dye stain with fluoresce too brightly to be effective to document ridge detail.

Avoid excess build-up of CA.

Do not use on a background that is yellow.

Items that fluoresce 500 nm range will be visually incompatible with this dye stain.

Materials and chemicals (United States Department of Justice, Federal Bureau of United States Department of Justice Federal Bureau of Investigation, 2001)

- Ardrox P133 D—2 mL
- Acetone—10 mL
- Methanol—25 mL
- Isopropanol—10 mL

- Acetonitrile—8 mL
- Petroleum Ethe—945 mL
- Scales/beakers/graduated cylinders
- Squirt bottle/glass tray/ALS
- Dark bottles

Mixing procedure (United States Department of Justice, Federal Bureau of United States Department of Justice Federal Bureau of Investigation, 2001)

- Stock solution
  - Ardrox stain does not use a stock solution. Ardrox is used undiluted directly from the container3.
- Working solution
  - Ardrox P133 D—2 mL
  - Acetone—10 mL
  - Methanol—25 mL
  - Isopropanol—10 mL
  - Acetonitrile—8 mL
  - Petroleum ether—945 mL

Combine the ingredients in the order listed. Do not use a magnetic stirrer.

Processing procedure (Sirchie Technical Information, a)

- Submerge the item in a tray for approximately 1 minute, or
- Spray the item approximately 6–9″ away from the surface.
- Allow the dye stain to set on the item, approximately 1 minute.
- Using running water, thoroughly rinse off any excess stain.
- View under an ultraviolet lamp in the 280–365 nm range:
  - Use ultraviolet goggles
- View under an ALS in the 435–480 nm range:
  - Use yellow colored goggles

Collection/documentation

Using a yellow filter, the latent evidence should then be photographed utilizing proper photography techniques for documenting latent evidence.

Shelf-life and disposal

Ardrox should be stored in clear or dark bottles.

The shelf-life of the working solution is up to 6 months.

Excess Ardrox working solution should be discarded in a waste container marked flammable.

2.3 Basic Yellow 40 (Fig. 2.3)

FIGURE 2.3

Basic Yellow 40.

Basic Yellow 40 is used to dye CA-developed latent prints on various colored surfaces. These prints can be viewed under an ALS and documented with a camera and yellow filter. This method is effective on nonporous surfaces and has a yellow fluorescence (Raleigh/Wake City-County Bureau of Identification, d).

Basic Yellow can be used to develop fingerprints on both the sticky and smooth side of duct tape as well as electrical tape. The duct tape should be fumed first, then frozen (preferably with liquid nitrogen), and then refumed. For the duct tape, the Basic Yellow solution must contain 25% water.

Basic Yellow dye stain yielded good results on a variety of substrates including: glossy paper, plastic grocery bag, aluminum can, glass beer bottle, gun magazine, unfinished wood, and finished wood (Richards & Thomas, 2014).

Basic Yellow 40 may be used prior to treatment with a RAY dye stain (Chesapeake Bay Division International Association of Identification, 2019c).

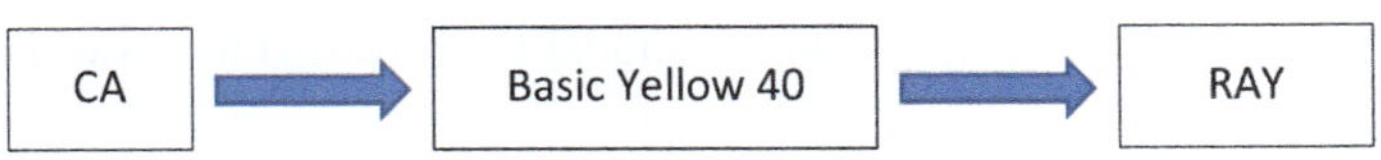

Precautions and incompatibilities

Surfaces that absorb too much of the dye stain with fluoresce too brightly to be effective to document ridge detail.

Avoid excess build-up of CA.

Do not use on a background that is yellow.

Items that fluoresce 490 nm range (Chesapeake Bay Division International Association of Identification, 2019c).

Misting the item with Basic Yellow 40 solution from an aerosol spray eliminates excessive background staining.

Materials and chemicals (Sirchie Technical Information, b)

- Basic Yellow 40 powder—1 g
- Methanol—500 mL, additional methanol for rinse (Chesapeake Bay Division International Association of Identification, 2019c).
- Scales/beakers/graduated cylinders
- Squirt bottle/glass tray/ALS
- Dark bottles

Mixing procedure

- Working solution (Sirchie Technical Information, b).
  - Dissolve Basic Yellow 40 in methanol.

Processing procedure

- Tray immersion or rinse bottle for approximately 10 s.
- View under an ultraviolet lamp around 365 nm (Sirchie Technical Information, b).
  - Use orange goggles
- View under an ALS in the 450–485 nm range (Sirchie Technical Information, b).
  - Use yellow colored goggles
- Use a methanol rinse if fluorescence is too bright

Collection/documentation

Using a yellow filter, the latent evidence should then be photographed utilizing proper photography techniques for documenting latent evidence.

Shelf-life and disposal

Basic Yellow should be stored in clear or dark bottles.

The shelf-life of the working solution is up to 6 months.

Excess Basic Yellow working solution should be discarded in a waste container marked flammable.

2.4 MBD (Fig. 2.4)

FIGURE 2.4

MBD.

MBD is used to dye CA-developed latent prints on various colored surfaces. These prints can be viewed under an ALS and documented with a camera and orange filter. This method is effective on non-porous surfaces and has an orange fluorescence.

Latent blood prints deposited on some oil and latex painted surfaces may easily be detected by applying the MBD solution to the surface being examined (Raleigh/Wake City-County Bureau of Identification, c).

MBD dye stain yielded good results on a variety of substrates including: glossy paper, plastic grocery bag, aluminum can, glass beer bottle, gun magazine, unfinished wood, and finished wood (Richards & Thomas, 2014).

The manufacturer recommends this dye stain on plastic bags (MedTech Forensics, a).

This reagent is available commercially; follow manufacturer's instructions.

Precautions and incompatibilities

Surfaces that absorb too much of the dye stain with fluoresce too brightly to be effective to document ridge detail (Chesapeake Bay Division International Association of Identification, 2019d).

Do not use on a background that is orange.

Avoid excess build-up of CA.

Items that fluoresce in the 515 nm range will interfere with the dye stain's fluorescence.

Materials and chemicals (Raleigh/Wake City-County Bureau of Identification, c)

- MBD powder—10 mL
- Acetone—1L
- Methanol—30 mL, plus additional for rinse
- Isopropanol—10 mL
- Petroleum ether—950 mL
- Scales/beakers/graduated cylinders
- Squirt bottle/glass tray/ALS
- Dark bottles

Mixing procedure

- Stock solution
    - MBD (United States Department of Justice, Federal Bureau of United States Department of Justice Federal Bureau of Investigation, 2001) powder is dissolved into the acetone.
- Working solution
    - MBD stock solution—10 mL
    - Methanol—30 mL
    - Isopropanol—10 mL
    - Petroleum ether—950 mL

Combine the ingredients in the order listed. Do not place on a magnetic stirrer.

Processing procedure

- Spray, immerse, or use a squirt bottle to apply the MBD solution.
- View under an ALS in the 435–535 nm range.
    - Use orange colored goggles
- Use a methanol rinse if fluorescence is too intense.

Collection/documentation

Using an orange filter, the latent evidence should then be photographed utilizing proper photography techniques for documenting latent evidence.

Shelf-life and disposal United States Department of Justice, Federal Bureau of United States Department of Justice Federal Bureau of Investigation (2001)

MBD should be stored in clear or dark bottles.

The shelf-life of the stock solution is indefinite.

The shelf-life of the working solution is up to 6 months.

Excess MBD working solution should be discarded in a waste container marked flammable.

2.5 RAY (Fig. 2.5)

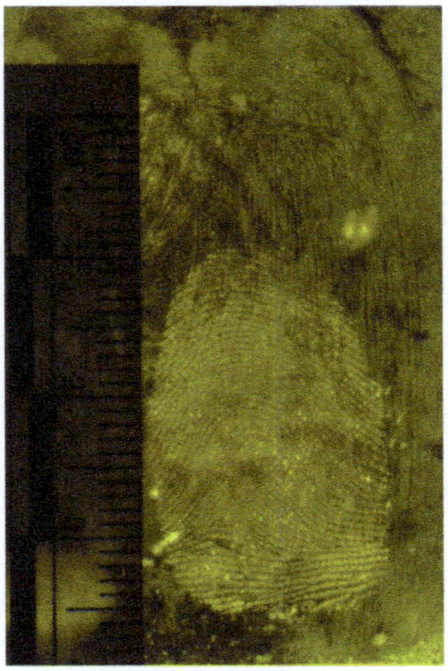

FIGURE 2.5

RAY.

RAY is used to dye CA-developed latent prints on various colored surfaces. RAY dye stain is a combination of Basic Yellow 40, Rhodamine 6G, and Ardrox dye stains (Raleigh/Wake City-County Bureau of Identification, e). These prints can be viewed under an ALS and documented with a camera and orange/red filter. This method is effective on nonporous surfaces and has an orange fluorescence.

RAY dye stain outperformed both gentian violet and alternate powder on the adhesive side of tape following CA fuming. The best method for processing the adhesive side of tape after CA fuming is gentian violet, followed by alternate powder, and then RAY dye stain (Wilson, 2010).

An Ardrox, a Rhodamine 6G, a Basic Yellow 40, or a TEC dye stain may be used prior to treatment with RAY (Chesapeake Bay Division International Association of Identification, 2019e).

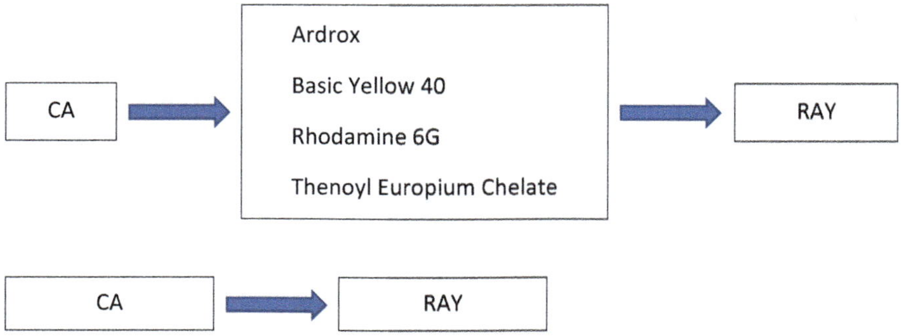

Precautions and incompatibilities

Surfaces that absorb too much of the dye stain with fluoresce too brightly to be effective to document ridge detail.

Do not use on a background that is orange/red.

Avoid excess build-up of CA.

Items that fluoresce 490–555 nm range.

Materials and chemicals (Chesapeake Bay Division International Association of Identification, 2019e)

- Basic Yellow 40 dye—0.5 g
- Glacial acetic acid—10 mL
- Rhodamine 6G dye—0.5 g
- Ardrox P133D—4 mL
- Isopropanol or denatured ethanol—450 mL
- Acetonitrile—40 mL
- Scales/beakers/graduated cylinders
- Squirt bottle/glass tray/ALS
- Dark bottles

Mixing procedure (Chesapeake Bay Division International Association of Identification, 2019e)

- Working solution
  - Basic Yellow 40 dye—0.5 g
  - Glacial acetic acid—10 mL
  - Rhodamine 6G dye—0.05 g
  - Ardrox P133D—4 mL
  - Isopropanol or denatured ethanol—450 mL
  - Acetonitrile—40 mL

  Combine the ingredients in the order listed.

Processing procedure

- Spray, immerse, or use a squirt bottle to apply the RAY solution.

- View under an ALS in the 450–550 nm range.
  - Use orange/red colored goggles
- Use a methanol rinse if fluorescence is too bright

Collection/documentation

Using an orange or red filter, the latent evidence should then be photographed utilizing proper photography techniques for documenting latent evidence.

Shelf-life and disposal

RAY should be stored in clear or dark bottles.

The shelf-life of the working solution is up to 6 months.

Excess RAY working solution should be discarded in a waste container marked flammable.

2.6 Red-Yellow (Fig. 2.6)

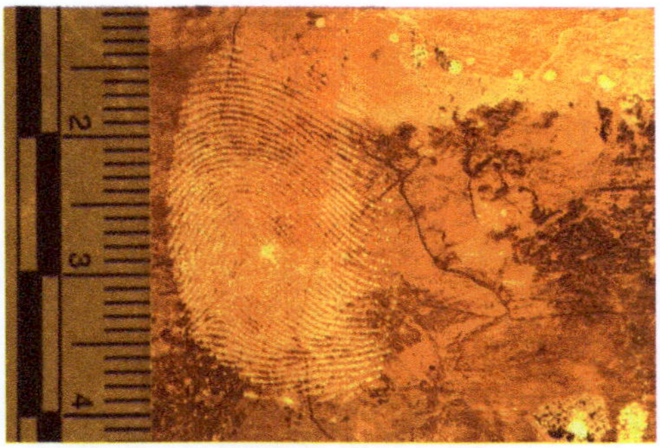

FIGURE 2.6

Red Yellow.

Red-Yellow is used to dye CA-developed latent prints on various colored surfaces. These prints can be viewed under an ALS and documented with a camera and orange filter. This method is effective on nonporous surfaces and has an orange fluorescence (Raleigh/Wake City-County Bureau of Identification, f).

Red-Yellow dye stain is a commercially available combination of Basic Red 28 stain and Basic Yellow 40 stain (MedTech Forensics, b); follow manufacturer's instructions.

Precautions and incompatibilities

Surfaces that absorb too much of the dye stain with fluoresce too brightly to be effective to document ridge detail.

Do not use on a background that is red/yellow/orange.

Avoid excess build-up of CA.

Materials and chemicals

- Manufacturer's premixed Red-Yellow dye stain

Mixing procedure

None.

Processing procedure

- Spray, immerse, or use a squirt bottle to apply the Red-Yellow solution.
- View under an ALS in the 435–535 nm range.
  - Use orange colored goggles
- Use a methanol rinse if fluorescence is too bright.

Collection/documentation

Using an orange filter, the latent evidence should then be photographed utilizing proper photography techniques for documenting latent evidence.

Shelf-life and disposal

Red-Yellow should be stored in clear or dark bottles.

The shelf-life of the working solution is up to 6 months.

Excess Red-Yellow working solution should be discarded in a waste container marked flammable.

2.7 Rhodamine 6G (Fig. 2.7)

FIGURE 2.7

Rhodamine 6G.

Rhodamine 6G is used to dye CA-developed latent prints on various colored surfaces (Raleigh/Wake City-County Bureau of Identification, g). These prints can be viewed under an ALS and documented with a camera and an orange filter. This method is effective on nonporous surfaces and has an orange fluorescence (Raleigh/Wake City-County Bureau of Identification, g).

Rhodamine 6G in conjunction with Oil Red O allows the development and the visualization of lipid-deposited fingerprints on dark, porous surfaces that have been previously wet. This process is done in two distinct steps: fingerprint staining (Oil Red O) and background staining (Rhodamine 6G).

Rhodamine 6G dye stain may be used prior to treatment with a RAY dye stain (Chesapeake Bay Division International Association of Identification, 2019f).

Precautions and incompatibilities

Surfaces that absorb too much of the dye stain with fluoresce too brightly to be effective to document ridge detail.

Do not use on a background that is orange/red.

Avoid excess build-up of CA.

Items that fluoresce 555 nm range.

Materials and chemicals (United States Department of Justice, Federal Bureau of United States Department of Justice Federal Bureau of Investigation, 2001)

- Rhodamine 6G—1g
- Methanol—1015 mL
- Acetone—15 mL
- Acetonitrile—10 mL
- Isopropanol—32 mL
- Petroleum ether—925 mL
- Scales/beakers/graduated cylinders
- Squirt bottle/glass tray/ALS
- Dark bottles

Stock solution

- Rhodamine 6G powder—1 g
- Methanol—1000 mL

Working solution

- Rhodamine 6G stock solution—3 mL
- Acetone—15 mL
- Acetonitrile—10 mL
- Methanol—15 mL
- Isopropanol—32 mL
- Petroleum ether—925 mL

Mixing procedure (United States Department of Justice, Federal Bureau of United States Department of Justice Federal Bureau of Investigation, 2001)

- Stock solution
  - Rhodamine 6G powder—1 g
  - Methanol—1000 mL

Combine the ingredients and place on a stirring device until the Rhodamine 6G powder is dissolved.

- Working solution
  - Rhodamine 6G stock solution—3 mL
  - Acetone—15 mL

- Acetonitrile—10 mL
- Methanol—15 mL
- Isopropanol—32 mL
- Petroleum ether—925 mL

Combine the ingredients in the order listed.

Processing procedure (Raleigh/Wake City-County Bureau of Identification, g)

- Spray, immerse, or use a squirt bottle to apply the Rhodamine 6G solution.
- View under an ALS in the 495–540 nm range.
  - Use orange/red colored goggles
- Use a methanol rinse if fluorescence is too bright.

Collection/documentation

Record development with photography and an orange/red filter.

Shelf-life and disposal

Rhodamine 6G should be stored in clear or dark bottles.

The shelf-life of the stock solution is definite (Chesapeake Bay Division International Association of Identification, 2019f).

The shelf-life of the working solution is up to 6 months.

Excess Rhodamine 6G working solution should be discarded in a waste container marked flammable.

2.8 Thenoyl europium chelate (Fig. 2.8)

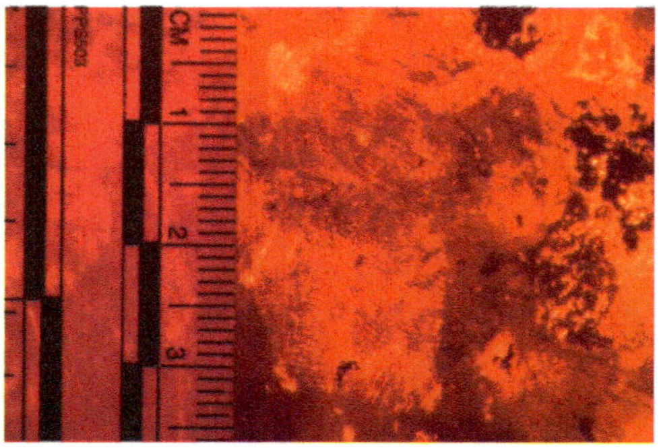

FIGURE 2.8

Thenoyl europium chelate.

Thenoyl europium chelate is used to dye CA-developed latent prints (Raleigh/Wake City-County Bureau of Identification, h). These prints can be viewed under an ALS and documented with a camera and red filter. This method is effective on nonporous surfaces and has a yellow fluorescence.

Thenoyl europium chelate produces a brighter fluorescence or ridge detail with less interfering background luminescence than other dye stains including

Rhodamine 6G and Ardrox (Chesapeake Bay Division International Association of Identification, 2019g).

TEC may be used prior to a RAY dye stain treatment.

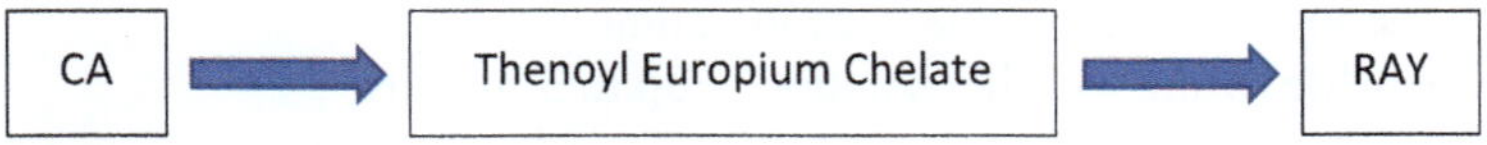

Precautions and incompatibilities

Do not mix the working solution using a magnetic stirrer.

Surfaces that absorb too much of the dye stain with fluoresce too brightly to be effective to document ridge detail.

Avoid excess build-up of CA.

Do not use on a background that is yellow.

Items that fluoresce in the ultraviolet range.

Materials and chemicals (Chesapeake Bay Division International Association of Identification, 2019g)

- Thenoyltrifluoroacetone—1 g
- Methyl ethyl ketone—200 mL
- Europium chloride hexahydrate—0.5 g
- Distilled water—800 mL
- Scales/beakers/graduated cylinders
- Squirt bottle/glass tray/ALS
- Dark bottles

Mixing procedure

- Stock solution A:
  - 1 g of thenoyltrifluoroacetone in 200 mL of methyl ethyl ketone
- Stock solution B:
  - 0.5 g of europium chloride hexahydrate dissolved in 800 mL of distilled water
- Working solution:
  Combine the stock solutions.
- Combined stock solution—100 mL
- Methyl ethyl ketone—180 mL
- Distilled water—720 mL

Combine the ingredients in the order listed.

Processing procedure

- Tray immersion or rinse bottle application for about 2 minutes (MedTech Forensics, c).
- View under an ALS at the long wave ultraviolet range around 350 nm.
  - Use ultraviolet goggles or red goggles

Collection/documentation
Record development with photography and a red filter.

Shelf-life and disposal
Thenoyl europium chelate should be stored in a tightly stopped dark bottle to eliminate the loss of solution due to evaporation.

The shelf-life of the working solution is up to 3 months.

Excess TEC working solution should be discarded in a waste container marked flammable.

2.9 White-Star (Fig. 2.9)

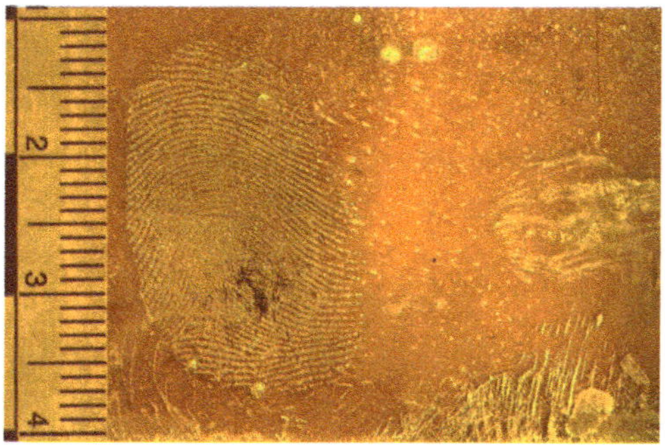

FIGURE 2.9
White-Star.

White-Star is used to dye CA-developed latent prints on dark-colored surfaces (Raleigh/Wake City-County Bureau of Identification, i). These prints can be viewed under an ALS and documented with a camera and an orange filter (MedTech Forensics, d). This method is effective on nonporous surfaces and has an orange fluorescence.

This reagent is available commercially; follow manufacturer's instructions.

Precautions and incompatibilities
Surfaces that absorb too much of the dye stain with fluoresce too brightly to be effective to document ridge detail.

Do not use on a background that is white.

Avoid excess build-up of CA.

Materials and chemicals
- White-Star premixed dye stain
- Methanol, for rinse as needed
- Squirt bottle/glass tray/ALS
- Dark bottles

Mixing procedure

None.

Processing procedure (Raleigh/Wake City-County Bureau of Identification, i)

- Spray, immerse, or use a squirt bottle to apply the White-Star dye stain solution.
- View under an ALS in the 495–540 nm range.
  - Use orange/red colored goggles
- Use a methanol rinse if fluorescence is too bright.

Collection/documentation

Using an orange or red filter, the latent evidence should then be photographed utilizing proper photography techniques for documenting latent evidence.

Shelf-life and disposal

White-Star should be stored in clear or dark bottles.

The shelf-life of the stock solution is indefinite.

Excess White-Star working solution should be discarded in a waste container marked flammable.

3. Nonporous substrates - Wet

3.1 Small particle reagent

Small particle reagent (SPR) is commonly used to develop or enhance latent prints on wet, nonporous surfaces; this process is ideal for vehicles covered with condensation or latent prints that are on surfaces that have been exposed to rain or other moisture (Raleigh/Wake City-County Bureau of Identification, j). Items that are dusty or oily or which would be otherwise difficult to process with powder can be processed with SPR (Cohen & Cohen, 2010). SPR has been successful in processing oxidized and galvanized metals.

SPR is a solution comprised of detergent and finely ground particles of molybdenum disulfide. The reagent reacts with fatty deposits and sebaceous lipids.

SPR does not interfere with DNA collection for analysis; the mechanical action or rinses and washes during the SPR procedure may remove portions of biological material from an item (Zamir et al., 2002).

SPR can be purchased in black, white, and luminescent. Depending on the surface color(s), the appropriate SPR should be utilized to maximize contrast. Light SPR has been used successfully to process black-handled knives for blood impressions (Bouwmeester et al., 2011).

SPR follows Sudan Black in the sequential process (Chesapeake Bay Division International Association of Identification, 2019i).

Premixed solutions are available commercially and are commonly used.

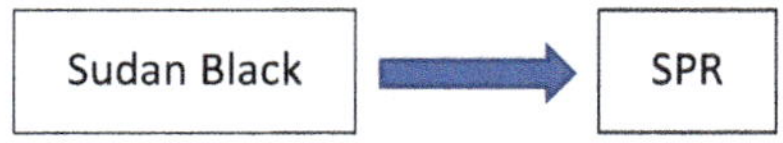

Precautions and incompatibilities

SPR is typically applied by spraying onto surfaces that are wet so a large work area may be required and run-off can be messy. As with other latent processes, the quality and of the latent detail is dependent of the amount of residue deposits left by the friction ridge skin.

The nozzle of the spray bottle can become clogged resulting in uneven application.

Materials and chemicals

- SPR is available in premixed kits with spray bottles
- Spray bottle with clean water

Mixing procedure

- Agitation of the solution is recommended before and in between spraying

Processing procedure (Sirchie Technical Information, c)

- Tray method: Mix the reagent well then submerge the item in a tray and keep it stationary for approximately 1 minute.
- Spray method: Mix the reagent well then spray directly onto the item, for approximately 1 min.
- Tap water is used to rinse excess reagent off the processed item for approximately 15 s.
- Development is complete when repeated applications of the reagent no longer produce development or enhancement.
- Allow the item to air dry at room temperature.

Collection/documentation

The latent evidence should then be photographed utilizing proper photography techniques for documenting latent evidence. Once dry, the latent print can be lifted with tape and placed on a lift backer.

Shelf-life and disposal

The mixed reagent can be retained in the provided spray bottle with an indefinite shelf-life.

3.2 Sudan Black

Sudan Black is a lysochrome, meaning that it is a compound that has the ability to dye fatty acids (Castello et al., 2002). This dye is used to develop sebaceous perspiration latent prints on nonporous surfaces. It can aid in the development of latent prints on smooth or rough surfaces that have been contaminated with oil or greasy substances.

Sudan Black can also be used to develop latent prints on wax surfaces such as candles. It can also be used to enhance prints post-CA fuming (Chesapeake Bay Division International Association of Identification, 2019j).

The benefit of this reagent is its inexpensive cost and its ability to successfully process items that are too contaminated with oils for powder processing (Sirchie Technical Information, d).

Precautions and incompatibilities

Sudan black should not be used on porous surfaces or absorbent surfaces as the entire item will be stained. The dye will stain most surfaces so clean up can be difficult (Sirchie Technical Information, d).

This process should be done after all biological and DNA collection is completed.

Ethanol is flammable, and, therefore, the mixed solution is flammable.

Processed items should be air dried and not exposed to intense heat to accelerate the drying process (Sirchie Technical Information, d).

Materials and chemicals (Raleigh/Wake City-County Bureau of Identification, k)

- Sudan black powder—15g
- Ethanol—1L
- Deionized/distilled water—500 mL
- Tap water or distilled water for rinse
- Laboratory stirring device
- Mixing container

Mixing procedure

- Mix Sudan Black with ethanol. Place the solution on the laboratory stirring device for approximately 15 min, until the powder has dissolved.
  - Add the distilled water to the solution. Stir until solution is mixed evenly; some of the Sudan Black may not dissolve fully.

Processing procedure

- Pour the solution into a glass tray.
- Submerge the surface to be processed in the solution for approximately 2 min.
- Remove the evidence and rinse using a slow stream of tap water being careful to not directly rinse the ridge detail.

Processing is complete when ridge detail appears dark blue after the water rinse and is allowed to air dry.

Collection/documentation

The latent evidence should then be photographed utilizing proper photography techniques for documenting latent evidence.

Shelf-life and disposal

The working solution should be stored in a clean, properly labeled, glass bottle with a tight-fitting cover.

The working solution is flammable and should be stored in a proper flammable cabinet when not in use.

4. Porous substrates

4.1 Iodine fuming (Fig. 2.10)

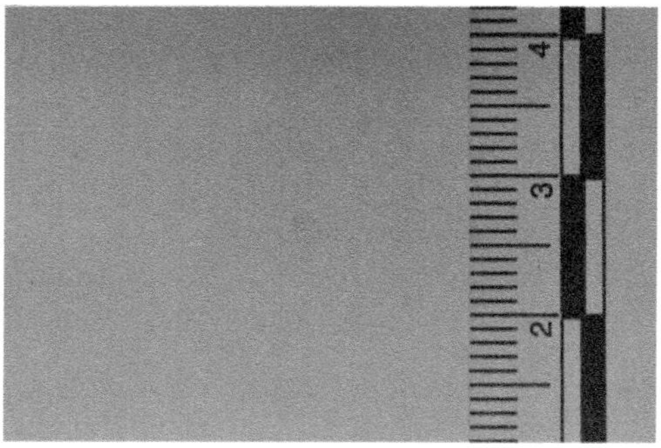

FIGURE 2.10

Iodine fuming.

Iodine fuming is a method for developing latent fingerprints on porous surfaces such as paper, cardboard, and raw wood. Iodine fumes react with the fatty and oily substances deposited by the fingers (Raleigh/Wake City-County Bureau of Identification, n).

Iodine fuming is a technique considered nondestructive, therefore precedes other procedures sequentially, such as DFO, ninhydrin, and 1,2-indanedione (Saferstein, 1998, p. 451).

Iodine is a solid crystal that upon being heated is transformed into a vapor without passing through a liquid phase. This transformation is called sublimation. Development is complete when the maximum yellow-brown detail is developed upon exposure to the Iodine fumes (Austin Police Department Forensic Science Bureau, 2019d).

As the iodine will evaporate from a treated surface, the development will no longer be visible. It is necessary to photograph results immediately for documentation (Austin Police Department Forensic Science Bureau, 2019d).

Iodine kits are available commercially and are commonly used, follow manufacturer's instructions.

Precautions and incompatibilities

Sufficient low temperature heat is required to create the violet-colored iodine fumes from the iodine crystals.

Moisture removing agents (calcium carbonate) are needed to assure the dry fumes are created.

Items cannot be processed with CA prior to iodine fuming.

Metal items can corrode upon exposure to iodine fumes.

Developed detail may not be seen on visibly dark surfaces.

Do not allow iodine fumes to get in contact with any photography equipment (Chesapeake Bay Division International Association of Identification, 2017m).

Materials and chemicals

- Iodine crystals
- Fuming chamber, ceramic/glass dish, heat source
- Disposable fuming gun
- Clear, sealable plastic bag large enough to contain the processed item

Mixing procedure

Not applicable, used as needed.

Processing procedure

Iodine fuming gun

- Remove the fuming gun from the plastic bag and keep the bag for the disposal of the used fuming gun
- The ampoule-containing iodine crystals will be visible inside the fuming gun
- Grasp the fuming gun in the palms of your hands for at least 1 minute (body heat will accelerate sublimation of crystals)
- Open the stopper cap on the front end of the fuming gun
- Attach the blowing tube to the red cap at the other end
- Crush the enclosed ampoule by squeezing between the thumb and the forefinger
- Aim the nozzle of the tube toward the area to be fumed (should not exceed 1 inch from processed area)
- Extend the blowing tube and blow steadily, a purple vapor will be seen coming from the nozzle
- Move the nozzle across the surface in a sweeping circular motion
- Faint prints can be refumed
- Starch can be sprayed to fix an iodine developed latent print

Modified fuming chamber

- Place crystals in bottom of clear, sealable plastic bag
- Place specimen in zip lock plastic bag
- Apply heat from hands or heat lamp to sublimate the crystals into a vapor

Collection/documentation

The latent evidence should then be photographed utilizing proper photography techniques for documenting latent evidence.

Shelf-life and disposal

Iodine crystals should be stored in a dark brown bottle with a plastic lid. The shelf-life of the iodine crystals is indefinite.

Small amounts of iodine crystals and the plastic bag that contain the used fuming gun (close the stopper cap and tie a knot in the blowing tube) can be wrapped in several layers of paper and discarded in a waste receptacle.

Large amounts of iodine crystals should be treated as caustic material.

4.2 DFO (1,8-diazafluoren-9-one) (Fig. 2.11)

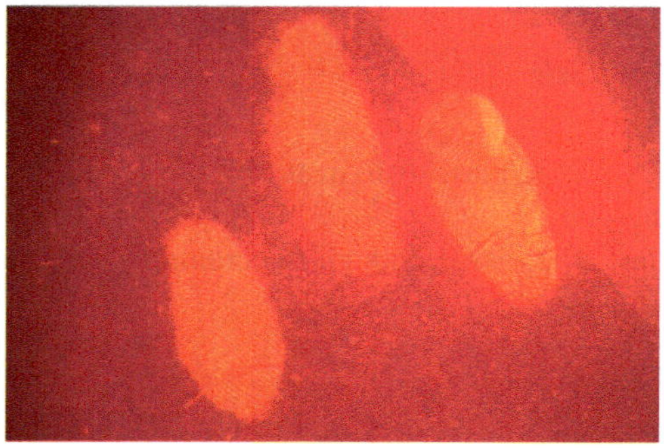

FIGURE 2.11

DFO.

Commonly referred to as DFO, 1,8-diazafluoren-9-one is used to develop latent prints on porous surfaces (Raleigh/Wake City-County Bureau of Identification, m). DFO reacts with nonspecific amino acids, specifically L-alanine that is a component of sweat. DFO is considered to be more sensitive to amino acids than Ninhydrin (McMullen & Beaudoin, 2013). When DFO reacts with amino acids, a pale red/pink color develops that also has a robust luminescence (Wallace-Kunkel et al., 2004).

With its fluorescent properties, DFO is useful on items with a variety of backgrounds. DFO can be applied to raw wood and dry porous surfaces (Chesapeake Bay Division International Association of Identification, 2019l).

A DFO stock solution can be created and stored with petroleum ether being added to create a working solution when ready to use the reagent.

Premixed solutions are available commercially and are commonly used.

Precautions and incompatibilities

It is suggested that DFO does not consume all of the amino acids present on an item and that continuing the processing sequence with Ninhydrin (D'Elia et al., 2015).

This reagent may cause inks to bleed and may interfere with biological evidence examination.

Yellow legal pad paper is best viewed at 570–590 nm with a red barrier filter (Sirchie Technical Information, f).

When a processed item is stored improperly, environmental humidity may decrease the luminescence of the ridge detail; heating the item for a few minutes can restore the luminescence (Chesapeake Bay Division International Association of Identification, 2019L).

Materials and chemicals (United States Department of Justice, Federal Bureau of United States Department of Justice Federal Bureau of Investigation, 2001)

- DFO powder—1g
- Methanol—200 mL
- Ethyl acetate—200 mL
- Glacial acetic acid—40 mL
- Petroleum ether—add to stock solution until working solution totals 2L
- Glass beaker/graduated cylinder
- Magnetic stirrer
- Glass pan
- Laboratory oven
- Dark plastic storage bottles

Mixing procedure (United States Department of Justice, Federal Bureau of United States Department of Justice Federal Bureau of Investigation, 2001)

- Stock solution
  - Combine 1g DFO powder into 200 mL methanol, 200 mL ethyl acetate, and 40 mL glacial acetic acid to create a stock solution.
  - Stir with a magnetic stirrer until all of the ingredients are dissolved.
- Working solution
  - When preparing to use the reagent, create the working solution by adding petroleum ether to the stock solution until it totals 2 L.

Processing procedure (Raleigh/Wake City-County Bureau of Identification, m)

Before any attempt is made to accelerate development by heating methods, the item must be completely dry.

- DFO can be applied to a surface by spraying or dipping for approximately 5 seconds.
- Place the item in an oven for 10–30 min at 100°C (212°F).

Development is complete when ridge detail becomes visible as a light pink color after baking the item (Wallace-Kunkel et al., 2004).

Examine the item with an ALS between 495 and 550 nm using an orange or red barrier filter.

Collection/documentation

The latent evidence should then be photographed utilizing proper photography techniques for documenting latent evidence.

Shelf-life and disposal

DFO should be stored in powder form until needed. As a solution, DFO should be store in a plastic-coated dark stoppered bottle up to 6 months.

This reagent is flammable and is a harmful irritant.

4.3 Ninhydrin (Fig. 2.12)

FIGURE 2.12

Ninhydrin.

Ninhydrin is used to develop latent prints on porous surfaces. Ninhydrin reacts with nonspecific amino acids in body fluids and frequently found in perspiration (Sirchie Technical Information, g). Fresh fingerprints can be developed; however, fingerprints that have aged one-to-two weeks develop more quickly than a fresh print, as the aged print has a higher initial concentration of "available" amino acids (Shulenberger, 2015).

Ninhydrin can be used to enhance bloody impressions.

Ninhydrin can be used to develop latent fingerprints on porous stones (Hefetz et al., 2015).

Ninhydrin can be used in several solvents: acetone, ethyl ether, methyl alcohol, ethyl acetate, etc. Acetone and ethyl ether dry quickly and therefore minimize the effect of solvent-soluble inks on the evidence. Porous surfaces more resistant to penetration, such as stiff brown paper, may require a slower drying solvent such as ethyl acetate.

Heptane-based ninhydrin reagents are recommended for items that may be examined as questioned documents as the heptane carrier may prevent inks running.

There is a commercially available ninhydrin-based reagent directed specifically at processing carbonless and heat-transfer (thermal) papers. Whereas acetic acid, ethyl acetate, and/or ethyl alcohol in standard ninhydrin will permanently darken specialty papers like receipts, the ninhydrin HT formula is free of these chemicals (Sirchie Technical Information, h).

The most widely used temperature used to heat documents after ninhydrin treatment is 80°C (176°F) as it develops the print quickly. Room temperature application over two-to-seven days produces the clearest prints through "slow curing."

Items processed with ninhydrin should be exposed to a humid environment. This can be achieved with the use of a humidity chamber or an iron on the steam setting.

Ninhydrin may be applied by dipping or spraying. Studies have shown aerosol mist spray produces clearer impressions than the dipping method. The spraying method, however, does increase safety hazards where exhaust fuming is not available.

Premixed solutions are available commercially and are commonly used.

Ninhydrin is used after DFO treatment and before 1,2-indanedione treatment (Raleigh/Wake City-County Bureau of Identification, o).

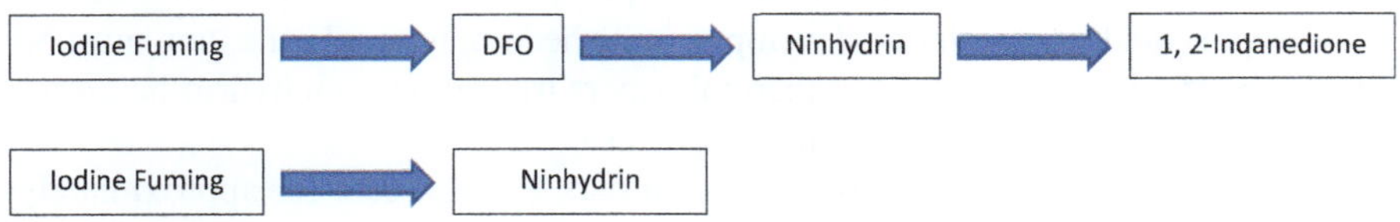

Precautions and incompatibilities

Nitrile gloves are recommended for handling items in ninhydrin as nitrile is more resistant to chemicals than latex (Wertheim, 2014).

A fuming hood is required when preparing and using this reagent as it is an inhalant and an irritant.

Ninhydrin follows DFO in the sequential process.

Items that have high animal or plant protein (leather, paper currency) may have excessive background staining (Chesapeake Bay Division International Association of Identification, 2019n).

Some solvents, like acetone, will cause inks to bleed.

Materials and chemicals

Alcohol-based solution (Raleigh/Wake City-County Bureau of Identification, o)

- Ninhydrin crystals—12g
- Alcohol solvent—1000 mL
- Glass beaker/graduated cylinder
- Stirring rod
- Glass pan
- Dark storage bottles

Heptane-based solution (Wertheim, 2014)

- Ninhydrin crystals—5g
- Ethanol—75 mL
- Ethyl acetate—25 mL
- Acetic acid—3 mL
- Heptane—1L

Mixing procedure

Alcohol-based solution

- Mix ninhydrin crystals into the alcohol solvent.
- The ninhydrin crystals will dissolve readily; minimal stirring is required.
- Store in dark storage bottles.

Heptane-based solution

- Mix the ninhydrin crystals into the combined chemicals.
- The ninhydrin crystals will dissolve readily; minimal stirring is required.
- Store in dark storage bottles.

Processing procedure

Ninhydrin can be applied to a surface by spraying, dipping, or painting. Before any attempt is made to accelerate development by heating methods, the item must be completely dry. Do not add heat to thermal papers treated with ninhydrin-based reagents specifically directed for thermal paper use.

Store the treated item in a plastic bag in a dark environment for approximately 36–72 h to allow for "slow cure" (Shulenberger, 2015).

The addition of humidity to the item can accelerate the development process. If a humidity chamber is available, set the humidity between 60% and 70% humidity for best results. While using an iron, use the highest steam setting and place a towel in between the item and the iron.

Development is complete when ridge detail becomes visible as a purple color and the item's background begins to stain purple (Wallace-Kunkel et al., 2004).

Collection/documentation

The latent evidence should then be photographed utilizing proper photography techniques for documenting latent evidence.

Shelf-life and disposal

Ninhydrin can be stored in dark bottles up to 1 year (United States Department of Justice, Federal Bureau of United States Department of Justice Federal Bureau of Investigation, 2001).

This reagent is flammable and is a harmful irritant.

4.4 1,2-indanedione (Fig. 2.13)

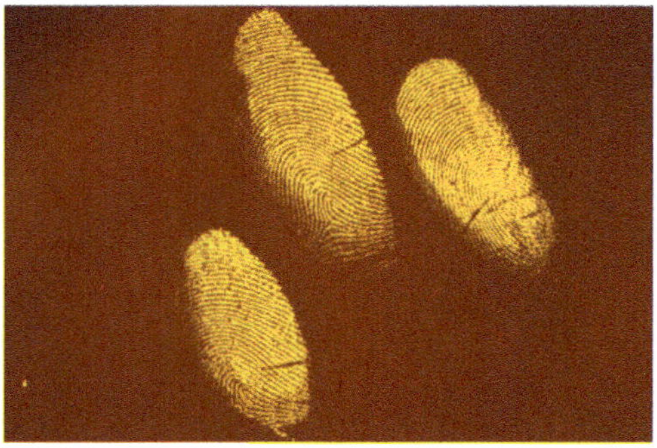

FIGURE 2.13

1,2-Indanedione.

1,2-Indanedione (IND) is used to develop latent prints on porous surfaces (Raleigh/ Wake City-County Bureau of Identification, l). IND reacts with alpha amino acids in fingerprint secretions creating a light pink reaction known as Joúllie's pink (Holt, 2013). With its fluorescent properties, IND is useful on items with a variety of backgrounds.

1,2-Indanedione can be applied to raw wood, brown paper bags, manila products, cardboard, kraft paper, and dry porous surfaces.

1,2-Indanedione is preferred to DFO as a processing tool as it creates less yellowish discoloration of the item than DFO-treated paper items. 1,2-Indanedione is less expensive than DFO and is less toxic than the carrier solvent used in DFO (D'Elia et al., 2015).

1,2-Indanedione is preferred to ninhydrin as a processing tool as it is a more sensitive detection method and the developed prints do not fade as quickly as ninhydrin-developed prints (Smith et al., 2011). However, in order to fully consume virtually all of the amino acids present on an item, the surface should be treated with IND and followed by Ninhydrin (Mangle et al., 2015).

A post-treatment zinc chloride fixing solution can be applied to the item to reduce fading of the developed print over time (Marriott et al., 2014).

Premixed solutions are available commercially and are commonly used.

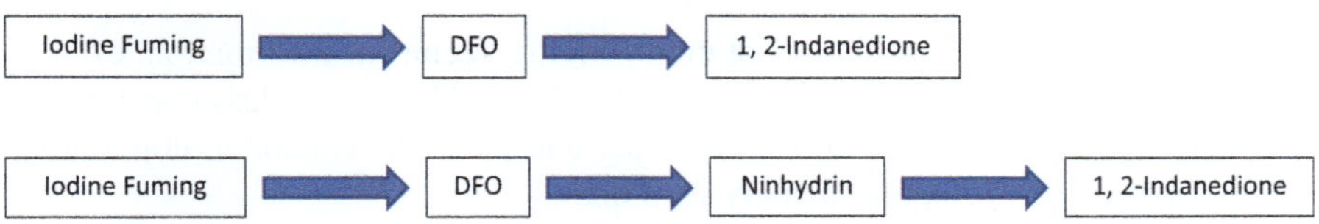

Precautions and incompatibilities

A fuming hood is required when preparing and using this reagent as it is flammable and an irritant.

Avoid exposing processed items to intense light or sunlight as photochemical reactions may cause a less-intense fluorescence. Store treated items in a dark, cool place.

This reagent may cause inks to bleed and may interfere with biological evidence examination.

Prolonged immersion in Ind-Zn (approximately 5 s) negatively affected subsequent processing with Oil Red O; the Oil Red O development may be fainter with less clearly defined detail (Frick et al., 2013).

Materials and chemicals

- Glass beakers
- Glass pans
- Dark glass storage bottle

- Dark chemical-resistant spray bottle
- Laboratory oven
- Laboratory mixer and magnetic stirrer
- ALS, orange/red filters, and goggles
- 1,2-Indandione working solution
  - 1,2-indanedione powder—2g
  - Ethyl acetate—70 mL
  - HFE-7100 fluid or petroleum ether solvent—930 mL
- (Optional) Zinc chloride fixing solution (Sirchie Technical Information, e)
  - Zinc chloride—30g
  - Methyl-tert-butylether (MTBE)—500 mL
  - Petroleum ether—500 mL

Mixing procedure

- 1,2-Indanedione working solution ((Raleigh/Wake City-County Bureau of Identification, l)
  - Add 70 mL ethyl acetate to 2g 1,2-indanedione powder into a dark glass bottle.
  - Gently swirl or shake the bottle until the powder is dissolved.
  - Add 930 mL of the petroleum ether solvent to the mixture.
  - Store in dark glass storage bottles.
- (Optional) zinc chloride fixing solution (Sirchie Technical Information, e)
  - Dissolve 30g of zinc chloride into 500 mL of MTBE in a glass container.
  - Add a magnetic stirrer to the container and place the container atop a laboratory mixer for approximately 20 min.
  - Remove the container from the mixer and stirrer.
  - Add 500 mL Petroleum ether to the mixture.

Processing procedure

- 1,2-Indanedione working solution ((Raleigh/Wake City-County Bureau of Identification, l)
  - Dip, spray, or wash the item in the reagent briefly (one-to-two seconds).
  - Air dry the item.
  - Bake the item in the laboratory oven at 100°C (212°F) for approximately 10–20 min at 60% humidity, or with no added humidity.

Development is complete when ridge detail becomes visible as a light pink color after baking the item.

- (Optional) Zinc chloride fixing solution (Sirchie Technical Information, e)
  - Add the solution to a chemical-resistant spray bottle.
  - Spray the item, left to right, and work down the item until it is saturated.
  - Air dry the item.
  - Bake the item in the laboratory oven at 100°C (212°F) for approximately 20 min.

- Examine the item with an ALS at 515 nm using an orange barrier filter.
- For manila, cardboard, brown paper bags, and kraft paper examine at 515—570 nm with an orange or red barrier filter (Chesapeake Bay Division International Association of Identification, 2019k).

Collection/documentation

The latent evidence should then be photographed utilizing proper photography techniques for documenting latent evidence.

Shelf-life and disposal

1,2-Indanedione should be stored in a dark glass stoppered bottle.

This reagent is flammable and is a harmful irritant.

4.5 Physical developer

Commonly referred to as PD, physical developer is used to develop latent prints on porous and semi-porous surfaces (Raleigh/Wake City-County Bureau of Identification, p). PD is a silver-based aqueous reagent that reacts upon the interaction of fatty acids and lipids in sweat with colloidal silver particles (Sodhi & Kaur, 2016). These components of fingerprints are insoluble in water and are stable for long periods of time; fingerprints that are several years old or that have been subjected to water may be visualized with PD. Metallic silver deposits on the water-insoluble components, thus allowing for fingerprint visualization (De Puit et al., 2011). Success has been achieved with PD in processing latent fingerprints that are over 30 days old (Frick et al., 2013).

Due to the elements of this reagent, this process is not recommended to be used in conjunction with silver nitrate. Furthermore, PD should not be used as the initial method of latent print development as additional latent detail may develop that were not discovered when amino acid-targeting processes were used (Sirchie Technical Information, i). PD follows DFO, ninhydrin, and Oil Red O in the sequential process6.

PD is considered to be very effective in developing latent prints on paper currency. PD is applicable to paper, cardboard, raw wood, tissue paper, paper based adhesive tapes, and some manufactured fibrous materials. Items that are wet, or that were wet and later dried may be subjected to the PD process (Raleigh/Wake City-County Bureau of Identification, p).

This processing technique is not recommended for thermal papers, photographs, or blueprints, as they may become permanently stained (Chesapeake Bay Division International Association of Identification, 2019o).

Premixed solutions are available commercially and are commonly used.

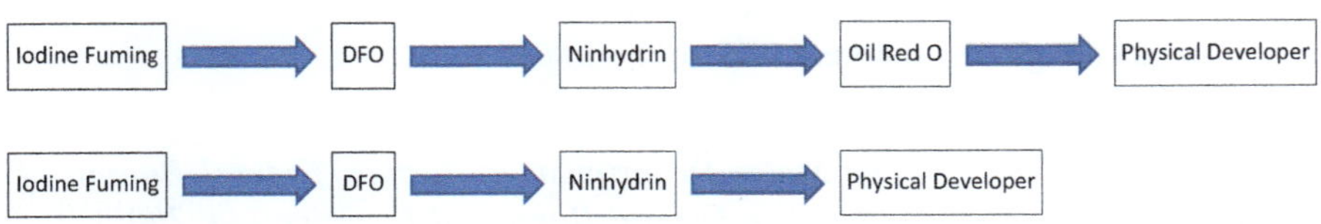

Precautions and incompatibilities

This process is expensive and time consuming, and requires a level of skill and knowledge in order to produce optimal results (Marriott et al., 2014). If an item is exposed to the reagent too long in the developer bath, metallic silver is deposited throughout the item's surface and ridge detail will be lost (De Puit et al., 2011).

A fuming hood is required when preparing and using this reagent as it is flammable and an irritant.

Laboratory glassware must be completely clean prior to initiating the development process.

When mixing the solutions, the chemicals must be combined in order of the recipe.

Processing should be done away from direct sunlight.

This processing technique should not be used on items that will be destroyed in water solutions.

If the item is to be examined as a questioned document, this processing technique is not recommended.

In an effort to mitigate the costs of using American Chemical Society (ACS)-grade silver nitrate, research has been conducted and found that technical grade or U.S. Pharmacopeia (USP)-grade silver nitrate produces results of similar quality as the ACS grade (Coppes et al., 2018).

Materials and chemicals (United States Department of Justice, Federal Bureau of United States Department of Justice Federal Bureau of Investigation, 2001)

- Maleic acid—25g
- Distilled water—4000 mL
- Ferric nitrate—30g
- Ferrous ammonium sulfate—80g
- Citric acid—20g
- N-dodecylamine acetate—3g
- Synperonic-N—4g
- Silver nitrate—200g
- Glass beakers:
  - Thoroughly cleaned
- Nonmetallic tongs:
  - With no serrated or sharp edges
- Laboratory rocker
- Magnetic stirrer
- Three glass pans:
  - Thoroughly cleaned and scratch free
  - Large enough that the item will not be folded
- Dark plastic storage bottles

Mixing procedure (United States Department of Justice, Federal Bureau of United States Department of Justice Federal Bureau of Investigation, 2001)

- Solution 1:
  - Maleic acid—25g
  - Distilled water—1000 mL
- Solution 2:
  - Ferric nitrate—30g
  - Ferrous ammonium sulfate—80g
  - Citric acid—20g
  - Distilled water—1000 mL
- Solution 3:
  - N-dodecylamine acetate—3g
  - Synperonic-N—4g
  - Distilled water—1000 mL
- Solution 4:
  - Silver nitrate—200g
  - Distilled water—1000 mL

Processing procedure (United States Department of Justice, Federal Bureau of United States Department of Justice Federal Bureau of Investigation, 2001)

Each solution should be thoroughly dissolved prior to beginning the process.

- Tray 1: solution 1—maleic acid
  - Submerge the item for 5 min.
  - If the item begins to emit bubbles, the item must be submerged until the bubbling concludes.
- Tray 2: solution 2—redox working solution
  - Add 1000 mL of solution two to glass pan with a stirring device.
  - Combine 40 mL of solution three to the glass pan and mix for 3–5 min.
  - Combine 50 mL of solution four to the glass pan and mix for 3–5 min.
  - Place tray two onto a laboratory rocker.
  - Submerge the item for 5–15 min, ensuring a continuous rocking motion.
- Tray 3: Water rinse
  - Submerge processed item to remove excess solution for 5 min; failure to do this will cause the item to become brittle when dried and vulnerable to destruction.
  - After the rinse, air dry the item.

Development is complete when background staining of the item is apparent. Ridge detail will appear gray/black.

Collection/documentation

The latent evidence should then be photographed utilizing proper photography techniques for documenting latent evidence.

Shelf-life and disposal

The shelf-life of this reagent is indefinite.

This reagent is flammable and is a harmful irritant.

4.6 Silver nitrate

Silver nitrate is used to develop latent prints on porous surfaces. The reagent that reacts with nonspecific sodium chloride, or salts, found in perspiration1. Silver nitrate follows ninhydrin in the sequential process (Chesapeake Bay Division International Association of Identification, 2019p). Due to the elements of this reagent, this process is not recommended to be used in conjunction with PD.

Silver nitrate can be prepared with a water or an alcohol carrier. The alcohol-based reagent can be used to process porous items that repel water such as waxed paper, styrofoam, and other items with waxy surfaces (United States Department of Justice, Federal Bureau of United States Department of Justice Federal Bureau of Investigation, 2001). This reagent is suited for porous items that have not been wet.

This processing technique is not recommended for photographs or blueprints as the reagent cannot be removed without destroying the item. Latent prints that are developed on glossy paper treated with silver nitrate may disappear hours after treatment (Sirchie Technical Information, j).

Due to the potential for over development and excessive background staining, this reagent is not widely used.

Premixed solutions are available commercially and are commonly used.

Precautions and incompatibilities

This is a costly process as there have been significant increases in the cost of silver nitrate in recent years (Coppes et al., 2018).

A fuming hood is required when preparing and using this reagent as it is flammable and an irritant.

This method is not recommended for items that have been wet.

Materials and chemicals (United States Department of Justice, Federal Bureau of United States Department of Justice Federal Bureau of Investigation, 2001)

- Silver nitrate (reagent grade purity $\geq$99%)
- Distilled water
- Ethanol
- Glass beakers
- Magnetic stirrer
- Dark glass storage bottles
- Ultraviolet light source ($\sim$360 nm)

Mixing procedure (United States Department of Justice, Federal Bureau of United States Department of Justice Federal Bureau of Investigation, 2001)

- 3% Silver nitrate water–based solution:
  - Silver nitrate—30g
  - Distilled water—1000 mL

Combine the silver nitrate and distilled water and stir for approximately 10 min, or until the crystals have disappeared.

- Alcohol-based solution:
  - Silver nitrate—30g
  - Distilled water—100 mL
  - Ethanol—1000 mL

Combine the silver nitrate and distilled water and stir for approximately 10 min, or until the crystals have disappeared. Add this solution to the ethanol.

Processing procedure

Silver nitrate can be applied to a surface by dipping or painting. Before any attempt is made to continue development, the item must be completely dry.

If exposed to room light, latent prints will develop over several hours (Sirchie Technical Information, j).

To accelerate development, the item should be exposed to an ultraviolet light source, at approximately 360 nm, and monitored continuously until development occurs. Development may occur between 10 and 60 min. Excessive high-intensity light or sunlight will cause severe background staining (Chesapeake Bay Division International Association of Identification, 2019p).

Development is complete when ridge detail becomes visible as a dark brown color and before the item's background begins to stain dark brown.

When storing the treated item, it should be packaged in a light-resistant container (Sirchie Technical Information, j).

Collection/documentation

The latent evidence should then be photographed utilizing proper photography techniques for documenting latent evidence.

Shelf-life and disposal

The shelf-life of this reagent is 12 months.

This reagent is flammable and is a harmful irritant.

5. Porous substrates - Wet

5.1 Oil Red O (Fig. 2.14)

FIGURE 2.14

Oil Red O.

Oil Red O (ORO) is used to develop latent prints on porous surfaces that have been wet (Raleigh/Wake City-County Bureau of Identification, q). Oil Red O is a lysochrome meaning that it is a compound that has the ability to dye fatty acids; it reacts with lipid proteins (Castello et al., 2002). Because lipids diffuse more slowly in paper, Oil Red O will react with porous items which have been wet (Beaudoin, 2012).

ORO treatment has been applied to developing lip prints with much success (Rawji & Beaudoin, 2006).

Successful development in the laboratory has been observed on deeply porous surfaces such as paper, cardboard, and kraft paper.

ORO is recommended to be performed prior to PD as it is less expensive and stains lipids, making it less destructive to the item than PD (Guigui & Beaudoin, 2007).

Premixed solutions are available commercially and are commonly used.

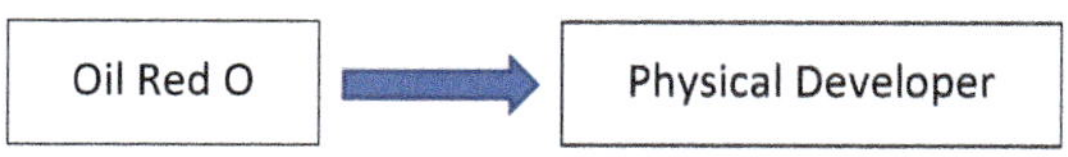

Precautions and incompatibilities

This is a time-consuming process.

A fuming hood is required when preparing and using this reagent as it is an inhalant and an irritant.

ORO requires a buffer solution to halt the development process.

ORO may be used prior to treatment with PD but ORO may cause higher background staining and can negatively affect PD's results (Marriott et al., 2014; Simmons et al., 2014).

Prolonged immersion in 1,2-Indanedione (approximately 5 s) negatively affected subsequent processing with Oil Red O; the Oil Red O development may be fainter with less clearly defined detail (Frick et al., 2013).

Materials and chemicals (Sirchie Technical Information, k)

- Laboratory mixer, magnetic stirrer
- Electric shaker
- Glass beaker/graduated cylinder
- Glass pans
- Dark storage bottles
- Oil Red O powder—1.54g
- Methanol—770 mL
- Sodium hydroxide—9.2g
- Distilled water
- Sodium phosphate monobasic monohydrate—101.55g
- Sodium phosphate dibasic heptahydrate—338.79g

Mixing procedure (Sirchie Technical Information, k)

- Developer
  - Dissolve 1.54g of Oil Red O into 770 mL of methanol.
  - Dissolve 9.2g of sodium hydroxide into 230 mL of distilled water. Add this mixture to the first mixture.
  - Place the mixture on an electric stirrer for approximately 20–30 min.
  - Filter the solution into a dark bottle away from light.
- Buffer solution
  - Dissolve 101.55g of sodium phosphate monobasic monohydrate into 1L of distilled water.
  - Dissolve 338.79g of sodium phosphate dibasic heptahydrate into 1L of distilled water.
  - Add these mixtures together and add enough water to increase the volume to 4L. Fully mix.

Processing procedure

The evidence item may be air-dried or wet at the time of processing.

- Oil Red O is applied by covering the item in a stain-resistant tray with the developer solution and agitated for 60-to-90 min, until development is observed (Raleigh/Wake City-County Bureau of Identification, q).

Development is complete when ridge detail becomes visible as a red color, and the item's background begins to stain pink.

- Remove the item from the developer tray and place it in a readied glass pan of the buffer solution. This will stabilize the pH of the document.
- Rinse the item in a readied glass pan distilled water and air dry or place in an oven at 50°C (122°F) to accelerate drying (Sirchie Technical Information, k).

Collection/documentation

The latent evidence should then be photographed utilizing proper photography techniques for documenting latent evidence.

Shelf-life and disposal

The two mixtures of the Oil Red O developer and buffer solutions can be stored in separate dark bottles up to 1 year.

This reagent is flammable and is a harmful irritant.

6. Adhesive

6.1 Crystal violet (gentian violet)

Crystal violet, also known as gentian violet, is a dye stain that can be utilized to develop latent evidence on the adhesive side of tape (Raleigh/Wake City-County Bureau of Identification, r). The dye stain is effective on duct tape, masking tape, clear plastic tape, plastic surgical tape, packing labels, and black electrical tape (Chesapeake Bay Division International Association of Identification, 2019q). This solution can be used on oily and greasy items, such as hand tools or car parts (Sirchie Technical Information, l).

The dye stain reacts with sebaceous material and dead skin cells that have been deposited on the tape through contact with friction ridge skin. This stain also reacts with protein and may be used to enhance protein residues in blood impressions (Aronson, 2010; Olenik, 2015)

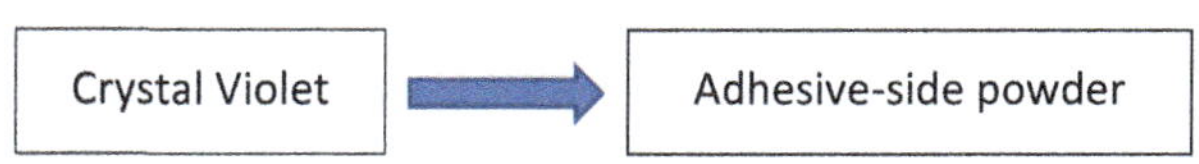

Precautions and incompatibilities

The nonadhesive side of the tape must be processed prior to the use of crystal violet. Crystal violet is a carcinogen, and, as a result, the solution can be harmful if inhaled or ingested.

Materials and chemicals (United States Department of Justice, Federal Bureau of United States Department of Justice Federal Bureau of Investigation, 2001)

- Crystal violet crystals—1g
- Distilled water—1L
- Tap water

Mixing procedure

- Combine the crystal violet crystals and distilled water.
- Mix until all crystal violet crystals are dissolved.

Processing procedure

- Pour the solution in a glass tray.
- Submerge the adhesive item in the solution for one-to-two minutes.
- Rinse the item with tap water being careful to avoid running water directly on the ridge detail. Allow to dry.

Processing is complete when ridge detail is visible as an intense, purple color.

Collection/documentation

The latent evidence should then be photographed utilizing proper photography techniques for documenting latent evidence.

Shelf-life and disposal

The mixed 1solution can be stored in a dark nonbreakable container indefinitely.

6.2 Adhesive-side powder

Adhesive-side powder, or sticky-side powder, is used to develop latent prints on the adhesive side of tapes and labels (Raleigh/Wake City-County Bureau of Identification, s). The powder is suspended in a detergent solution; after application, it reacts with sebaceous deposits and lipid components to develop latent detail.

It is highly effective on duct tape, plastic tapes, vinyl shipping labels and packing tape. Adhesive-side powder is used on nonporous surfaces and develops dark gray latent prints. The powder is mixed with a solution, which may be provided with a kit or can be mixed with equal parts water and detergent.

Adhesive-side powder may be used after gentian violet processing (Chesapeake Bay Division International Association of Identification, 2019r). This reagent can be post-CA fumigation with considerations given to the nonadhesive side of the item.

Premixed solutions are available commercially and are commonly used; follow the manufacturer's instructions.

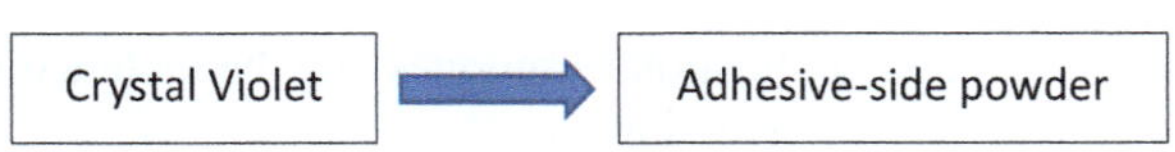

Considerations and incompatibilities

As adhesive-side powder develops dark gray latent prints, it is not recommended for use on dark surfaces due to lack of contrast.

Poor results may also be found when adhesive-side powder is used on adhesives that are gummed or water activated.

It can be used post-CA fuming, but the use of the regent may affect the ability to process the nonadhesive side of the tape. As such, considerations should be made to process or protect the nonadhesive surfaces prior to processing with adhesive-side powder.

Extended exposure of the mixed solution on an item may cause the excess staining to be difficult to rinse off (Chesapeake Bay Division International Association of Identification, 2019r).

Materials and chemicals (Sirchie Technical Information, m)

- Adhesive-side powder (light or dark option)
- Commercially available premixed detergent solution (EZFLO or Photo-Flo 200)
- Tap water
- Dish for mixing solution
- Small, camel hair brush (United States Department of Justice, Federal Bureau of United States Department of Justice Federal Bureau of Investigation, 2001) for application
- Clear plastic sheet for evidence retention

Mixing procedure

- Place 1 tsp (5 mL) of the powder in the mixing dish (Sirchie Technical Information, m).
- Add one tsp (5 mL) of the prepared detergent solution to the powder.
- Mix rigorously forming a thin, frothy, charcoal-colored paste.

Processing procedure (United States Department of Justice, Federal Bureau of United States Department of Justice Federal Bureau of Investigation, 2001)

- Using a small brush, apply the mixture by "painting" the solution onto the adhesive-side of the evidence.
- Let sit for 30–60 s.
- Rinse with slow stream of water, avoiding direct contact with the developed ridge detail.
- Processing is complete when dark-gray latent detail is visible following the water rinse.
- Can be reapplied if further development is needed.

Additional recommended application techniques may be included with the manufacturer's procedure, such as immersion.

Collection/documentation

The latent evidence should then be photographed utilizing proper photography techniques for documenting latent evidence.

Once dry, the latent print can be secured to a piece of clear plastic and retained as evidence.

Shelf-life and disposal

Mix as needed as storage is not recommended. Unused solution should be placed in paper and discarded.

7. Blood search

7.1 Bluestar

Bluestar is used as a searching tool that is designed to reveal trace amounts or diluted blood on porous and nonporous surfaces (Raleigh/Wake City-County Bureau of Identification, t). When Bluestar comes into contact with the peroxidase-like activity of the iron in the hemoglobin in blood; visible light as a blue-white luminescence is produced (Sorum, 2013).

The solution's widely reported sensitivity of 1:10,000 to 1:100,000 dilutions allows for the detection of trace amounts of blood (Sorum, 2013).

The chemiluminescence develops steadily and lasts from one-to-three minutes (Sorum, 2013). Total darkness is not required, though environmental light should be limited for ideal visibility and photography.

Bluestar has been reported not to harm blood samples for DNA tests (Sirchie Technical Information, n).

Bluestar was able to penetrate two layers of lacquer on finished wood flooring. The grooved areas sitting below the surface reacted heavily along the entire length of the wood sections (Smith, 2015).

Bluestar is available commercially; follow the manufacturer's instructions.

Precautions and incompatibilities

False positives may occur due to iron-rich soils, some copper and iron objects, iron compounds or rust, household cleaning products containing hypochlorite, bleach, some paints, some carpets, and a variety of vegetable compounds such as turnips, bananas, radishes, leeks, green beans, ginger, potatoes, and tomatoes.

The best results from the mixed reagent occur within 3 h of creation (Austin Police Department Forensic Science Bureau, 2019e).

An excessive amount of spray may dilute the impression.

Materials and chemicals (Sorum, 2013)

- Bluestar commercially available kit (2 catalyst tablets: one beige, one white)
- Distilled water—4oz should cover approximately 250 sq. ft. (Add a set of tablets for each 4oz of distilled water used.)
- Spray bottle

Mixing instructions (Sorum, 2013)

- Add 4oz of distilled water to the spray bottle.
- Add one beige tablet and one white tablet to the spray bottle.

- Gently swirl the spray bottle until the tablets have completely dissolved, approximately 2 minutes. Do not shake.

Processing procedure

- For indoor scenes, block all outside light sources and turn off the lights.
- For outdoor scenes, wait for dusk and limit light sources, that is, street lights, a bright moon.
- Establish camera settings to nighttime exposure to prevent using an excess of Bluestar that may dilution of the blood stain.

From approximately two feet away from the target, spray lightly and horizontally ahead of you.

Move the spray bottle side-to-side in a sweeping motion above the target area.

Processing is complete when an intense light-blue luminescence is observed in the 420–440 nm range. Be alert for false positives.

Collection/documentation

The low-level light technique should then be photographed utilizing proper photography techniques for documenting low-level light scenes.

Using a tripod, prepare the camera perpendicular to the target area to be photographed.

Use the following settings as a reference point.

- Manual setting
- ISO 400
- Large aperture—f/2.8 or f/4
- Shutter speed to bulb (30–90 s)
- No flash

Respray the activated area to document the chemiluminescence. Take several photographs with varying shutter speeds.

Shelf-life/disposal

Unmixed tablets have a shelf-life of 3 years.

7.2 Lumiscene

Lumiscene is a chemiluminescent reagent that is known as a catalytic presumptive test for blood (Raleigh/Wake City-County Bureau of Identification, u). Luminescence occurs when Lumiscene comes into contact with the peroxidase-like activity of the hemoglobin in blood; visible light as a blue luminescence is produced (Sirchie Technical Information, o). This reagent is a searching tool, not an enhancement tool.

This application must be used in the dark to visualize the results.

Lumiscene's chemical luminescence emission peaks around 525 nm providing higher visibility than standard luminol solutions. The reagent contains a low percentage of peroxide chemistry, thus protecting against DNA degradation (Sirchie Technical Information, o).

Lumiscene provided slightly better results in regard to DNA degradation than BlueStar at a dilution of 1:100 at 30 days (Nicloux & Bressler, 2014); Lumiscene has lower concentration of hydrogen peroxide of 0.12% (Andersson, 2017).

Lumiscene is commercially available as a premixed kit.

Precautions and incompatibilities

Multiple false positives to include: oxidants, catalysts, copper, nickel, iodine, rust, bleach, formalin, horseradish, citrus fruits, bananas, watermelon, and numerous vegetables.

To visualize the reagent the environment must be dark.

Overspraying dilutes the sample.

The reagent should be used within 4 hours of creation (Sirchie Technical Information, o).

Materials and chemicals

- Manufacturer's kit (16oz. bottle of stock solution, two Activator tablets)
- Distilled water
- Spray bottle
- Beaker

Mixing procedure

- Working Solution (Sirchie Technical Information, o).
  - Add the two activator tablets to the 16oz bottle of stock solution.
  - Swirl the solution gently for 1 min, then let stand for 5 min.
  - Repeat the swirl/stand instruction three times.

If needed, transfer the solution from the stock bottle to a fine mist spray bottle.

Processing procedure

Spraying is the most effective method of application; approximately 6–8 inches from the area being processed. When spraying, use the finest mist possible because an excess of application may cause over development.

Spray the area of interest, the development should occur within 30 s.

Do not overspray the area; the area will need to be tested with phenolphthalein.

Processing is complete when the suspected area when a blue-white luminescence is observed.

Collection/documentation

The low-level light technique should then be photographed utilizing proper photography techniques for documenting low-level light scenes.

Shelf-life and disposal

Lumiscene should be stored in dark bottles. The shelf-life of the solution is limited to a day or two, and the tablets will have an expiration date of the box. Make the solution as you need it.

Excess Lumiscene can be discarded in the properly marked waste container.

8. Blood enhancements

8.1 Acid Yellow 7

Acid Yellow 7 is a reagent that can be used to develop or enhance bloody impression on nonporous surfaces (Sirchie Technical Information, p). Acid Yellow 7 is a sensitive acid dye that reacts with the protein components found in blood on nonporous surfaces. This process requires the use of an ALS to visualize the latent detail; the fluorescing ridge detail appears under blue/blue-green light (BVDA a, 2019).

Once the item has been processed, the stain can be examined with the ALS and lifted with a gel lifter.

Premixed solutions are available commercially and are commonly used, follow manufacturer's instructions.

Considerations and incompatibilities

Acid Yellow 7 should not be used on absorbent materials such as carpet, linen, or paper as the background staining cannot be removed (Sears et al., 2005).

Before staining, the surface should be fixed to prevent the blood from running.

Acid Yellow 7 is not considered as a hazardous material, and since the working solution is a water/ethanol mixture, there are no harmful flumes in normal use. The solution is flammable and should be used where the surface and air temperatures do not exceed 28° C (82.4°F) (Sears et al., 2005).

Material and chemicals (BVDA a, 2019)

- 5-Sulfosalicylic acid fixative—20g
- Distilled water—2400 mL
- Acid Yellow 7 powder—1g
- Ethanol (98% +)—500 mL
- Glacial acetic acid—100 mL
- ALS
- Yellow filter/goggles
- Orange filter/goggles
- Gel lifters

Mixing procedure (BVDA a, 2019)

- 5-Sulfosalicylic acid fixative:
  - 5-Sulfosalicylic acid dihydrate—20g
  - Distilled water—1L
  - Combine 50g of 5-sulfosalicylic acid dihydrate with 1 liter of distilled water.
- Acid Yellow working solution
  - Acid Yellow 7 powder—1g
  - Distilled water—700 mL

- Ethanol—250 mL
- Glacial acetic acid—50 mL
- Add acid yellow 7 powder to distilled water and stir until the powder is dissolved.
- Once the powder is dissolved, add ethanol and glacial acetic acid.

- Rinse solution
  - Distilled water—700 mL
  - Ethanol—250 mL
  - Glacial acetic acid—50 mL
  - Combine all of the ingredients.

Processing procedure (Sirchie Technical Information, p)

- Fix the impression with the fixing solution of 5-sulfosalicylic acid with a pump sprayer and allow to completely dry, approximately 15 min. Fresh blood's color will change from dark red to dark brown when fixation occurs.
- Spray the working solution on the item from a distance of six″ to 9"; do not spray directly at the latent evidence, but from parallel to the item's surface. Allow the stain to remain on the item for approximately 5–10 min.
- Allow approximately 1 min for the solution to dry.
- Wash lightly with the rinse solution to remove background staining.
- Processing is complete when ridge detail appears yellow in color. Under an ALS between 455 and 470nm, the ridge detail will fluoresce bright yellow when examined with an amber filter. The impression may be examined with an ALS at 520–560 nm with an orange filter.

Collection/documentation

- The latent/impression evidence should be photographed utilizing proper photography techniques for documenting latent/impression evidence.
- A gel lifter can be used to collect the impression; allow the lifter to remain on the surface for only 1 minute before removing (BVDA a, 2019).

Shelf-life and disposal

- The premixed formula has a 12-month shelf-life.

8.2 Amido Black

Amido Black is a protein dye stain that can be used on nonporous and some porous surfaces to enhance bloodstained fingerprints and footwear impressions. Specifically, this stain is a disulfonic acid that reacts with the lysine, arginine, and histidine pendant groups of a hemoglobin molecule (Marchant & Tague, 2007). When applied, Amido Black leaves a blue-black impression when it comes into contact with the protein serum and amino acids in blood (Praska & Langenburg, 2013). This process should only be used where blood is visible on an item or within a scene.

Amido Black can be created in two forms: a methanol or an aqueous solution. The methanol-based formula produces a clearer stain on an item, but due to its toxicity, may not be ideal in all environmental settings. The aqueous formula is preferred for use in the field processing, or when the target surface is painted (Raleigh/Wake City-County Bureau of Identification, v).

Premixed solutions are available commercially and are commonly used, follow manufacturer's instructions.

Precautions and incompatibles

Some denser porous surfaces can absorb too much of the dye stain and turn the surfaces dark (Chesapeake Bay Division International Association of Identification, 2019s).

Amido Black should be used after all DNA samples have been collected, and after all, other fingerprint development methods have been attempted.

The methanol-based method is highly flammable and toxic; this may damage some surfaces including painted surface.

Materials and chemicals

- Laboratory stirring device
- Clear or dark stoppered bottles
  - Methanol-based formula (United States Department of Justice, Federal Bureau of United States Department of Justice Federal Bureau of Investigation, 2001):
    - Developer solution:
      - Naphthol blue black powder (or commercially available Amido Black powder)—2g
      - Glacial acetic acid—100 mL
      - Methanol—900 mL
    - Rinse solution:
      - Glacial acetic acid—100 mL
      - Methanol—900 mL
    - Final rinse solution:
      - Distilled water—1L (tap water can be used)
  - Aqueous-based formula (Sirchie Technical Information, q):
    - Rinse solution:
      - Citric acid—38g
      - Distilled water—2000 mL
    - Developer solution:
      - Naphthol blue black powder (or commercially available Amido Black powder)—2g
      - Liqui-Nox detergent—2 mL
      - Amido Black aqueous rinse solution—1000 mL

Mixing procedure

- Methanol-based developer formula:

- Combine the powder, the glacial acetic acid, and the methanol. Place the solution on a stirring device for approximately 30 min, until the powder is dissolved.
- Methanol-based rinse solution:
  - Combine the glacial acetic acid and methanol.
- Aqueous-based developer formula:
  - Combine powder, the detergent, and the rinse solution. Place the solution on a stirring device for approximately 30 min, until the powder is dissolved.
- Aqueous-based rinse solution:
  - Combine the citric acid and the distilled water.

Processing procedure

Prior to processing, the item or area should be completely dried.

- Methanol-based formula:
  - Apply the developer solution by dipping the item or a squirt bottle.
  - Leave the solution on the item for approximately 10 s to I minute.
  - Apply the methanol solution with a squirt bottle to remove excess dye.
  - Apply a final rinse of distilled water.
  - Allow to air dry.
- Aqueous-based formula:
  - Apply the developer solution by dipping the item or a squirt bottle.
  - Leave the solution on the item for approximately 2 min until desired development has been achieved.
  - Rinse the item or immerse in the rinse solution for approximately 1 min to remove background staining.
  - These steps may be repeated until maximum clarity is achieved. Apply the rinse solution again.
  - Allow to air dry.

Development is complete when maximum contrast of the black-blue stain.

Collection/documentation

The latent evidence should be photographed utilizing proper photography techniques for documenting latent evidence.

There have been several cases were the impression have been lifted with a gel lifter.

Shelf-life/disposal

Amido Black should be store in a dark container and marked with reagents name and date made.

Amido Black has been recorded to have an indefinite shelf-life.

Solutions are flammable and therefore should be store in a flammable cabinet.

Small spills can be collected with absorbent paper, wrapped in layers of the paper, and discarded.

8.3 Hungarian Red

Hungarian Red is a dye solution in a water–acetic acid mixture that is used for enhancing impression evidence in blood on porous and nonporous surfaces (Petretei & Angyal, 2015).

Hungarian Red can be used to recover blood prints from human skin without the risk of poisoning or long-lasting coloring of the body (Petretei & Angyal, 2015).

Lifted and/or weak traces of Hungarian Red will fluoresce under a green ALS (520–560nm) when viewed with a yellow or orange filter (Sirchie Technical Information, r).

After the solution has dried, the impression can be collected on a gel lifter (BVDA b, 2019).

Hungarian Red is a premixed, commercially available solution; follow manufacturer's instructions.

Precautions and incompatibles

Collect all DNA samples prior to using this reagent for processing. Do not use Hungarian Red on items that may be subject to other forms of forensic examinations such as hair, fiber, physiological fluid, handwriting, or ink analyses.

Stains caused by Hungarian Red may be difficult to remove.

When the results are collected with a gel lifter, the solution may be absorbed by the gel lifter over time. The gel lift of the impression will be the reverse of the actual impression.

Material and chemicals

- Manufacturer's Hungarian Red solution
- Distilled water
- Hair dryer
- ALS
- Yellow filter/goggles
- Orange filter/goggles
- Gel lifters

Mixing procedure

None.

Processing procedure

- Immerse or use a rinse bottle to apply the stain. If spraying the surface, spray from a distance of 6–9″ from the object (Sirchie Technical Information, r).
- Allow approximately 1 min for the solution to dry.
- Wash lightly with distilled water.
- Remove any excess water residue with hair dryer on low heat.
- The impression may be examined with an ALS at 520–560 nm with an orange or yellow filter (Sirchie Technical Information, r).

Collection/documentation

The latent evidence should be photographed utilizing proper photography techniques for documenting latent evidence.

A gel lifter can be used to collect the impression; allow the gel lifter to remain on the surface for 15–30 min (BVDA b, 2019).

Shelf-life and disposal

Hungarian Red can be stored in dark bottles up to 1 year.

8.4 Leuco crystal violet (LCV)

Leuco crystal violet (LCV) is a stain used on porous and nonporous evidence for the development and enhancement of blood evidence. When LCV and hydrogen peroxide come into contact with hemoglobin in blood, a catalytic reaction occurs, and the color reaction is a purple/violet color (Bodziak, 1995).

The stain application can be used on bloodstains that are not visible and to enhance and provide additional contrast to blood stain patterns that are visible.

Other blood enhancement techniques can be used after the application of LCV including Amido Black.

Advantages of LCV compared to other blood enhancement chemicals include the ease of application and the variety of surfaces that the stain can be applied to. The reaction of LCV with blood results in an almost instant visualization of the reaction.

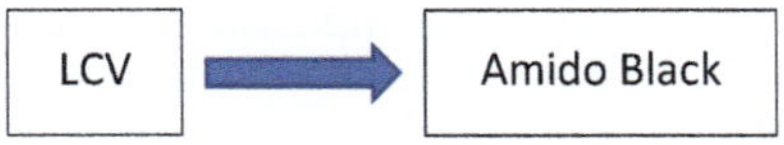

Precautions and incompatibilities

Background development of the item may occur under the intense light due to photoionization of the stain. Photograph any enhanced impressions subject to sunlight after development due to photoionization (Chesapeake Bay Division International Association of Identification, 2019t).

LCV may react to other substances not specific to blood; there are several oxidizing substances that will produce a false positive for the presence of blood.

This reagent is not recommended for excessively blood-stained items.

The application of the excess reagent may result in leaching of the impression, apply the reagent using the fines misting device available. LCV is an aqueous solution and can distort ridge pattern if sprayed in excessive amounts.

CA fuming may be detrimental to this procedure.

Materials and chemicals (Austin Police Department Forensic Science Bureau, 2019f)

- LCV crystals—1 g
- 5-Sulfosalicylic acid—10 g
- Hydrogen peroxide—500 mL
- Sodium acetate—3.7 g

- Fine mist sprayer
- Paper towels
- Laboratory stirrer
- Coffee filter

Mixing procedure

- Combine 5-sulfosalicylic acid to the hydrogen peroxide and fully dissolve.
- Add the sodium acetate and fully dissolve.
- Add the LCV crystals and fully dissolve.
- Place the solution on a stirring device for approximately 30 min.
- Strain the mixed solution through a coffee filter and a funnel into a spray bottle; this step reduces the spray bottle's chances of getting clogged.

Processing procedure

Spraying is the most effective method of application; spray approximately 6–8 inches from the area being processed.

When spraying use the finest mist possible because excess application may cause over development or ruining of the print. Spray the area of interest, the development should occur within 30 s and then blot the area with a paper towel.

The solution should be blotted after positive results and prior to documenting.

Steps can be repeated when the area is dry to improve contrast.

Collection/documentation

The latent/impression evidence should be photographed utilizing proper photography techniques for documenting latent/impression evidence.

Shelf-life and disposal

LCV should be stored in dark bottles. The shelf-life of the solution is limited to a day or two; however, the LCV dye in powder form is indefinite. Make the solution as you need it.

Small amounts of LCV powder can be wrapped in paper and discarded in the waste receptable and excess LCV mixed reagent can be discarded in the properly marked waste container.

8.5 Phloxine B

Phloxine B is a protein dye and is commonly used to enhance bloodstained impression evidence on nonporous surfaces (Raleigh/Wake City-County Bureau of Identification, x). Phloxine B is a biological stain that also acts as an acid-base indicator (Sodhi et al., 2004). The reagent will not enhance a print composed solely of normal latent print residues, however is used in cases with blood contaminated impressions. Phloxine B is used on dark colored or multicolored surfaces.

When examined with an ultraviolet light, Phloxine B provides optimum results in the long wavelength UV range on white and multicolored surfaces (Sodhi et al., 2004).

Phloxine B is a premixed commercially available reagent, follow manufacturer's instructions.

Precautions and incompatibilities

Phloxine B should not be used on absorbent surfaces; it works well on surfaces like linoleum, glass, tiles, painted surfaces, and PVC floor covering (Sodhi et al., 2004).

Reaction time is slow.

Phloxine B contains ethanol and formic acid, ethanol is highly flammable and toxic, and formic acid is caustic.

Overspray dilutes the sample that may need to be tested/collected as a blood sample.

Materials and chemicals

- Manufacturer's phloxine B solution
- Spray bottle
- Beaker

Mixing procedure

None.

Processing procedure

Spraying is the most effective method of application; approximately 6–eight″ from the area being processed.

When spraying use the finest mist possible because excess application may cause over development.

Spray the area of interest, allow the stain to react with the impression for 2–3 min or until the impression becomes a reddish-orange colored stain.

Do not overspray the area, the area will need to be tested with phenolphthalein.

Collection/documentation

The latent evidence should then be photographed utilizing proper photography techniques for documenting latent evidence.

Shelf-life and disposal

Phloxine B should be stored in dark bottles. The shelf-life of the solution is limited, make the solution as you need it.

Excess phloxine B can be discarded in the properly marked waste container.

9. Gun bluing

Gun bluing is chemical process that is typically used to maintain the metal finish on firearms by preventing oxidation or rust. This chemical process can also be used to develop latent ridge detail on metal surfaces and, in particular, brass and nickel fired and unfired shell casings. The gun bluing solution is comprised of three chemical components; an acid, cupric salt, and selenious acid (Morrissey et al., 2017).

The solution reacts with metal surfaces it comes in contact with, effectively causing the metal to gray or darken.

When oily or fatty deposits from friction ridge skin are present on the metal or a shell casing, they create a barrier between the solution and the casing. As such, the surface of the casing without oily or fatty deposits will darken and latent detail will develop.

There are various manufactures of gun blue products that may be utilized for this process. As most of the available solutions are designed to treat and preserve metal on firearms, you will need to dilute the solution for a forensic application. A ratio of 50/50 dilution is commonly used, but it will vary depending on manufacture and, therefore, testing and controls should be utilized to determine the best working ratio.

There are gun bluing kits that are sold that are designed specifically for forensic applications. In the event a forensic gun bluing kit is utilized, follow the manufacture's recommended procedure for application. The gun bluing process can be done prior to or post CA processing. Morrissey et al. found that best results were obtained if gun bluing was done after a short CA cycle of around 5 min, or if done prior to CA.

Precautions and incompatibilities

The gun bluing reaction occurs relatively quickly, within 20–60 s. Close monitoring of the development is required to avoid the over processing of the casing. If the chemical solution is left on the metal cartridge too long, this can result in the loss of latent detail.

This procedure may interfere with breech face markings that are used in firearms examinations (Chesapeake Bay Division International Association of Identification, 2019h).

Materials and chemicals

- Beaker or clear container for mixing the solution
- Gun blue reagent
- Distilled water

Or

- Gun bluing kit including bluing solution and acetic acid

Mixing procedure

- The ratio will vary depending on the manufacturer

Start with 50:50 gun blue to distilled water (Morrissey et al., 2017).
Or

- Follow manufactures instructions for preparing solution for forensic gun bluing kits

Processing procedure

- Pour the solution in a clear glass beaker
- Submerge the casing in the solution

- Closely monitor the darkening of the casing, approximately 20–60 s
- Once the casing begins to darken, remove it from the solution
- Rinse thoroughly with tap water to stop development

Development is complete when black ridge detail is visible.

Collection/documentation

The latent evidence should be photographed utilizing proper photography techniques for documenting latent evidence.

Shelf-life and disposal

Follow manufacture's recommendations for disposal and storage.

This solution should be made fresh prior to processing (Chesapeake Bay Division International Association of Identification, 2019h).

10. Conclusion

In summary, there are various methods for developing latent ridge detail. The surface the latent print has been deposited on will be the primary factor in deciding the best processing method. Other considerations may include the color of the surface, the texture of the surface, as well as if the surface is wet, greasy, sticky, or other contaminants are present. Other factors and limitations that may impact the processing method are the environment and the availability of specialized equipment and reagents in the field or in the laboratory.

The aforementioned processes in this chapter are intended to serve as a guide. Although this is a thorough list of processes and reagents, there may be alternative processes developed as forensic science and accompanying technologies continues to advance. Regardless of the process used, the examiner must be sure that their decisions on how to proceed, and the techniques utilized are supported with documented studies, and all methods should be practiced and tested prior to being utilized in actual case work.

References

Andersson, R. (2017). *An evaluation of two presumptive blood tests and three methods to visualize blood (bachelor thesis)*. Linköping, Sweden: Linköping University.

Aronson, C. (2010). Development of bloody prints on the adhesive side of duct tape. *Journal of Forensic Identification, 61*(3), 250–259.

Austin Police Department Forensic Science Bureau b. (February 01, 2019). *CA (cyanoacrylate) fuming-heat acceleration*. Technical Manual.

Austin Police Department Forensic Science Bureau e. (February 01, 2019). *BlueStar*. Technical Manual.

Austin Police Department Forensic Science Bureau a. (February 01, 2019). *CA (cyanoacrylate) fuming-fuming wand.* Technical Manual.

Austin Police Department Forensic Science Bureau c. (February 01, 2019). *CA (cyanoacrylate) fuming-gel pack.* Technical Manual.

Austin Police Department Forensic Science Bureau d. (February 01, 2019). *Iodine fuming.* Technical Manual.

Austin Police Department Forensic Science Bureau f. (February 2019). *Leucocrystal violet.* Technical Manual, 01.

Beaudoin, A. (2012). Fingerprint staining technique on dark and wetted porous surfaces: Oil red O and rhodamine 6G. *Journal of Forensic Identification, 62*(4), 315–329.

Bodziak, W. J. (1995). The use of Leuco crystal violet to enhance shoe prints in blood. In *European meeting for shoe print and tool mark examiners* (pp. 8–11). Helsinki, Finland.

Bouwmeester, M., Gorré, S., Rodriguez, C., & de Puit, M. (2011). A comparison of reagents for the visualization of blood prints on knives with black handles. *Journal of Forensic Identification, 61*(4), 353–362.

BVDA a. (December 12, 2019). *"Acid yellow 7", staining blood traces.*

BVDA b. (December 12, 2019). *"Hungarian red", staining blood traces.*

Castello, A., Alvarez, M., Miquel, M., & Verdu, F. (2002). Long-lasting lipsticks and latent prints. *Forensic Science Communications, 4*(2).

Chesapeake Bay Division International Association of Identification a. (June 22, 2017). *"Cyanoacrylate ester", interactive chemical reagents program.*

Chesapeake Bay Division International Association of Identification b. (June 22, 2019). *"Ardrox", interactive chemical reagents program.*

Chesapeake Bay Division International Association of Identification c. (June 22, 2019). *"Basic yellow 40", interactive chemical reagents program.*

Chesapeake Bay Division International Association of Identification d. (June 22, 2019). *"MBD", interactive chemical reagents program.*

Chesapeake Bay Division International Association of Identification e. (June 22, 2019). *"RAY", interactive chemical reagents program.*

Chesapeake Bay Division International Association of Identification f. (June 22, 2019). *"Rhodamine 6G", interactive chemical reagents program.*

Chesapeake Bay Division International Association of Identification g. (June 22, 2019). *"Thenoyl Europium chelate", interactive chemical reagents program.*

Chesapeake Bay Division International Association of Identification h. (August 29, 2019). *"Gun bluing", interactive chemical reagents program.*

Chesapeake Bay Division International Association of Identification i. (September 23, 2019). *"Small particle reagent", interactive chemical reagents program.*

Chesapeake Bay Division International Association of Identification j. (August 29, 2019). *"Sudan black", interactive chemical reagents program.*

Chesapeake Bay Division International Association of Identification k. (July 10, 2019). *"1, 2-indanedione", interactive chemical reagents program.*

Chesapeake Bay Division International Association of Identification l. (June 22, 2019). *"D.F.O.", interactive chemical reagents program.*

Chesapeake Bay Division International Association of Identification m. (June 22, 2017). *"Iodine fuming", interactive chemical reagents program.*

Chesapeake Bay Division International Association of Identification n. (June 18, 2019). *"Ninhydrin", interactive chemical reagents program.*

Chesapeake Bay Division International Association of Identification o. (August 16, 2019). *"Physical developer", interactive chemical reagents program.*

Chesapeake Bay Division International Association of Identification p. (August 26, 2019). *"Silver nitrate", interactive chemical reagents program.*

Chesapeake Bay Division International Association of Identification q. (September 23, 2019). *"Gentian violet", interactive chemical reagents program.*

Chesapeake Bay Division International Association of Identification r. (August 29, 2019). *"Sticky side powder", interactive chemical reagents program.*

Chesapeake Bay Division International Association of Identification s. (September 20, 2019). *"Amido black - methanol", interactive chemical reagents program.*

Chesapeake Bay Division International Association of Identification t. (June 22, 2019). Leucocrystal violet (LCV). In *Interactive chemical reagents program.*

Cohen, D., & Cohen, E. H. (2010). A significant improvement to the SPR process: More latent prints were revealed after thorough wiping of small particle reagent-treated surface. *Journal of Forensic Identification, 60*(2), 152–157.

Coppes, A., Ramotowski, R. S., Jones, B. A., Manna, M. E., Chervinsky, E. V., & Smith, KimD. (2018). Silver nitrate grade and its effect on physical developer performance – a validation study. *Journal of Forensic Identification, 68*(1), 11–27.

De Puit, M., Koomen, L., Bouwmeester, M., de Gift, M., Rodriguez, C., van Wouw, J., & de Haan, F. (2011). Use of physical developer for the visualization of latent fingerprints. *Journal of Forensic Identification, 61*, 166–170.

D'Elia, V., Materazzi, S., Iuliano, G., & Niola, L. (2015). Evaluation and comparison of 1,2-Indanedione and 1,8-diazafluoren-9-one solutions for the enhancement of latent fingerprints on porous surfaces. *Forensic Science International, 254*, 205–214.

Frick, A. A., Fritz, P., Lewis, S. W., & van Bronswijk, W. (2013). Sequencing of a modified oil red O development technique for the detection of latent fingermarks on porous surfaces. *Journal of Forensic Identification, 63*, 369–385.

Gardner, Ross M. (2005). *Practical Crime Scene Processing and Investigation, 9*, 238–241.

Guigui, K., & Beaudoin, A. (2007). The use of oil red O in sequence with other methods of fingerprint development. *Journal of Forensic Identification, 57*(4), 550–573.

Hefetz, I., Pertsey, R., & Bar-Sheshet, E. (2015). Development of latent fingerprints from stones: Field work provides identifications. *Journal of Forensic Identification, 65*(3), 214–218.

Holt, D. (2013). Determining the quality and sustainability of friction ridge deposits on envelopes sent through the postal system. *Journal of Forensic Identification, 63*(3), 247–253.

Kent, T. (2013). Letter to the editor Re: Forced condensation of cyanoacrylate with temperature control of the evidence surface to modify polymer formation and improve fingerprint visualization. *Journal of Forensic Identification, 63*(1), 2–3.

Mangle, M. F., Xu, X., & de Puit, M. (2015). Performance of 1, 2-Indanedione and the need for sequential treatment of fingerprints. *Science & Justice, 55*, 343–346.

Marchant, B., & Tague, C. (2007). Developing fingerprints in blood: A comparison of several chemical techniques. *Journal of Forensic Identification, 57*(1), 76–93.

Marriott, C., Lee, R., Wilkes, Z., Comber, B., Spindler, X., Roux, C., & Lennard, C. (2014). Evaluation of fingermark detection sequences on paper substrates. *Forensic Science International, 236*, 30–37.

McMullen, L., & Beaudoin, A. (2013). Application of oil red O following DFO and ninhydrin sequential treatment: Enhancing latent fingerprints on dry, porous surfaces. *Journal of Forensic Identification, 63*(4), 387–423.

MedTech Forensics a. MBD mixture, premixed liquid.

MedTech Forensics b. Red-yellow, premixed liquid.

MedTech Forensics c. Thenoyl europium chelate.

MedTech Forensics d. White-star mixture, premixed liquid.

Montgomery, L., Spindler, X., Maynard, P., Lennard, C., & Roux, C. (2012). Pretreatment strategies for the improved cyanoacrylate development of dry latent fingerprints on nonporous surfaces. *Journal of Forensic Identification, 62*(5), 517–542.

Morrissey, J., Larrosa, J., & Birkett, J. W. (2017). A preliminary evaluation of the use of gun bluing to enhance friction ridge detail on cartridge casings. *Journal of Forensic Identification, 67*(3), 313–322.

Mutter, N., Deacon, P., & Farrugia, K. (2018). The effect of cyanoacrylate fuming on subsequent protein stain enhancement of fingermarks in blood. *Journal of Forensic Identification, 68*(4), 545–556.

Nicloux, C., & Bressler, J. (2014). Effect of four latent blood visualization products of DNA. *Forensic Science Sem, 4*(1), 30–34.

Olenik, J. (2015). Dye staining of duct tape: An overlooked procedure. *Journal of Forensic Identification, 65*(3), 219–221.

Petretei, D., & Angyal, M. (2015). Recovering bloody fingerprints from skin. *Journal of Forensic Identification, 65*(5), 813–826.

Praska, N., & Langenburg, G. (2013). Reactions of latent prints exposed to blood. *Forensic Science International, 224*, 51–58.

Raleigh/Wake City-County Bureau of Identification a. Super glue fuming wand (cyanowand). Laboratory Manual.

Raleigh/Wake City-County Bureau of Identification b. Super glue fuming (Cyano-Shot). Laboratory Manual.

Raleigh/Wake City-County Bureau of Identification c. MBD dye stain. Investigations Division Technical Procedures Manual.

Raleigh/Wake City-County Bureau of Identification d. Basic yellow dye stain. Investigations Technical Procedures Manual.

Raleigh/Wake City-County Bureau of Identification e. RAY dye stain. Investigations Technical Procedures.

Raleigh/Wake City-County Bureau of Identification f. Red-yellow dye stain. Investigations Division Technical Procedures Manual.

Raleigh/Wake City-County Bureau of Identification g. Rhodamine 6G dye stain. Investigations Technical Procedures Manual.

Raleigh/Wake City-County Bureau of Identification h. Thenoyl Europium chelate. Investigations Division Technical Procedures Manual.

Raleigh/Wake City-County Bureau of Identification i. White-star dye stain. Investigations Division Technical Procedures Manual.

Raleigh/Wake City-County Bureau of Identification j. Small particle reagent (molybdenum disulfide). Investigations Division Technical Procedures Manual.

Raleigh/Wake City-County Bureau of Identification k. Sudan black. Investigations Division Technical Procedures.

Raleigh/Wake City-County Bureau of Identification l. 1, 2-Indanedione. Investigations Division Technical Procedures Manual.

Raleigh/Wake City-County Bureau of Identification m. DFO (1, 8-Diazafluoren-9-one). Investigations Division Technical Procedures Manual.

Raleigh/Wake City-County Bureau of Identification n. Iodine fuming. Investigations Technical Procedures Manual.

Raleigh/Wake City-County Bureau of Identification o. Ninhydrin. Investigations Division Technical Procedures Manual.

Raleigh/Wake City-County Bureau of Identification p. Physical developer. Investigations Division Technical Procedures Manual.

Raleigh/Wake City-County Bureau of Identification q. Oil red O. Investigations Division Technical Procedures Manual.

Raleigh/Wake City-County Bureau of Identification r. Crystal violet. Investigations Division Technical Procedures Manual.

Raleigh/Wake City-County Bureau of Identification s. Sticky-side powder. Investigations Division Technical Procedure Manual.

Raleigh/Wake City-County Bureau of Identification t. Bluestar. Investigations Division Technical Procedures Manual.

Raleigh/Wake City-County Bureau of Identification u. Lumiscene. Investigations Technical Procedures Manual.

Raleigh/Wake City-County Bureau of Identification v. Investigations Technical Procedures Manual.

Raleigh/Wake City-County Bureau of Identification x. Phloxine B. Investigations Division Technical Procedures Manual.

Rawji, A., & Beaudoin, A. (2006). *Oil Red O Versus Physical Developer on Wet Papers: A Comparative Study, 56*(1), 33–54.

Richards, D., & Thomas, J. (2014). Nonporous fluorescent dye stains: A comparative analysis. *Journal of Forensic Identification, 64*(3), 239–254.

Saferstein, Richard (1998). *Criminalistics an introduction to forensic science* (6th ed.).

Schwarz, L., & Hermanowski, M. (2012). The effect of humidity on long-term storage of evidence prior to using cyanoacrylate fuming for the detection of latent fingerprints. *Journal of Forensic Identification, 62*(3), 227–231.

Sears, Butcher, & Fitzgerald. (2005). Enhancement of fingerprints in blood Part 3: Reactive techniques, acid yellow 7, and process sequences. *Journal of Forensic Identification, 55*(6), 741–761.

Shulenberger, W. (2015). Present status of the ninhydrin process for developing latent fingerprints. *Journal of Forensic Identification, 65*(4), 417–422.

Simmons, R. K., Deacon, P., & Farrugia, K. (2014). J. Water-soaked porous evidence: A comparison of processing methods. *Journal of Forensic Identification, 64*(2), 157–173.

Sirchie Technical Information a. Ardrox TI02-71ENG-REV6.

Sirchie Technical Information b. Basic yellow fluorescent enhancement dye. TI02-77ENG-REV5.

Sirchie Technical Information c. Small particle reagent kit. TI03-238ENG-REV4.

Sirchie Technical Information d. Sudan black. TI02-76ENG-REV7.

Sirchie Technical Information e. 1, 2-Indanedione. TI02-129ENG-REV6.

Sirchie Technical Information f. Dfo. TI02-28ENG-REV7.

Sirchie Technical Information g. Ninhydrin. TI02-30ENG-REV7.

Sirchie Technical Information h. Ninhydrin HT. TI04-369ENG-REV1.

Sirchie Technical Information i. Physical developer. TI02-46ENG-REV7.

Sirchie Technical Information j. Latent print development manual. TB02-102ENG-REV5.

Sirchie Technical Information k. Oil red O. TI06-526ENG-REV2.
Sirchie Technical Information l. Crystal violet. TI02-51ENG-REV6.
Sirchie Technical Information m. Adhesive-side powder development. TI02- 32ENG-REV5.
Sirchie Technical Information n. BlueStar forensic kit.
Sirchie Technical Information o Lumiscene. TI11-683ENG-REV1.
Sirchie Technical Information p. Acid yellow Vol. 7, TI11-684ENG-REV1.
Sirchie Technical Information q. Amido black. TI02-44ENG-REV8.
Sirchie Technical Information r. Hungarian red. TI02-49ENG-REV6.
Smith, K. (2015). The efficacy of blue star forensic on wood floors coated with lacquer and shellac: A cold case in progress. *Journal of Forensic Identification, 65*(2), 97−106.
Smith, S., Sebetan, I. M., & Stein, P. (2011). Development of aged latent prints on envelopes. *Journal of Forensic Identification, 61*(4), 363−372.
Sodhi, G. S., & Kaur, J. (2016). Physical developer method for detection of latent fingerprints: A review. *Egyptian Journal of Food Science, 6*, 44−47.
Sodhi, G. S., Kaur, J., & Garg, R. K. (2004). Fingerprint powder formulations based on organic, fluorescent dyes. *Journal of Forensic Identification, 54*, 4−8.
Sorum, E. D. (2013). Identifying a false positive reaction from bluestar on nonporous surfaces. *Journal of Forensic Identification, 63*(6), 660−673.
Steele, C., Hines, M., Rutherford, L., & Wheeler, A. (2012). Forced condensation of cyano-acrylate with temperature control of the evidence surface to modify polymer formation and improve fingerprint visualization. *Journal of Forensic Identification, 62*(4), 335−348.
United States Department of Justice, Federal Bureau of Investigation. (2001). *Processing guide for developing latent prints.*
Wallace-Kunkel, C., Roux, C., Lennard, C., & Stoilovic, M. (2004). The detection and enhancement of latent fingermarks on porous surfaces − a survey. *Journal of Forensic Identification, 54*(6), 687−705.
Wertheim, P. (November 2014). *Ninhydrin: Basic to advanced* (Vol 15). Iowa Division International Association of Identification.
Wilson, H. (2010). RAY dye stain versus genetian violet and alternate powder for development of latent prints on adhesive side of tape. *Journal of Forensic Identification, 60*(5), 510−523.
Zamir, A., Oz, C., Leifer, A., & Geller, B. (2002). The effect of small particle reagent employed as a fingerprint enhancement technique of subsequent STR typing from bloodstains. *Journal of Forensic Identification, 52*(6), 691−695.

CHAPTER

3

Artificial intelligence in forensic anthropology: State of the art and Skeleton-ID project

Rubén Martos[1,2], Oscar Ibáñez[1,3,5], Pablo Mesejo[1,4]

[1]Panacea Cooperative Research S. Coop., Ponferrada, Spain; [2]Department of Physical Anthropology, University of Granada, Granada, Spain; [3]Andalusian Research Institute in Data Science and Computational Intelligence, University of Granada, Granada, Spain; [4]Department of Computer Science and Artificial Intelligence and Research Centre for Information and Communications Technologies of the University of Granada, Granada, Spain; [5]Faculty of Computer Science, CITIC, University of A Coruña, A Coruña, Spain

1. Introduction

Human identification (ID) is not only of great importance in medicolegal contexts, resolving serious legal and social predicaments, but also provides a resolution to grieving families who need closure to their sadness. The untraceable (and shameful) number of unidentified people worldwide is staggering and keeps growing due to repeated mass disasters, war conflicts, forced disappearances, criminal investigations of dead and missing people, etc. All these factors contribute to the increasing need for accurate and efficient tools that allow for establishing and verifying human identity. The number of examples is appalling. Natural disasters have caused over 1.3 million deaths in the last 2 decades (Ritchie & Roser, 2014). For instance, the recent cyclone in Mozambique (2019) resulted in over 700 deaths, and the devastating earthquake of 2010 in Haiti killed more than 160,000 people that have yet to be identified. Countries with recent wars, such as Chile, Argentina, Panama, and South Africa, have established Truth Commissions (Hayner, 2006), which is one of their key goals for the identification of their victims. Within the EU, similar initiatives exist in Spain (Association for the Recovery of Historical Memory, ARMH) in the Balkans (International Commission on Missing People, ICMP); and according to the UN, only in Spain, it is estimated that there are more than 100,000 unidentified people in mass graves from the civil war (UN Human Rights Council, 2014) (second country in the world, after Cambodia). In certain countries in Latin America, the situation is particularly dramatic due to their high levels of violent deaths and enforced disappearances (Jaramillo, 2020). Only in Mexico, according to the country's National Search Commission (CNB), there are more than 26,000 unidentified bodies and over 40,000 missing persons (Mexico's Missing

Methodological and Technological Advances in Death Investigations. https://doi.org/10.1016/B978-0-12-819394-5.00006-7

People Agency Searching, 2019), and social and political movements are demanding solutions to this epidemic and the victims' identification problem. Neighboring countries count by thousands the number of missing persons as well, Colombia (over 83,000), Guatemala (45,000), Argentina (>30,000), Peru (>20,000), El Salvador (>8000), and Chile (>3200). On the other hand, new challenges have emerged in the domain of ID of living people, in which accurate identification techniques can be instrumental. In recent years, the EU is facing an unprecedented wave of mass migration, which is creating a strain at our borders, and fast-growing numbers of unidentified dead (Missing Migrants, 2019) in the Mediterranean. Besides, one of the most sensitive associated challenges is the estimation of the living age of unaccompanied minor migrants: more than 20,000 during 2017, around 90% 15–17 years old, mostly undocumented (UNICEF, 2019). Forensic age estimation of the living is requested by courts and other government authorities, so that immigrants—in most cases, unaccompanied refugees who may be minors and whose real age is unknown—do not suffer unfair disadvantages because of their guesstimated age. According to the United Nations High Commissioner for Refugees (UNHCR), almost half the people forcibly displaced from their homes are children, representing a demographic at a particular risk of "abuse, neglect, violence, exploitation, trafficking or forced military recruitment" and in need of international protection. Additionally, another set of methods that have a relationship with the underlying anatomical structures, identification methods based on facial photographs, can be used in crimes with the presence of video surveillance cameras or other image evidence to identify criminals and detect the presence of minors on pedophile material or in border control, among others.

Governments struggle to approach this titanic task, being utterly overflowed and lacking the resources and adequate forensic tools required. Although all legal and societal issues are hard to solve, the implementation of efficient and affordable identification systems would contribute to bringing closure to many families and to protect vulnerable sectors of society. DNA and fingerprints are the most common ID methods. However, DNA requires a comparison sample, which may not always be available. The main limitation of fingerprints identification is that postmortem friction ridge skin may not always be available, and the disaster victims may not always have antemortem fingerprints available in a searchable database. Hence, the efficiency of these gold-standard ID techniques can be dramatically decreased in DVI scenarios.

Forensic anthropology (FA) represents an alternative and counterpart with a much broader range of applicability. According to the Scientific Working Group for Forensic Anthropology (SWGANTH), forensic anthropologists contribute to identification at two levels. The first level is through methods that establish an identification. The second level is through methods that contribute to identification by limiting potential matches to the individual. Among the former group, the SWGANTH includes comparative radiology (CR) and the comparison of surgical implants, while it leaves for the second level, the following techniques or lines of evidence: Craniofacial superimposition (CFS), biological profile (BP), medical

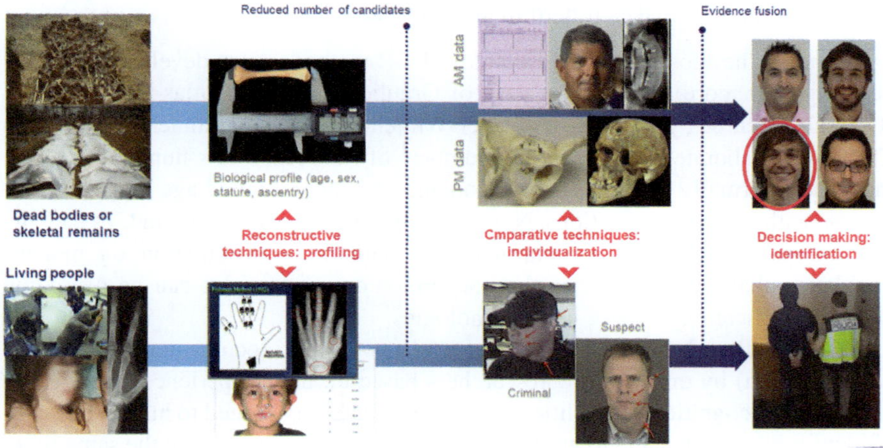

FIGURE 3.1

Application of forensic anthropology techniques to dead and living people cases.

Credit: Original.

and/or dental records, congenital abnormalities and pathological conditions, and comparative photography (Scientific Working Group for Forensic) See Fig. 3.1 for a schematic visualization of the applicability range of FA techniques.

Surgical implant identification involves locating the manufacturer's symbol along with the device's unique serial number that is not an easy task as older implants are not easily traced. The remaining methods are largely complex to apply. We summarize below the main difficulties forensic practitioners experience when applying these techniques. Sometimes, they are not seen as difficulties since they are assumed as limitations of the nature of the problem at hand. However, there are empirical evidences in related scientific fields that those limitations can be transformed into challenges that can be tackled following an interdisciplinary approach.

1.1 Reconstructive techniques (profiling)

- Manual (caliper-based) measurements in which there may be intra- and interobserver variation.
- Subjective and inaccurate comparison of forms (atlas-based categorization) (Greulich & Pyle, 1959; Schmeling et al., 2016).
- Unknown patterns and/or hidden relationships in a large amount of multidimensional data.
- Lack of international consensus and good practices in validation studies. For this reason, the Organization of Scientific Area Committees (OSAC) for Forensic Science, administered by the National Institute of Standards and Technology (NIST), is working actively to strengthen forensic practice through improved international standards (gov, 2016)

- Manual filtering makes it hard to apply to mass disasters.

Some of the most commonly employed BP methods were developed 50–100 years ago (or more), as it is the case of Greulich and Pyle's atlas-based method (GP) (Greulich & Pyle, 1959) or Tanner-Whitehouse (TW2) (Tanner et al., 1975). They were elaborated with a limited number[1] of samples (a few hundred to a few thousand), normally biased by a common ancestry and a limited age range in comparison with modern populations. Nowadays, the access to antemortem CTs and virtual autopsies will provide anthropologists with more information on modern population than ever before, so that the limitations of the past can be overcome with the application of these new technologies.

Additionally, phases or patterns were observed and documented (atlas-based categorization) by one or a few researchers based on their experience, knowledge, and pattern recognition capabilities. On the one hand, it is limited to human capacity of identifying patterns and to work with a huge data set of samples at the same time. The application of this atlas-based method is linked to subjectivity (by the nature of the problem of holistically matching a pattern/shape with a sketch of the average pattern/shape) and intra- and interobserver dispersion (Cameriere et al., 2012; Ritz-Timme et al., 2011). A large group of methods rely on a series of linear measurements directly taken from the clean bone with the caliper or in radiographic images. Finally, the number of published BP methods can be counted by hundreds. However, there is currently no clear consensus on how to calculate, express, and interpret the error when validating methods for age estimation, while at the same time, there exist empirical evidence about the inadequacy of some age estimation methods in calculating, expressing, and interpreting the errors obtained (Valsecchi et al., 2019).

1.2 Comparative techniques (individualization)

- Complex and subjective visual observations.
- Need to acquire image of postmortem (PM) bone in the same pose and conditions as antemortem (AM) bone.
- Very dependent on the knowledge and experience of the anthropologist.
- Very high variability in precision and little or no validation.
- Lack of standardization and international agreements.
- Generic image processing software, very limited, introduces new errors.

[1] Although a data set of a few thousand samples it is probably considered an ideal (rarely achieved) situation in the FA field, other forensic and life sciences research fields develop their models using larger datasets, as it is the case of fingerprints (up to 500.000 pairs are employed to validate the system in Peralta et al. (2016)), facial recognition (3.7 million images of 58,207 subjects in Ranjan et al. (2017)) or medical image classification (two million of X-rays were employed in Laserson et al. (2018) for pathological classification; 129,450 clinical images in Esteva et al. (2017) for dermatologist-level classification of skin cancer).

The characteristics involved in physical matching and matching achieved in patterned evidence existing in the state of nature are not events amenable for counting; instead these are ensemble of visible units occupying the entire pattern area stretching the probability of re-occurrence of a verisimilitude pattern into infinity offering epistemic support to uniqueness (Jayaprakash, 2013). The application of comparative techniques used to be reduced to subjective comparison of the above pattern types by methods that are observational such as physical matching, superimposition, or side-by-side visual evaluation.

Standardization is a big issue in comparative techniques and at the decision-making stage. While there are meritorious examples of individual or team proposals for standardization, for example in craniofacial anthropometry nomenclature (Caple & Stephan, 2016) or CR-based identification (Ross et al., 2016), there is a gap of international/multicenter initiatives, as for example, MEPROCS EU initiative (Damas et al., 2015).

The main difficulty and source of errors is the different acquisition moments (from months to years), different acquisition settings (subject-to-camera-distance, focal distance, relative pose, etc.), different acquisition devices (different camera or X-ray models), and even different nature of the AM and PM materials to be compared, as it is the case of CFS technique where one or more photographs of the face are compared with a skull. In any case, the side-by-side comparison should be preceded by a PM data acquisition process trying to mimic the AM acquisition conditions. This task is normally approached in a trial-and-error process, which is time-consuming, and the error cannot be measured or estimated, that is, its validity strongly depends on the knowledge and experience of the anthropologist (Ibáñez et al., 2015).

1.3 Decision-making (identification)

- Decisions based on partial and approximate knowledge with a high presence of uncertainty and conjectures.
- Difficult visualization of data and interpretation of results.
- Different categorical degrees in decision-making.
- Strongly dependent on the expert and difficult to defend in legal processes.
- Lack of reproducibility. Absence of solid reliability studies
- Time constraints: unapproachable for multiple comparisons/mass disasters/mass graves.

Finally, the decision-making process leading to the final identification decision is normally expressed in varying linguistic degrees (strong, moderate or limit support; presumptive or positive, etc.), which account for the presence of uncertainty and incomplete information. How different evidence is combined and weighted by the expert cannot be expressed quantitatively, depends on the expert's knowledge and experience. The whole identification process lacks reproducibility, and it is almost impossible to be applicable to a multiple comparison scenario (unless a team of experts is available during an extended period of working time).

Large reliability studies are not common in the FA field as there are still ethical and legal concerns not overcome for the acquisition and sharing of public data sets. Additionally, the lack of standardization and reproducibility involve contradictory conclusions concerning the reliability of the techniques. This is at least the case of CFS where the reliability studies reported in the literature are fraught with limitations. The absence of an objective measure of the skull face overlay match, technical limitations of the equipment, disregard for accurate landmarks location while performing landmark based methods, absence of soft tissue data for the tested population, insufficient quality of the 3D cranial models, postmortem photographs, reduced samples, absence of appropriate statistical analysis, the absence of inter- and intraobserver studies are but a few (Huete et al., 2015).

We summarize all the limitations identified in the existing methods in a single challenge: the need of automatic, objective, and more accurate methods. This seems to be the perfect environment for computerized systems based on artificial intelligence (AI) techniques (Russell & Norvig, 1995), due to their ability to model human behavior in solving specific problems and their capacity to process extremely large amounts of data and discover hidden patterns.

Despite the theoretical and empirical convenience of applying AI techniques to FA, only a limited number of AI-based papers have been published in the last decade. However, they have demonstrated their precision and robustness, hence their feasibility for forensic identification applications in humans. The purpose of this chapter is to give visibility and increase the awareness of the FA community about the potential of AI to solve problems in this field, by carrying out the first bibliographic review. In fact, we considered that there is a problem of lack of interdisciplinary research. This claim stems from the fact that there are only a few multidisciplinary research groups worldwide where forensic anthropologists work alongside AI specialists. On the other hand, we also think that there is a lack of technological development in the FA community that, together with the high complexity of some of the anthropology techniques, has led to errors and inaccuracies. As a consequence of these, the use of techniques such as CFS has been relegated and discouraged. Despite the proven benefits, the use of AI techniques in daily forensic casuistry is practically null.

The content of this chapter is organized as follows. Section 2 is an introduction to an important group of AI techniques, those that we consider most appropriate to address the main challenges in the field of FA and on which the majority of the proposals to date are based. Section 3 represents the central part of this work, the study of the state-of-the-art applications of AI techniques in the field of FA. This in turn is divided into five parts that collect, almost exhaustively, the approaches based on AI techniques to address: the estimation of the BP from the study of the skeleton and the sex and age estimation from facial photographs, the trauma and pathology analysis, CR, CFS, and finally facial approximation. For each of these FA methods, a summary of the fundamentals and reference works is also included (it is not intended to be exhaustive or precise at all), with the aim that this chapter serves not only to bring FA closer to AI, but also the reverse path, which is capable of attracting the interest of the AI community to the FA research field. Section 4 includes a description of the Skeleton ID project, as a representative paradigm of fulfilling the gap between FA and AI communities while providing technological means accessible for practitioners. Finally, Section 5 includes some concluding observations and a discussion of the actions that the authors consider most important in order to advance in the field of FA.

2. Artificial intelligence: Techniques and fundamentals

The following are some specific branches of AI, which, in our opinion, can address all the challenges of the FA field cited above. Importantly, these AI research fields do not correspond to disjoint or hermetic categories, but there is a high degree of permeability and hybridization between them.

2.1 Computer vision

Computer vision (CV) is the scientific discipline that deals with the automatic interpretation of images (Forsyth & Ponce, 2002). It covers different levels of abstraction. First, low-level CV, also called image processing, involves primitive operations that consider local properties of an image. This level takes as input an image and gives as output the same image transformed according to the aforementioned operation (e.g., image restoration and image enhancement). Second, mid-level CV, also called image analysis, involves intermediate steps prior to image semantic understanding. This level takes as input an image and a set of features, characterizing the image, is provided as output (e.g., image segmentation and feature detection). Finally, high-level CV aims to "give meaning" to the input image/video and to develop cognitive functions related with the human vision system (e.g., object recognition and image registration).

Within the CV, among the specific techniques with the greatest potential for application in the field of FA, we highlight the following:

Image segmentation (IS), which is defined as the division of an image into regions that are homogeneous with respect to some visual feature. More precisely, it is the process of assigning a label (class) to each pixel in the image so that the pixels that share the same label will also have certain similar visual characteristics, such as color, intensity, or texture. In addition to the individual properties of each pixel, in more complex segmentation problems, it will be necessary to take into account information at different hierarchical levels, from the pixel to regions and even the entire image, were changes in pixel characteristics, distances or shapes. Fig. 3.2 shows an example of multiclass segmentation, that is, different classes of objects, specifically lungs, clavicles, and heart, are segmented on an X-ray. Precise segmentation of organs and bones on radiographs is especially difficult due to the overlap

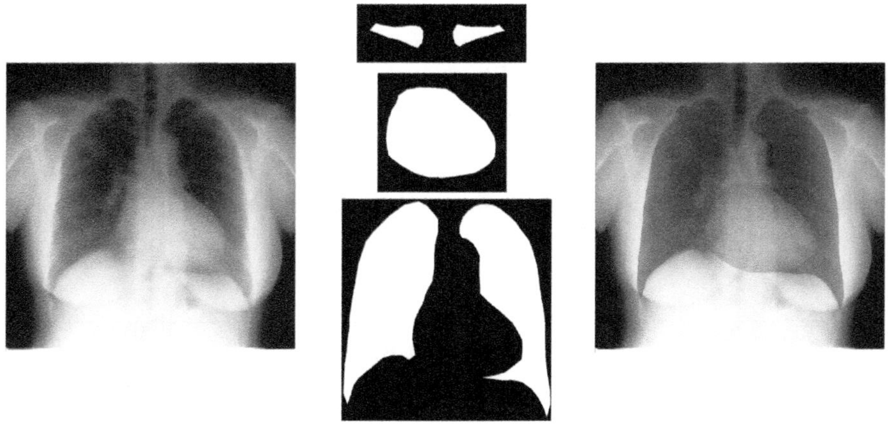

FIGURE 3.2

IS example where the original image is a chest radiograph (a). Using the automatic IS algorithm in (Gómez et al., 2020), the clavicles, heart and lungs are extracted (b). The image on the right (c) represents the organs and bones segmented over the original image with different colors.

Credit: Original.

that exists between them and the diffuse contours of the "objects" to be segmented in many areas of the image. In fact, in this specific problem a learning process has been necessary (machine learning methods will be explained later) where, from hundreds of radiographs previously segmented by a radiologist manually (using image processing software, the contours of the lungs, heart and clavicles were carefully delimited), one learns the characteristics of each of the "objects" of interest (typical shape and possible variations, location within the image and with respect to other objects, range of intensities and textures).

The detection, classification, and understanding of images: strongly related and dependent on the IS, consists of detecting/locating objects within an image (drawing, for example, a rectangle around them), categorizing those objects and even mathematically describing properties of the detected objects (Forsyth & Ponce, 2002). Image understanding is the process of actually interpreting those regions/objects to find out what is really happening in the image. This may ultimately include making some decision for future action. Fig. 3.3 shows an example of the latter, a system that detects firearms from video surveillance images and activates an alarm when that happens.

Image registration (IR), which aims to find a geometric transformation that superimposes two images taken at different times, from different points of view, and/or by different sensors (Markelj et al., 2012). Depending on the nature of the acquisition systems, we can distinguish IR methods of different modalities (monomodality/multimodality) and dimensions. Within this latter version, we can

FIGURE 3.3

In the image on the left, we can see an example of weapon detection (Olmos et al., 2018). In this example, the algorithm developed is capable of detecting weapons and classifying them by assigning a probability (as can be seen in the image with the pistol class) in real time, that is, on frames of a video while it is displayed. The image on the right shows the result of an algorithm for the automatic detection and classification of cephalometric landmarks (Gómez et al., 2019a).

Credit: Original.

distinguish: 2D-2D (that is, between two photos or two radiographs), 3D-3D (between two 3D models, for example, two intraoral scans of the same person 1 month apart), and 3D-2D (between a 3D model and a 2D image, for example, a 3D model of a skull and a photograph of a person's face). Other possible classification of IR methods includes: the intersubject registration (images of different people, for example, to study the morphometry of the skull and later relate it to variables such as sex or ancestry) and different methods according to the reference information used (extrinsic/intrinsic) and the similarity metrics used to measure the registration error (intensity-based/feature-based).

CV could be extremely valuable in FA. Take for example, the comparison of an AM X-ray image and a 3D PM model to determine if the bone that appears in both belongs to the same person. First, we would need to isolate the anatomical structure of interest in the AM and PM data. This involves an IS process (see Fig. 3.3). We could then automatically align the projection of the segmentation resulting from the PM data onto the segmented AM X-ray image. This process is known as IR (see Fig. 3.4).

2.2 Machine learning

Machine learning (ML) is the branch of AI whose objective is the development of techniques that allow computers to learn directly from data (Bishop, 2006). ML represents a vast field of research that includes, without claiming completeness.

- Supervised learning: where the data set employed to train the models includes inputs and desired outputs.

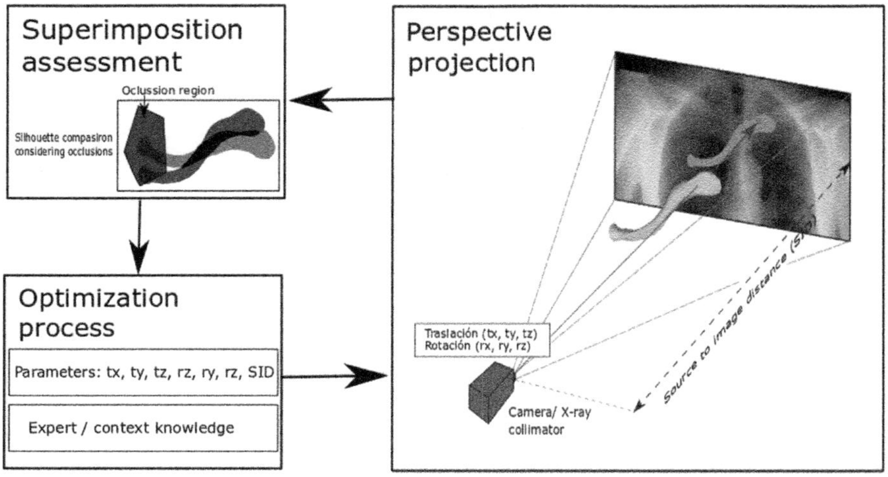

FIGURE 3.4

Example of an iterative IR process where a 3D model of a clavicle is registered on a chest (2D) radiograph. In this iterative process, an optimization algorithm seeks to reproduce the acquisition parameters of the AM radiograph, it searches for the translation, rotation and X-ray source (collimator) to image (plate) distance values. This search process is guided by the overlapping error (error minimization process) between the 3D model contour (once projected onto the radiograph) and the clavicle contour (obtained by an IS process) on the radiograph.

Credit: Original.

- Unsupervised learning: where the system, according to a notion of similarity, has to be able to recognize patterns based solely on the input examples.
- Reinforcement learning: where the system learns through a trial-and-error procedure, interacting with the environment, based on a generic feedback signal about how well or badly the task in question is being performed.

Data are cheap and abundant, while knowledge is expensive and scarce; hence, ML techniques are used to solve those problems in which there is no human experience (for example, sailing on Mars), where humans are unable to explain their experience (speech recognition), when the solution must be tailored to particular cases (user biometrics), or the size of the problem is too large for our limited reasoning capabilities (calculating the ranges of web pages).

From a practical point of view, ML deals mainly with the resolution of regression problems (i.e., the estimation of continuous values), classification problems (i.e., the estimation of discrete values or classes) and clustering (which consists in grouping a set of objects in such a way that the members of the same group, or cluster, are as similar as possible according to certain criteria).

In the more than 70 years of existence of the ML field, a multitude of methods have been developed, among which we can highlight artificial neural networks,

Bayesian networks, statistical classifiers, rule-based systems, decision trees, or support vector machines. Today, the most prolific and revolutionary field of AI is the so-called deep learning (DL) (LeCun et al., 2015). This represents a family of ML algorithms that, over the last decade, have dramatically improved the results provided by existing techniques in tasks such as speech recognition (Hinton et al., 2012), machine translation (Sutskever et al.), and image classification (Krizhevsky et al., 2017) or that have directly exceeded human capacity facing complex activities (Silver et al., 2016).

The ability shown by these algorithms to solve problems of all kinds presupposes their potential in also solving problems in FA, such as the estimation of the BP, the location of cephalometric landmarks, or the automation of certain tasks involved in a forensic decision-making process.

2.3 Soft computing

Opposite to traditional computing methods (*hard computing*), **soft computing (SC)** (also called computational intelligence) techniques are not based on closed-form solutions (e.g., a formula which solves a specific equation), but mostly on search/optimization procedures (heuristics) and other "approximate" techniques, which are able to solve problems in the presence of qualitative, uncertain, imprecise, and incomplete data (Engelbrecht, 2020). Such techniques try to emulate humans' ability to deal with such situations effectively. The main SC paradigms are analyzed below.

Artificial neural networks (ANNs) are powerful and flexible ML approaches that are able to approximate complex functions. They are bioinspired models, that is, they are inspired by the neural networks of the brain (see Fig. 3.5), although they do not necessarily seek to imitate their behavior.

The first models of ANNs are from the year 1943 (Engelbrecht, 2020; McCulloch & Pitts, 1943), and since then hundreds of models and applications have emerged, but it has not been until the last decade when their use has become more popular thanks to the increase in the capabilities of computers, which has allowed the development of models with many more layers and neurons. They are the so-called deep

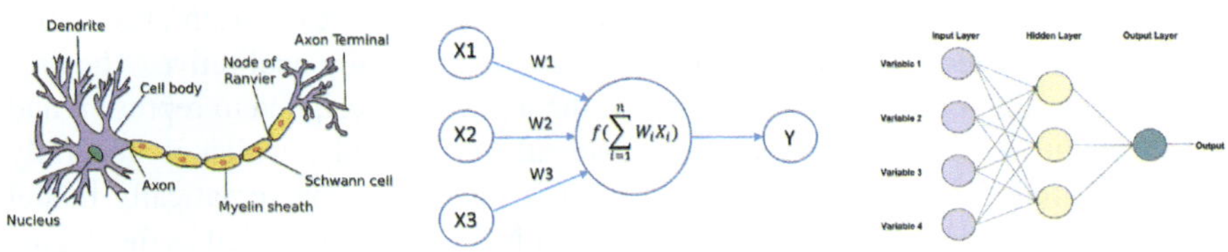

FIGURE 3.5

From left to right, representation of a biological neuron (dendrites, nucleus, and axon), an artificial neuron (different input variables X_i, weights w_i associated with the inputs, and an information processing function *f* and output Y), and an ANN (input, output and hidden layers with different number of artificial neurons and connectivity between them).

Credit: Original.

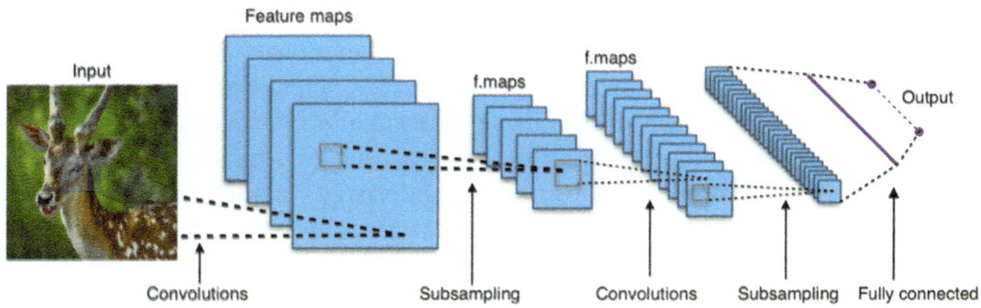

FIGURE 3.6

Simplified representation of a ConvNets where multiple layers can be seen that act (convolve) at all times on an nxn matrix of the input image.

Credit: Original.

neural networks, or DL, paradigm of ML that we have talked about previously. Within these networks, it is worth highlighting a family of concrete models, convolutional neural networks (or ConvNets), models of deep ANNs that explicitly assume that the inputs have a topology similar to that of a grid (for example, images), and that they are especially suitable for analyzing visual images without any preprocessing or feature extraction steps (see Fig. 3.6).

Evolutionary algorithms (EAs) are optimization, search, and learning algorithms inspired by the processes of natural selection and genetic evolution. They stand out for their ability to efficiently solve NP-hard and multimodal problems and do not require a priori information on the error function. The way these algorithms work is very simple, populations of individuals that represent potential solutions to problems evolve. In this evolution process, individuals (parents) are selected based on a model that combines randomness and adaptation to the environment (which is measured with a mathematical function of how good an individual is at solving the problem, error function), they cross to generate some new descendants (exchange of genetic information) and these mutate (generation of new information), with a certain probability (see Figs. 3.7 and 3.8).

Fuzzy Logic extends Boolean logic to the continuous domain [0, 1], where a fuzzy expression is not necessarily true or false (various degrees of truth/class membership are accepted). This allows concepts that are essentially qualitative to be processed, according to rigorous mathematical theory. It was designed to represent and reason about knowledge expressed linguistically or verbally, which is generally "vague," "imprecise," "diffuse," or "fuzzy." It allows us to mathematically model phenomena (for which a probability distribution is unknown) as varied as the degree of support in decision-making (for example, limited, moderate or strong) or how the body mass index affects the reliability of a certain morphological criterion (for example, reliable up to a body mass index less than 25, unreliable after 35, but with different degrees of reliability between both measurements).

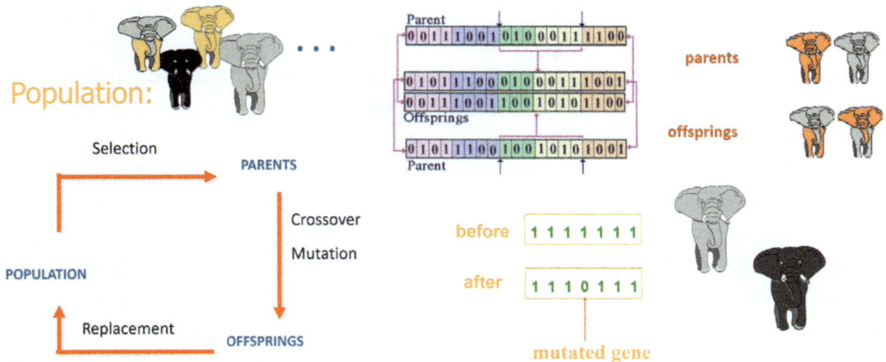

FIGURE 3.7

Representation of the evolution process of an EA, from an initial population, individuals (chromosomes) are selected, crossed, and mutated to generate a new population that replaces the previous one, and so on.

Credit: Original.

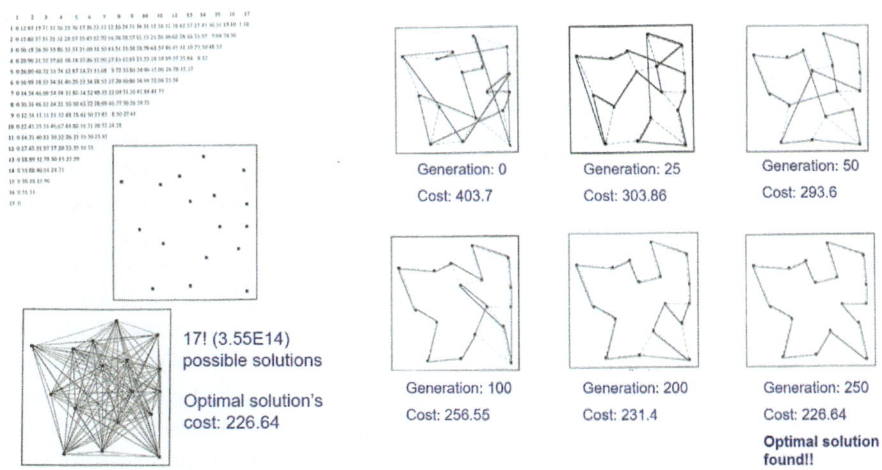

FIGURE 3.8

Example of solving the traveling salesman problem (TSP) using an EA. In the TSP problem, given a set of cities (nodes of a graph) connected by different paths (edges of arches), find the path of the minimum cost (least number of Kms) passing all of them once and returning to the starting point. Each individual of the EA, chromosome, encodes in their genes the order in which cities are visited. The adaptation function of each individual is the number of Kms traveled to pass through all the cities. On the left, cost (Kms) of travel between each city/node and connection map. On the right, the best EA solution in different generations (initial, 25, 50, 100, 200, and 250, where the ideal solution is found).

Credit: Original.

Finally, probabilistic reasoning, which is based on a data structure called the Bayesian network (also called a probabilistic network, a causal network, or a belief network), which allows us to take an event that has occurred and to predict the probability of any of the several possible known causes of the contributing factor.

Both SC techniques with each other, and these, with the rest of the AI paradigms mentioned in the previous pages, are often combined (hybridized) to address the resolution of more complex problems. In the specific case of FA, EA can be very useful to solve optimization problems that usually arise in CV tasks, such as IS or IR (for example, in CFS or CR); while fuzzy logic may be the underlying paradigm used to increase the explainability and interpretability of computer-assisted decision support systems that analyze data and images using ML and CV techniques.

The following section collects the publications that develop approaches based on one or more of these AI techniques to tackle a specific FA problem.

3. Overview of the existing artificial intelligence approaches for forensic anthropology techniques

For the last 2 decades, techniques like DNA or fingerprints have been employed in many ID scenarios. However, the application of these methods fails when there is not enough AM or PM information available due to the lack of data (second DNA sample) or to the state of preservation of the corpse. While the skeleton usually survives both natural and non-natural decomposition processes (fire, salt, water, etc.), the soft tissue progressively degrades and is lost. This is the most frequent case in disaster victim ID scenarios. In fact, the experience of several practitioners in these scenarios indicates the poorer effectiveness of DNA analysis (around 3% of IDs) and dactyloscopy (15%–25%) against skeleton-based forensic identification (SFI) techniques (70%–80%) (Beauthier et al., 2009), which are the daily practice of FA experts. These techniques involve the assessment of human osseous remains to identify the deceased person's identity and cause of death (Bethard, 2014). SFI methods employed by forensic anthropologists, odontologists, and pathologists are crucial in AM data collection and BP, and even more important they represent the victim's last chance for ID using techniques such as CR (including dental comparison), CFS or facial approximation.

Challenges have recently emerged in the ID of living people in which accuracy and robustness are fundamental. Facial imaging methods (Stephan et al., 2018) are indispensable in many circumstances, as they provide means for police investigation and valuable evidence in judicial instances. With the increasing number of surveillance cameras, there is a larger demand for facial recognition systems. However, differences in photographic conditions (e.g., lighting, camera angle, and lens), head position, facial expression, and resolution between reference and test images are common and severely complicate the whole procedure (Edmond et al., 2015). Another recent problem related to the ID of living people is that the increase of cross-border migration movements has also led to an increase in the number of experts' reports on age assessment for living juveniles and young adults in numerous countries. These minors, who usually carry invalid identity papers, can give inaccurate information about their age, which is of paramount importance in legal proceedings (Schmeling et al., 2016). The legally relevant age limits are between 12 and 21 years, setting the legal age at 18 in most countries (Jayaraman et al., 2016). According to the recommendations of the Study Group on Forensic Age Diagnostics (AGFAD), a physical examination, an X-ray examination of the hand, and a dental examination (including orthopantomogram) should be used for age assessment. If the skeletal development of the hand is completed, an additional CT scan of the medial clavicle should be carried out (Schmeling et al., 2008, 2016). It is important to remark that in order to prevent the violation of minor's rights, an anamnesis survey (in which growth-influencing diseases or medications are asked) and a physical examination (body height, body weight, and recognizable signs of sexual maturity) are carried out at the beginning of the diagnostic procedure. The main purpose of this initial physical examination is to determine growth and developmental disorders. The conclusion from the biological age (skeletal age, tooth age) to the chronological age is only justified for persons who are inconspicuous in this respect (Schmeling et al., 2016).

The following subsections summarized both the most relevant and novel AI approaches to the different FA techniques. We have included in this group traditional methods based on the direct analysis of the skeleton such as BP- and FA-related methods such as Sex and Age estimation in Facial Images, Traumatism and Pathologies description, CR, CFS, and Facial Approximation.

3.1 Overview of the existing artificial intelligence approaches for biological profile estimation

BP has been studied for more than 300 years, and nowadays, it plays a crucial role in narrowing the range of potential matches during the ID process. This step is previous to the corroboration by any ID technique. BP involves the study of skeletal remains with the aim of finding characteristic traits that support determining the identity of the individual. These traits include: (1) age estimation, by analyzing appearance, ossification patterns, dental development, and rib and pelvic morphology (Todd, 1920); (2) sex estimation, based on morphometrical and morphological studies, that is, shape of the skull and the hip bone (Ubelaker, 1999); (3) ancestry, by analyzing the skull both morphologically and metrically (Byers, 2011); and (4) stature, by measuring long bones length (femur) and extrapolating the measurements to estimate living height.

Assessing the BP from skeletal remains is a complex task, especially when estimating the age of a subject as there are different methods to be applied depending on the individual's development stage. Most individualizing traits can be identified in several structures as the skull sutures, pubis symphysis, and the external rib extremity. Variations in bone morphology are well known, but they do not happen at the same time in different individuals as they are subjected to genetic and environmental conditions. For all these reasons, BP is assessed as a sequential procedure commencing by determining ancestry, followed in turn by biological sex, age, stature, and finally individualizing characteristics.

With the goal of reproducing the previously consolidated methods in physical anthropology, radiological imaging, mainly CT scanning, is gaining popularity for BP since it is a noninvasive (in the sense that the human expert do not need to have direct visual access to the bone) approach, and it allows better possibilities for observation and metric calculations (Ubelaker, 1999). Estimation of BP from X-ray images has been approached from three different scientific communities with three different purposes. In clinical medicine, the biological age is important when determining endocrinological diseases in adolescents or for optimally planning the time-point of pediatric orthopedic surgery interventions. Nevertheless, in legal medicine, it is used to approximate unknown chronological age, when determining age in cases of criminal investigations or for asylum-seeking procedures, where identification documents of children or adolescents are missing. Finally, physical and forensic anthropologists are interested in determining sex, age, stature, and ancestry of any human remain.

The bigger international efforts have been focused on the development of accurate and objective automatic approaches for assessing whether living individuals have reached the threshold age that signifies legal adulthood. There are different computer-based proposals to assist the assessment procedure by using radiological imaging methods. Usually, MRI or X-ray images of the hand/wrist are employed in some AI-based proposals using SC techniques such as fuzzy decision trees (Aja-Fernández et al., 2004), random forest (RF) (Stern et al., 2014), or ANNs (Mansourvar et al., 2013). Recently, the proliferation of ConvNets has attracted interest in medical imaging analysis. DL techniques overcome many of these limitations by allowing to automatically learn the features useful for image interpretation without any direct human intervention during the training process.

Nevertheless, to our knowledge, there is no automatic approach facing a complete forensic BP assessment considering different stages of the procedure and a whole age range. Most published automatic methods operate only with X-ray scans of Caucasian subjects younger than 10 years, with a few approaches dealing with subjects less than 18 years old. There are neither automatic methods performing age estimation of adults and just a few automatic sex estimation methods from X-ray. For this reason, the following subsections will focus on the main BP methods (sex estimation and age estimation), mainly applied to living individuals and addressed through AI techniques.

3.1.1 Artificial intelligence approaches for sex estimation of skeletal structures

The sex estimation is a fundamental pillar of the BP. If the sex estimation is incorrect, then the identification may be delayed. Current methods for sex estimation are mainly based on morphometric or morphological criteria (Haas et al., 1994; Krishan et al., 2016). The morphometric approach involves the measurements of hands, feet, and the extremities corresponding to the upper, lower, and long bones. On the other hand, the morphological approach finds its foundation in the sexual dimorphism presented in certain degrees in most of the bones in human body. In particular, the most common and popular parts of human body for sex estimation are skull and the pelvis area (Pinto et al., 2016). However, these methods are subject to analyst bias, require a high degree of expertise, are complex, time consuming (Sierp & Henneberg, 2015), and are not always adequate, mainly due to the presence of significant damage (chemical and/or physical) in the bone.

Among the few studies published in this regard, ML approaches stand out, either combined with other CV methods (Abdullah et al., 2017; Darmawan et al., 2015; Pinto et al., 2016) or in isolation, using DL techniques (Bewes et al., 2019; Kaloi & He, 2018). DL techniques offer a flexible and powerful solution for sex estimation from images of skeletal structures. One of the advantages of DL techniques is that they automatically and autonomously discover the characteristics of an image that are most useful for classification (Goodfellow et al., 2016; Oakden-Rayner et al., 2017).

Of these five papers that apply AI techniques to sex estimation, only one focuses on children (Kaloi & He, 2018). The body of an adult is mature enough to point out significant clues which can help to distinguish its sex but may not be suitable for sex estimation in children.

In Darmawan et al. (2015), the authors used a combination of an artificial neural network with a hybrid particle Swarm technique (an SC technique for optimization) for sex estimation of individuals. They used a dataset of left hand X-ray images of Asian population. Their data set was small, and their results suggest a different accuracy for different age groups. Pinto et al. (Pinto et al., 2016) introduced a methodology for objective quantification of sexually dimorphic features on images of skull and pelvis using the Wavelet Transform, which is a multiscale mathematical tool that allows for measurements of shape variations that are hidden at different scales of resolution. Authors claimed that their method had been successfully applied for sex estimation on a pilot sample of 3D meshes of the supraorbital morphology. This information can be used by experts to improve the accuracy of BP assessment and to describe the geographic and temporal variations within and among populations. In Abdullah et al. (2017), the authors presented an automated Haversian canal detection system based on the histomorphology, which uses only bone fragments to estimate age and sex. They divided their detection system into two parts. In the first part, they manually analyzed and observed differences in the parameters of male and female sample of bones. In the second part, they applied microstructural image processing techniques to identify the gender. Bewes et al. (Bewes et al., 2019) addressed the problem of sex estimation of skeletal remains by adapting a very popular deep network, called GoogLeNet (Szegedy et al., 2015), and designed to analyze 2D input images. They trained the network with images of 900 skulls virtually reconstructed from hospital CT scans. When tested on previously unseen images of skulls, the deep network showed 95% accuracy at sex estimation.

On the other hand, only the authors of Kaloi and He (2018) have focused on the estimation of sex in children. They proposed a technique called Gender Estimation with Convolutional Neural Networks (GDCNN), where left-hand radiographs of the children between a wide range of ages (ranging from 1 month to 18 years old) are examined to estimate the gender. To identify the area of attention (part of the hand), they used Class Activation Maps, discovering that the lower part of the hand around carpals (wrist) is more important than other factors for child sex estimation. They obtained an accuracy of 98%, identifying the gender of a child even with half of the lower part of the hand, which is impressive considering the incompletely grown skeleton of the children.

3.1.2 Artificial intelligence approaches for age estimation of skeletal structures

It is well-known for the forensic anthropologists that certain bone areas show a definite sequence of modification, which is strictly associated with age. The bone structures commonly used for estimating age in adults include the pubic symphysis (Brooks & Suchey, 1990; Todd, 1920, 1921), the fourth rib (Işcan et al., 1984, 1985), the cranial sutures (Meindl & Lovejoy, 1985), or the teeth (Lamendin et al., 1992). In the twenties of the last century, changes in the pubic symphysis were first studied by Todd (Todd, 1920, 1921) in a collection of male skeletons of known age. He proposed an age estimation method based on 10 age categories, and he also provided a really thorough description of the morphological aspects of the pubic symphysis on each of them. Seventy years later, Brooks and Suchey (Brooks & Suchey, 1990) used a sample of 739 males and 273 females, whose symphysis were obtained from a well-documented modern sample of autopsy individuals in Los Angeles, establishing 6 phases with their characteristics (for both males and females), with the mean and standard deviation and age range. Another structure used for age estimation in adults is the fourth rib. Iscan et al. (Işcan et al., 1984) studied 230 right ribs extracted from individuals of known age, proving to be a reliable and relatively easy to apply method, although it is dependent of the population. Another method used, this time in the skull, is the closure of the cranial sutures and their relationship to the age of the individual. Meindel and Lovejoy (Meindl & Lovejoy, 1985) proposed a method based on the study of 10 points located in the cranial calotte, establishing four stages of closure. The teeth are commonly used in relation to age too; Lamendin et al. (Lamendin et al., 1992) carried out their work on 360 single-root teeth, obtained from 208 individuals aged between 22 and 90 years, and assessed periodontitis and root transparency.

It is important to note that when it comes to estimating age in an FA case, the conditioning factors of each method and its variants must be taken into account in terms of the population of origin that has given rise to the method and the particular conditions of each case.

The majority of AI-based proposals use SC techniques, but we can distinguish two different approaches. On the one hand, those proposals that take a classical FA model as a starting point and try to automate and/or improve it, such as (Aja-Fernández et al., 2004) and (Stern et al., 2014), where different approaches based on fuzzy logic are proposed to automate the methods of Tanner et al. (TW2) (Tanner et al., 1983), (TW3) (Tanner et al., 2001), or Todd's (Todd, 1920, 1921). On the other hand, and mainly in the last 5–6 years, approaches called end-to-end are approaches where the only input of the algorithm is an image (radiography or MRI of the hand/wrist) and the output is the chronological age predicted by the algorithm. These approaches are only possible, thanks to the use of ConvNets trained with hundreds of images whose precise chronological age is known (Kim et al., 2017; Larson et al., 2018; Lee et al., 2017; Li et al., 2019; Mutasa et al., 2018; Štern et al., 2019).

Within the first group, some studies use the fuzzy integral for age estimation in adults (Anderson et al., 2010). These methods consider the manual application of different age assessment methods based on different bones: Todd's method using the pubic symphysis and other two using the auricular surface and the cranial suture closure. These three independent estimations are combined by a fuzzy integral in order to obtain a more accurate estimation. Villar et al. (Villar et al., 2017) propose a preliminary fuzzy rule-based classification system (Ishibuchi et al., 2005) for age estimation of skeletal remains in FA based in the pubic symphysis, following Todd's method. Their aim was to simplify the process, detecting the main characteristics of the problem and learning a compact system for classifying new cases according to such characteristics. They generated a labeled dataset with very promising results. Apart from these two works based exclusively on techniques from fuzzy logic, we highlight a last work that hybridizes the latter with supervising learning techniques, in particular, decision trees. In Aja-Fernández et al. (2004), the authors propose the use of fuzzy decision trees to automate the method of Tanner et al. (TW2) (Tanner et al., 1983).

Also in this first group of proposals, but focused on estimating the age in subadults, the automated approaches that reproduce the TW2 method can be classified mainly according to whether they use image processing or knowledge-based techniques, and an exhaustive exam can be found in Mansourvar et al. (2013). Most methods based on image processing date back to the 2000s. These methods use hand radiographs of living people as a source of knowledge for classifier training. In Aja-Fernández et al. (2004), a classifier for evaluating skeleton maturity based on computation with words is proposed. In Hsieh et al. (2007), the proposal is based on a classifier and on the output of a diffuse filter. In Mansourvar et al. (2013), a fuzzy inference system is used for the evaluation of age.

Beyond FA, there are several contributions in age estimation for both clinical and legal medicine applications. In legal medicine, when identification documents of children or adolescents are missing, as may be the case in asylum seeking procedures or in criminal investigations. Estimation of physical maturation is used as an approximation to assess unknown chronological age. The established radiological methods estimating unknown age in children and adolescents are based on visual examinations of bone ossification in X-ray images of the hand. Ossification is best followed in the hand due to the large number of assessable bones that are visible in X-ray images from this anatomical region, together with the fact that aging progress is not simultaneous for all hand bones. From the level of ossification assessed by the radiologist, the most common methods for the estimation of physical maturation of an individual are the GP method (Greulich & Pyle, 1959) and the TW2 method (Tanner et al., 1983). The GP method is the approach used by the majority of radiologists due of its simplicity and speed. This method is based on the comparison between the X-ray image of the hand and an atlas of normal hand and wrist at various chronological ages. The patient's radiograph is compared to the suitable image in the atlas. The TW2 method analyzes specific bones, instead of the whole hand as in the GP method. In particular, this method takes into account a set of specific regions of interest divided into epiphysis/metaphysis regions and carpal regions.

Within this framework, we can find most of the few laboratories with a multidisciplinary composition and orientation that have developed end-to-end approaches based on the latest AI techniques. In this way, and through the main use of ConvNets, they have demonstrated the enormous possibilities of this paradigm for bone age estimation.

A first group of publications have focused on the age estimation of subadults subjects based on the fundamentals of the GP method regarding the strong correlation between the processes of the ossification of the hand and the chronological age (Kim et al., 2017; Larson et al., 2018; Lee et al., 2017; Lee & Kim, 2018; Mutasa et al., 2018).

Larson et al. (Larson et al., 2018) used a ConvNet over a total of 14,036 clinical hand radiographs and their corresponding reports, obtained from two children's hospitals to train and validate the model. For the first test set, composed of 200 examinations, the mean of bone age estimates from the clinical report, and three additional human reviewers was used as a reference standard. Overall model performance was assessed by comparing the root mean square error (RMS) and the mean absolute deviation (MAD) between the model estimates and the reference standard bone ages. The RMS of a second test set composed of 1377 examinations from the publicly available GP Digital Hand Atlas (Gertych et al., 2007; Zhang et al., 2009) was compared with published reports of an existing automatic model (Thodberg et al., 2010). The mean difference between bone age estimates by the model and by the reviewers was 0 years, with a mean RMS and MAD of 0.63 and 0.50 years, respectively. The estimates of the model, the clinical report, and the three reviewers were within the 95% limits of agreement. RMS for the Digital Hand Atlas data set was 0.73 years, compared with 0.61 years of a previously reported model.

In Kim et al. (2017), the authors used a GP method-based DL technique to develop an automatic software system for bone age estimation. Using that software, they estimated the bone age from left-hand radiographs of 200 patients (3–17 years old) using first-rank bone age (only the software), computer-assisted bone age (two radiologists with software assistance), and GP atlas-assisted bone age (two radiologists with GP atlas assistance). The reference bone age was determined by the consensus of two experienced radiologists. The first-rank bone ages determined by the automatic software system showed a 69.5% of concordance rate and significant correlations with the reference bone age ($r = 0.992$; $P < .001$). The concordance rates also increased with the use of the automatic software for both reviewers (around 8.0% from the GP atlas assisted for the computer-assisted bone age), and the X-ray images evaluation time required by the radiologists were reduced between 18.0% and 40.0%. Their results suggested that automatic software system reliably showed accurate bone age estimations and appeared to enhance efficiency by reducing evaluation times without compromising diagnostic accuracy.

In Lee et al. (2017), the authors created a DL system to automatically detect and segment the hand and wrist. They perform automated bone age assessment with a trained ConvNet on a set of 4278 female and 4047 male radiographs (with chronological age of 5–18 years old). The images were labeled by skeletal age and generate structured radiology reports with the final decision by a radiologist. This system automatically standardizes all hand radiographs of different formats, vendors, and quality to be used as a training dataset for future model enhancement. Their model achieves 57.32% and 61.40% accuracies for the female and male cohorts, respectively. Female test radiographs were assigned a bone age within 1 year in 90.39% of cases and within 2 years in 98.11% of cases. Male test radiographs were assigned in 94.18% of cases within 1 year and in 99.0% of cases within 2 years.

In Lee and Kim (2018), the authors presented a way to use DL for age estimation from a subject's hand X-ray images, employing a set of feature points on the hand. These points have to be defined, to serve as a reference to crop a certain region that is informative in terms of aging-induced morphological changes. They obtained a mean absolute error (MAE) of 18.9 months on a test set of 200 radiographs (the model was trained with a different set consisting of 400).

The most common in the field of DL is to use a pretrained (on a set of hundreds of thousands of images to millions) and designed deep ANN for a similar problem and, after a training phase on images of the problem to be solved (in this case X-ray of the hand and chronological age), measure the precision of the network on a set of test images of the specific problem. This has been the approach followed in the previously reviewed works. However, Mutasa et al. (Mutasa et al., 2018) developed their own customized ANN architecture trained on 10,289 images of different skeletal age (0–15 years, half boys and half girls). Their good results with an MAE of 0.536, support the hypothesis that purpose-built ANNs provide improved performance over networks derived from pretrained imaging data sets.

The emergence and proliferation of ConvNets using hand radiographs have provided new applications for the evaluation of age using other bones. Spampinato et al. (Spampinato et al., 2017) proposed and tested various approaches of DL. In particular, they used several existing pretrained ConvNets to automatically assess skeletal bone age, based on the TW2 method and using a dataset of about 1400 X-ray images. The results showed a medium discrepancy between manual evaluation and automatic of about 0.8 years. They also designed and trained a custom ConvNet from scratch, which proved to be the most effective and robust solution for assessing bone age across all ethnic groups, age ranges, and gender. Furthermore, this was the first automated skeletal bone age assessment work tested on a public dataset.

Apart from the pubic symphysis, the iliac crest apophysis provides an excellent subject for the application of forensic age diagnostics to the living, particularly for determining age thresholds of 14, 16, and 18 years. For this reason, Li et al. (Li et al., 2019) developed a DL system using transfer learning techniques to perform automatic bone age estimation based on 1875 clinical pelvic radiological images, particularly for individuals between 10 and 25 years old. It can handle all possible cases of automated skeletal bone age assessment, even for samples from individuals of 19, 20, and 21 years old. However, it may not be practical in determining ages over 22 years due to the little change in the mean score of ossification. Compared to the existing cubic regression model, their ConvNet model achieves better average performance (MAE = 0.89 and RMSE = 1.21) but are slightly higher than previous studies with DL architectures based on left-hand X-ray images, where the MAE values range were from 0.54 to 0.80 years (Kim et al., 2017; Larson et al., 2018; Mutasa et al., 2018; Spampinato et al., 2017). Their statistical analysis indicates a high positive correlation between the estimated and real age ($r = 0.916$; $P < .05$), but this number is less accurate than hand radiographic images methods ($r = 0.992$; $P < .001$).

On the other hand, as an alternative to the age estimation methods based on X-ray images, research in age estimation using MRI has gained tremendous interest in recent years. The interest in developing automatic MRI-based methods for age estimation is determined by addressing the problems of exposure to ionizing radiation, the necessity to define new MRI specific staging systems, and the subjective influence of the examiner (Štern et al., 2019). In Stern et al. (2014), the authors used RF ML technique to separately regress chronological age from intensity-based features extracted from 11 selected hand bones of adolescent subjects. A decision tree excluding metacarpal and phalanx information from older subjects served as a heuristic fusion strategy for age estimation, making this method ad hoc and dependent on parameter tuning. In Štern et al. (2016), the capability of RFs techniques for information fusion was explored by allowing it to internally decide from which bones to learn a subject's chronological age. Thus, they treated aging as a global developmental process without the need for heuristic fusion schemes, as in Stern et al. (2014), or predefined nonlinear functions, as in Tanner et al. (1983) or Thodberg et al. (2010).

As explained previously in the case of radiographs, the current trend in the area of ML from images has shift from feature extraction and the use of a classifier to relate those features to the image class, to an approach with a single element, the use of DL, capable of doing both tasks. Following this new paradigm, the authors of Štern et al. (2016) proposed a ConvNet architecture to combine age information from individual bones in an automatic fashion by letting the architecture learn directly the most relevant features for age estimation. More recently, in

Štern et al. (2019), the authors present a solution for automatic age estimation from 3D MRI scans of the hand. They evaluate ML methods, as RFs and ConvNets, with different variants of the image information used as input for learning. Trained on a dataset of 328 MRI images, they compare the performance of the different input strategies and demonstrate unprecedented results achieving the state-of-the-art accuracy compared with previous MRI-based methods. For estimating biological age, they obtain an MAE of 0.37 ± 0.51 years for the age range of subjects ≤ 18 years, that is, where bone ossification has not yet saturated. Finally, they adapted their best performing method to 2D images and applied it to a dataset of X-ray images in order to validate their findings, showing that their method is in line with the state-of-the-art methods developed specifically for X-ray data.

3.1.3 Overview of the existing artificial intelligence approaches for sex and age estimation in facial images

From a single face, humans are able to identify facial attributes such as age, gender, ethnicity, expression, etc. Automatic estimation of age and gender from facial images has received an increasing attention in recent years. In terms of soft biometrics, the developed systems are expected to process the real-world data obtained from uncontrolled environments, such as airports and stadiums, in varying conditions such as illumination changes or facial occlusion. Recent advancements in deep convolutional neural networks, increasing computational capabilities, and publicly available high amount of data have made it possible to have robust classifiers for age and gender classification as for many CV problems (Ozbulak et al., 2016).

CV-based classification methods for sex and age estimation were usually based on, first, extracting features from the given face image and, then, using these features to train a classifier that outputs the estimation. Such methods could be divided into two main categories: (1) geometry-based and (2) appearance-based methods. In the former category, the distance between different points in the facial image is used, while the latter category is based on the pixel values of the face image. Each of these approaches has its own advantages and disadvantages. Methods of the appearance-base category can be considered holistic, in which the feature vector is extracted from the whole face image. Such a representation has the advantage over geometric-based category that information is extracted from all regions of the face. A disadvantage of the holistic appearance-based representation, however, is its sensitivity to local appearance variations, which can be caused by variability in position, pose, expression, and illumination. On the other hand, due to their superior performance in several CV tasks, DL methods have been recently used and proposed for facial image analysis. Concretely, ConvNet-based methods are believed to find appropriate features for age and sex estimation by training the network with well-prepared datasets and suitable loss functions. In this category, an end-to-end solution is provided by learning a set of linear and nonlinear functions directly from the raw images.

Concerning to the geometric-based sex classification methods, these techniques extract and utilize geometric features from a face image to predict the sex. Burton et al. (Burton et al., 1993) presented a sex classification technique that relies on 73 facial points and uses discriminant analysis of point-to-point distances to infer the sex. They take photographs of 91 male and 88 female faces in full face and profile, and they measured them in several ways: (1) simple distances between key points in the pictures and (2) ratios and angles; 3D distances derived by combination of full-face and profile photographs. The discriminant function analysis showed that the best discriminators were derived from simple distance measurements in the full face (85% accuracy with 12 variables) and 3D distances (85% accuracy with six variables). Combining measures taken from the picture plane with those derived in 3D produced a discriminator approaching human performance (94% accuracy with 16 variables). On the other hand, appearance-based methods rely on extracting features from either or both of: (1) the whole face image (holistic features) and (2) regions of the face image (local features). Following the appearance-based method, Li et al. (Li et al., 2012) introduced a method based on five individual facial components in addition to the hair and clothing of the person and then used multiple classifiers to classify the gender based on the individual features.

Combining both methods (geometric-based and appearance-based), Mozaffari et al. (Mozaffari et al., 2010) presented a technique that extracts both geometry-based and appearance-based features. They used two facial databases: AR and ethnic. AR database consist of different facial images of 56 females and 70 males (total 126) (PDF The AR face database, 2436). They built the ethnic database (with the same distribution as AR) with facial images of Iranian persons. Combining both methods they obtain a very high overall accuracy classifying the gender for both ethnic (97,1%) and AR (96,0%) databases. In Tapia and Perez (2013), the authors propose the use of feature selection based on mutual information and fusion of intensity, shape, and texture features, as well as different spatial scales to improve gender classification of face images. The method was assessed using unconstrained images from the LFW database (Huang et al.) (they used 2943 female and 4500 male images) and on face images taken under controlled conditions such as those in the FERET (Phillips et al., 1997) (they used a subset of 199 female and 212 male images) and UND (186 female and 301 male images) databases. They obtain a classification rate of 99.13% on the FERET database, 94.01% on the UND database, and 98.01% on the LFW database. Rai et al. (Rai & Khanna, 2014) presented a gender classification system that works for nonoccluded face images to face images occluded up to 60%. Local information of the face, which carries the most discriminative features to find the gender, is gathered by dividing the face image into M x N sub-images. The proposed approach gives a 98.4% classification rate on FERET database for nonoccluded face images. For occluded face images, occlusions ranging from 10% to 60% results are quite competitive with accuracies around 90%. In Moeini and Mozaffari (2017), the authors proposed to learn separate dictionaries of male and female features. Then, an automatic feature extractor was proposed by fusion of local binary patterns and gray pixels for gender classification. Finally, two dictionary learning methods were proposed to learn both male and female dictionaries. The proposed methods were tested on public databases with a wide subject on FERET (5000 female and 5000 male images), LFW (6505 female and 6505 male images), and Groups (28,231 face images) databases, the results of which are 91.9%, 94.9%, and 84.4% overall gender classification rates, respectively.

On the other hand, deep ANNs are becoming increasingly ubiquitous in many classification problems, as gender estimation, according to the remarkable improvements recently achieved. Levi and Hassner (Levi & Hassncer, 2015) classified both gender and age via a simple ConvNet that was applied to the Adience benchmark (Eidinger et al., 2014) for age and gender classification in a holistic manner. The Adience collection includes 26,000 images of 2284 subjects in unconstrained conditions (see Table 3.1), reflecting many of the real-world challenges of faces appearing in Internet images. They obtain a mean accuracy of 86.8 ± 1.4 for gender classification and a mean accuracy of 50.7 ± 5.1 for the exact age estimation and 84.7 ± 2.2 with 1-off. Mansanet et al. (Mansanet et al., 2016) proposed a model called Local Deep Neural Network (Local-DNN), which is based on two key concepts: local features and deep architectures. The model learns from a small overlapping region in the visual field using discriminative feedforward networks with several layers. They evaluate their approach in the LFW (13,233 images) and Groups (Gallagher & Chen, 2009) (14,760 images) databases. Using the LFW for training and the Groups for testing, they obtain an overall accuracy of 83.04%. On the other hand, using the Groups for training and the LFW for testing, they obtain an overall accuracy of 94.48% in the gender classification task. Juefei-Xu et al. (Juefei-Xu et al., 2016) undertake the task of occlusion and low-resolution robust facial gender classification. Inspired by the trainable attention model via deep architecture, and the fact that the periocular region is proven to be most salient region for gender classification purposes, they designed a progressive ConvNet training paradigm to enforce the attention shift during the learning process. They obtain a high overall accuracy on the large-scale Pinellas County Sheriff Office (PCSO) mugshot database (1.4 million images) in a subset of 400K images under occlusion (93,12%) and low-resolution settings (95,67%).

As we can see, most of the prior work in gender classification was depending on extracting large number of local features per image. On the contrary, Afifi and Abdelhamed (Afifi & Abdelhamed, 2017) proposed a method that only uses four highly discriminative facial components (i.e., two eyes, nose, and mouth) and, in

Table 3.1 Total number of facial images in the most commonly employed face databases.

Dataset	Total number of face images
Groups (Gallagher & Chen, 2009)	28,231
Adience (Eidinger et al., 2014)	26,580
LFW (Huang et al.)	13,233
FERET (Phillips et al., 1997)	5786

Credit: Original.

opposition to prior work (dependent on hand-crafted features), relied on deep learned features extracted after fine-tuning ConvNets. They applied their proposed method (AFIF[4]) to unconstrained types of face images, that is, frontal images, near-frontal images, nonfrontal images, and images with large poses and occlusions. Table 3.2 shows the overall accuracy reported by the authors for unconstrained types of face images from the LFW, Groups, and Adience datasets in comparison with the dictionary methods reported in Moeini and Mozaffari (2017).

Age estimation from a single image is an interesting but challenging task in human and CV, which has many applications such as in forensic or social media. In the literature, there are two types of age estimation problems. The first one addresses real age estimation, which is to predict the biological age of a subject using his or her face image. The second one addresses age group estimation. In this type, the objective is to predict the age group in which the person's age falls (Levi & Hassncer, 2015).

Two categories of approaches can be differentiated for solving the age estimation from images depending on the type of image representation: (1) ML algorithms to estimate a person's age based on features (color, texture, edges, contours, etc.) extracted from face images (Levi & Hassncer, 2015; Eidinger et al., 2014; Guo et al.) or measurements/indexes calculated from landmarks (Machado et al., 2017) and (2) ConvNet-based methods (Dornaika et al., 2020; Rothe et al., 2018; Shen et al., 2017; Taheri & Toygar, 2019).

Recent works have shown that deep ConvNets can be very effective for image-based age estimation due to their superior performance (Dornaika et al., 2020; Rothe

Table 3.2 Comparison of cross-dataset evaluation of the method proposed in Afifi and Abdelhamed (2017) against the results reported by Moeini and Mozaffari (2017). The values represent the overall gender classification accuracy (%).

Training set	Testing set	DL-GC (Moeini & Mozaffari, 2017)	SDL-GC (Moeini & Mozaffari, 2017)	AFIF[4] (Afifi & Abdelhamed, 2019)
LFW	LFW	93.60	94.90	**95.98**
	Groups	69.70	72.40	**76.67**
	FERET	88.80	89.70	**92.71**
Groups	LFW	80.60	83.10	**91.74**
	Groups	83.30	84.40	**90.73**
	FERET	85.20	87.10	**92.90**
FERET	LFW	71.70	73.50	**85.78**
	Groups	59.50	61.90	**85.67**
	FERET	99.50	**99.90**	99.49

Credit: Redrawn from Afifi and Abdelhamed (2017).

et al., 2018; Shen et al., 2017; Taheri & Toygar, 2019) over the ML algorithms feature-based methods.

In Rothe et al. (Rothe et al., 2018), the authors introduced a DL method for age prediction. They generated a large database (IMDB-WIKI database), which is among the largest public age databases. Their solution adopted the use of age groups, but the final estimation provides a real number since the expected age can be estimated from the obtained probability distribution. They evaluate the performance of their method for age group estimation on the Adience dataset (Eidinger et al., 2014), achieving an accuracy (exact age) of 64.0% ± 4.2. When predicting the 1-off accuracy they achieve 96.6% ± 0.9, that is, their method is nearly always able to predict at least the adjacent age group.

Shen et al. (Shen et al., 2017) introduced the use of Deep Regression Forest (DRFs) and used it as end-to-end solution for age prediction. These DRFs receive as input the output of a given deep ConvNet or any other image representation. They evaluated their DRFs on three standard benchmarks: MORPH (55,000 face images with age range from 16 to 77 years) (Ricanek & Tesafaye, 2006), FG-NET (1002 images of 82 persons with ages from 0 to 69 years) (Panis et al., 2016), and the Cross-Age Celebrity Dataset (CACD) (160,000 facial images of 2000 celebrities) (8). The performance of age estimation was evaluated in terms of MAE as well as Cumulative Score (CS), achieving a 3.85 MAE on the FG-NET, 2.87 MAE on MORPH, and 5.768 on CACD.

In Taheri et al., 2019, the authors proposed an architecture for age estimation method based on multistage fusion of information. Multistage learned features from different layers of a ConvNet are automatically combined together by score-level fusion method by using DAG-CNN architecture (a normal ConvNet and some branches from its different layer to fuse multi-stage learned features). They selected two public available ConvNets, VGG-16, and GoogleNet architectures. They tested their method's accuracy on the MOPRH and FG-NET datasets. The robustness and effectiveness of the proposed methods were studied in terms of MAEs, achieving a 2.81 MAE (DAG-VGG16) and 2.87 (DAG-GoogleNet) on the MORPH dataset. For the FG-NET dataset, they obtain 3.08 MAE (DAG-VGG16) and 3.05 (DAG-GoogleNet).

In Dornaika et al. (2020), the authors introduced the use of robust loss functions for training deep ConvNets in regression-based age estimation. Their experimental results over four public databases demonstrate that learning a deep ConvNet with robust losses can improve the age estimation. Concretely, they conduct age estimation experiments on the following public databases: FG-NET (Panis et al., 2016), PAL (1046 images of different subjects with ages from 18 to 93 years) (Minear & Park, 2004), MORPH (Ricanek & Tesafaye, 2006), and FACES (2052 images from 171 subjects with age range from 19 to 8o years) (Ebner et al., 2010). They achieved an MAE (years) for FGNET, PAL, MORPH, and FACES models of 3.05, 2.74, 2.75, and 3.55, respectively.

3.2 Overview of the existing artificial intelligence approaches for trauma and pathology

In recent years, the success of DL to classify images has caused great interest in its application to medical image analysis in several fields, including the detection of skin cancer (Esteva et al., 2017), diabetic retinopathy (Gulshan et al., 2016), mammographic lesions (Kooi et al., 2017), or lung nodules (Hua et al., 2015). However, one example of pathology that is of high interest, but also rare, is bone lesions (Franchi, 2012). To our knowledge, there are just a few works in the field of orthopedics related to the application of DL to detect bone lesions or pathologies in X-ray images.

Olczack et al. (Olczak et al., 2017) extracted 256,000 wrists, hand, and ankle radiographs from Danderyd's Hospital and identified four classes: the presence or absence of fracture, left or right laterality, body part (ankle, wrist and hand, the latter also had subgroups of scaphoids, thumb or finger), and examination view (antero-posterior/frontal, lateral, oblique, and, in the case of scaphoids, proximal, distal, ulnar, and radial). Then, they evaluated the diagnostic accuracy of five openly available DL networks adapted to this task. All networks exhibited an accuracy of at least 90% when identifying laterality, body part, and exam view. The final accuracy for fractures was estimated at 83% for the best performing network. The network behaved similarly to two very experienced orthopedic surgeons when images were presented to them with the same resolution as the network.

Chung et al. (Chung et al., 2018) evaluated the ability of AI techniques (ConvNets) for detecting and classifying proximal humerus fractures using plain antero-posterior shoulder radiographs. The dataset evaluated was composed of 1891 images (1 image per person) of normal shoulders (n = 515) and four proximal humerus fracture types (greater tuberosity, 346; surgical neck, 514; 3-part, 269; four part, 247) classified by three specialists. They trained a ConvNet after augmenting the training dataset. The ability of the ConvNet was measured by top-1 accuracy in comparison with humans (28 general physicians, 11 general orthopedists, and 19 orthopedists specialized in the shoulder) to detect and classify proximal humerus fractures. Their results showed 96% accuracy, for distinguishing normal shoulders from proximal humerus fractures, and 65%–86% accuracy for classifying the fracture type.

In Gupta et al. (Gupta et al., 2019), the authors address the problem of classifying bone lesions from X-ray images. As in most DL-based works, it is necessary to artificially augment the training dataset because the few hundred or thousands of images are usually insufficient for the network to be able to generalize properly. This augmentation of data usually involves a simple task of generating thousands of new images, rotating, zooming, or adding noise to the original images. In this case, the authors propose a generative data augmentation approach based on a cycle-consistent generative adversarial network (a type of DNN that is capable of creating synthetic images that closely resemble real images) that synthesizes bone lesions on images without pathology. They pose the generative task as an image-patch translation problem that they optimize specifically for distinct bones (humerus, tibia, and femur). In experimental results, they confirm that the described method mitigates the class imbalance problem in the binary classification task of bone lesion detection. They show that the augmented training sets enable the training of superior classifiers achieving better performance on a held-out test set. Additionally, they demonstrate the feasibility of transfer learning and apply a generative model that was trained on one body part to another. The results of its best mode in terms of sensitivity and specificity are 0.84 and 0.80 in the case of the humerus, 0.75 and 0.46 in the case of the tibia, and 0.66 and 0.67 in the case of the femur.

3.3 Overview of the existing artificial intelligence approaches for comparative radiography

CR involves the direct comparison of AM radiographs, acquired with clinical purposes, with PM radiographs, acquired specifically for the ID. Both radiographs are visually evaluated for similarity in osseous shapes and densities, to determine whether they represent one of the same subject (Stephan et al., 2014). The most common and valuable bones for individualizing are teeth, frontal cranium bones, vertebras, and clavicles, although dental-based ID is the most employed and discriminative technique. Also, the most commonly AM and PM images employed with the CR technique (Christensen et al., 2018; Hatch et al., 2014; Thali et al., 2003) include radiographs, CT images, and 3D surface models.

Methodological approaches for performing CR-based identification are divided into three groups according to the dimensionality of the data employed: 2D-2D (radiograph-radiograph), 2D-3D (radiograph-CT or 3D surface image), and 3D-3D (CT—CT or 3D model). The greater the dimensionality, the greater the accuracy and robustness of the methods. Within each of these groups, methods can be further classified into manual approaches and semi-automatic approaches. In this section, we will focus on the semi-automatic methods, those in which some tasks of the identification process are automatized by means of some of the AI-based techniques already mentioned.

3.3.1 2D-2D approaches for comparative radiography

The comparison of AM and PM radiographs is the most extended approach in forensic literature. In order to highlight the applicability of CR-based forensic ID, it is important to remark that X-ray images represent the most commonly employed medical imaging modality (Sandström et al., 2003). In particular, chest X-rays (CXRs) are the most commonly performed radiology examination worldwide (Daffner & Hartman, 2013) because they are able to produce images of the heart, lungs, airways, blood, vessels, spine, and chest (Rigby & Hacking, 2018) and because of their diagnosis and treatment potential (Daffner & Hartman, 2013; Van Ginneken et al., 2001). In order to quantify the importance of CXR analysis, it is important to notice that 2.02 million CXRs were performed in 2015/16 by the National Health Service of United Kingdom (Statistics, 2020), and that 150 million CXRs are annually acquired in the United States alone (Laserson et al., 2018).

There are several works that semi-automatically compare different skeletal structures between AM and PM radiographs. These skeletal structures include frontal sinus (Christensen, 2005a, 2005b), cranial vault (Maxwell & Ross, 2014), and teeth (Jain & Chen, 2004; Nomir & Abdel-Mottaleb, 2007). These methods are based on the comparison of the silhouettes of skeletal structures in radiographs using geometric morphometric techniques. The elliptical Fourier analysis (Caple et al., 2017) is used to compare AM and PM silhouettes obtaining a shortlist of the most probable PM matches for each AM one. The segmentation of the skeletal structures (silhouette marking) in AM and PM radiographs is required in all these methods, and it is done manually.

Related to that, there are a few computational approaches that automate the manual segmentations using ad-hoc rule-based segmentation methods, as the automated algorithm for frontal sinuses segmentation (Tabor et al., 2009).

Another approaches do not require the IS stage as they perform a direct comparison of the intensities, as it is the case of the computer-assisted decedent identification (CADI) (Derrick et al., 2018) for vertebrae comparison. However, the latter approach suffers from the elapsed time between the AM and PM radiographs and the consequent change in the intensities of the skeletal structures. CADI reduces its impact via the manual selection of a region of interest around each vertebra, the equalization of the pixels within these areas (e.g., with a histogram equalization filter), and lastly, the comparison of AM and PM vertebrae using the Jaccard similarity metric.

3.3.2 3D-2D approaches for comparative radiography

In the manual approach, the comparison methodology requires the acquisition of PM simulated radiographs from a CT trying to simulate the AM radiographs (Hatch et al., 2014; Kahana, 2009; Pfaeffli et al., 2007; Shinkawa et al., 2017), either directly on the corpse with an X-ray acquisition device. The acquisition of these simulated radiographs is a time-consuming, error-prone, and subjective task.

However, there are just a few automatic approaches for the comparison of AM radiographs and 3D images (Stephan et al., 2014; Niespodziewanski et al., 2016; D'Alonzo et al., 2017). These approaches are based on the use of 3D laser range scanners for the acquisition of 3D surface models of the skeletal structures of interest, particularly, clavicles in Stephan et al. (2014), D'Alonzo et al. (2017) and patellae in Niespodziewanski et al. (2016). They follow a procedure where a set of 2D projected images are obtained from these PM 3D surface models through the 3D model rotation. These 2D projections only contain the silhouette of the target skeletal structure. Finally, this set of PM projections is automatically compared to the manually segmented silhouette of the skeletal structure in the AM radiographs using elliptical Fourier analysis descriptors. However, the limitation of these methods lies in the set of predefined 2D projections, and in the assumption that the parameters that modulate the perspective distortions are known.

Alternatively, Gómez et al. (Gómez et al., 2018), developed an evolutionary IR method using EAs which successfully solved this image comparison problem. The

AM data are clinical radiographies (2D images) of a particular bone that have to be compared against the actual PM bone (a 3D model). The promising results achieved led them to recently design a methodology to fully automate the ID process by CR (see Fig. 3.9). This method was tested with simulated CTs and radiographs of frontal sinuses, clavicles, and patellae obtaining a superb performance. The average overlap error in synthetic positive cases is less than 2% of the silhouette pixels according to the DICE metric. The worst results were obtained with the patellas due to the lower singularity of the visible region with an average error of 0.761 mm and 1.5% of pixels badly superimposed according to the mRPD and DICE metrics, respectively. The mean recorded error of the clavicle was 0.055 mm and 0.2% of poorly overlapping pixels. The best results were obtained with the frontal sinuses, with an average error of 0.028 mm and 0.2% of poorly overlapping pixels. In addition, they carried out two studies to measure the discriminatory capacity of the developed IR method (without any subsequent analysis, only based on the overlap error). In the first experiment, in which 10 simulated radiographs were used against 10 head CT scans, positive cases were always ranked first in the ranking resulting from ordering each AM projection against all 3D PM models according to the DICE metric. However, in a second experiment using 10 real radiographs, the percentage of positive cases in the first position of the ranking dropped to 58%. This is mainly due to the low visibility of the frontal sinuses in five of the 10 AM radiographs that do not obtain the first position in the ranking. In this regard, the authors conclude that a protocol for the segmentation of the bone/cavity region and occlusion could help improve the results of cases with low visibility.

In addition to the dependence on well contour marking, the method showed the following drawbacks: (1) none of the considered projective projections reproduced the perspective distortion of radiographs where the X-ray generator was not perpendicular to the image receptor (e.g., in the Water's projection of radiographs of frontal

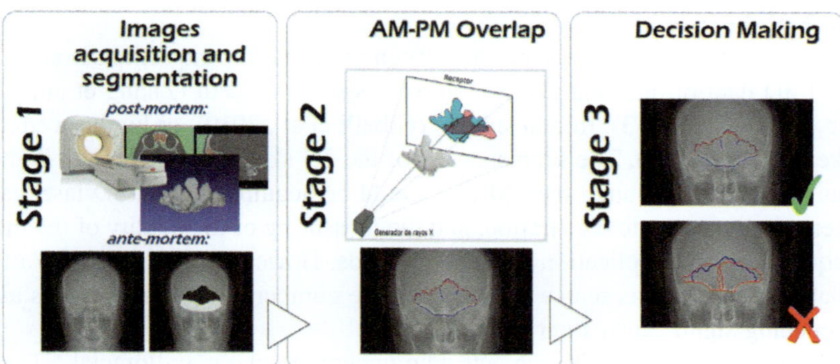

FIGURE 3.9

Three stages proposed for automating forensic identification using comparative radiography.

Credit: Original.

sinuses (Thali et al., 2003)); (2) the robustness of the EA employed, differential evolutionary (DE), especially with clavicles and patellae, that in some runs led to bad superimpositions due to the stochastic nature of DE and the highly multimodal search space tackled; and (3) the large amount of time required to obtain a superimposition with DE (1800 s on average).

Finally, they also tackled the problem of segmenting multiple organs (hearts, lungs, and clavicles) in chest X-ray images using ConvNets (Gómez et al., 2019b). They proposed several new deep architectures to deal with this complex problem. Their best performing proposal obtained better results than the competitor methods on clavicles with 0.0884, 0.939, and 18.022 for Jaccard Index, Dice Similarity Coefficient, and Hausdorff Distance metrics, respectively. This performance is in line with the ability of expert radiologists to accurately delimitate the contour of clavicles in X-ray images.

3.3.3 3D-3D approaches for comparative radiography

The CT–CT comparison approach is the most accurate and reliable and does not have any of the above limitations, since the 3D shapes can be directly compared (Deloire et al., 2019; Hacl et al., 2017; Iino et al., 2016; Ruder et al., 2016). Thus, when AM and PM CTs are available, this approach is recommended over the latter two due to their greater reliability and forensic potential (Gascho et al., 2018).

In manual approaches (although supported by software), identification is done through visual comparison of their 3D shapes, avoiding occlusions or perspective distortions, or through anthropological measurements, where distances can be compared directly since CTs maintain the original physical units. In fact, in Kim et al. (2013), 15 measurements were studied on head CTs of 119 Korean corpses. It was observed that the total volume of the frontal sinuses, some nonmetric characteristics and the bilateral asymmetry index in men differed significantly from those of women ($P < .05$). With a combination of these measures, they were able to identify 98% of the individuals.

A few computerized approaches have been proposed for the comparison of AM and PM 3D data of different skeletal structures such as teeth (Zhang et al., 2015; Zhong et al., 2011, 2013), frontal sinuses (Gibelli et al., 2019), or lumbar vertebrae (Decker & Ford, 2019). The segmentation of the 3D skeletal structures in both the AM and PM CTs (although the PM data could be acquired with a 3D laser range scanner), their automatic registration, and the measuring of the quality of the match are required for the application of these methods. However, the availability of 3D AM data (such as CT) is scarce compared to the number of AM radiographs available reducing significantly their applicability.

In Gibelli et al. (2019), 30 subjects who underwent two maxillofacial CT scans (interval: 1 month to 5 years) were selected from a hospital database. The frontal sinuses were automatically segmented using the open source ITK-SNAP software and the three-dimensional models belonging to the same patient were automatically superimposed according to the smallest point-to-point difference between the two surfaces. Two hundred patients were randomly selected from the same database and underwent the same procedure to perform 200 frontal sinus overlays belonging to different individuals, divided equally between men and women (negative cases). The statistically significant differences in the RMS point to point between the group of positive cases, on the one hand, and that of negative cases, on the other, as well as the possible differences according to sex, were evaluated. In the group of positive cases, the RMS ranged from 0.07 to 0.96 mm (mean RMS 0.35 ± 0,23 mm), while in the group of negative cases, it ranged from 0.96 to 10.29 mm (mean RMS 2,59 ± 1,79 mm), with a statistically significant difference ($P < .0001$).

In Decker and Ford (2019), the objective was to document the effectiveness of the part-to-part comparison of 3D models of the lumbar spine obtained by CT scans in forensic identification. This study aimed to provide a new quantifiable positive identification technique (through a percentage coincidence) that met the explicit requirements of the Daubert judgment and the challenges established in the 2009 NAS report. The AM and PM simulated PM models were compared with the lumbar vertebrae (L1-L5) of 30 individuals by means of part comparison analysis. A threshold of ±0.5 mm, with at least 90% coincidence, was considered a positive identification. Using this threshold, the part comparison results had a perfect identification rate with no false positives or negatives. An ROC curve with a score of one was generated which means "perfect" sensitivity and specificity, with a cut-off value of 65.5%. On average, positive identifications had a coincidence of 94.7% within the established threshold, while negative identifications had an average of 21.4%. Observing the impact of the different components of the BP, the age and sex of the unknown individual played a minimal role in the percentage of coincidence for both positive and negative identification.

3.4 Overview of the existing artificial intelligence approaches for craniofacial superimposition

CFS is probably the most challenging SFI method (Iscan & Helmer, 1993). It involves the superimposition of an image of a skull with a number of AM face images of an individual and the analysis of their morphological correspondence. This skull-face overlay (SFO) process is usually done by corresponding anatomical (anthropometrical) landmarks located in the skull (craniometric) and the face (cephalometric). Thus, differently to CR, two objects of different nature are compared (a face and a skull). CFS has been used for one century, yet it is not a mature and fully accepted technique due to the absence of solid scientific approaches, significant reliability studies, and international standards. On the other hand, this technique is widely employed in developing countries because its application is inexpensive and the only AM data required is one or more photographs of the face.

The most recent comprehensive surveys of the CFS field differentiate three consecutive stages (see Fig. 3.10) for the whole CFS process (Damas et al., 2011; Huete et al., 2015): (1) the acquisition and processing of the materials, that is, skull (or skull 3D model) and the AM facial photographs with the corresponding location

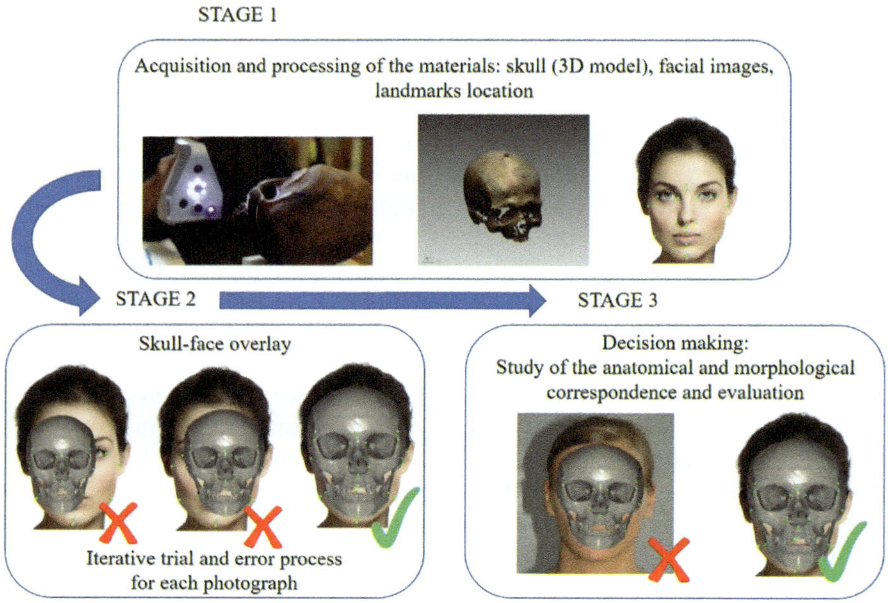

FIGURE 3.10

General overview of the craniofacial superimposition (CFS) forensic identification technique.

Credit: Original.

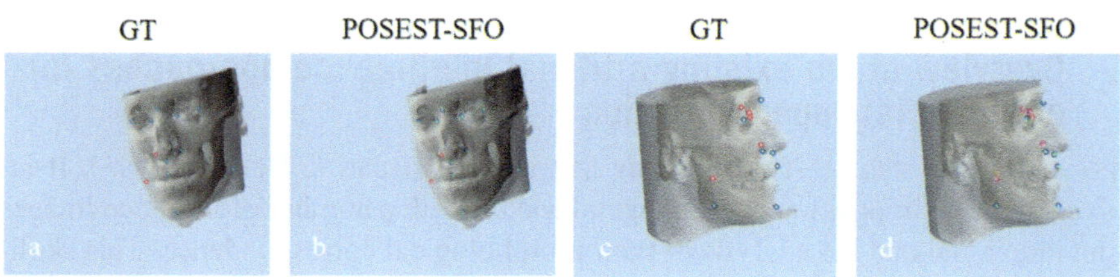

FIGURE 3.11

Two simulated SFO scenarios involving subject X with a nearly frontal and lateral pose. The (a) and (c) images shows the ground truth solution, followed by the automatic SFO computed by POSEST-SFO, (b) and (d).

Credit: Original.

of anthropometric landmarks on both; (2) the SFO process, which deals with accomplishing the best possible superimposition of the skull on a single AM photograph of a missing person. This process is repeated for each available photograph, obtaining different overlays; (3) the decision-making which evaluate the degree of support of being the same person or not (exclusion) based on the previous SFOs. This decision is influenced by the morphological correlation between the skull and the face, the matching between the corresponding landmarks according to the soft tissue depth, and the consistency between asymmetries. These criteria can vary depending on the region and the pose (Damas et al., 2015).

The following subsections review the main existing computer-aided CFS approaches for each of the three stages, specially emphasizing on the automatic methods developed over the last 10 years.

3.4.1 Acquisition and processing of the materials

The computerized systems developed for the first stage of CFS are related to face enhancement and skull modeling procedures. Skull 2D images, skull live images (video superimposition), and more frequently nowadays skull 3D models can be used in CFS. With the use of scanning devices, like laser range scanners, the forensic anthropologist can get a skull 3D model with a precision lower than 1 millimeter in a reasonable time (Park et al., 2006). The use of a 3D model instead of a skull 2D image is more recommended because it is a more accurate representation of the real skull. It has already been shown that 3D models are more informative in other forensic identification tasks (De Angelis et al., 2009). In the biomedical field, CT scanning images are the starting data to reconstruct the skull (Fantini et al., 2008; Singare et al., 2009).

Since the first proposal to use a skull 3D model to tackle the CFS problem (Nickerson et al., 1991), 3D image reconstruction software is a real need to construct the 3D model by aligning the views in a common coordinate frame. In this sense, Santamaria et al. (Santamaría et al., 2007b; Santamaría et al., 2007a; Santamaría et al., 2009), proposed a method, based on EAs, for the automatic alignment of skull range images. Different views of the skull to be modeled were acquired by using a laser range scanner. A two-step pair-wise range IR technique was successfully applied to such images. The method is very robust since it reconstructs the skull 3D model even if there is no turntable, and the views are wrongly scanned. In (Ballerini et al.), the authors proposed the automatic reduction of the data provided by the laser range scanner used in the skull 3D model reconstruction task. The dense point cloud corresponding to every skull view is synthesized by considering heuristic features that are based on the curvature values of the skull surface. Those features guide the automatic skull 3D model reconstruction by means of an EA. Today's technology, that is, current 3D acquisition devices and corresponding software, automatically solves the alignment of the different acquisition views without the need of turntables or any additional device.

Finally, a different related task was presented in Campomanes-Álvarez et al. (2012). The authors proposed a new algorithm to deal with the 3D open model mesh simplification problem from an evolutionary multiobjective point of view. An open model refers to a surface with open ends. The problem is based on the location of a certain number of points in order to approximate a mesh as accurately as possible to the initial surface. The algorithm considers two conflicting objectives, the accuracy and the simplicity of a simplified 3D mesh.

On the other hand, this stage also encompasses the tasks of marking cephalometric and craniometrics landmarks. A problem very similar to the former, the location of facial landmarks in photographs, has been widely addressed in the CV community, and more recently with DL techniques (Johnston & Chazal, 2018). DL approaches are able to fully automate the process, with an accuracy similar to that of an expert eve "in the wild" photographs, that is to say, totally realistic photographs, without any type of restriction regarding pose, lighting, occlusions, etc. However, the landmark sets used in these works are not the same as those used in FA, and we can only find a single publication that focuses on the automatic location of cephalometric landmarks in photographs (Porto et al., 2019) (there are several in radiographs (Lindner et al., 2016; Song et al., 2020)). In Porto et al. (2019), the authors use CV and ML techniques on a set of 1000 photos and the manual marking of landmarks on these by an expert, to detect a total of 28 cephalometric landmarks. The proposed methodology achieves a normalized mean distance error (in pixels) of 0.014, similar to the average dispersion among experts (0.009). The main drawback of this method is that it is designed for frontal images that comply with the ICAO 9303 standard (ISO/IEC 19794, 2020). Furthermore, in the case of the gonion, zygion, nasion, and glabella, the localized landmark is not the standard and the authors give their own definition.

3.4.2 Skull-face overlay

The automation of the SFO stage has attracted the interest of a very small group of researchers, standing out among all, due to the volume of publications and the progress they represent, the Soft Computing and Intelligent Information Systems (SOCCER) research group at the University of Granada. According to them, the most natural way to deal with the SFO problem is to replicate the original scenario of the AM photograph in which the living person was in a given pose somewhere inside the camera's field. Regarding computer-aided automatic methods, the task of replicating on a skull the pose and the remaining acquisition parameters of a given facial photograph is the main goal of the SFO process. This is similar to the classic CV problem of replicating the pose of a 3D object from a photo based on some reference points. Technically, we are given n points having 3D positions $a_1, \ldots, a_n$ and target 2D positions $b_1, \ldots, b_n$. The goal is to find a projection P so that every $P(a_i)$ is as close as possible to b_i. This problem is named as IR or camera calibration problem.

The first computer-aided approach for the SFO task was proposed by Nickerson et al. (Nickerson et al., 1991). The landmarks of the 3D skull mesh were selected to calculate the affine and perspective transformation (rotation, scaling and translation) to map with the landmarks of the 2D face image using real-coded genetic algorithms. Another automatic approach was presented in Ghosh and Sinha (2001), in which they considered two different ANNs for implement an objective assessment of the symmetry between two nearly frontal 2D images (skull and facial image).

In the last decade, the vast majority of proposals come from the SOCCER research group to tackle the SFO automation using EAs and fuzzy sets (Campomanes-Álvarez et al., 2015; Ibáñez et al., 2009, 2012a, 2012b). These approaches are based on overlaying a 3D model of the skull over a facial photograph by minimizing the distance among pairs of landmarks while handling the imprecision introduced by the location of facial landmarks (Cummaudo et al., 2013; Damas et al., 2015). The minimization process involves the search for a specific projection of the skull model leading to the best possible matching between corresponding landmarks. More recently, Valsecchi et al. (Valsecchi et al., 2018) proposed a novel automatic SFO algorithm called POSEST-SFO. Their previous works (Campomanes-Álvarez et al., 2015; Ibañez et al., 2011) solved the projection problem by an iterative optimization process, where multiple solutions are evaluated at every step, eventually converging to a high quality solution. Unlike these methods, POSEST-SFO algorithm solves a system of polynomial equations relating the distances between the points before and after the projection. This latter algorithm was tested on a synthetic data set comprised of nine CBCTs from nine different subject and 60 simulated photographs, 30 laterals, and 30 frontals (see Fig. 3.4), from each of them, that is, 540 SFOs. This method is extremely fast, since it lasts 78 ms to automatically perform a single SFO. In the most realistic scenario, considering soft tissue thickness (the mean distance was employed) and ± 5 pixels of error in facial landmarks, the mean back-projection error was 2.0 and 3.2 mm in frontal and lateral photos, respectively. However, this algorithm, contrary to previous publications (Bermejo et al., 2017; Campomanes-Álvarez et al., 2015), does not address the sources of uncertainty, that is, the articulation of the mandible, the estimation of the soft tissue thickness, and the intra- and intererror in landmark location. It is clear then that there is still a large margin for improvement.

3.4.3 Skull-face overlay assessment and decision-making

In the stage 3 of the CFS process (see Fig. 3.10), the forensic expert has to make a decision to determine the degree of support that the skull and facial photographs belong to the same person or not. This decision is made through the analysis of the previous SFOs and influenced by several criteria assessing the skull-face anatomical correspondence. This way, different authors have defined and classified those criteria in four different families.

1. Analysis of the consistency of the bony and facial outlines/morphological curves.
2. Assessment of the anatomical consistency by positional relationship.
3. Line location and comparison to analyze anatomical consistency.
4. Evaluation of the consistency of the soft tissue thickness between corresponding cranial and facial landmarks.

This is a subjective process that relies on the forensic expert's skills and the quantity and quality of the used materials. However, there are just a few works tackling the automation of the analysis of craniofacial correspondences within the framework of CFS identification (Ricci et al., 2006; Yoshino et al., 1997). Most of the existing literature was published more than 20 years ago, and the works are very basic and limited. In addition, they do not consider the use of either skull 3D models or computer techniques to perform the skull-face overlay. Besides, the employed technique for the shape analysis implies manual interaction. They provide a value that does not take into account the actual spatial relation between skull and face since the methods employed are invariant to translation, scale, and rotation. Finally, these systems only implement a single group of the criteria to assess the craniofacial correspondence, those of the first family, since what they do is to extract mathematical characteristics of the contours, using the Fourier Elliptic, for their subsequent quantification and comparison.

Recently, in Campomanes-Alvarez et al. (2016), (2018), members of the SOCCER research group presented a hierarchical system for the decision-making stage and CV algorithms to evaluate the anatomical consistence of morphological criteria between the face and the skull. This means that from a series of SFOs of the same individual, the decision support system (DSS) provides to the forensic expert a quantitative output value indicative of the morphological matching consistency of a given CFS problem. This quantitative value is based on the use of several skull-face anatomical criteria combined at different levels by means of fuzzy aggregation functions considering the evaluation of the anatomical correspondence between the skull and the face at three different levels: criterion evaluation (level 3), SFO evaluation (level 2), and CFS evaluation (level 1). The sources of uncertainty and degrees of confidence involved in the process (bone preservation and 3D model quality, image quality, discriminatory power of each individual criterion, BP influence) were modeled and taken into account at each level of the system (Campomanes-Alvarez et al., 2018). With the aim of comparing the performance of real forensic practitioners with our CFS DSS, we applied our system to the same experimental dataset of (Ibáñez et al., 2015). In that study, 26 participants from 17 different institutions were asked to deal with 14 identification scenarios, some of them involving the comparison of multiple candidates and unknown skulls. A total number of 60 SFO problems were tackled. The mean value of the results of the 26 experts, the result of the three best experts, and the outcomes of their automatic DSS are shown in Table 3.3. The designed DSS can be considered the first automatic tool for classifying couples of unknown faces and skulls as positive or negative cases with accuracy similar to the best performing forensic expert (Campomanes-Álvarez et al., 2018). However, one of the conclusions reached was that the identification results based on the performance of the DSS could be strongly influenced by the poor quality of some SFOs. In this particular system, all SFOs were automatically obtained by the method developed in Campomanes-Álvarez et al. (2015).

Finally, in Nagpal et al. (2017), Singh et al. (2018), the authors proposed a model for automated skull recognition without the need of superimposition. In this work, the authors used a dataset consisting of 464 photographs of deceased people and the same number of photographs of their respective skulls, to learn a mathematical model (semi-supervised and unsupervised learning) that was capable of relating pairs of skull and facial photos. The results achieved position this approach as a promising alternative to filter a significant number of possible candidates using only a frontal photograph of the skull.

Table 3.3 The table shows the mean value of the results of the 26 experts, the results of the three best experts, and the outcomes of our automatic DSS. Detailed performance indicators are shown, such as the percentage of correct decisions, the number of positive and negative decisions given in each case, and the corresponding rate of true and false positives and true and false negatives. Ground truth refers to the real nature of each CFS case (P = positive, N = negative).

Method	Correct decisions	Ground truth	Decision		Decision (%)	
			P	N	P	N
Expert mean	78.99%	P	100	90	52.63%	47.3%
		N	152	810	15.80%	84.20%
Best expert 1	93.33%	P	8	2	80.00%	20.00%
		N	2	48	4.00%	96.00%
Best expert 2	88.14%	P	6	3	66.67%	33.33%
		N	4	46	8.00%	92.00%
Best expert 3	86.21%	P	5	3	62.50%	37.50%
		N	5	45	10.00%	90.00%
Our DSS	**90.00%**	P	6	4	**60.00%**	40.00%
		N	2	48	4.00%	**96.00%**

Credit: Data from Campomanes-Álvarez et al. (2018).

3.4.4 3D-3D computer-aided approaches for craniofacial superimposition

In recent years, some authors have proposed a consistent 3D skull-3D face approach for CFS.

Duan et al. (Duan et al., 2014) proposed a novel ID method based on the correlation measure between 3D skull and 3D face in morphology. The mapping between skull and face is obtained using canonical correlation analysis. Unlike existing techniques, this method does not need the accurate relationship between skull and face and only measures the correlation between them. In order to measure the correlation between skull and face more reliably and improve the identification capability of the correlation analysis model, a region fusion strategy is adopted. Experimental results validate the proposed method and show that the region based method significantly boost the matching accuracy. The correct recognition rate reaches 100% using a CT dataset. The biggest problem with this approach is its low applicability, as it requires a 3D facial AM model.

In Tan et al. (2020), another 3D-3D superimposition approach was presented in an effort to contribute to computer-aided CFS. The proposed method emphasizes adherence to two important parameters: (1) maintaining the life-size of the face image in relation to the size of the skull and (2) orienting the skull on an anthropological basis using selected feature points. The proposed method commences by reconstructing the 3D face model from a given 2D face image using a mean simplified generic elastic model. Following a "leave-one-out" methodology, they studied the precision of the method of generating a facial 3D model from a photo based on public facial models "USF 3D face database," which contains 102 individuals. The root mean square error of the generated 3D models was close to 4 mm. Next, a 3D-3D registration step of the facial model with the skull model considering the jaw line is carried out using a B-spline model. The registration error is evaluated by six different methods to suggest the degree to which the 3D facial model (obtained from a photograph) corresponds to the 3D model of the skull. With the registered error, a precision index is calculated between 0 and 1; the result of comparing all the cases with each other is ordered in function of the positive case. Using a set of 29 3D skull models (CTs) and comparing each of them against 131 photographs (actually against the 3D model generated from each of these), the precision index reached an average value of 0.8, or what is the same, the proposed method places the correct candidate in position 27 on average. From these results, and in the absence of a more complete statistical analysis, it can be concluded that this method could serve to filter an indeterminate number of cases and never to identify.

3.5 Overview of the existing artificial intelligence approaches for forensic facial approximation

Forensic facial approximation, also called facial reconstruction, is an identification technique for unknown skeletal remains, or corpses encountered in criminal investigations, based on the estimation of a face from a skull with the aim to obtain information about the deceased person's identity. In Stephan et al. (2018), four different approaches to carry out facial estimation with a variety of techniques can be distinguished.

(1) Two-dimensional (2D) representation of the face over a photograph of the skull (Clement & Marks, 2005; IOS Press Ebooks, 2020; Stephan & Henneberg, 2001; Taylor, 2000).
(2) Three-dimensional (3D) manual construction of the face in clay or mastic over the skull or skull cast (Gatliff, 1984; Prag & Neave, 1997; Ullrich & Stephan, 2011; Wilkinson, 2004).
(3) Computerized sculpting of the face using haptic feedback devices and a 3D scan of the skull (Wilkinson, 2005; Wilkinson et al., 2006; Lee et al., 2012; Wilkinson & Rynn, 2012; Evenhouse et al.).
(4) Computerized construction of the face using more complex computer-automated 3D routines (Claes et al., 2006; Claes et al., 2010; Parks et al., 2013; Quatrehomme et al., 1997; Guyomarc'h et al., 2014; de Buhan & Nardoni, 2018; Vandermeulen et al., 2006; Imaizumi et al., 2019).

All these approaches have in common the dependence of soft tissue thickness measurements of the face.

Inside the fourth and last group, several works on the automation of this technique have been proposed during the last 10 years, giving rise to completely computerized and largely automated methods of facial approximation, often using CT scans as training sets (Guyomarc'h et al., 2014; de Buhan & Nardoni, 2018; Vandermeulen et al., 2006; Imaizumi et al., 2019; Tu et al., 2007; Liu & Li, 2018).

Vandermulen et al. (Vandermeulen et al., 2006) presented a fully automatic procedure for craniofacial reconstruction, using a reference database of head CT scans. All reference images are automatically segmented into head volumes (enclosed by the external skin surface) and bone/skull volumes, both represented by a signed distance transform (sDT) map. The reference skull sDTs are nonlinearly warped to the target skull sDT, and this warping is applied to all reference skin sDTs. A linear combination of the warped reference skin sDTs is proposed as the reconstruction of the external skin surface of the target subject. Results on a pilot reference database (N = 20) show the feasibility of this approach, although further investigations are required. First, metal streak artifacts need to be removed from the images, since they possibly distort the reconstructions to an unacceptable extent. Second, the warping procedure needs to be examined more carefully, paying attention, on the one hand, to better fitting the reference to the target skull and, on the other hand, to provide a smooth extrapolation of the warping. Third, other linear combinations besides the mere average need to be explored. Finally, a more extensive quantitative validation framework for the reconstructions needs to be carried out.

Tu et al. (Tu et al., 2007) proposed the automation of the reconstruction process through a data-driven 3D generative model of the face constructed using a database of CT head scans for a given skull. The reconstruction can be constrained based on prior knowledge such as age and/or weight. To determine whether or not these reconstructions have merit, geometric methods for comparing reconstructions against a gallery of facial images are proposed. First, active shape models (a CV technique that consist of defining the mean shape and statistical variability of a given object using a set of points) are used to automatically detect a set of facial landmarks on each image. These landmarks are associated with 3D points on the reconstruction. Direct comparison of the reconstruction is problematic since, in general, the camera geometry used for image capture is unknown, and there are uncertainties associated with the reconstruction and landmark detection processes. The first method of comparison uses constrained optimization to determine the optimal projection of the reconstruction onto the image. Residuals are then analyzed resulting in a ranking of the gallery. The second method uses boosting to learn which points are both reliable and discriminating. This results in a match/no-match classifier.

Claes et al. (Claes et al., 2010) described the common pipeline of modern facial approximation software. First, it is necessary that an expert examines the unknown skull in order to determine de BP. Then, a virtual replica of the skull is produced and represented according to the modeling parameters. A craniofacial template encoding face, skull, and soft tissue information are derived from a head database. Then, an admissible geometric transformation drives the adaptation of the craniofacial template onto the unknown skull, according to the "proximity" between the skulls. As a result, the template face is deformed onto the predicted face associated with the unknown skull, linking together information coming from both the database and the examination of the unknown skull. Finally, a skin texture and hairiness are added to the reconstructed face.

Guyomarc'h et al. (Guyomarc'h et al., 2014) developed a computerized method for estimating facial shape based on CT scans of 500 French individuals. Facial soft tissue depths are estimated based on age, sex, corpulence, and craniometrics and projected using reference planes to obtain the global facial appearance. Position and shape of the eyes, nose, mouth, and ears are inferred from cranial landmarks through geometric morphometrics. The 100 estimated cutaneous landmarks are then used to warp a generic face to the target facial approximation. A validation by resampling on a subsample of 500 CTs demonstrated an average accuracy of ~4 mm for the overall face. The resulting approximation is an objective probable facial shape, but is also synthetic (i.e., without texture), and therefore needs to be enhanced artistically prior to its use in forensic cases. This facial approximation approach is integrated in the TIVMI software,[2] is available freely for further testing.

De Buhan and Nardoni (de Buhan & Nardoni, 2018) present a new numerical method for facial reconstruction. Their approach combines classical features as the use of a skulls/faces database, and more original aspects: (1) an original shape matching method is used to link the unknown skull to the database templates and (2) the final face is seen as an elastic 3D mask that is deformed and adapted onto the unknown skull. In this method, the skull is considered as a whole surface and not restricted to some anatomical landmarks, allowing a dense description of the skull/face relationship. Also, the approach is fully automated. Various results are presented to show its efficiency.

Liu and Li (Liu & Li, 2018) developed a new algorithm to perform facial reconstruction from a given skull. Unlike most existing strategies that directly reconstruct the face from the skull, they utilize a database of portrait photos to create many face candidates (3D facial models) and then perform a superimposition with the skull from which they want to do the facial reconstruction. To support this pipeline, they employ deep neural nets: first, they build an effective autoencoder for image-based facial reconstruction and, second, they use a generative model for constrained face inpainting. Their experiments have demonstrated that the proposed pipeline was stable and accurate.

Imaizumi et al. (Imaizumi et al., 2019) developed a software solution for 3D facial approximation from the skull based on CT scans of the head obtained from 59 Japanese adult volunteers (40 males, 19 females). The positional relationship between the skull and head surface shape were analyzed by creating anatomically homologous shape models. Before modeling, skull shapes were simplified by concealing hollow structures of the skull using in house software. Surficial tissue thickness, represented by the distance between corresponding vertices of the simplified skull and head surface, was calculated for each individual and averaged for each sex. Although the approximate head shapes of known individuals showed a

[2] http://projets.pacea.u-bordeaux.fr/TIVMI/index.php?page=afa3d.

relatively good resemblance in both the shape of the whole head and facial parts, some errors were identified, particularly in areas with thick surficial tissue at the cheek, and thicker tissue at the glabella, nose, mouth, and chin. Moreover, they created referential models for CFS from average models of the skull and head surface shape for each sex.

Beyond and related to facial approximation from a skull, it seems important to us to point out the latest advances in facial reconstruction based on information from the genetic profile (Claes et al., 2014). Called "molecular photofitting" (Molecular Photofitting, 2008), these methods can supplement facial approximation methods to predict faces and are especially useful for morphologies with limited tangible relationships to the skeletal structure. In terms of specific face traits, red hair color and blue/brown colors of the iris are regarded as accurately predictable from genes alone (Kayser & Schneider, 2009). Approximately 70% accuracy has been recorded for red hair prediction (Sulem et al., 2007), whereas positive predictive intervals of colors of the iris ranged from 66% to 100% for blue eyes and 70%−100% for brown eyes (Kastelic et al., 2013; Pneuman et al., 2012; Walsh et al., 2011, 2012). Predictive models for skin color are also being investigated, tested, and validated (Maroñas et al., 2014; Spichenok et al., 2011).

4. Skeleton-ID: Artificial intelligence at the service of physical and forensic anthropology

Skeleton-ID (Skeleton-ID and https) is the main R&D project and first product of Panacea Cooperative Research, a young (founded in 2017) Spanish start-up, spin-off of the UGR. Free for educational and research purposes, it is a proprietary software commercialized to provide an integral support to forensic ID through physical anthropology techniques.

Skeleton-ID is a web platform (accessible from internet or installed in an institutional intranet), which means that only a web browser and Internet connection are needed to use it (there are no requirements concerning type of terminal or operating system). Due to its online nature, it facilitates remote networking, collaborative research, and secure case sharing among experts and institutions. Confidentiality and security are assured through storage and transmission of encrypted data as well as authentication and a hierarchical privileges system.

Skeleton-ID is conceived to be a complete and integral platform, offering the necessary tools to perform all the (reconstructive and comparative) FA techniques. In particular, it facilitates tools and functionalities to administrate: (1) users and their roles (access levels); (2) AM and PM databases, including the performance of complex queries to filter cases; (3) data sharing and compatibility with standardize forms/software (Interpol, ICRC); (4) case files and the corresponding reports including all relevant information (chain of custody log, evaluations and decisions, tables, images, etc.); and (5) institutional or professional preferences such as:

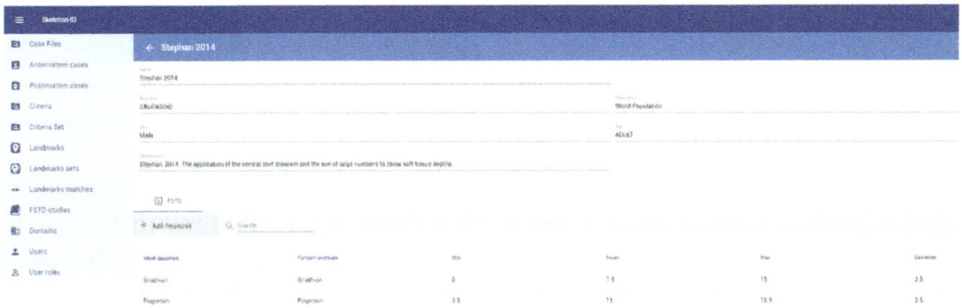

FIGURE 3.12

Skeleton-ID administration panel for the definition of soft tissue depth studies.

Credit: Original.

landmarks employed, soft tissue depth studies definition, morphological and morphometric criteria sets, etc. Figs. 3.12–3.14 depict some screenshots of the software related to the cited administrative tools.

Forensic experts can use Skeleton-ID to store information, perform searches, and filter candidates (based on different sources of information such as BP, dental records or physical observations over the skeletal remains), create new case files from them (for example, one skeleton and their compatible missing persons), annotate morphological and morphometric characteristics, perform the evaluation of the results obtained, provide partial and final decisions, or generate and print identification reports.

Alternatively, these same features will allow anthropologists and archaeologists from academia to use Skeleton-ID as a free software tool to digitally store and share all the information gathered from their own osteological collections. At the same time, it will allow to carry out more ambitious research studies involving data from several institutions collected in the same standard format.

On the other hand, in order to obtain all the benefits of Skeleton-ID AI technology, AM and PM images must be employed. During the last decade, there has been a boom in 3D photogrammetry-based acquisition devices together with the development of a novel field of research, the Virtopsy (Bolliger and Thali, 2015). Thus, imaging techniques, like 3D bone scanning, and radiological procedures, like CT, are being progressively incorporated to scientific research in forensic medicine, and today, they are part of the routine workflow in some forensic institutes. The software provides a web graphic engine allowing the visualization of almost any kind of 2D (photographs, X-rays) and 3D image (meshes and volumetric images such as CT or MRI). Together with the visualization capability, it brings a set of tools specifically designed to address FA tasks: (1) manage images of different nature in the same window: 2D, 3D, 2D-3D, and 3D-3D; (2) grids, reference lines, and multiple simultaneous views (Frankfurt, coronal and sagittal planes) to facilitate 2D and 3D landmark location; (3) 3D model rotation, translation, scaling and projection; (4) 2D-3D advanced operations: subject-to-camera distance, focal length and principal point; (5) 2D and 3D tools to measure distances, areas, perimeters and volumes; (6)

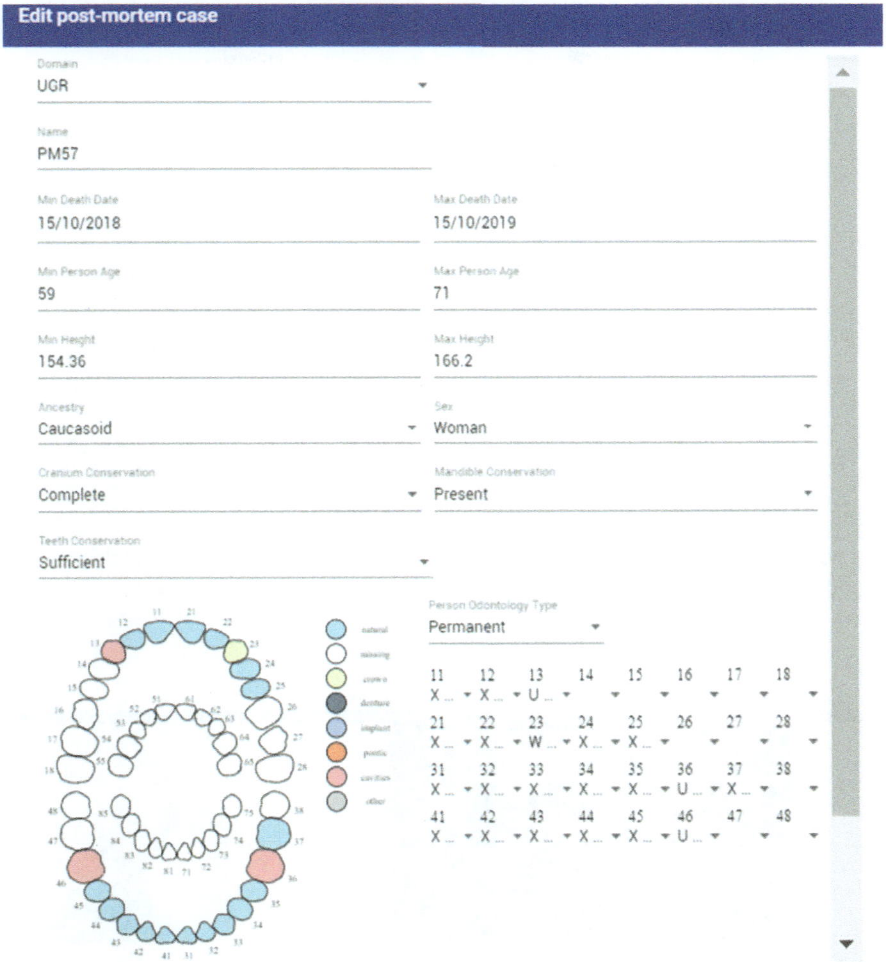

FIGURE 3.13

Form with all relevant information for a PM case, including death date, biological profile data, and skull and dental preservation information.

Credit: Original.

wipe and transparency mode in superimposition, etc. Figures below (Figs. 3.15 and 3.16) show some of the functionalities related to the graphic engine.

The use of AM and PM images implies a series of advantages: (1) automatic chain of custody over the digital version of the remains, since every action is recorded together with a time stamp and the ID of the user; (2) reproducibility of the task performed, the measurements taken, the analysis accomplished, etc.; (3) the possibility to easily share (digital) evidences with other experts and access them whenever required; and (4) the possibility to better support in court the reasons

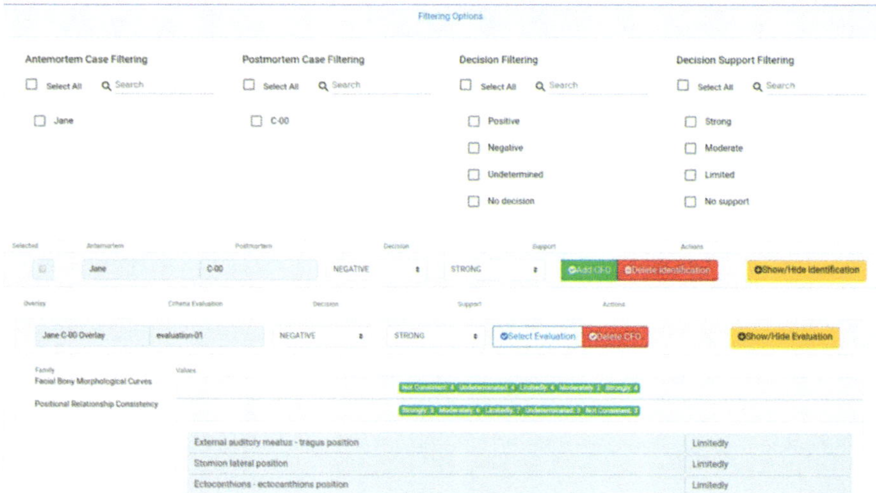

FIGURE 3.14

Identification reports panel with heterogeneous data (filtering options, CFS level decision support, SFO level decision support, anatomical consistency decision support).

Credit: Original.

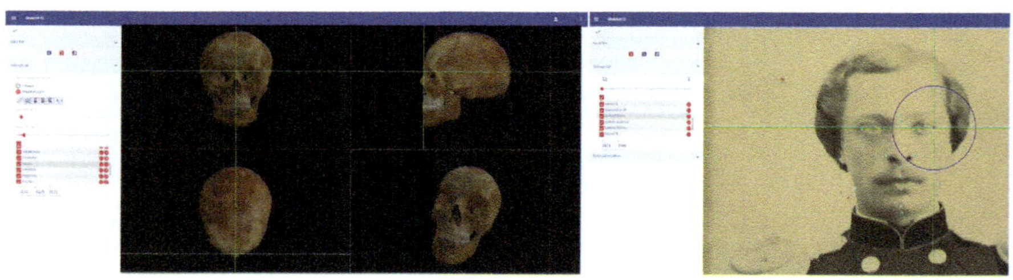

FIGURE 3.15

Craniometric landmark location tools. Once the Frankfurt plane has been established, the window splits in four to show and interact with the coronal, axial and sagittal planes, and the free 3D model (left). Cephalometric landmarks location tools. Perpendicular lines to reduce inter- and intraerror in landmark location (right).

Credit: Original.

behind a given decision, among others. However, the most significant advantage of working with digitalized data is the possibility to apply AI techniques on them. In the following subsections, we briefly explain the AI techniques currently included in Skeleton-ID, or in the process to be included, and those that are under research and development. They all are grouped into different modules, according to the technique they give support to.

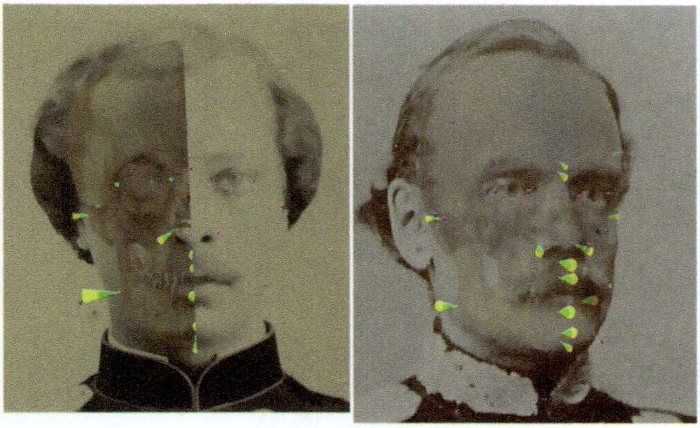

FIGURE 3.16

Wipe (first image) and transparency (second image) to facilitate the evaluation of craniofacial correspondence analysis in the craniofacial superimposition technique. The previous images also show the projection of colored cones according to the defined soft tissue depth study (green zone for the mean ± std and the yellow for the mean ± 3*std).

Credit: Original.

4.1 Artificial intelligence in the craniofacial superimposition module

This is the first module and, right now, the only module developed so far. It contains the state-of-the-art algorithms developed and published by the UGR, together with new algorithms not fully published yet, as they are under validation or development process.

Cephalometric landmark location: We have developed a DL algorithm able to identify which cephalometric landmarks (30) are visible and locate them into facial photographs showing "in the wild" characteristics (i.e., unconstrained poses, different illuminations and artifacts, like glasses, beard, hair and other type of occluding elements) (Gómez et al., 2019a). Currently, it has been trained using 3000 synthetic images (2D projections of 3D facial models) of 99 annotated 3D models (45 males, 54 females) but just 134 real facial photographs. Although the small number of real images employed, it achieved a root mean square error of 3.9 pixels. Fig. 3.17 (left) shows a graphical representation of such an error. There is still a lot of ground for improvement, beginning with the enlargement of the training set (number of photos with cephalometric landmarks previously located).

Craniofacial landmark location: A completely different approach is employed in this case mainly because of the availability of a skull 3D model. We employ a versatile template-based registration method that locates any number of predefined craniometric landmarks in 3D skull models, making use of the open source Meshmonk toolkit (White et al., 2019). An average representation of a human skull acts as a template model, whose geometry is locally deformed to warp into any (male or

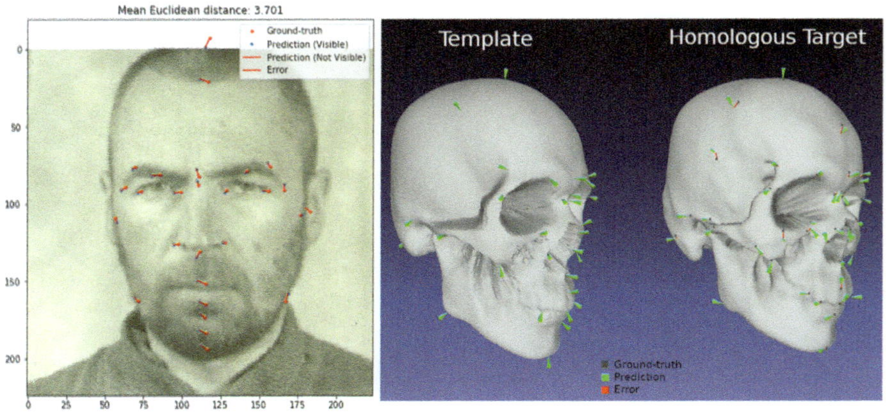

FIGURE 3.17

Left image: Graphical representation of the root mean square error on the automatic location of cephalometric visible landmarks into a face photograph. Right image: Graphical representation of the Euclidean distance error on the automatically transferred landmarks on a skull 3D model.

Credit: Original.

female) 3D skull model. The craniometric landmarks are direct correspondences from the template vertices to the homologous model and thus, can be directly transferred into the target skull. This approach has been preliminary tested with a set of 38 manually annotated landmarks on 45 annotated 3D skull models (25 males, 20 females). On average, it achieved a Euclidean distance error of 2.6 mm, which is graphically represented on Fig. 3.11 (right). Automatically transferred landmarks fit in general terms within the dispersion error resulting from manual labeling by forensic experts. Nevertheless, the precise localization will be improved in the future by considering a refinement based on the geometry of the model and the anatomical definition of the landmarks.

Skull-face overlay: This task has focused on the efforts of the researchers at the UGR during the last 10 years and is still an open and challenging research line where UGR and now also Panacea researchers continue working. The state of the art is represented by the algorithm developed by Valsecchi and collaborators in 2018 (Valsecchi et al., 2018), which is the one currently available in Skeleton-ID.

Since the publication of Valsecchi et al.'s work, UGR and Panacea researchers are working in its improvement and validation on a large data set. In particular, we are working with a data set of 500 CTs from Pierre Guyomarc'h's PhD dissertation. One of the preliminary results we can advance is the empirical demonstration of the uniqueness of the skull. We have performed more than a million cross-comparisons of simulated SFOs (3D skull landmarks from the CTs and 2D facial landmarks from the 2D projection of the CT). Using only the landmark matching error (no morphological criteria at all) obtained by Valsecchi et al.'s automatic

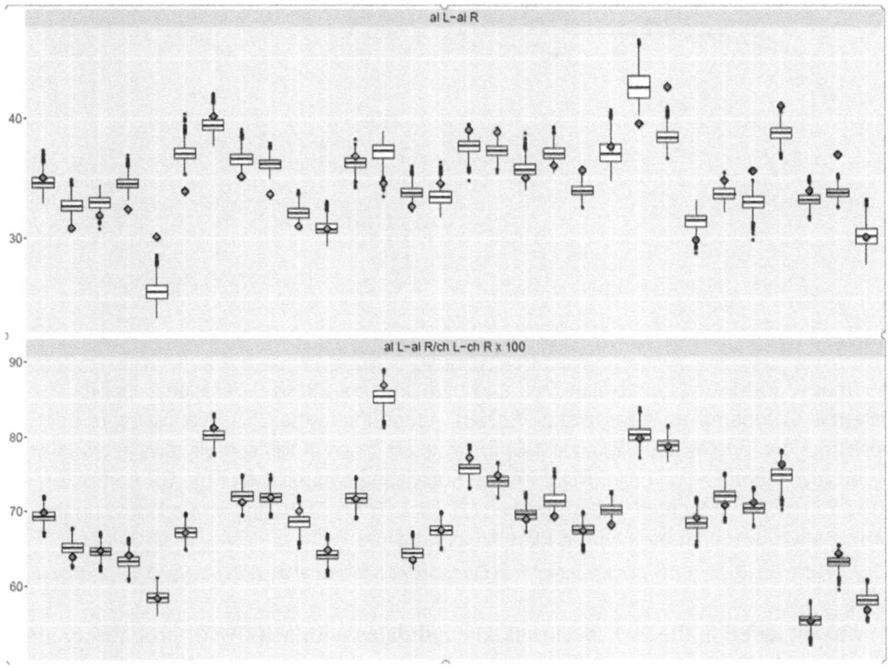

FIGURE 3.18

Top image: Estimated (boxplot) 3D distance between alare left and right in 30 different subjects in comparison with the real distance (colored diamond). Bottom image: Estimated (boxplot) Alar-Chelial index in 30 different subjects in comparison with the real index.

Credit: Original.

SFO algorithm, the lower SFO error always corresponds to a true positive case. Note that this experiment considers ideal and unrealistic conditions: known soft tissue thickness, no landmark location error, and no mandible articulation. In any case, it serves as a proof of concept and points out the need to continue researching in order to be able to transform CFS in a reliable identification technique.

Craniofacial correspondence evaluation and decision support system: The first and unique attempts to automate morphological evaluations of previously obtained SFOs, and to provide consequent support to the identification decision, have been made within the framework of C. Campomanes-Álvarez PhD dissertation. In this work, the authors modeled the automatic evaluation of nine skull-face morphological criteria and developed a hierarchical DSS as explained in Section 3.4.3. From the analysis of the experiment developed (Campomanes-Álvarez et al., 2018), the authors concluded that their system was suitable for (see Fig. 3.19, left).

- Filtering (sort-listing) cases: In 62.5% of the cases, the positive one is ranked in the first position. Besides, given a data set of initial candidates, the positive case

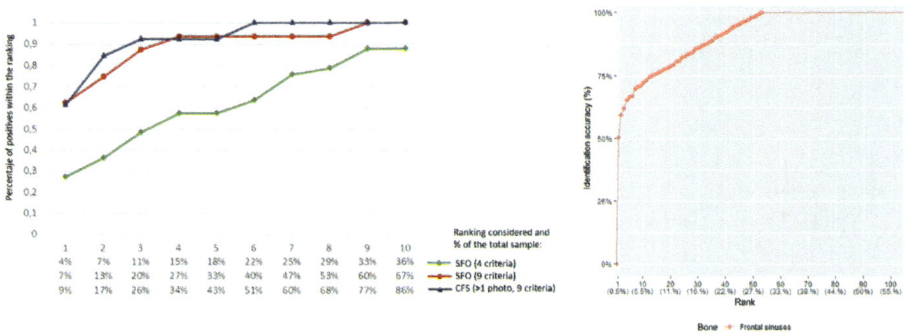

FIGURE 3.19

Left image: Sort-listing capabilities (red and blue lines) of the CFS decision support system in Campomanes-Álvarez et al. (2018). According to the CFS level (using or not more than one photo), the 22% (rank-6) first ranked cases in the sample always contain the positive identification case. Right image: Sort-listing capabilities of the CR computer-aided framework presented in Gómez et al. (2019c). The ~27% first ranked cases in the sample always contain the positive identification case.

Credit: Fig. 3.13_1 has been redrawn from Campomanes-Álvarez et al. (2018). Fig. 3.13_2 is original.

was included in the 60% best ranked candidates with a 100% of probability and within the 27% best ranked candidates with a 92% of probability.

- Establishing exclusion: The ability to determine a negative identity was performed with 97.4% of accuracy (97.4% of true negative over the test data set and 96.0% over the training data set).

Campomanes-Álvarez et al.'s algorithms will be integrated into Skeleton-ID along 2020, together with the graphical tools to delimit the facial and cranial regions subject to morphological correspondence automatic evaluation. The impact of this system in the application of the CFS technique is clear. Together with previous AI-based algorithms, it almost automates the whole process. It will provide the possibility to approach multiple-comparison scenarios, since all the SFO cross-comparisons will be automatically generated together with their morphological evaluation. The result will be an ordered list of candidates for each AM and/or PM case. In addition to saving a lot of time, it leads to a more objective process, as it allows including quantitative information and known error ranges in the decision-making process. This is especially significant in the case of estimating the parameters of the camera with which the photograph was taken.

Other tasks related to CFS: The previous three tasks have been associated to the main three stages of CFS as has been explained in Section 3.4. However, there is an intermediate task completely omitted by the AI-based proposals: the description of the morphometric and morphological features of the face and the skull. This is one of the main objectives of Rubén Martos' PhD dissertation, one of the authors of this chapter, whose results are also expected to be soon integrated into Skeleton-ID. On the one hand, Martos and collaborators (Martos et al., 2018) have proposed a novel methodology to estimate 3D dimensions and proportionality indices (DPIs) from 2D ones. The error in the estimation of the 3D DPIs can be as large as 35%, but both first and third quartiles are consistently inside the ±5% range. The next step in this research line involves the extension of the methodology to the comparison of skull and facial images. The most straightforward implementation is to simply compare cranial 3D DPIs with estimated 3D DPIs from 2D facial photographs. However, soft-tissue thickness must be considered when comparing those DPIs so an additional source of uncertainty will be introduced, with a presumably impact on its discriminatory power. On the other hand, as a continuation of Martos' PhD dissertation, we plan to automate facial and skull morphological description. In fact, as we explain in Section 4.4, we have already begun a research project aimed to automate facial morphological description for forensic facial comparison purposes in collaboration with the Federal Police of Brazil.

A transversal issue with relevant importance to all CFS stages refers to the estimation of facial soft tissue depth (FSTD). When tackling SFO as a craniofacial landmark matching problem (Valsecchi et al., 2018), the FSTD is calculated as the average depth per landmark from a certain sample of a particular population. In Urdín et al. (2019), we propose to avoid the mere use of this average and substitute this strategy by the regression of a series of 3D landmarks on the face from 3D landmarks on the skull, in order to estimate the thickness of the soft tissue that separates the skull from the face for each particular individual. Different regression methods are compared (linear regression, multilayer perceptron, RF, support vector machines, and partial least squares), and both the benefits of using imputation techniques for the missing values and the impact of adding additional landmarks are studied. The results indicated that our regression model based on a multilayer perceptron is a better estimator than the FSTD average with statistical significance. Further studies on the influence over automatic SFO and decision-making process are part of the work in progress.

Finally, Panacea research team is also working on providing automatic solutions based on AI algorithms to two tasks which will be initially applied to the CFS problem but with a direct application in other FA approaches, in particular, the 3D assembly of fragmented skulls and automatic CFS reporting by linguistic summarization. Regarding the former problem, there are only a few and preliminary approaches (Li et al., 2011; Zhang et al., 2015). We tried with our own implementation of the ideas provided in those publications, but the results were not satisfactory for a real casuistry. Concerning the automatic reporting system, our first goal has been to propose a CFS report template and try to promote it to a standard in the field (Ibáñez et al., 2019). We are also currently working in a linguistic summarization engine able to hierarchically summarize all the information available of a given CFS case or cases using natural language.

4.2 Artificial intelligence in the comparative radiography module

This module is estimated to be integrated in Skeleton-ID along 2020-21. It will initially provide all the AI-based algorithms developed by the UGR during the last 4 years. In particular, the image IR algorithm to estimate X-ray parameters and perform 3D bone model to X-ray superimposition (Gómez et al., 2018), and the DL models to automatically segment the contour of the bone of interest in X-ray images (Gómez et al., 2019b) (and other works under review).

The most recent results of this automatic comparative radiography framework have been presented during the IACI and AEAOF 2019 conferences (Gómez et al., 2019c, 2019d). In this work, the automatic framework considering frontal sinuses was evaluated. A cross-comparison scenario involving 180 individuals with their respective cranial CT and X-ray was considered, resulting in a total of 32.400 CT-X-ray comparisons. The results were provided in terms of ranking (see Fig. 3.19, right), the positive individual was ranked first 50% of the cases, within the first 10 individuals 73% of times, and always if we just consider the first 50 (up to 180) individuals. Note that the position in the raking was established according to the 3D-2D overlapping error after performing automatic superimposition. However, comparative radiography identification is based on a point-by-point comparison, in search of consistencies and inconsistencies in bone morphology, trabecular patterns, skeletal anomalies, dental characteristics, pathological conditions and trauma, etc. None of these features have been considered and its automatic analysis and comparison is an open future research line.

As in the case of the CFS hierarchical DSS, AI-based algorithms are already able to automatically filter many cases (63% of the candidates) in a multiple comparison scenario without human intervention. Additionally, they provide a precise superimposition for the following point-by-point comparison. In fact, the automatic of the latter is part of the future research lines, concerning this promising identification technique, which also includes the development of reliability studies using the anatomical regions more commonly employed in radiological forensic identification. Additionally, the 3D AM-3D PM scenario will be addressed given the increasing number of CTs and MRIs performed daily.

4.3 Artificial intelligence in the biological profile module

While Skeleton-ID will include along 2020 different forms to introduce the required quantitative and qualitative information to directly perform most of the state-of-the-art biological profiling estimation methods, AI-supported approaches are still under research. Four are the different research lines currently considered by Panacea and UGR: (1) age and sex estimation from photographs of the pubic symphysis; (2) age and sex estimation from 3D models of different bones; (3) age estimation from X-ray images; and (4) sex estimation in sub-adults from photographs of the Ilium. In all those cases, ML algorithms are expected to be able to outperform current established biological profiling methods due to its pattern recognition capabilities when a large and representative data set is available. As it has been summarized in Section 3.1.2, there are already a few works completely automating age estimation using ML techniques with outstanding performance. As long as the required data become more accessible, we firmly believe that BP estimation techniques will experiment a significant improvement in their accuracy.

4.4 Future modules supported by artificial intelligence

Panacea is intended to expand their research activities, in collaboration with both the UGR and other research centers, to the following topics.

Chronological Age Estimation of Unaccompanied Minors: The final objective is to increase the accuracy of chronological age estimation by practitioners, widely criticized by different NGOs because of their error rates, reducing estimation times and subjectivity. We will again follow a twofold approach. On the one hand, we will develop software and graphical tools to facilitate and optimize the application of the most accepted existing methods, that is, the analysis of the shape and size of the individual bone elements and the ossification state of the epiphyseal plates in X-ray images of the hand, the mineralization of third molars assessed by means of an orthopantomogram, and the assessment of the degree of ossification of the medial clavicular epiphysis in a CT. On the other hand, we have recently initiated a specific research line to totally automate this task from a given X-ray, CT, or MRI using DL techniques. We will initially focus on the same bones and images (hand, teeth, and clavicle), but we will also extend our study to other bones such as the pelvic bone due to the promising results recently achieved by Li et al. (Li et al., 2019). An additional challenge in this research line will be to include physical examination parameters into the ML models, that is, growth-influencing diseases, medications, anthropometric data such as body height, bodyweight, and body type as well as the externally recognizable signs of sexual maturity.

Forensic facial comparison (FFC): We aim to support, with ad-hoc tools and automatic algorithms, the forensic identification given a reduced set of candidates (as a result of a previous sort-listing process developed by a facial recognition system or because of the nature of the investigation), that is, FFC. This task is currently performed manually by trained policemen through the examination of facial images or videos with a little support of general-purpose image processing software. The two main groups in charge of the standardization and best practices in FFC are the ENFSI Digital Imaging Working Group (DIWG) and the Facial Identification Scientific Working Group (FISWG). Although four main different approaches have been studied, they only recommend the morphological analysis. We aim to develop a software solution to facilitate the traditional approach to morphological analysis. This implies tools for frames extraction from videos, filters to improve the image quality, cephalometric landmarks and anatomical regions detection, side-by-side and superimposition scenes, etc. Apart from these tools, we have initiated a research line to develop accurate and objective automatic algorithms to apply two of the approaches discouraged due to their subjectivity and associated errors:

morphological classification, and photo-anthropometry. In particular, we aim to automatically categorize the morphology and estimate 3D DPI from a given facial photograph. Concerning the latter, as explained in Section 4.1, we have proposed an ML algorithm able to estimate 3D DPI from 2D photographs (see Fig. 3.18) (Martos et al., 2018). Additionally, we have developed a methodology for filtering cases that has demonstrated to be useful in the task of reducing the list of possible candidates for a given photograph. It is able to remove on average (validated using cross-validation) up to 57% of the negative cases, depending on the amount of DPIs available. Regarding the automatic morphological classification, we have begun with the design of a new atlas to label hundreds of images to feed ML algorithms. Alternatively, to atlas-based proposals, where a few examples of facial features are given, we propose the use of synthetic facial images (Martos et al., 2019). We have used MakeHuman, a software solution specifically designed for the modeling of virtual humans, with a simple yet complete system including the simulation of muscular movement. Employing this software, we have developed a concise guide for morphological labeling with a set of 39 facial criteria, modeling all of them in a progressive scale (with 11 examples per criteria) including "normal" appearances and both deviation extremes. We have set-up inter- and intraobserver studies in which we have created a simulated scenario with 3D facial models of which we know the real value (numerical weights in MakeHuman software) assigned to all the facial features evaluated. Then, we ask the participants to match the criteria observed in the image with the most similar example of the guide, which has been assigned with a previous value to subsequently compare it with the ground truth (i.e., the correct value we expect to obtain). For the first time, in this work, we have developed a methodology to directly compare the results obtained by an observer with real data for a set of facial criteria. This allows us to determine which criteria are more objective and which are more discriminative. In our previous pilot study, and similar to the conclusions achieved in related scientific literature (Ritz-Timme et al., 2011), following the traditional methodology, we obtained several discrepancies between the participants and a high interexpert variability. Now, with this new approach, promising results have been obtained in a first pilot study, with low interexpert variability and a high precision (around 80%).

Pathology and traumatology: As introduced in Section 3.2, pathology and traumatology with forensic medicine purposes have attracted really limited attention from researchers in AI. However, we see this field as one of the most promising for the application of AI-based approaches due the following reasons.

- The extraordinary success of AI-based approaches in clinical medicine during the last few years. One paradigmatic example is the case of automatic chest X-ray diagnosis by means of ConvNets (Laserson et al., 2018; Liu et al., 2019; Wang et al., 2017). These algorithms are able to automatically classify up to 40 pathologies with a higher accuracy than an expert radiologist, since a team of radiologists agree on average more with the algorithm than with each other.

- The ease and relative low cost to acquire this type of data, X-rays. In addition, there is an increasing number of laboratories worldwide that perform virtual autopsies (virtopsy) as a daily practice. One common practice in some of them is to perform a CT scan of the whole cadaver. This involves a large and extremely rich source of data to accomplish this kind of research projects.

5. Conclusion and discussion

AI emerged in the middle of the last century as a result of the research work of a handful of scientists from different fields (mainly, mathematicians, psychologists, and engineers). Currently, it is present in a myriad of applications and services of all kinds, where AI techniques are applied with remarkable success in speech recognition, automatic translation, video games, transportation, and robotics, among many others, and very notably in healthcare and medical imaging. There is no doubt that AI has come to our society to stay. It is therefore surprising the technological delay of FA in relation to other medical disciplines, with respect to the use of intelligent systems to expand the capabilities of human experts. Indeed, AI techniques can be used to automate tedious tasks for humans, such as the segmentation of anatomical structures or facial regions, the alignment of images to study their overlap, or the marking of relevant information in images (landmarks, for instance). AI also provides tools to integrate and structure the information available on a certain problem, allowing inference and exploration for knowledge discovery. As consequence, AI techniques have the potentiality to improve existing manual approaches in terms of reproducibility, robustness, accuracy, and execution time. Machines are better than humans in repeatable/well-defined tasks and tasks that require high precision/execution speed. In turn, humans are better than machines in everything else. But, in particular, humans can deal with uncertainty, learn from examples and generalize knowledge, improve their performance based on experience, evolve, and cooperate to perform difficult tasks. Current AI systems are improving their efficiency in the aforementioned scenarios (ML, CV, and SC techniques are research fields devoted to make machines emulate those humans' abilities).

Since AI currently has a residual presence in FA, this chapter presents the first bibliographic review of the state of the art in the application of AI techniques to FA, as well as other strongly related identification techniques. The application of AI would reduce the time needed to perform human forensic identification. This would lead to solve more cases in a shorter time, allowing, for instance, the realization of multiple comparisons in CFS or CR (something unthinkable in the past due to the lack of this technology). On the other hand, decisions could be supported on objective and reproducible results that, perhaps, would have a stronger impact in a court of law. The studies mentioned along this book chapter show that ANNs can be trained to estimate the BP, describe trauma- or pathological conditions, of an individual from skeletal remains or radiographic images. They are able to estimate age, sex, or identify from photographs of living people with high accuracy and have the potential to remove human bias in all these tasks. However, it is important to highlight one of the main characteristics, and at the same time limitations, of these ML models: the result will be as good as the data available, so if the dataset used to train these systems is not broad and diverse enough, the results will surely be suboptimal.

In our opinion, two main issues are limiting the application and positive impact of AI techniques to the FA field.

(i) **The reduced number of multidisciplinary research groups including forensic researchers in anthropology and related sciences (odontology, forensic medicine, or anatomy) and AI experts.** This interaction is essential in order to establish a fluid and productive collaboration between different scientific disciplines. On the one hand, it allows unifying terminology and facilitating the useful transfer of knowledge among scientists. On the other hand, it allows joining forces in a common direction toward challenging research projects (including the acknowledgment of the possibilities and limitations of the different knowledge fields involved). This interdisciplinary collaboration should bear fruit in the recognition that machines are not here to replace human beings, but to complement them, help them, and assist them in those tasks that humans do not want perform or want to perform faster.

(ii) **The lack of large and open public data sets for research purposes in forensic anthropology.** Knowledge exchange and the possibility to improve existing approaches, and propose new methods to solve problems, are the main forces behind the evolution of science. Currently, when data-hungry approaches, like DL, are breaking barriers every week in the resolution of complex problems, data availability is the starting point and requirement for the validation of many AI techniques. The guarantee of objective procedures to evaluate the performance of those techniques is essential. To compare the performance of newly developed methods, a common forensic dataset of known case studies should be available. This is a common practice in other fields as close as clinical medicine and biomedical research, with representative examples such as classification and localization of common thorax diseases in chest X-ray (Wang et al., 2017), melanoma classification in skin photographs (Brinker et al., 2019), the cancer imaging archive (TCIA Collections, 2020), the Allen mouse and human brain atlases for combining genomics and neuroanatomy (Lein et al., 2007), classification of gastrointestinal lesions from regular colonoscopy (Mesejo et al., 2016), and the MIMIC critical care database that contains health data associated with approximately 40,000 critical care patients (Johnston & Chazal, 2018), the Alzheimer's Disease neuroimaging initiative (ADNI Alzheimer, 2020), or the OpenNeuro initiative for sharing MRI and fMRI data (Poldrack et al., 2013), among others. It is also important to recognize the fact that it is not only about acquiring and storing data, but how these data are compiled in order to meet ethical requirements and avoid machine bias (Dressel & Farid, 2018) (e.g., that due to having much more examples of men than women, the system classification works better with the first than with the second), among others. One novel public repository, The New Mexico Decent Image Database (New Mexico Decedent Image Database, 2020), could be the best existing example of the type of resource that can boost research and multidisciplinary in the field. This data base collects whole body CT scans of over 15,000 New Mexicans with a 0.5 mm resolution and metadata includes almost 60 variables about the individuals' demography, life and death. It opens the possibility of the development of new models (for example, relating extrinsic parameters and bone morphology for age estimation) and validation of the existing ones over and unprecedented number of samples.

Beyond the academic world, the impact of AI on the daily practice of ID is limited to biometrics (face, fingerprints, etc.) and DNA, but to date forensic experts have had no AI-based tool available to automate tasks related to human forensic identification using FA methods. In that sense, Skeleton-ID is the first commercial tool designed by and for FA. Skeleton-ID fills this technological gap by bringing a novel computer-aided automatic paradigm for ID based on FA methods, thanks to the innovative methodologies and AI-based automation algorithms developed by Panacea. This software solution employs CV, SC, and ML to automate identification techniques such as CFS and CR, through unbiased and accurate analysis and comparison of AM data (pictures, X-ray) with PM 3D bone models; and BP estimation, both dead and alive, from X-ray to 2D and 3D images. Moreover, this technology enables fast multiple comparisons and new use cases. Skeleton-ID offers a very efficient filtering tool using CFS and BP that can largely reduce the candidates of a database in minutes instead of days, thanks to its multiple comparison capabilities, hence enormously reducing (attending to our calculations, at least by 90%) the time employed in these forensic techniques.

In the context of forensic sciences, advances in computer processing power and the magnitude of emerging AI techniques during the last decade, such as machines learning, have shown an improvement in the capabilities of machines to understand images and recognize patterns with a similar or better accuracy of a human expert. Its great potential lies in the ability to automatically execute tasks that for the expert are tedious, time-consuming, and error-prone (such as the SFO task in CFS). The computing power and automatic algorithms will allow forensic experts to address and resolve a greater number of cases in less time, allowing the multiple comparisons of cases in databases of missing people, unidentified skeletal remains, mass disaster victims, terrorism, etc. They also facilitate the numerical analysis of subjective tasks by making the ID methods more objective, supporting the expert in decision making and serving as a better legal guarantee in judicial proceedings.

The main motivation of this article is to make known what AI already is able to do, and to present some contributions, it can provide in the short term in the field of FA. The human tragedy of missing persons and unidentified remains needs solutions on a par with the circumstances, where the forensic experts have to lean on technology to be able to reliably address the enormous number of cases they face. As conclusion, we consider that FA can enormously benefit from science and technology. Afterall, as Garry Kasparov said after losing against the chess-playing computer Deep Blue in 1997, a good human plus a machine is likely to be the best combination.

Acknowledgments

This work was supported by the "Instituto para la Competitividad Empresarial de Castilla y León" under grant 07/18/LE/0001, "línea: desarrollo de la industria tic", and the Spanish Ministry of Science, Innovation and Universities under grant EXASOCO (PGC2018-101216-B-I00), both including ERDF funds. Pablo Mesejo is funded by the European Commission H2020-MSCA–IF–2016 through the Skeleton-ID Marie Curie Individual Fellowship [Grant Number 746592].

References

donna.sirk@nistgov. The organization of scientific area Committees for forensic science. NIST, https://www.nist.gov/topics/organization-scientific-area-committees-forensic-science. 2016.

(6) (PDF) The AR face database. ResearchGate. https://www.researchgate.net/publication/243651904_The_AR_face_database.

Abdullah, H., Jamil, M. M. A., & Nor, F. M. (2017). Automated haversian canal detection for histological sex determination. In *2017 IEEE Symposium on Computer Applications Industrial Electronics* (pp. 69–74). ISCAIE).

ADNI Alzheimer's disease neuroimaging initiative.(2020). http://adni.loni.usc.edu/. (Accessed 7 May 2020).

Afifi, M., & Abdelhamed, A. (2017). *AFIF4: Deep gender classification based on AdaBoost-based fusion of isolated facial features and foggy faces*. ArXiv170604277 Cs. http://arxiv.org/abs/1706.04277. (Accessed 15 May 2020).

Aja-Fernández, S., de Luis-García, R., Martín-Fernández, M.Á., et al. (2004). A computational TW3 classifier for skeletal maturity assessment. A computing with words approach. *Journal of Biomedical Informatics, 37*, 99–107.

Anderson, M. F., Anderson, D. T., & Wescott, D. J. (2010). Estimation of adult skeletal age-at-death using the Sugeno fuzzy integral. *American Journal of Physical Anthropology, 142*, 30–41.

Ballerini, L., Cordón, O., Damas, S., et al. Automatic 3D modeling of skulls by scatter search and heuristic features. In E. Avineri, M. Köppen, K. Dahal, et al. (Eds.), Applications of soft computing (pp. 149–158). Berlin, Heidelberg: Springer Berlin Heidelberg.

Beauthier, J.-P., Valck, E., Lefevre, P., et al. (2009). Mass disaster victim identification: The tsunami experience. *The Open Forensic Science Journal, 2*. https://benthamopen.com/ABSTRACT/TOFORSJ-2-54. (Accessed 3 May 2020).

Bermejo, E., Campomanes-Álvarez, C., Valsecchi, A., et al. (2017). Genetic algorithms for skull-face overlay including mandible articulation. *Information Sciences, 420*, 200–217.

Bethard, J. D. (2014). Forensic anthropology: An introduction. Edited by MariaTeresa A. Tersigni-Tarrant and Natalie R. Shirley. Boca Raton, FL: CRC press. 2013. 462 pp. ISBN 978-1-4398-1646-2. $99.95 (hardcover). *American Journal of Physical Anthropology, 154*, 166–167.

Bewes, J., Low, A., Morphett, A., et al. (2019). Artificial intelligence for sex determination of skeletal remains: Application of a deep learning artificial neural network to human skulls. *Journal of Forensic and Legal Medicine, 62*, 40–43.

Bishop, C. (2006). *Pattern recognition and machine learning*. New York: Springer-Verlag. https://www.springer.com/gp/book/9780387310732. (Accessed 2 May 2020).

Bolliger, S. A., & Thali, M. J. (2015). Imaging and virtual autopsy: Looking back and forward. *Philosophical Transactions of the Royal Society B: Biological Sciences, 370*. https://doi.org/10.1098/rstb.2014.0253. Epub ahead of print 5 August 2015.

Brinker, T. J., Hekler, A., Enk, A. H., et al. (2019). Deep learning outperformed 136 of 157 dermatologists in a head-to-head dermoscopic melanoma image classification task. *European Journal of Cancer, 113*, 47–54.

Brooks, S., & Suchey, J. M. (1990). Skeletal age determination based on the os pubis: A comparison of the acsádi-Nemeskéri and suchey-Brooks methods. *Human Evolution, 5*, 227–238.

de Buhan, M., & Nardoni, C. (2018). A facial reconstruction method based on new mesh deformation techniques. *Forensic Sciences Research, 3*, 256–273.

Burton, A. M., Bruce, V., & Dench, N. (1993). What's the difference between men and women? Evidence from facial measurement. *Perception, 22*(2), 153–176. https://doi.org/10.1068/p220153. Epub ahead of print 25 June 2016.

Byers, S. N. (2011). *Introduction to forensic anthropology*. Pearson Education.

Cameriere, R., De Luca, S., De Angelis, D., et al. (2012). Reliability of Schmeling's stages of ossification of medial clavicular epiphyses and its validity to assess 18 years of age in living subjects. *International Journal of Legal Medicine, 126*, 923–932.

Campomanes-Álvarez, B. R., Damas, S., & Cordón, Ó. (2012). Mesh simplification for 3D modeling using evolutionary multi-objective optimization. In *2012 IEEE congress on evolutionary computation* (pp. 1–8).

Campomanes-Álvarez, B. R., Ibáñez, O., Campomanes-Álvarez, C., et al. (2015). Modeling facial soft tissue thickness for automatic skull-face overlay. *IEEE Transactions on Information Forensics and Security, 10*, 2057–2070.

Campomanes-Alvarez, C., Ibáñez, O., & Cordón, O. (2016). Design of criteria to assess craniofacial correspondence in forensic identification based on computer vision and fuzzy integrals. *Applied Soft Computing, 46*, 596–612.

Campomanes-Alvarez, C., Ibáñez, O., Cordón, O., et al. (2018). Hierarchical information fusion for decision making in craniofacial superimposition. *Information Fusion, 39*, 25–40.

Campomanes-Álvarez, C., Martos-Fernández, R., Wilkinson, C., et al. (2018). Modeling skull-face anatomical/morphological correspondence for craniofacial superimposition-based identification. *IEEE Transactions on Information Forensics and Security, 13*, 1481–1494.

Caple, J., Byrd, J., & Stephan, C. N. (2017). Elliptical fourier analysis: Fundamentals, applications, and value for forensic anthropology. *International Journal of Legal Medicine, 131*, 1675–1690.

Caple, J., & Stephan, C. N. (2016). A standardized nomenclature for craniofacial and facial anthropometry. *International Journal of Legal Medicine, 130*, 863–879.

Christensen, A. M. (2005a). Assessing the variation in individual frontal sinus outlines. *American Journal of Physical Anthropology, 127*, 291–295.

Christensen, A. M. (2005b). Testing the reliability of frontal sinuses in positive identification. *Journal of Forensic Sciences, 50*, 18–22.

Christensen, A. M., Smith, M. A., Gleiber, D. S., et al. (2018). The use of X-ray computed tomography technologies in forensic anthropology. *Forensic Anthropol, 1*, 124–140.

Chung, S. W., Han, S. S., Lee, J. W., et al. (2018). Automated detection and classification of the proximal humerus fracture by using deep learning algorithm. *Acta Orthopaedica, 89*, 468–473.

Claes, P., Liberton, D. K., Daniels, K., et al. (2014). Modeling 3D facial shape from DNA. *PLoS Genetics, 10*, e1004224.

Claes, P., Vandermeulen, D., De Greef, S., et al. (2006). Craniofacial reconstruction using a combined statistical model of face shape and soft tissue depths: Methodology and validation. *Forensic Science International, 159*, S147–S158.

Claes, P., Vandermeulen, D., De Greef, S., et al. (2010). Computerized craniofacial reconstruction: Conceptual framework and review. *Forensic Science International, 201*, 138–145.

Clement, J. G., & Marks, M. K. (2005). *Computer-graphic facial reconstruction*. Elsevier.

Cummaudo, M., Guerzoni, M., Marasciuolo, L., et al. (2013). Pitfalls at the root of facial assessment on photographs: A quantitative study of accuracy in positioning facial landmarks. *International Journal of Legal Medicine, 127*, 699–706.

Daffner, R. H., & Hartman, M. S. (2013). *Clinical radiology: The essentials*. Wolters Kluwer Lippincott Williams and Wilkins Health.

D'Alonzo, S. S., Guyomarc'h, P., Byrd, J. E., et al. (2017). A large-sample test of a semi-automated clavicle search engine to assist skeletal identification by radiograph comparison. *Journal of Forensic Sciences, 62*, 181–186.

Damas, S., Cordón, O., Ibáñez, O., et al. (2011). Forensic identification by computer-aided craniofacial superimposition: A survey. *ACM Computing Surveys, 43*(27), 1–27.

Damas, S., Wilkinson, C., Kahana, T., et al. (2015). Study on the performance of different craniofacial superimposition approaches (II): Best practices proposal. *Forensic Science International, 257*, 504–508.

Darmawan, M. F., Yusuf, S. M., Rozi, M. A., et al. (2015). Hybrid PSO-ANN for sex estimation based on length of left hand bone. In *2015 IEEE Student Conference on Research and Development* (pp. 478–483). SCOReD).

De Angelis, D., Sala, R., Cantatore, A., et al. (2009). A new computer-assisted technique to aid personal identification. *International Journal of Legal Medicine, 123*, 351–356.

Decker, S. J., & Ford, J. M. (2019). Forensic personal identification utilizing part-to-part comparison of CT-derived 3D lumbar models. *Forensic Science International, 294*, 21–26.

Deloire, L., Diallo, I., Cadieu, R., et al. (2019). Post-mortem X-ray computed tomography (PMCT) identification using ante-mortem CT-scan of the sphenoid sinus. *Journal of Neuroradiology, 46*, 248–255.

Derrick, S. M., Hipp, J. A., & Goel, P. (2018). Chapter 23 - the computer-assisted decedent identification method of computer-assisted radiographic identification. In K. E. Latham, E. J. Bartelink, & M. Finnegan (Eds.), *New Perspectives in Forensic Human Skeletal Identification* (pp. 265–276). Academic Press.

Dornaika, F., Bekhouche, S. E., & Arganda-Carreras, I. (2020). Robust regression with deep CNNs for facial age estimation: An empirical study. *Expert Systems with Applications, 141*, 112942.

Dressel, J., & Farid, H. (2018). The accuracy, fairness, and limits of predicting recidivism. *Science Advances, 4*, eaao5580.

Duan, F., Yang, Y., Li, Y., et al. (2014). Skull identification via correlation measure between skull and face shape. *IEEE Transactions on Information Forensics and Security, 9*, 1322–1332.

Ebner, N. C., Riediger, M., & Lindenberger, U. (2010). FACES-a database of facial expressions in young, middle-aged, and older women and men: Development and validation. *Behavior Research Methods, 42*, 351–362.

Edmond, G., Davis, J. P., & Valentine, T. (2015). Expert analysis. In *Forensic facial identification* (pp. 239–262). John Wiley and Sons, Ltd.

Eidinger, E., Enbar, R., & Hassner, T. (2014). Age and gender estimation of unfiltered faces. *IEEE Transactions on Information Forensics and Security, 9*, 2170–2179.

Engelbrecht, A. P. (2020). *Computational intelligence: An introduction* (2nd ed.). Wiley. *Wiley.com* https://www.wiley.com/en-us/Computational+Intelligence%3A+An+Introduction%2C+2nd+Edition-p-9780470035610. (Accessed 2 May 2020).

Esteva, A., Kuprel, B., Novoa, R. A., et al. (2017). Dermatologist-level classification of skin cancer with deep neural networks. *Nature, 542*, 115–118.

Evenhouse, R. J., Rasmussen, M., & Sadler, L. L. Computer-aided forensic facial reconstruction. In Biostereometric technology and applications (pp. 147–156). International Society for Optics and Photonics.

Fantini, M., de Crescenzio, F., Persiani, F., et al. (2008). 3D restitution, restoration and prototyping of a medieval damaged skull. *Rapid Prototyping Journal, 14*, 318–324.

Forsyth, D. A., & Ponce, J. (2002). *Computer vision: A modern approach*. Prentice Hall Professional Technical Reference.

Franchi, A. (2012). Epidemiology and classification of bone tumors. *Clinical Cases in Mineral and Bone Metabolism, 9*, 92–95.

Gallagher, A. C., & Chen, T. (2009). Understanding images of groups of people. In *2009 IEEE Conference on Computer Vision and Pattern Recognition* (pp. 256–263).

Gascho, D., Philipp, H., Flach, P. M., et al. (2018). Standardized medical image registration for radiological identification of decedents based on paranasal sinuses. *Journal of Forensic and Legal Medicine, 54*, 96–101.

Gatliff, B. P. (1984). Facial sculpture on the skull for identification. *The American Journal of Forensic Medicine and Pathology, 5*, 327–332.

Gertych, A., Zhang, A., Sayre, J., et al. (2007). Bone age assessment of children using a digital hand atlas. *Computerized Medical Imaging and Graphics, 31*, 322–331.

Ghosh, A. K., & Sinha, P. (2001). An economised craniofacial identi®cation system. *Forensic Science International, 11*.

Gibelli, D., Cellina, M., Cappella, A., et al. (2019). An innovative 3D-3D superimposition for assessing anatomical uniqueness of frontal sinuses through segmentation on CT scans. *International Journal of Legal Medicine, 133*, 1159–1165.

Gómez, O., Ibáñez, O., Mesejo, P., et al. (2019c). Automatic segmentation of skeletal structures in X-ray images using deep learning: Towards a computer-aided decision support system for comparative radiography. In *Proceedings of the 18th Meeting of the International Association for Craniofacial Identification (IACI)* (p. 49). Baton Rouge, USA.

Gómez, O., Ibáñez, O., Mesejo, P., et al. (2019d). Towards a computer-aided decision support system for comparative radiography. In *Proceedings of the XI Reunión Cientıfica Internacional de la Asociación Española de Antropologiá y Odontologiá Forense (AEAOF)*. Spain: Pastrana.

Gómez, O., Ibáñez, O., Valsecchi, A., et al. (2018). 3D-2D silhouette-based image registration for comparative radiography-based forensic identification. *Pattern Recognition, 83*, 469–480.

Gómez, O., Mesejo, P., Ibáñez, O., et al. (2019b). Deep architectures for high-resolution multi-organ chest X-ray image segmentation. *Neural Computing and Applications, 32*, 15949–15963. https://doi.org/10.1007/s00521-019-04532-y. Epub ahead of print 21 October 2019.

Gómez, O., Mesejo, P., Ibáñez, O., et al. (2020). Deep architectures for the segmentation of frontal sinuses in X-ray images: Towards an automatic forensic identification system in comparative radiography. *Neurocomputing, 456*, 575–585.

Gómez, G., Mesejo, P., Ibáñez, O., et al. (2019a). Automatic cephalometric landmarks localization using deep convolutional neural networks. In *Proceedings of the 18th Meeting of the International Association for Craniofacial Identification (IACI)* (p. 48). Baton Rouge, USA.

Goodfellow, I., Bengio, Y., & Courville, A. (2016). *Deep learning*. https://mitpress.mit.edu/books/deep-learning. (Accessed 4 May 2020).

Greulich, Iannaccone G. W. W., & Pyle, S. I. (1959). Radiographic atlas of skeletal development of the hand and wrist. In *I volume-atlante di 256 pagine* (2nd ed.). Stanford, California: Stanford University Press. Acta Genet Medicae Gemellol Twin Res.

Gulshan, V., Peng, L., Coram, M., et al. (2016). Development and validation of a deep learning algorithm for detection of diabetic retinopathy in retinal fundus photographs. *JAMA, 316*, 2402–2410.

Guo, G., Mu, G., Fu, Y., et al. Human age estimation using bio-inspired features. Vol 8.

Gupta, A., Venkatesh, S., Chopra, S., et al. (2019). *Generative image translation for data augmentation of bone lesion pathology*. ArXiv190202248 Cs Stat. http://arxiv.org/abs/1902.02248. (Accessed 14 May 2020).

Guyomarc'h, P., Dutailly, B., Charton, J., et al. (2014). Anthropological facial approximation in three dimensions (AFA3D): Computer-assisted estimation of the facial morphology using geometric morphometrics. *Journal of Forensic Sciences, 59*, 1502–1516.

Haas, J., Buikstra, J. E., Ubelaker, D. H., et al. (1994). *Standards for data collection from human skeletal remains: Proceedings of a seminar at the field museum of natural history, organized by jonathan haas*. Arkansas Archeological Survey.

Hacl, A., Costa, A. L. F., Mayara Oliveira, J., et al. (2017). Three-dimensional volumetric analysis of frontal sinus using medical software. *Journal of Forensic Radiology and Imaging, 11*, 1–5.

Hatch, G. M., Dedouit, F., Christensen, A. M., et al. (2014). RADid: A pictorial review of radiologic identification using postmortem CT. *Journal of Forensic Radiology and Imaging, 2*, 52–59.

Hayner, P. B. (2006). Truth commissions: A schematic overview. *International Review of the Red Cross, 88*, 295–310.

Hinton, G., Deng, L., Yu, D., et al. (2012). Deep neural networks for acoustic modeling in speech recognition: The shared views of four research groups. *IEEE Signal Processing Magazine, 29*, 82–97.

Hsieh, C.-W., Jong, T.-L., Chou, Y.-H., et al. (2007). Computerized geometric features of carpal bone for bone age estimation. *Chinese Medical Journal, 120*, 767–770.

Hua, K.-L., Hsu, C.-H., Hidayati, S. C., et al. (2015). Computer-aided classification of lung nodules on computed tomography images via deep learning technique. *OncoTargets and Therapy, 8*, 2015–2022.

Huang, G. B., Ramesh, M., Berg, T., et al. Labeled faces in the wild: A database for studying face recognition in unconstrained environments. 11.

Huete, M. I., Ibáñez, O., Wilkinson, C., et al. (2015). Past, present, and future of craniofacial superimposition: Literature and international surveys. *Legal Medicine Tokyo Japan, 17*, 267–278.

Ibáñez, O., Ballerini, L., Cordón, O., et al. (2009). An experimental study on the applicability of evolutionary algorithms to craniofacial superimposition in forensic identification. *Information Sciences, 179*, 3998–4028.

Ibáñez, O., Cordón, O., & Damas, S. (2012). A cooperative coevolutionary approach dealing with the skull–face overlay uncertainty in forensic identification by craniofacial superimposition. *Soft Computing, 16*, 797–808.

Ibañez, Ó., Cordon, Ó., Damas, S., et al. (2011). Modeling the skull–face overlay uncertainty using fuzzy sets. *IEEE Transactions on Fuzzy Systems, 19*, 946–959.

Ibáñez, O., Cordón, O., Damas, S., et al. (2012). An advanced scatter search design for skull-face overlay in craniofacial superimposition. *Expert Systems with Applications, 39*, 1459–1473.

Ibáñez, O., Martos, R., Campomanes-Álvarez, C., et al. (2019). An identification report template for linguistic summarization in Craniofacial Superimposition. In *Proceedings of the 18th Meeting of the International Association for Craniofacial Identification (IACI)* (p. 39). Baton Rouge, USA.

Ibáñez, O., Vicente, R., Navega, D. S., et al. (2015). Study on the performance of different craniofacial superimposition approaches (I). *Forensic Science International, 257*, 496–503.

Iino, M., Fujimoto, H., Yoshida, M., et al. (2016). Identification of a jawless skull by superimposing post-mortem and ante-mortem CT. *Journal of Forensic Radiology and Imaging, 6*, 31–37.

Imaizumi, K., Taniguchi, K., Ogawa, Y., et al. (2019). Development of three-dimensional facial approximation system using head CT scans of Japanese living individuals. *Journal of Forensic Radiology and Imaging, 17*, 36–45.

IOS press Ebooks - computer–aided forensics: Facial reconstruction.(2020). http://ebooks.iospress.nl/publication/10639. (Accessed 7 May 2020).

Iscan, M. Y., & Helmer, R. P. (1993). *Forensic analysis of the skull: Craniofacial analysis.* Wiley-Liss.

Işcan, M. Y., Loth, S. R., & Wright, R. K. (1984). Age estimation from the rib by phase analysis: White males. *Journal of Forensic Sciences, 29*, 1094–1104.

Işcan, M. Y., Loth, S. R., & Wright, R. K. (1985). Age estimation from the rib by phase analysis: White females. *Journal of Forensic Sciences, 30*, 853–863.

Ishibuchi, H., Nakashima, T., & Nii, M. (2005). *Classification and modeling with linguistic information granules: Advanced approaches to linguistic data mining*. Berlin Heidelberg: Springer-Verlag. https://doi.org/10.1007/b138232. Epub ahead of print 2005.

ISO/IEC 19794-5:2011(en), Information technology — biometric data interchange formats — Part 5: Face image data.(2020). https://www.iso.org/obp/ui/#iso:std:iso-iec:19794:-5:ed-2:v1:en. (Accessed 7 May 2020).

Jain, A. K., & Chen, H. (2004). Matching of dental X-ray images for human identification. *Pattern Recognition, 37*, 1519–1532.

Jaramillo, K. (2020). Latin America: The region with the highest number of enforced disappearances - LatinAmerican Post https://latinamericanpost.com/23187-latin-america-the-region-with-the-highest-number-of-enforced-disappearances. (Accessed 2 May 2020).

Jayaprakash, P. T. (2013). Practical relevance of pattern uniqueness in forensic science. *Forensic Science International, 231*, 403.e1–403.e16.

Jayaraman, J., Roberts, G. J., Wong, H. M., et al. (2016). Ages of legal importance: Implications in relation to birth registration and age assessment practices. *Medicine, Science & the Law, 56*, 77–82.

Johnston, B., & Chazal, P de (2018). A review of image-based automatic facial landmark identification techniques. *EURASIP J Image Video Process, 2018*, 86.

Juefei-Xu, F., Verma, E., Goel, P., et al. (2016). DeepGender: Occlusion and low resolution robust facial gender classification via progressively trained convolutional neural networks with attention. In *2016 IEEE Conference on Computer Vision and Pattern Recognition Workshops (CVPRW)* (pp. 136–145). Las Vegas, NV, USA: IEEE.

Kahana, T. (2009). *El aporte de la radiología al avance de la Antropología forense: Perspectiva profesional*. https://digibug.ugr.es/handle/10481/2603. (Accessed 4 May 2020).

Kaloi, M. A., & He, K. (2018). *Child gender determination with convolutional neural networks on hand radio-graphs*. ArXiv181105180 Cs. http://arxiv.org/abs/1811.05180. (Accessed 4 May 2020).

Kastelic, V., Pośpiech, E., Draus-Barini, J., et al. (2013). Prediction of eye color in the Slovenian population using the IrisPlex SNPs. *Croatian Medical Journal, 54*, 381–386.

Kayser, M., & Schneider, P. M. (2009). DNA-based prediction of human externally visible characteristics in forensics: Motivations, scientific challenges, and ethical considerations. *Forensic Science International: Genetics, 3*, 154–161.

Kim, D.-I., Lee, U.-Y., Park, S.-O., et al. (2013). Identification using frontal sinus by three-dimensional reconstruction from computed tomography. *Journal of Forensic Sciences, 58*, 5–12.

Kim, J. R., Shim, W. H., Yoon, H. M., et al. (2017). Computerized bone age estimation using deep learning based program: Evaluation of the accuracy and efficiency. *American Journal of Roentgenology, 209*, 1374–1380.

Kooi, T., Litjens, G., van Ginneken, B., et al. (2017). Large scale deep learning for computer aided detection of mammographic lesions. *Medical Image Analysis, 35*, 303–312.

Krishan, K., Chatterjee, P. M., Kanchan, T., et al. (2016). A review of sex estimation techniques during examination of skeletal remains in forensic anthropology casework. *Forensic Science International, 261*, 165.e1–165.e8.

Krizhevsky, A., Sutskever, I., & Hinton, G. E. (2017). ImageNet classification with deep convolutional neural networks. *Communications of the ACM, 60*, 84–90.

Lamendin, H., Baccino, E., Humbert, J. F., et al. (1992). A simple technique for age estimation in adult corpses: The two criteria dental method. *Journal of Forensic Sciences, 37*, 1373–1379.

Larson, D. B., Chen, M. C., Lungren, M. P., et al. (2018). Performance of a deep-learning neural network model in assessing skeletal maturity on pediatric hand radiographs. *Radiology, 287*, 313–322.

Laserson, J., Lantsman, C. D., Cohen-Sfady, M., et al. (2018). TextRay: Mining clinical reports to gain a broad understanding of chest X-rays. In A. F. Frangi, J. A. Schnabel, C. Davatzikos, et al. (Eds.), *Medical image computing and computer assisted intervention – MICCAI 2018* (pp. 553–561). Cham: Springer International Publishing.

LeCun, Y., Bengio, Y., & Hinton, G. (2015). Deep learning. *Nature, 521*, 436–444.

Lee, J. H., & Kim, K. G. (2018). Applying deep learning in medical images: The case of bone age estimation. *Healthcare Informatics Research, 24*, 86–92.

Lee, H., Tajmir, S., Lee, J., et al. (2017). Fully automated deep learning system for bone age assessment. *Journal of Digital Imaging, 30*, 427–441.

Lee, W.-J., Wilkinson, C. M., & Hwang, H.-S. (2012). An accuracy assessment of forensic computerized facial reconstruction employing cone-beam computed tomography from live subjects. *Journal of Forensic Sciences, 57*, 318–327.

Lein, E. S., Hawrylycz, M. J., Ao, N., et al. (2007). Genome-wide atlas of gene expression in the adult mouse brain. *Nature, 445*, 168–176.

Levi, G., & Hassncer, T. (2015). Age and gender classification using convolutional neural networks. In *2015 IEEE Conference on Computer Vision and Pattern Recognition Workshops* (pp. 34–42). CVPRW.

Li, Y., Huang, Z., Dong, X., et al. (2019). Forensic age estimation for pelvic X-ray images using deep learning. *European Radiology, 29*, 2322–2329.

Li, B., Lian, X.-C., & Lu, B.-L. (2012). Gender classification by combining clothing, hair and facial component classifiers. *Neurocomputing, 76*, 18–27.

Lindner, C., Wang, C.-W., Huang, C.-T., et al. (2016). Fully automatic system for accurate localisation and analysis of cephalometric landmarks in lateral cephalograms. *Scientific Reports, 6*, 1–10.

Liu, C., & Li, X. (2018). *Superimposition-guided facial reconstruction from skull.* ArXiv181000107 Cs. http://arxiv.org/abs/1810.00107. (Accessed 7 May 2020).

Liu, J., Zhao, G., Fei, Y., et al. (2019). Align, attend and locate: Chest X-ray diagnosis via contrast induced attention network with limited supervision. In *2019 IEEE/CVF International Conference on Computer Vision (ICCV)* (pp. 10631–10640).

Li, X., Yin, Z., Wei, L., et al. (2011). Symmetry and template guided completion of damaged skulls. *Computer Graphics, 35*, 885–893.

Machado, C. E. P., Flores, M. R. P., Lima, L. N. C., et al. (2017). A new approach for the analysis of facial growth and age estimation: Iris ratio. *PLoS One, 12*, e0180330.

Mansanet, J., Albiol, A., & Paredes, R. (2016). Local deep neural networks for gender recognition. *Pattern Recognition Letters, 70*, 80–86.

Mansourvar, M., Ismail, M. A., Herawan, T., et al. (2013). Automated bone age assessment: Motivation, taxonomies, and challenges. *Computational and Mathematical Methods in Medicine, 2013*, e391626.

Markelj, P., Tomaževič, D., Likar, B., et al. (2012). A review of 3D/2D registration methods for image-guided interventions. *Medical Image Analysis, 16*, 642–661.

Maroñas, O., Phillips, C., Söchtig, J., et al. (2014). Development of a forensic skin colour predictive test. *Forensic Science International: Genetics, 13*, 34–44.

Martos, R., Ibáñez, O., & Alemán, I. (2019). A new atlas of facial features for morphological analysis employing synthetic facial images. In *Proceedings of the 18th Meeting of the International Association for Craniofacial Identification (IACI)* (p. 38). Baton Rouge, USA.

Martos, R., Valsecchi, A., Ibáñez, O., et al. (2018). Estimation of 2D to 3D dimensions and proportionality indices for facial examination. *Forensic Science International, 287*, 142–152.

Maxwell, A. B., & Ross, A. H. (2014). A radiographic study on the utility of cranial vault outlines for positive identifications. *Journal of Forensic Sciences, 59*, 314–318.

McCulloch, W. S., & Pitts, W. (1943). A logical calculus of the ideas immanent in nervous activity. *Bulletin of Mathematical Biophysics, 5*, 115–133.

Meindl, R. S., & Lovejoy, C. O. (1985). Ectocranial suture closure: A revised method for the determination of skeletal age at death based on the lateral-anterior sutures. *American Journal of Physical Anthropology, 68*, 57–66.

Mesejo, P., Pizarro, D., Abergel, A., et al. (2016). Computer-aided classification of gastrointestinal lesions in regular colonoscopy. *IEEE Transactions on Medical Imaging, 35*, 2051–2063.

Mexico's missing people agency searching for trafficking victims. (March 15, 2019). Reuters. https://www.reuters.com/article/us-mexico-trafficking-government-intervi-idUSKCN1QW2CG. (Accessed 2 May 2020).

Minear, M., & Park, D. C. (2004). A lifespan database of adult facial stimuli. *Behavior Research Methods, Instruments, & Computers, 36*, 630–633.

Moeini, H., & Mozaffari, S. (2017). Gender dictionary learning for gender classification. *Journal of Visual Communication and Image Representation, 42*, 1–13.

Epub ahead of print. *Molecular photofitting* (2008). Elsevier. https://doi.org/10.1016/B978-0-12-088492-6.X5001-4

Mozaffari, S., Behravan, H., & Akbari, R. (2010). Gender classification using single frontal image per person: Combination of appearance and geometric based features. In *2010 20th International Conference on Pattern Recognition* (pp. 1192–1195).

Mutasa, S., Chang, P. D., Ruzal-Shapiro, C., et al. (2018). Mabal: A novel deep-learning architecture for machine-assisted bone age labeling. *Journal of Digital Imaging, 31*, 513–519.

Nagpal, S., Singh, M., Jain, A., et al. (2017). On matching skulls to digital face images: A preliminary approach. In *2017 IEEE International Joint Conference on Biometrics (IJCB)* (pp. 813–819).

New Mexico decedent image database - welcome home.(2020). https://nmdid.unm.edu/. (Accessed 7 May 2020).

Nickerson, B. A., Fitzhorn, P. A., Koch, S. K., et al. (1991). A methodology for near-optimal computational superimposition of two-dimensional digital facial photographs and three-dimensional cranial surface meshes. *Journal of Forensic Sciences, 36*, 480–500.

Niespodziewanski, E., Stephan, C. N., Guyomarc'h, P., et al. (2016). Human identification via lateral patella radiographs: A validation study. *Journal of Forensic Sciences, 61*, 134–140.

Nomir, O., & Abdel-Mottaleb, M. (2007). Human identification from dental X-ray images based on the shape and appearance of the teeth. *IEEE Transactions on Information Forensics and Security, 2*, 188–197.

Oakden-Rayner, L., Carneiro, G., Bessen, T., et al. (2017). Precision radiology: Predicting longevity using feature engineering and deep learning methods in a radiomics framework. *Scientific Reports, 7*, 1–13.

Olczak, J., Fahlberg, N., Maki, A., et al. (2017). Artificial intelligence for analyzing orthopedic trauma radiographs. *Acta Orthopaedica, 88*, 581–586.

Olmos, R., Tabik, S., & Herrera, F. (2018). Automatic handgun detection alarm in videos using deep learning. *Neurocomputing, 275*, 66–72.

Ozbulak, G., Aytar, Y., & Ekenel, H. K. (2016). How transferable are CNN-based features for age and gender classification?. In *2016 International Conference of the Biometrics Special Interest Group* (pp. 1–6). BIOSIG.

Panis, G., Lanitis, A., Tsapatsoulis, N., et al. (2016). Overview of research on facial ageing using the FG-NET ageing database. *IET Biometrics, 5*, 37–46.

Park, H.-K., Chung, J.-W., & Kho, H.-S. (2006). Use of hand-held laser scanning in the assessment of craniometry. *Forensic Science International, 160*, 200–206.

Parks, C. L., Richard, A. H., & Monson, K. L. (2013). Preliminary performance assessment of computer automated facial approximations using computed tomography scans of living individuals. *Forensic Science International, 233*, 133–139.

Peralta, D., Triguero, I., García, S., et al. (2016). DPD-DFF: A dual phase distributed scheme with double fingerprint fusion for fast and accurate identification in large databases. *Information Fusion, 32*, 40–51.

Pfaeffli, M., Vock, P., Dirnhofer, R., et al. (2007). Post-mortem radiological CT identification based on classical ante-mortem X-ray examinations. *Forensic Science International, 171*, 111–117.

Phillips, P. J., Moon, H., Rauss, P. J., et al. (1997). The FERET evaluation methodology for face-recognition algorithms. *Proceedings - IEEE Computer Society Conference on Computer Vision and Pattern Recognition*. https://doi.org/10.1109/CVPR.1997.609311. Epub ahead of print 1997.

Pinto, S. C. D., Urbanová, P., & Cesar, R. M., Jr. (2016). Two-dimensional wavelet analysis of supraorbital margins of the human skull for characterizing sexual dimorphism. *IEEE Transactions on Information Forensics and Security, 11*, 1542–1548.

Pneuman, A., Budimlija, Z. M., Caragine, T., et al. (2012). Verification of eye and skin color predictors in various populations. *Legal Medicine, 14*, 78–83.

Poldrack, R. A., Barch, D. M., Mitchell, J. P., et al. (2013). Toward open sharing of task-based fMRI data: The OpenfMRI project. *Frontiers in Neuroinformatics, 7*. https://doi.org/10.3389/fninf.2013.00012. Epub ahead of print 8 July 2013.

Porto, L. F., Correia Lima, L. N., Pinheiro Flores, M. R., et al. (2019). Automatic cephalometric landmarks detection on frontal faces: An approach based on supervised learning techniques. *Digital Investigation, 30*, 108–116.

Prag, J., & Neave, R. (1997). *Making faces: Using forensic and archaeological evidence*. Trustees of the British Museum.

Quatrehomme, G., Cotin, S., Subsol, G., et al. (1997). A fully three-dimensional method for facial reconstruction based on deformable models. *Journal of Forensic Sciences, 42*, 649–652.

Rai, P., & Khanna, P. (2014). A gender classification system robust to occlusion using Gabor features based (2D)2PCA. *Journal of Visual Communication and Image Representation, 25*, 1118–1129.

Ranjan, R., Sankaranarayanan, S., Castillo, C. D., et al. (2017). An all-in-one convolutional neural network for face analysis. In *2017 12th IEEE International Conference on Automatic Face and Gesture Recognition (FG 2017)* (pp. 17–24). Washington, DC, USA: IEEE.

Ricanek, K., & Tesafaye, T. (2006). Morph: A longitudinal image database of normal adult age-progression. In *7th International Conference on Automatic Face and Gesture Recognition (FGR06)* (pp. 341–345).

Ricci, A., Marella, G. L., & Apostol, M. A. (2006). A new experimental approach to computer-aided face/skull identification in forensic anthropology. *The American Journal of Forensic Medicine and Pathology, 27*, 46–49.

Rigby, D.-M., & Hacking, L. (2018). Interpreting the chest radiograph. *Anaesthesia and Intensive Care Medicine, 19*, 50–54.

Ritchie, H., & Roser, M. (2014). *Natural disasters*. Our World Data. https://ourworldindata.org/natural-disasters. (Accessed 2 May 2020).

Ritz-Timme, S., Gabriel, P., Obertovà, Z., et al. (2011). A new atlas for the evaluation of facial features: Advantages, limits, and applicability. *International Journal of Legal Medicine, 125*, 301–306.

Ross, A., Lanfear, A., & Maxwell, A. (2016). Establishing standards for side-by-side radiographic comparisons. *The American Journal of Forensic Medicine and Pathology, 37*, 86–94.

Rothe, R., Timofte, R., & Van Gool, L. (2018). Deep expectation of real and apparent age from a single image without facial landmarks. *International Journal of Computer Vision, 126*, 144–157.

Ruder, T. D., Brun, C., Christensen, A. M., et al. (2016). Comparative radiologic identification with CT images of paranasal sinuses – development of a standardized approach. *Journal of Forensic Radiology and Imaging, 7*, 1–9.

Russell, S. J., & Norvig, P. (1995). *Artificial intelligence: A modern approach.* Englewood Cliffs, N.J: Prentice Hall.

Sandström, S., Ostensen, H., Pettersson, H., et al. (2003). *The WHO manual of diagnostic imaging: Radiographic technique and projections.* https://apps.who.int/iris/handle/10665/42720. (Accessed 4 May 2020).

Santamaría, J., Cordón, O., & Damas, S. (2007a). Evolutionary approaches for automatic 3D modeling of skulls in forensic identification. In M. Giacobini (Ed.), *Applications of evolutinary computing* (pp. 415–422). Berlin, Heidelberg: Springer Berlin Heidelberg.

Santamaría, J., Cordón, O., Damas, S., et al. (2007b). A scatter search-based technique for pair-wise 3D range image registration in forensic anthropology. *Soft Computing, 11*, 819–828.

Santamaría, J., Cordón, O., Damas, S., et al. (2009). Performance evaluation of memetic approaches in 3D reconstruction of forensic objects. *Soft Computing, 13*, 883–904.

Schmeling, A., Dettmeyer, R. B., Rudolf, E., et al. Forensic age estimation. Dtsch Arzteblatt Int Epub ahead of print 2016. DOI: 10.3238/arztebl.2016.0044.

Schmeling, A., Grundmann, C., Fuhrmann, A., et al. (2008). Criteria for age estimation in living individuals. *International Journal of Legal Medicine, 122*, 457.

Scientific working group for forensic anthropology (SWGANTH). Vol 6.

Shen, W., Guo, Y., Wang, Y., et al. (2017). *Deep regression forests for age estimation.* ArXiv171207195 Cs. http://arxiv.org/abs/1712.07195. (Accessed 15 May 2020).

Shinkawa, N., Hirai, T., Nishii, R., et al. (2017). Usefulness of 2D fusion of postmortem CT and antemortem chest radiography studies for human identification. *Japanese Journal of Radiology, 35*, 303–309.

Sierp, I., & Henneberg, M. (2015). The difficulty of sexing skeletons from unknown populations. *Journal of Anthropology, 2015*, e908535.

Silver, D., Huang, A., Maddison, C. J., et al. (2016). Mastering the game of Go with deep neural networks and tree search. *Nature, 529*, 484–489.

Singare, S., Lian, Q., Ping Wang, W., et al. (2009). Rapid prototyping assisted surgery planning and custom implant design. *Rapid Prototyping Journal, 15*, 19–23.

Singh, M., Nagpal, S., Singh, R., et al. (2018). *Learning A shared transform model for skull to digital face image matching.* ArXiv180804571 Cs. http://arxiv.org/abs/1808.04571. (Accessed 7 May 2020).

Skeleton-ID. https://skeleton-id.com/.

Song, Y., Qiao, X., Iwamoto, Y., et al. (2020). Automatic cephalometric landmark detection on X-ray images using a deep-learning method. *Applied Sciences, 10*, 2547.

Spampinato, C., Palazzo, S., Giordano, D., et al. (2017). Deep learning for automated skeletal bone age assessment in X-ray images. *Medical Image Analysis, 36*, 41–51.

Spichenok, O., Budimlija, Z. M., Mitchell, A. A., et al. (2011). Prediction of eye and skin color in diverse populations using seven SNPs. *Forensic Sci Int Genet, 5*, 472–478.

Statistics » diagnostic imaging dataset 2015-16 data.(2020). https://www.england.nhs.uk/statistics/statistical-work-areas/diagnostic-imaging-dataset/diagnostic-imaging-dataset-2015-16-data/. (Accessed 4 May 2020).

Stephan, C. N., Amidan, B., Trease, H., et al. (2014). Morphometric comparison of clavicle outlines from 3D bone scans and 2D chest radiographs: A shortlisting tool to assist radiographic identification of human skeletons. *Journal of Forensic Sciences, 59*, 306–313.

Stephan, C. N., Caple, J. M., Guyomarc'h, P., et al. (2018). An overview of the latest developments in facial imaging. *Forensic Sciences Research, 4*, 10–28.

Stephan, C. N., & Henneberg, M. (2001). Building faces from dry skulls: Are they recognized above chance rates? *Journal of Forensic Sciences, 46*, 432–440.

Stern, D., Ebner, T., Bischof, H., et al. (2014). Fully automatic bone age estimation from left hand MR images. *Med Image Comput Comput-Assist Interv MICCAI Int Conf Med Image Comput Comput-Assist Interv, 17*, 220–227.

Štern, D., Payer, C., Lepetit, V., et al. (2016). Automated age estimation from hand MRI volumes using deep learning. In S. Ourselin, L. Joskowicz, M. R. Sabuncu, et al. (Eds.), *Medical image computing and computer-assisted intervention – MICCAI 2016* (pp. 194–202). Cham: Springer International Publishing.

Štern, D., Payer, C., & Urschler, M. (2019). Automated age estimation from MRI volumes of the hand. *Medical Image Analysis, 58*, 101538.

Sulem, P., Gudbjartsson, D. F., Stacey, S. N., et al. (2007). Genetic determinants of hair, eye and skin pigmentation in Europeans. *Nature Genetics, 39*, 1443–1452.

Sutskever, I., Vinyals, O., Le, Q. V. Sequence to sequence learning with neural networks. In Z. Ghahramani, M. Welling, C. Corte , et al. (Eds.), Advances in neural information processing systems 27(pp. 3104–3112). Curran Associates, Inc..

Szegedy, C., Liu, Wei, Jia, Yangqing, et al. (2015). Going deeper with convolutions. In *2015 IEEE Conference on Computer Vision and Pattern Recognition* (pp. 1–9). CVPR.

Tabor, Z., Karpisz, D., Wojnar, L., et al. (2009). An automatic recognition of the frontal sinus in X-ray images of skull. *IEEE Transactions on Biomedical Engineering, 56*, 361–368.

Taheri, S., & Toygar, Ö. (2019). On the use of DAG-CNN architecture for age estimation with multi-stage features fusion. *Neurocomputing, 329*, 300–310.

Tan, J. S., Liao, I. Y., Venkat, I., et al. (2020). Computer-aided superimposition via reconstructing and matching 3D faces to 3D skulls for forensic craniofacial identifications. *The Visual Computer, 36*, 1739–1753. https://doi.org/10.1007/s00371-019-01767-7. Epub ahead of print 30 October 2019.

Tanner, J. M., Healy, M. J. R., Cameron, N., et al. (2001). *Assessment of skeletal maturity and prediction of adult height (TW3 method)*. W.B. Saunders.

Tanner, J. M., Whitehouse, R. H., Marshall, W. A., et al. (1975). Prediction of adult height from height, bone age, and occurrence of menarche, at ages 4 to 16 with allowance for midparent height. *Archives of Disease in Childhood, 50*, 14–26.

Tanner, J. M., Whitehouse, R. H., Marshall, W. A., et al. (1983). *Assessment of skeletal maturity and prediction of adult height* (Subsequent edition). London; New York: Academic Pr.

Tapia, J. E., & Perez, C. A. (2013). Gender classification based on fusion of different spatial scale features selected by mutual information from histogram of LBP, intensity, and shape. *IEEE Transactions on Information Forensics and Security, 8*, 488–499.

Taylor, K. T. Forensic art and illustration. CRC Press. Epub ahead of print 15 September 2000. DOI: 10.1201/9781420036954.

TCIA collections - the cancer imaging archive (TCIA).(2020). https://www.cancerimagingarchive.net/collections/. (Accessed 7 May 2020).

Thali, M. J., Braun, M., & Dirnhofer, R. (2003). Optical 3D surface digitizing in forensic medicine: 3D documentation of skin and bone injuries. *Forensic Science International, 137*, 203–208.

Thodberg, H. H., Neuhof, J., Ranke, M. B., et al. (2010). Validation of bone age methods by their ability to predict adult height. *Hormone Research in Paediatrics, 74*, 15–22.

Todd, T. W. (1920). Age changes in the pubic bone. I. The male white pubis. *American Journal of Physical Anthropology, 3*, 285–334.

Todd, T. W. (1921). Age changes in the pubic bone. *American Journal of Physical Anthropology, 4*, 1–70.

Tu, P., Book, R., Liu, X., et al. (2007). Automatic face recognition from skeletal remains. In *2007 IEEE Conference on Computer Vision and Pattern Recognition* (pp. 1–7).

Ubelaker, D. H. (1999). *Human skeletal remains: Excavation, analysis, interpretation* (3rd ed.). Washington: Taraxacum.

Ullrich, H., & Stephan, C. N. (2011). On Gerasimov's plastic facial reconstruction technique: New insights to facilitate repeatability*: GERASIMOV'S plastic facial reconstruction technique. *Journal of Forensic Sciences, 56*, 470–474.

Urdín, D., Mesejo, P., Ibáñez, O., et al.Urdín, D., Mesejo, P., Ibáñez, O., Valsecchi, A., Guyomarc'h, P., & Coqueugniot, H. (2019). Facial soft tissue depth estimation using machine learning techniques. In *Proceedings of the 18th Meeting of the International Association for Craniofacial Identification (IACI)* (p. 50). Baton Rouge, USA, 2019.

Valsecchi, A., Damas, S., & Cordón, O. (2018). A robust and efficient method for skull-face overlay in computerized craniofacial superimposition. *IEEE Transactions on Information Forensics and Security, 13*, 1960–1974.

Valsecchi, A., Irurita Olivares, J., & Mesejo, P. (2019). Age estimation in forensic anthropology: Methodological considerations about the validation studies of prediction models. *International Journal of Legal Medicine, 133*, 1915–1924.

Van Ginneken, B., Ter Haar Romeny, B. M., & Viergever, M. A. (2001). Computer-aided diagnosis in chest radiography: A survey. *IEEE Transactions on Medical Imaging, 20*, 1228–1241.

Vandermeulen, D., Claes, P., Loeckx, D., et al. (2006). Computerized craniofacial reconstruction using CT-derived implicit surface representations. *Forensic Science International, 159*(Suppl. 1), S164–S174.

Villar, P., Alemán, I., Castillo, L., et al. (2017). A first approach to a fuzzy classification system for age estimation based on the pubic bone. In *2017 IEEE International Conference on Fuzzy Systems* (pp. 1–6). FUZZ-IEEE.

Walsh, S., Liu, F., Ballantyne, K. N., et al. (2011). IrisPlex: A sensitive DNA tool for accurate prediction of blue and brown eye colour in the absence of ancestry information. *Forensic Science International: Genetics, 5*, 170–180.

Walsh, S., Wollstein, A., Liu, F., et al. (2012). DNA-based eye colour prediction across Europe with the IrisPlex system. *Forensic Science International: Genetics, 6*, 330–340.

Wang, X., Peng, Y., Lu, L., et al. (2017). ChestX-Ray8: Hospital-Scale chest X-ray database and benchmarks on weakly-supervised classification and localization of common thorax diseases. In *2017 IEEE Conference on Computer Vision and Pattern Recognition (CVPR)* (pp. 3462–3471).

White, J. D., Ortega-Castrillón, A., Matthews, H., et al. (2019). MeshMonk: Open-source large-scale intensive 3D phenotyping. *Scientific Reports, 9*, 1–11.

Wilkinson, C. Forensic facial reconstruction. Cambridge Core Epub ahead of print May 2004. DOI: 10.1017/CBO9781107340961.

Wilkinson, C. (2005). Computerized forensic facial reconstruction: A review of current systems. *Forensic Science, Medicine and Pathology, 1*, 173–177.

Wilkinson, C., & Rynn, C. (2012). *Craniofacial identification*. Cambridge University Press.

Wilkinson, C., Rynn, C., Peters, H., et al. (2006). A blind accuracy assessment of computer-modeled forensic facial reconstruction using computed tomography data from live subjects. *Forensic Science, Medicine and Pathology, 2*, 179–187.

Yoshino, M., Matsuda, H., Kubota, S., et al. (1997). Computer-assisted skull identification system using video superimposition. *Forensic Science International, 90*, 231–244.

Zhang, A., Sayre, J. W., Vachon, L., et al. (2009). Racial differences in growth patterns of children assessed on the basis of bone age. *Radiology, 250*, 228–235.

Zhang, K., Yu, W., Manhein, M., et al. (2015). 3D fragment Reassembly using integrated template guidance and fracture-region matching. In *2015 IEEE International Conference on Computer Vision (ICCV)* (pp. 2138–2146).

Zhong, X., Yu, D., Foong, K. W. C., et al. (2011). Towards automated pose invariant 3D dental biometrics. In *2011 International Joint Conference on Biometrics (IJCB)* (pp. 1–7).

Zhong, X., Yu, D., Wong, Y. S., et al. (2013). 3D dental biometrics: Alignment and matching of dental casts for human identification. *Computers in Industry, 64*, 1355–1370.

CHAPTER

A medicolegal approach to postmortem interval estimation

4

Lerah Sutton[1], Tim Gallagher[2] and Haley Russo[3]

[1]*University of Florida Maples Center for Forensic Medicine, Gainesville, FL, United States;* [2]*District 1 Office of the Medical Examiner, Pensacola, FL, United States;* [3]*Cook County Office of the Medical Examiner, Chicago, IL, United States*

1. Introduction

The postmortem interval, also referred to as the time since death, is the amount of time that has accrued between the moment of death and the time of discovery. It is one of the most sought out questions in a death investigation as it can assist investigators with recognizing the circumstances and timing surrounding the death event. The postmortem interval can be established through the analysis of physical and chemical decompositional changes of the body. While there is a plethora of research that attempts to quantify the qualitative process of decomposition, despite these efforts, the accuracy of postmortem interval estimation has been relatively low.

1.1 Historical review of postmortem interval estimation methods

To understand current literature on the postmortem interval, it is first necessary to recognize the historical influences behind forensic medicine. The first anatomic descriptions for forensic medicine came from the observation of animal anatomy in fourth century BC in Babylonia. At this time, autopsies were limited to animals as human bodies were regarded as sacred (Choo & Choi, 2012). During this period, Aristotle became one of the first noteworthy figures in the study of anatomy. Despite never having undertaken human dissection, his assertions on the topic were considered significant in both fact and influence. He believed that the body was composed of simple and compound forms of blood, fat, marrow, brain, flesh, and bone with the final form being the soul. He ultimately proclaimed that decomposition begins when the soul leaves the body (O'Malley, 1964). In ancient Greek medicine, the humoral theories of disease were of significant interest. This theory claimed that the humors—black bile, yellow bile, phlegm, and blood—composed the body, and all diseases were a result of an imbalance of the humors to other elements in the body (Choo & Choi, 2012). This philosophy was widely accepted for centuries throughout Europe, but it limited investigations from correlating anatomy and disease. This was in part due to the focus on clinical observations of disease through the evaluation of wounds rather than the effect of the disease on the body through dissection (Finkbeiner & Ursell, 2009). However, as the ideologies of

Methodological and Technological Advances in Death Investigations. https://doi.org/10.1016/B978-0-12-819394-5.00002-X

the ancient world evolved, new outlooks on the dead began to form, and the fear of desecrating a human body through dissection started to ease.

While the end of the ancient times showed a more liberal attitude toward death, the Dark Ages of the medieval times in Europe halted this advancement as autopsies were forbidden. It was not until 1231 that the first law approving human dissection was established. From this point forward, autopsy restrictions began to open up throughout Europe with the first recorded medicolegal autopsy being performed in 1302 in Bologna. Meanwhile in Asia, forensic medicine was a progressive concept where postmortem autopsies were conducted as early as the end of the 11th century (Choo & Choi, 2012). One of the earliest available publications on forensic medicine is the 13th-century Chinese handbook *The Washing Away of Wrongs by Sung Tz'u*. The handbook contains guidelines on postmortem examinations and dissection techniques as well as investigation methods for suspicious deaths. Its utility provided an understanding of forensic medicine at that time and laid a foundation for future forensic medicine endeavors (Tz'u, 1981).

With the arrival of the Renaissance period, the doctrines of Galen began to transform the ideology of medicine and medicolegal science. While these doctrines were rooted on the study of ancient texts rather than the physical dissection of a corpse, the popularity of them led to undisputable claims of medicine (Benini & Bonar, 1996). Despite these claims, by the 1500s, autopsies were generally accepted by the Catholic Church, and many scholarly works on forensic medicine became available. In 1507, the recordings of Antonia Benivieni were published as *The Hidden Causes of Disease,* which utilized anatomic dissection as a means of establishing the cause of death (Choo & Choi, 2012). In 1543, Andreas Vesaluis, who is often referred to as the founder of modern anatomy, published one of the most influential books on human anatomy *De humani corporis fabrica (On the Fabric of the Human Body).* Contrary to Galen, Vesaluis believed that anatomic knowledge could only be achieved through dissection of a human corpse rather than studying traditional texts. He was a witness to the difficulties of proposing new science when the doctrines of Galen were heavily trusted but overcame the adversity to establish a modern understanding of anatomy (Benini & Bonar, 1996).

Toward the end of the 16th century, autopsies were commonly associated with death investigations where physicians in Europe were often called to aid with solving fatal crimes. Around this time, autopsies began to be recorded in the United States. During the 20th century in the United States, prominent leaders in medicine emphasized the importance of using autopsies for education which led to the advancement of forensic medicine throughout the United States (Choo & Choi, 2012). Through the evaluation of death and decomposition, the postmortem interval arose as a topic of interest for years to come.

1.2 The importance of postmortem interval estimation in a medicolegal death investigation

Having an understanding of the postmortem interval can be of significant help to a death investigation. While it is extremely difficult to determine an exact time since death, an estimation can prove invaluable. Being able to effectively provide an estimation as to how long someone has been dead for allows a timeframe to be associated with the death-causing event and time of discovery. The timeline can then be used to implicate or exclude suspects. For instance, if a suspect has an alibi for three of the 5 days a decedent has been missing, the postmortem interval estimation can narrow down the time of death which can then be used determine if the suspect could have been involved in the crime. Similarly, the postmortem interval can be used to corroborate or disprove witness testimony. Such that if a witness claims they last saw the decedent 2 days prior, but the postmortem interval indicates they have been dead for at least 5 days, it can be presumed that the witness is not a reliable source of information.

Furthermore, the postmortem interval can imply when a crime may have occurred. However, this must be considered with caution as it is possible that the time of assault is different from the time of death. There are instances in where the decedent received injuries when the crime occurred, but had a period of survival time before succumbing to their injuries. In these cases, the postmortem interval provides an understanding of when the death happened but fails to consider when the crime that eventually led to their death transpired. Accordingly, it is more appropriate to use the postmortem interval to identify the minimum time, rather that the exact time, of when the crime may have occurred.

Aside from the criminal component of the investigation, the postmortem interval can assist investigators in the identification of a decedent. While the postmortem interval itself cannot identify an individual, it can provide investigators with a foundation for their investigation. That is to say if an individual is found in an advanced state of decomposition and the postmortem interval indicates they have been deceased for approximately 28 days; the investigators can use this information, along with missing person reports, to identify who went missing around that time.

Overall, the postmortem interval gives vital leads to investigators regarding the timing and circumstances surrounding a death. However, its applicability goes beyond criminal cases and has shown helpful in civil cases as well. In civil cases, knowing when the death occurred can be an important factor in deciding who will inherit property and whether an insurance policy was in force at the time of death. Ultimately, the postmortem interval can influence the livelihood of many individuals. Thus, while it is difficult to attain, it is necessary so that there can be a deeper understanding of the death.

2. Postmortem change and time since death determination

Time since death determination, also known as postmortem interval estimation, is crucial in death investigations. While there is currently no single method that can determine the postmortem interval with 100% certainty, postmortem changes that occur after death can provide a range of time in which the death may have occurred. Using the estimated range of time in conjunction with scientific evidence, witness testimonials, and circumstantial evidence, it is possible to establish how long someone has been deceased for. However, postmortem changes can vary based on individual and environmental factors, so these methods must be used with caution when used as a basis for postmortem interval estimation.

2.1 Autolysis and putrefaction

Human decomposition starts approximately 4 min after death, with the onset beginning with a process known as autolysis or self-digestion (Vass, 2001). Autolysis is defined as the breakdown of cells and organs through a chemical process caused by intracellular enzymes (DiMaio & DiMaio, 2001). It is responsible for the initial breakdown of tissue during decomposition. After death, the cells in the body become deprived of oxygen, which results in an increase of carbon dioxide in the blood, a decrease in pH, and an accumulation of waste in the body that ultimately poisons the cells (Vass, 2001). When the cells die, lysosomes release a mixture of enzymes. These intracellular enzymes released are self-destructive in nature and destroy the cells (Child, 1995). When this process occurs, the tissues soften and lose cellular details that result in the destruction of tissue (Spitz et al., 2006). As autolysis affects the internal organs, it facilitates the movement of bacteria into the bloodstream, which results in it being spread throughout the entire body (Zhou & Byard, 2011).

Autolysis eventually affects all of the cells in the body, but early autolytic changes begin in organs rich in enzymes, like the pancreas, and organs high in water concentration, like the brain. However, the pattern in which autolysis spreads is most affected by temperature. The process is accelerated by heat, delayed by cold, and stopped with freezing or severe heat due to the inactivation of enzymes (DiMaio & DiMaio, 2001). Because autolysis occurs internally within the cells and organs, it is difficult to describe the gross appearance. However, autolysis is generally visible a few days after death, with its presence being indicative of skin blisters and skin slippage (Vass, 2001). While autolysis occurs shortly after death, it becomes progressively apparent as the postmortem interval increases.

Putrefaction is the other main component of decomposition. It follows autolysis and occurs due to bacteria and fermentation that breaks down tissue. When a death occurs, gastrointestinal bacteria spreads throughout the body and produces putrefaction (DiMaio & DiMaio, 2001). These changes are primarily dependent on the environmental temperatures and the decedent's state of health. Advanced putrefaction may be seen in less than 12 h following death, but the timing is reliant on the decedent's weight, clothing, physical environment, etc. Due to all of these variable factors, it is difficult to standardize a time of death with reference to putrefaction (Spitz et al., 2006). The general gross appearance of putrefaction includes green discoloration followed by red-black discoloration. Occasionally, the bacteria will multiply in the blood vessels, which absorbs into linear red streaks known as marbling. The bacteria of putrefaction can also influence body distortion and bloating (Fig. 4.1).

Autolysis and putrefaction are the two primary endogenous processes that influence decomposition. Despite the lack of ability to utilize these processes for

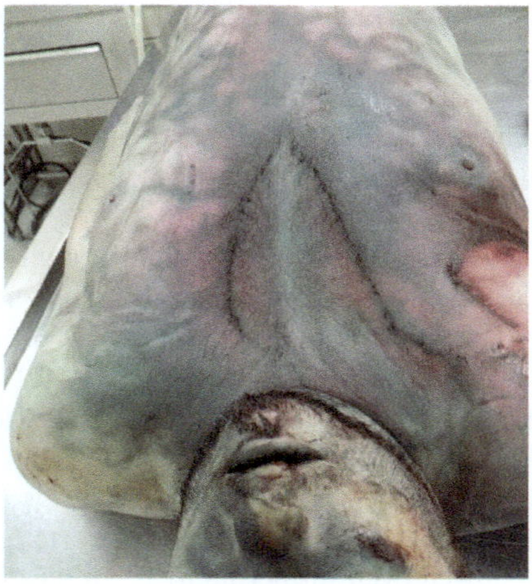

FIGURE 4.1

Putrefactive decomposition is generally characterized by green-gray discoloration of the skin, marbling, bloating, and a putrid odor.

Courtesy of Dr. Tim Gallagher.

postmortem interval estimation, they initiate the visual postmortem changes that can be used in the early postmortem period to establish a range of time since death.

2.2 Vitreous humor

Vitreous humor is commonly analyzed when estimating the postmortem interval (Chandrakanth et al., 2013). It is a transparent, gelatinous tissue that fills the eyeball behind the lens. Each human has approximately 4–5 mL of vitreous humor, which is composed of 99% water and the rest a mixture of collagen, proteins, salts and sugars. Due to the large volume and ease of accessibility, vitreous humor is a regarded as a simple method in postmortem interval estimation, but the reliability of it is still in question (Baniak et al., 2015).

Vitreous humor is relatively stable and less susceptible to rapid chemical changes and contamination due to its isolated topography and resistance to microbiological contamination that may occur as a result of postmortem changes. This makes it popular for analysis among forensic scientists. Certain substances that reside in the vitreous humor, such as sodium, calcium, chloride, phosphate, magnesium, creatinine, urea, and lactate, have been analyzed to estimate the postmortem interval, but it is the potassium ion ($K+$) concentration that is most frequently used (Chandrakanth et al., 2013).

The first person to evaluate the association between death and contents of vitreous humor was Hans Naumann in 1959. In this study, he compared several vitreous humor and cerebrospinal fluid postmortem concentrations including urea, glucose, creatinine, chlorine, calcium, sodium, and potassium. He found that the postmortem concentrations of these chemicals increased more in the cerebrospinal fluid than in the vitreous humor. Specifically, 9 h after death, the K+ concentration was twice the initial concentration in the vitreous humor and seven times the concentration in the cerebrospinal fluid (Naumann, 1959). While this research provided a foundation for future evaluations of vitreous humor, it did not associate the findings with the postmortem interval.

In 1962, Jaffe was the first to publish a study that recognized the association between increased levels of K+ concentration in the vitreous humor and its applicability for postmortem interval estimation. In his study, 31 deceased individuals with known times of death had their vitreous humor K+ concentration levels measured throughout the postmortem period. The results concluded that there was a steady increase and positive correlation between the K+ concentration levels and the postmortem interval. At 9 h postmortem, the levels of K+ approximately doubled in concentration. Between 9- and 30 h postmortem, the levels increased but at a slower rate and slowed even further up to 125 h postmortem. A linear relationship was ultimately identified between K+ concentration levels in the vitreous humor and the postmortem interval (Jaffe, 1962). Since the discovery of the relationship between the postmortem interval and the K+ concentration of the vitreous humor, there have been many studies that have attempted to quantify the rate of change in order to establish the postmortem interval.

One of the most noteworthy studies was conducted by Sturner in 1963. The results of this study concluded that there was a 95% confidence interval of ±9.5 h. However, subsequent studies have had differing 95% confidence intervals. Hughes (1965) states ±20 h, Hansson et al. (1966) states ±40 h, and Coe (1989) states ±12 h. Generally, the research has shown a variation among 95% confidence intervals between ±9.5 h to ±40 h of the postmortem interval up to 100 h and ±6 h to ±12 h of the postmortem interval up to 24 h (Madea, 2016a, 2016b, 2016c). These inconsistencies among researchers show that using vitreous K+ concentration for postmortem interval estimation is a highly variable method (Fig. 4.2).

Along with the variation in research, there are other limitations of this method. For instance, the starting levels of the potassium concentration in the vitreous humor vary heavily from person to person. Those who consume larger amounts of potassium throughout their lifetime will have higher K+ levels in their vitreous humor than those who do not. This makes it difficult to standardize the linear relationship between potassium levels and time since death since the initial potassium levels after death are not consistent for everyone. Another limitation resides in the acquisition methods of the vitreous sample. According to the recommendations of Coe (1989), the vitreous humor should be carefully collected via a needle and small syringe. Syringes with strong suction should not be used since fragments of the retina or other tissues may contaminate the sample and skew the biochemical values. Decomposition can alter the color of the fluid to be brown and cloudy; however, the only samples suitable for analysis are ones where the fluid is colorless and clear. These restrictions make using this method time-consuming and costly.

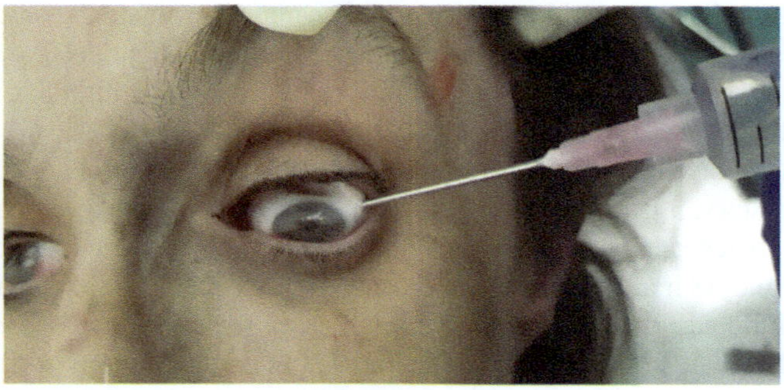

FIGURE 4.2

Aspiration of vitreous humor from eye of decedent. It is important the sample be colorless with a minimum of blood contamination. The fluid should be drawn expeditiously as it degrades over the course of a several days making result interpretation challenging.

Courtesy of Dr. Tim Gallagher.

2.3 Rigor mortis

Rigor mortis, also known as postmortem rigidity, is a chemical cellular process that causes a gradual onset of muscle stiffening followed by relaxation (DiMaio & DiMaio, 2001). In 1811, French physician P.H. Nysten was the first to publish a scientific evaluation of rigor mortis. He recognized that rigor mortis follows a specific progression pattern beginning in the trunk and neck, followed by the upper extremities and ending with the lower extremities. This ultimately became known as Nysten's law, which describes the onset and resolution of rigor mortis (Krompecher, 2016). More than a century later, Bendall and Bate-Smith (1947) conducted a study that confirmed the breakdown of adenosine triphosphate (ATP) influenced the onset and development of rigor mortis. ATP is a required source of energy for muscles to contract. Since ATP only sustains muscle contractions for a few seconds, it is necessary that there is a continuous supply. When death occurs, the creation of ATP stops, however, the body's consumption of ATP continues. After all of the ATP in the body is depleted, the actin and myosin filaments become fixed, which causes rigor mortis to set in. Then, as proteins in the body are broken down through decomposition, the fixed chemical bridges between the actin and myosin break down, which lead the muscles to relax again (Fisher & Fisher, 2012). Individuals who exert ATP prior to death will have a sped-up onset of rigor mortis. In rare cases, the instantaneous appearance of rigor mortis, known as cadaveric spasm, can occur (DiMaio & DiMaio, 2001).

One of the earliest studies to assess the timeline of rigor mortis was conducted in 1872 by P F. Niderkorn, who evaluated 113 cases of rigor mortis. Of these cases, 67% reached their maximum, where all muscles are fully stiffened, in 4–7 h. The range of all cases was between 2 and 13 h. This study also recognized that temperature affects rigor mortis, noting that rigidity lasts longer in cold, dry environments than hot, wet ones (Krompecher, 2016). One of the more comprehensive studies done on the chronology of rigor mortis development was conducted by Mallach, where he surveyed

108 publications between 1811 and 1960 to compare and evaluate the observations of rigor mortis statistically. He found that overall, there was a 3-hour delay period before the onset of rigor mortis, and the maximum rigidity was seen within 8 h; it persisted for 57 h and resolved around 76 h (Kori, 2018).

While there have been variations in the timeline of rigor mortis among scientists throughout history, it is generally agreed-upon that rigidity becomes apparent 4–6 h postmortem, reaches its maximum between 12 and 24 h postmortem, and dissipates between 24 and 48 h after death. However, there are several intrinsic and extrinsic factors that influence the onset and duration of rigor mortis. In many cases, rigorous exercise and high fevers leading up to death result in the rapid onset of rigidity and a shorter overall duration. The amount of muscle in a body also dictates the duration, such that a child will undergo rigor mortis more quickly than a heavy adult. Extrinsic factors including death from electrocution, drowning, and strychnine poisoning have been known to accelerate rigor mortis (Hayman & Oxenham, 2016a, 2016b). Temperature also heavily influences rigidity in that heat accelerates the onset and progression and cold slows it down. Since there are many influential factors for rigidity, it must be used with caution as a postmortem interval estimation method. Rigor mortis may be used more appropriately and accurately to determine the body's position at the time of death (Figs. 4.3 and 4.4).

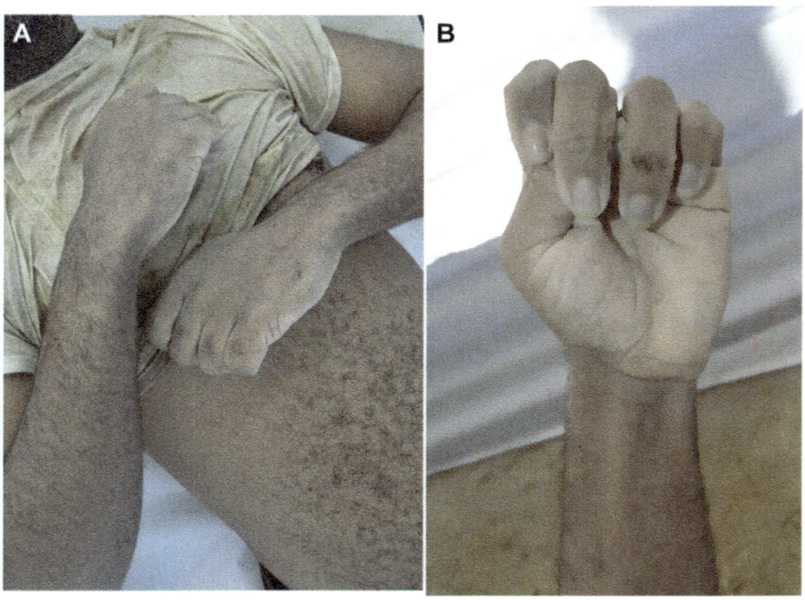

FIGURE 4.3

(a) Rigor mortis of the upper extremities. The hands are clenched and the elbows are flexed. (b) Typical rigor mortis pattern in the hand. The thumb flexes medially and the remaining four fingers overlie the distal portion of the thumb.

Courtesy of Dr. Tim Gallagher.

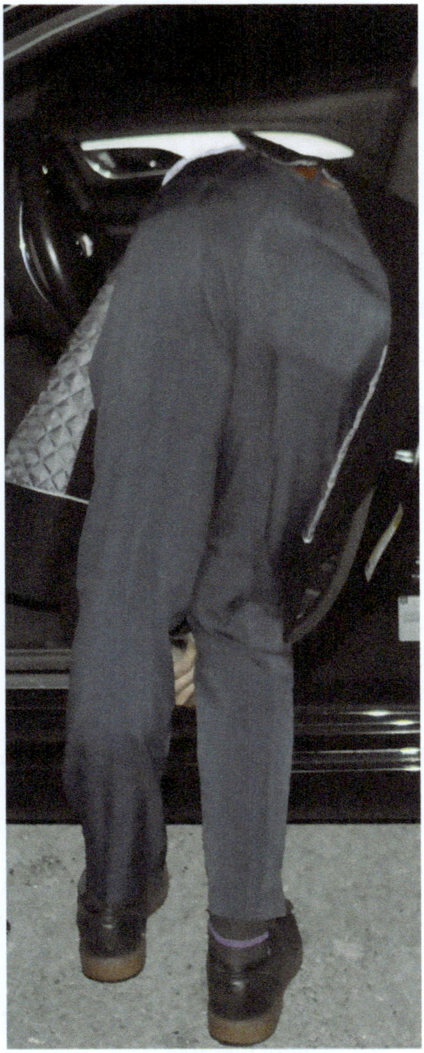

FIGURE 4.4

Rigor mortis of the lower extremities. Rigor of the legs is usually the last to dissipate secondary to the large proportion of muscle in the lower extremities when compared to the remainder of the body. In this case the decedent appeared to be standing for several hours after death.

Courtesy of Dr. Tim Gallagher.

2.4 Livor mortis

Livor mortis, also referred to as lividity or hypostasis, is a postmortem change that occurs immediately after the cessation of blood circulation. The skin becomes

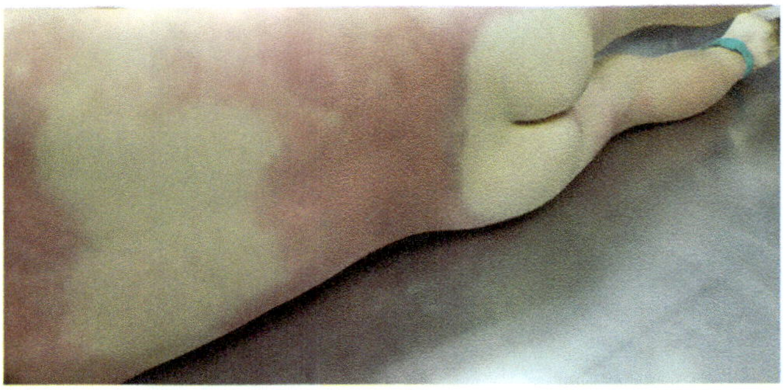

FIGURE 4.5

Posterior lividity. After death the blood in the vasculature settles to the gravity dependent areas of the body. The areas of pallor between the shoulder blades and the gluteal region are pressure points where the body was in contact with a hard surface. The vasculature becomes compressed and impedes the passive blood flow creating the lighter areas.

Courtesy of Dr. Tim Gallagher.

discolored due to the pooling of the blood in gravity dependent areas both externally in the skin capillaries and venules and also in the internal organs. If the skin is exposed to direct pressure, such as the ground, objects, or tight clothing, lividity will not be seen in the area of contact due to the blood being pushed out of the vessels. These areas are known as contact pallors (Hayman & Oxenham, 2016a, 2016b) (Fig. 4.5).

Understanding lividity and its timeline can help investigators determine the postmortem interval of an individual because it happens at relatively consistent rate. Although the onset begins immediately after death, livor mortis is not readily apparent until approximately 2 h after death. From that point, it becomes more prominent over the next several hours. As a general rule of thumb, lividity becomes fixed after 6 h postmortem. However, the actual amount of time lividity takes to fix itself varies among several studies (Fig. 4.6).

Adelson (1952) reports that it becomes fixed at 8–12 h, Vanezis and Trujillo (1996) state approximately 48 h, Kaatsch et al. (1994) note 40 h, and Usumoto et al. (2019) say 72 h. Despite conflicting reports of when lividity becomes fixed, to determine if the lividity is fixed, an investigator should press their thumb into an area of pooled blood to determine if there is a presence or absence of skin blanching. Nonfixed lividity will turn lighter when pressed into, while fixed lividity will not change color. Once the lividity is fixed, it will remain so until the process of decomposition breaks down the capillaries. The color of the lividity may change from the purple/pink/red to green/gray, but this color change is not beneficial in determining the postmortem interval, as it is a result of putrefaction changes.

The notion of livor mortis has been around since the mid-13th-century. The earliest reference was in Sung Tz'us comprehensive handbook for forensic investigators, where Tz'u stated "Generally, dead persons have a slight red coloration on

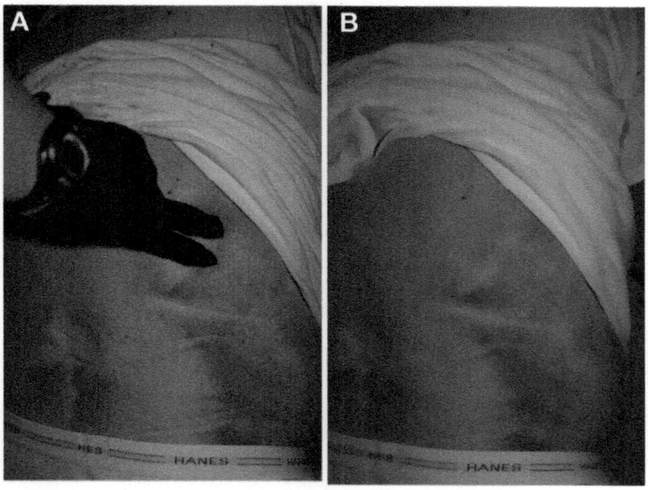

FIGURE 4.6

(a) Fixed lividity. A medicolegal death investigator (MDI) presses two fingers into an area of lividity on the skin in order to determine if it is fixed or unfixed. This information can be used in approximating the time of death. (b) After the fingers of the MDI are removed from the surface of the skin the compressed area is observed for pallor. If pallor is absent the lividity is determined to be fixed, as depicted in the photograph.

Courtesy of Dr. Tim Gallagher.

the back of the neck, on the top of the back, on the ribs, the back of the waist, the insides of the legs, the knees, the feet and the stomach … The collapse of the blood vessels may cause this slight red coloration, which does not indicate any other cause of death" (Tz'u, 1981). Since then, livor mortis has primarily been the topic of research in relation to its use as a method to determine the postmortem interval. However, considering the physiological mechanisms of blood pooling, coagulation, and dissociations of hemoglobin are variable and that the assessment of lividity is based on observations which are subjective and prone to error, this method is relatively unreliable (Knight, 2002). Nevertheless, research is still being conducted on lividity in order to better understand why and when this phenomenon occurs (Fig. 4.7).

One of the more unique research studies focused on evaluating lividity and its relationship to the postmortem interval used a colorimeter measuring system. In this study, lividity was measured using a tristimulus colorimeter in 93 cadavers. During a 4-h period, the intensity of the lividity was measured in order to find a rate of change for the lightness of lividity. It was found that when these data were measured against the time of death, there was a positive correlation between the darkening of lividity and the postmortem increase. Within the first 12 h after death, the lividity color shifted the most. From 12 to 28 h after death, the rate of change was slow but visible, and after 48 h, it was very low. This shows that lividity can be a useful

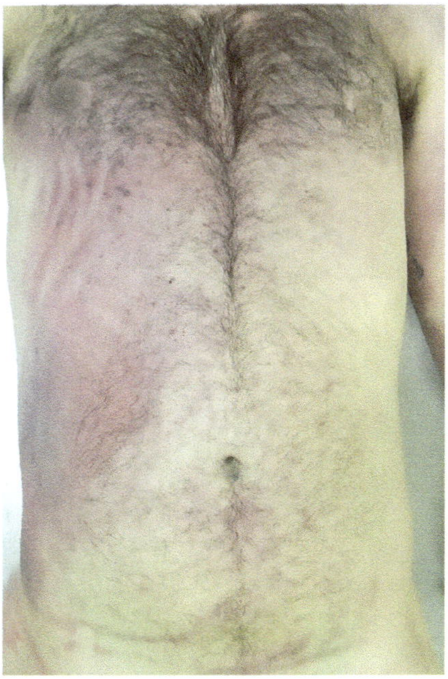

FIGURE 4.7

Lividity is concentrated on the right side of the torso. This is an indication the position of the body was on its right chest when death occurred and lividity became fixed.

Courtesy of Dr. Tim Gallagher.

source to determine the postmortem interval up to 48 h after death. It was also noted in the study that factors, such as body size, cause of death, age, sex, and color of skin, can affect the color intensity change (Vanezis & Trujillo, 1996). Another study utilized photometric measurements of pressure-induced blanching to analyze livor mortis and its relation to the postmortem interval. To execute this study, they applied increasing levels of defined magnitudes of pressure to the lividity in 50 cadavers. The surface area under the pressure applied points were then calculated and plotted into 10-h postmortem time categories. It was found that there were distinct differences between the time categories of blanching up to 40 h in which pressure did not create blanching. It was also concluded, like the previous study, that many factors play a role in the data variations (Kaatsch et al., 1994). One of the most recent studies—a pilot study in 2019—looked at creating a predictive equation of the postmortem interval based on the spectrophotometric values of postmortem lividity. 86 cadavers were measured spectrophotometrically to obtain a chroma and hue value. These data were then analyzed to develop an equation regarding the relationship between the color of control skin, blood colors, and postmortem lividity. Although blood color itself proved to not correlate to the color of lividity and the control skin, the researchers were still able to develop equations that estimate postmortem lividity color using control skin. The equation established, without using the blood color values, was able to estimate the postmortem interval within ±10.29 h and be useful up to 72 h post death (Usumoto et al., 2019). Each of these studies recognize the uncontrollable factors that play a role in lividity but acknowledge the potential for lividity to be used as a postmortem interval estimation method.

Similar to rigor mortis, lividity is affected by a multitude of variables, which makes its utility for postmortem estimation unreliable. If this method is employed, other methods should be used to further support the time since death estimation.

2.5 Postmortem muscle excitability

Postmortem muscle excitability is a measurement that is used to determine time since death by testing a corpse's muscle reaction to stimulation. The two primary methods utilized to assess this measure are mechanical and electrical stimulation. In older investigations of mechanical stimulation, muscles were excited in a variety of ways, including pinching and hitting with a hand or knife. Generally, the harder the strike, the stronger the reaction (Madea, 2016a, 2016b). Dowler (1846) was the first to observe the mechanical muscle stimulation effects on postmortem limbs. He recognized that when bicep muscles were struck 2 h after death, the extended arm would contract into the chest (Hayman & Oxenham, 2016a, 2016b). Following this discovery, other researchers noticed that skeletal muscles react to mechanical stimulation in the early postmortem period. Madea (2002) found that when the lower thigh is struck, the muscles respond to the mechanical stimuli with strong contractions for 1.5–2.5 h postmortem (Madea, 2002). The muscle contractions then gradually dissipate until 12 h postmortem, when there is no more response. Further studies, a comprehensive study evaluating 270 cases of mechanically stimulated skeletal muscles indicates that the upper time limit of mechanical muscle response is 13 h (Warther et al., 2012). According to Madea (2016a), (2016b), the most useful information for the practical use of mechanical excitability states that there are three phases with corresponding postmortem timeframes. Phase one is indicated by the complete contraction of the muscle and occurs 1.5–2.5 h postmortem. Phase two happens 4–5 h postmortem and is recognized by the development of a strong idiomuscular pad. The last phase is seen 8–12 h postmortem and is characterized by the development of a weak idiomuscular pad. The mode of excitement for this information is a strike to the bicep with the back of a knife (Madea, 2016a, 2016b).

Electrical stimulation holds similar methodology to mechanical stimulation but instead uses electrodes as the mode of excitement. Galvani (1781) first documented electrical muscle excitability in a study that evaluated the electrical stimulation of disassociated frog legs. The thighs were completely removed, but the legs and feet were still attached to the spinal column via the sciatic nerves. In the series of experiments, Galvani electrically stimulated the sciatic nerves which caused the muscles to contract. He regarded this phenomenon as "animal electricity." Further studies focused on using electrical muscle excitability as a means of postmortem interval estimation but were regarded as incomparable due to the inconsistencies among the research variables (Hayman & Oxenham, 2016a, 2016b). Madea and Henssge (1990) further reviewed the association between electrical stimulation of muscles and the postmortem interval. They found that the strength of contraction in the orbicularis oculi, orbicularis, and hand muscles declined as the postmortem interval increased. In this review, they also noted that in order for this method to have a practical use, the methodology must be standardized with regard to grading the contractions, electrode positioning, and physical characteristics of excitement (Madea & Henssge, 1990). In 1992, Madea attempted to create an accurate and consistent means of using electrical muscle stimulation for postmortem interval estimation. In this study, human muscles were stimulated and their contractions were measured. It was found that the muscles had a period of maximum contraction that was followed by relaxation until the muscles no longer responded to the stimulus, which was approximately 13 h after death. The decrease in stimulated contractions and increase in relaxation period were then measured to be used for postmortem interval estimation purposes (Madea, 1992).

While electrical stimulation can be readily preformed on scene in a timely manner, the variation in mode of excitement and grading of contractions among researchers proves this method to be unreliable as the sole measurement. To increase the accuracy of the postmortem interval, electrical stimulation is best coupled with the Henssge nomogram method. More appropriately, this method should be used in conjunction with other postmortem changes to establish the postmortem interval.

3. Temperature-based methods

One of the most influential variables that affect decomposition is temperature. Almost every postmortem artifact is temperature dependent, so it is essential that temperature is considered when estimating the postmortem interval. Typically, cooler temperatures slow the rate of decomposition, while warmer temperatures accelerate the process. This general understanding has led researchers to thoroughly investigate how temperature relates to the postmortem interval. However, due to the numerous environmental and individual variables associated with temperature-based postmortem interval methods, the applicability of the research has been limited in producing reliable results.

3.1 Algor mortis

One of the most understood concepts in regard to temperature and decomposition is algor mortis. Algor mortis is commonly defined as the postmortem cooling of the body, but it is better described as the postmortem change in body temperature until it reaches the ambient temperature. While in most cases, the body will cool to reach the ambient temperature, the reverse is possible.

As a general rule of thumb, the body cools at approximately 1.5–2°F per hour during the first 12 h and then slows to a rate of 1.0°F per hour until the ambient

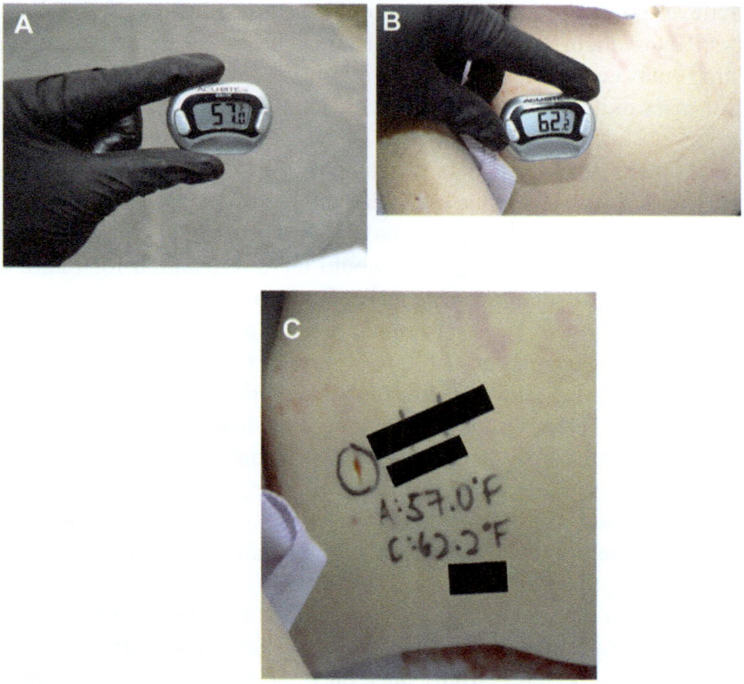

FIGURE 4.8

(a) A medicolegal death investigator measuring the ambient temperature near the location of a death scene. (b) Method by which a body temperature core sample is obtained on a decedent. A small incision is created with a scalpel blade over the liver on the right lateral portion of the body. A temperature probe is then inserted through the incision and into the liver to obtain a core body temperature. (c) The body is subsequently marked with the ambient temperature, the body core temperature, and other identifying data. The incision where the probe was inserted into the liver is circled.

Courtesy of Dr. Tim Gallagher.

temperature is reached (Prahlow, 2010). In most instances, the body takes 18–20 h to reach the ambient temperature (Fisher & Fisher, 2012). It is necessary that when analyzing algor mortis, investigators are familiar with local climate data as that heavily influences the rate and duration of algor mortis. Similarly, algor mortis is highly variable based on clothing, perimortem activity level, drug use, and illness (Fisher and Fisher, 2012). This results in the need for investigators to not only evaluate the body temperature but the characteristics surrounding the death as well (Fig. 4.8).

The earliest documentation of using body temperature after death as a basis for postmortem interval estimation comes from a study done by Dr. John Davy in 1839. In this study, the bodies of 10 soldiers who died in 1828 and nine soldiers who died in 1838 were evaluated. During the autopsies, Dr. Davy found that in all cases, the internal body temperature was raised above the ambient room temperature. This led him to believe that body temperature may be used as a means of establishing the postmortem interval. In Dr. Davy's publication, he stated that the findings from this research "may enable the enquirer ... to arrive at a tolerably positive conclusion, in doubtful cases of death, as to the time which may have elapsed, between the fatal event and the postmortem examination" (Davy, 1839). Following Dr. Davy's findings, several other researchers began conducting similar studies. In 1863, Drs. Taylor and Wilks recorded the surface body temperature of 100 decedents and observed the temperature changes as time progressed. Despite a lack of controlled variables, they made several notable findings that would lay a foundation for future studies. Such that, "fat" bodies retained a higher body temperature for a longer period of time, bodies retained heat for approximately 12 h postmortem with an apparent plateau phase, and the environment and coverings on the body played a role in the rate at which it cooled (Hayman & Oxenham, 2016a, 2016b). Subsequent studies have attempted to develop equations that can establish a postmortem interval based on temperature changes, but due to the numerous variables that affect body temperature after death, these methods have had varying degrees of success.

While there are several different equations that express the rate of cooling in regard to the postmortem interval estimation, the standard is the Glaister equation that states: postmortem interval (hours)=(96.8°F body temperature before death) - (rectal temperature after death)/1.5. This equation is based on the premise that the body cools at 1.5°F per hour. This equation, along with many others, is limited to the early postmortem period (<18 h) since once the body reaches ambient temperature, algor mortis proves useless as a method to estimate the time of death. It also does not account for any variables that influence the change in body temperature, which increases the error rate (Prahlow, 2010).

A more advanced equation was established by Marshall and Hoare (1962). This equation incorporates the postmortem temperature plateau that is commonly noted in algor mortis research and the succeeding temperature drop. It is represented by

$$Q=(T{\downarrow}r-T{\downarrow}a)\,/\,(T{\downarrow}0-T{\downarrow}a)=A\,x\,\mathbf{exp}\,[(B\,x\,t)+(1-A)\,x\,\mathbf{exp}(AxB\,/\,(A-1))xt]$$

in which, Q = standardized temperature; T = rectal temperature at any time t; T = rectal temperature at death ($t=0$); T = ambient temperature; A = constant; B = constant; t = death time. While this equation poses some difficulties in identifying certain values, it is regarded as one of the most successful mathematical equations for achieving the time since death using body temperature change (Henssge, 1998).

Marshall and Hoare's model provided a foundation for the nomogram method. The nomogram method, which is based on a single rectal temperature measurement, was developed by Claus Henssge. This method is regarded as the gold standard for time of death determination as it represents the relationship between cooling of the body and associated variables such as the rectal temperature, the ambient temperature of the air, body weight, clothing, and air movement (Madea, 2016a, 2016b). A nomogram is a visual diagram that depicts the relationship between three or more variables based on a relationship between scales. Henssge recognized that a nomogram could be utilized to evaluate other prediction equations, environmental variables, and the body's physical processes to establish a postmortem interval. When utilized appropriately, Henssge's nomogram can be used to approximately determine the postmortem interval with error rates of ±2.5 h within the first 12 h postmortem and increasing beyond that (Henssge, 1988). It is the most statistically accurate method of measuring algor mortis. However, any method that utilizes rectal temperature must be used with caution as attaining body temperature through this method can alter or destroy evidence, especially in cases of sexual assault.

3.2 Accumulated degree days

Literature and research regarding the postmortem interval suggests that temperature is a crucial factor in the estimation of time since death. Accumulated degree days (ADD) are often used in forensic entomology when estimating the postmortem interval. ADD, also known as thermal units, heat units, or growing degree days, are defined as the number of degrees above a certain threshold temperature required for growth within 24 h (Capinera, 2008). In forensic entomology, ADD represent chronological time in combination with temperature data as a means of measuring the growth and development of arthropods (Kumara et al., 2017). Essentially, ADD represent the amount of time that an insect, or stage of decomposition, spends at a temperature above and below a developmental threshold. ADD are then used to refer to the accumulated amount of time that it takes a particular stage to complete development based on temperature history and data (Capinera, 2008). Megyesi et al. (2005) recognized that just as insect growth is dependent on accumulated temperature, decomposition follows a similar pattern. This research suggests that decomposition is better modeled through accumulated temperature rather than time.

In 1855, a French doctor, Louis François Étienne Bergeret, was the first to use forensic entomology to estimate the postmortem interval in a criminal case. Bergeret was tasked with determining the postmortem interval of a child found deceased in a house. The primary assumption during this time was that the metamorphosis of any particular insect was 1 year; the females lay their eggs in the summer, the larvae pupate in the spring, and they eclose the following summer. Two generations of insects were present on the corpse, which Bergeret assumed meant the death had occurred 2 years prior. Bergeret established the time since death to be approximately 2 years. While the current understanding of forensic entomology and insect succession recognizes Bergeret's assumptions as inaccurate, this case exemplifies the utilization of insects as a method of developing a postmortem interval (Benecke, 2001).

Forensic entomology research has shown that different species of insects arrive and depart from a body at various times throughout decomposition. This arrival and departure of insects provides a timeline that is helpful in the estimation of the postmortem interval. The pattern of visitation, also known as seres, is dependent on season and geographic location, which may also indicate not only when, but where a death occurred (Byrd & Tomberlin, 2019). Previous research provides investigators and entomologists with general guidelines as to which insect species are likely to be present at each stage of decomposition. Additionally, based on previously conducted research, forensic entomologists are able to identify which species are present at or around a body and utilize developmental data to determine the age of the insect larvae present.

The rate of development of insects' immature stages is dependent on ambient temperature; therefore, their age is positively correlated with the accumulated thermal units they acquire during growth. The equation for calculating an insect's accumulated degree days is the average temperature minus the lower determined threshold for a particular species and then multiplied by a unit of time (days or hours). Each specific insect species has an upper and lower temperature threshold determined through intensive laboratory research (Amendt et al., 2007). To utilize accumulated degree days, temperature data should be retrieved from closest certified weather station to the scene.

4. Artifacts of decomposition

Decomposition is a continuous process that begins immediately after a death event and essentially ends when the body becomes a skeleton. The stages of decomposition are often marked by gross observational benchmarks, and virtually every study designates these benchmarks as a series of stages. The number and classification of stages vary throughout research. For instance, Cornaby (1974) recognized only one stage of decomposition, while studying lizards and toads in Costa Rica; conversely, a 19th century study on female corpses acknowledges nine stages of decomposition (Chin, 1998).

There is importance in recognizing the different stages of decomposition. The separation of the decomposition process into stages allows scientists and researchers to easily organize new research based on a particular stage. For example, forensic entomologists and other scientists studying Calliphorid insects may focus and organize their research on the fresh stage of decomposition, as Calliphorid flies tend to appear on the body very quickly after death. Additionally, there is a benefit to using the stages of decomposition in a courtroom setting during trial. It is easy to explain the stages of decomposition to members of a jury, due to the qualitative nature of these stages (i.e., physical description of each stage and/or specific insect activity at each stage). Jurors are able to use the stages of decomposition for reference in any death or decomposition case.

4.1 General stages of decomposition

There is not a general consensus among forensic practitioners regarding the number and division of stages of decomposition. On the least divided end, some forensic pathologists will assess decomposition in only three stages—early, moderate, and advanced—with regards to the degree of putrefactive decomposition. On the more heavily divided end, some forensic entomologists will access decomposition in as many as 12 stages based on unique insect succession and colonization data. Despite the lack of truly uniform agreement regarding the stages of decomposition within the scientific community, the majority of decomposition-focused research suggests there are five broad stages of decomposition: fresh, bloat/early decay, active decay, advanced decay, and dry remains. These stages are classified based on general characteristics and appearance.

4.1.1 Fresh

The fresh stage of decomposition begins immediately after death occurs and lasts until bloating becomes apparently visible. Remains are considered fresh when there is no observed discoloration, with the exception of lividity, and any maggot activity is not yet externally visible. Generally, in cooler months, remains stay fresh beyond the first day after death. During this time, insects will begin to colonize the body and may arrive as early as 15 min after death. Insects colonize a fresh body in a head-down pattern, laying their eggs in natural openings of the body, such as the eyes, nose, mouth, ears, and genitals, as well as sites of trauma and wounds. The first insects to arrive to a body during the fresh stage of decomposition include Calliphoridae (blow flies) and Sarcophagidae (flesh flies). Eggs may hatch during the fresh stage, and larvae may begin feeding on the body; however, typically, there is little evidence of feeding observed on the external surface of the body during the fresh stage (Fig. 4.9).

4.1.2 Bloat/early decay

The bloat/early decay stage is the second recognized stage of decomposition. During this stage, the skin will change from looking "fresh" to having a green or purple coloration. This is often referred to as "marbling." Putrefaction, one of the two main components of decomposition, begins during the bloat/early decay stage due to the anaerobic bacteria in the body beginning to digest the tissue. This

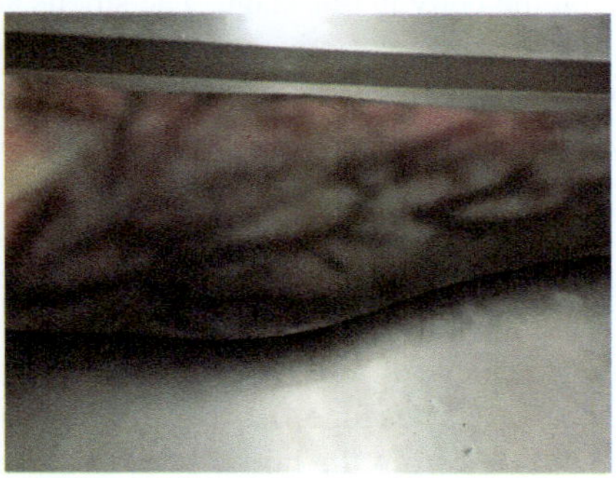

FIGURE 4.9

Early decomposition includes the breakdown products of blood within the vasculature and their absorption into the skin causing a red-green "marbling" coloration.

Courtesy of Dr. Tim Gallagher.

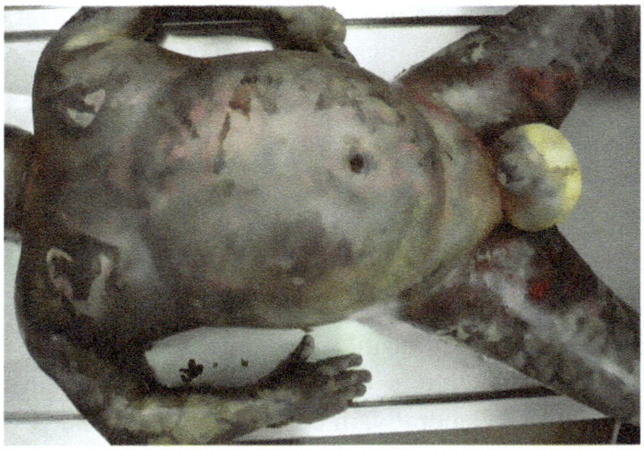

FIGURE 4.10

Gas produced by bacterial metabolic activity accumulates and is trapped under the skin causing the abdomen and scrotum to bloat in the early stages of decomposition.

Courtesy of Dr. Tim Gallagher.

metabolic process produces gases—typically hydrogen sulfide, methane, cadaverine, and putrescine—that cause the abdomen to inflate, hence the term "bloating." Gases continue to absorb into the body, causing the rest of the body, including the face, neck, and extremities, to bloat. Putrefaction and the building up of the aforementioned gases within the body are the processes responsible for emitting the unique smell commonly associated with death and decomposition (Fig. 4.10).

A great deal of maggot activity is typically observed within the bloat/early decay stage of decomposition unless the body is in an area of where flies are not present. During this stage, insect larvae are present internally within and externally upon the body while feeding. Larvae typically feed on the body in masses, so it is easy to spot many fly larvae feeding on the body in this stage. The smells and further decay associated with decomposition are very attractive to flies and other insects, so it is common to see plenty of adult insect species on and around the body during the bloat/early decay stage, as well.

4.1.3 Active decay

While most of the stages of decomposition are heavily subjective, there is a clear gross observation that indicates the active decay stage. Active decay occurs when the maggot feeding and putrefaction break the outer layer of the skin, which allows the gases inside the body to escape. At this point, the body "deflates," and strong, putrid odors are emitted from the body. The "deflation" is very prominent in the abdomen, and the skin on the body begins to turn dark-colored, or black. During this stage, bodily fluids may be present surrounding the body due to the breakdown and liquefication of bodily tissue as a result of deflation.

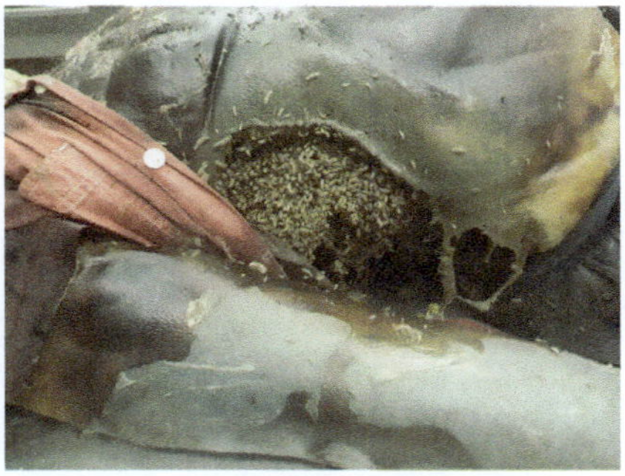

FIGURE 4.11

During the active decay stage, extensive insect colonization may be present in the form of a large maggot mass responsible for tissue loss. Skin coloration changes from green to black are also present and skin sloughing or slippage is often observed.

Courtesy of Dr. Tim Gallagher.

Toward the end of the active decay stage, the first insects that arrived during the fresh stage will have fully developed and left the remains to pupate. However, large numbers of Diptera (true flies) larvae are present during this stage to remove the last of the internal flesh from the body. Other insects, such as beetles, may be present during the active decay stage, too (Fig. 4.11).

4.1.4 Advanced decay

The advanced decay stage is a relatively moist phase of decomposition, characterized by the caving in of bodily tissue and widespread insect larvae activity. A majority of the bodily tissue is gone due to insect activity, scavenging, or natural decomposition processes, and bones, cartilage, ligaments, and hair remain. During the advanced stage of decomposition, the remains may begin to skeletonize, mummify, or saponify based on the environmental conditions (Fig. 4.12).

This stage has an increased number and variety of parasites and predatory insects present on and near the body. Because any bodily tissue left may be difficult to break down for fly larvae, this stage typically attracts insects with chewing mouthparts, like necrophagous beetles. At this stage, it is likely that fly larvae will have left the body in order to pupate, so it is important to check the soil up to several feet away from the body for fly pupae.

4.1.5 Dry remains

The final stage of decomposition is referred to as the dry remains stage. During this stage, the remains generally end up in one of three ways: skeletonized, mummified, or saponified. Skeletonization occurs when the majority of bones are exposed and the majority of soft tissue is absent. Desiccated material, however, may still remain on the body near muscle points and ligament attachments. The visible bones may have a greasy appearance. Skeletonization can occur in many different environments.

FIGURE 4.12

Decomposition has advanced to partial skeletonization. Focal areas of soft tissue remain in the torso area, this can be important in DNA and toxicology studies used to identify the individual and assist in determining the cause of death.

Courtesy of Dr. Tim Gallagher.

Mummification occurs when bodily tissues are dehydrated and dry up. This state is characterized by dry, brittle skin that is generally brown but may have areas of white, green, or black due to the colonization of fungus. Mummification is generally observed throughout the whole body. Mummification occurs when the environment is dry. Mummification is often seen in individuals who decompose in dry, outdoor environments and in hanging deaths.

Saponification refers to the process in which adipocere forms on a dead body. Adipocere, also known as "grave wax," comes from the Latin language; "adipo-" means fat, while "cera" means wax. Adipocere is a waxy material that is often observed to be yellow or off-white. Adipocere gives off a distinct odor. This process takes several weeks to begin, and it is difficult to undo the consequences of the process of saponification. Saponification is often seen in individuals who have been buried underground (Fig. 4.13).

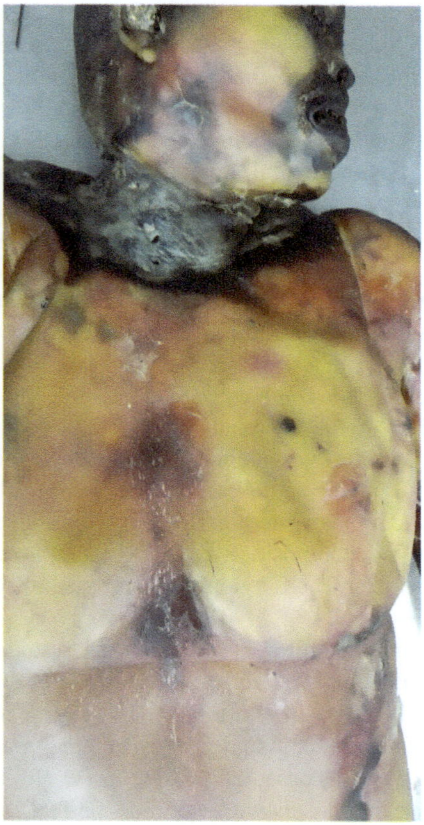

FIGURE 4.13

Adiposcere production and mummification can occur simultaneously. This decedent was located face-down in a indoor dwelling several months after she was last seen alive. Adopocere production can be observed as the yellow areas on the chest and abdomen. Areas of mummification can be observed as dark colored areas on the neck and facial areas.

Courtesy of Dr. Tim Gallagher.

4.2 Progressive method index using total body score

To combat the subjective nature of classifying remains, total body score is a progressive method that can be utilized to quantify the stages of decomposition. Considering most postmortem interval estimation methods are only useful within the early postmortem period, the total body score method creates a standardized means of measuring decomposition that can be used for postmortem interval estimation, in conjunction with temperature, from the fresh stage to skeletonization.

The concept of total body score was first recognized in 1989 when Galloway et al. evaluated the decomposition process of 189 cases of human remains found in arid environments. In order to quantify the rate of decomposition, they developed a table that appoints a number value to the stages of decomposition and the secondary classifications that further define those stages. In the table, a point value is associated with each defining characteristic beginning the "1" as fresh and increasing one point per characteristic as the decomposition advances in each stage. The total point value then quantifies the overall condition of the decomposition (Galloway et al., 1989).

While the premise of Galloway et al.'s table was sound, modifications needed to be made in order for it to be more effective. Megyesi et al. (2005) adjusted Galloway et al.'s table in several ways during their study on using accumulated degree days and total body score to evaluate decomposition. The first change was placing the stages and secondary classifications in a sequential order of when they most likely occur in the decomposition process. This contributed to the final decomposition score being a more accurate reflection of the accumulated amount of decomposition that has occurred. Since decomposition does not occur equally throughout the body, the other significant change was to independently score three areas of the body: the head and neck, the trunk, and the limbs. The classifications during each stage were then adjusted to represent the decomposition process of that specific region (Megyesi et al., 2005). The scores from each region are combined to produce the total body score.

Megyesi et al.'s scoring method was validated by two studies that found the total body score method to have high reliability (Gelderman et al., 2018). Dabbs et al. (2016) examined the reliability of the total body scoring method by examining the interobserver error rates. In their study, 16 participants were asked to determine the total body score for 59 cases based off of Megyesi et al.'s total body score table. It was found that the participants displayed "almost perfect" agreements among the total body scores. The average absolute correlation coefficient was 0.99, and the average consistent correlation was 0.991. This indicated that the interobserver error rate was low, and the reliability of this method is high (Dabbs et al., 2016). Similarly, Nawrocka et al. (2016) evaluated the reliability of the total body scoring method by analyzing the inter-rater reliability. Totally, 120 participants, who were trained in using the total body scoring method, were asked to score decomposition of pig carcasses through photographs. The results concluded that the total body scoring method was homogeneous among the participants regardless of their qualifications. This study further proved that the total body scoring method can be noted as inter-rater reliable (Nawrocka et al., 2016).

While the total body scoring method has proved reliable in measuring decomposition, in order for a postmortem interval estimation to be made, temperature must also be considered. In the study conducted by Megyesi et al. (2005), they established an equation that utilized the total body scoring method to predict the accumulated degree days that would have occurred from the time of death to the time of discovery. Once the ADD is established, a PMI can be determined, or in this study confirmed, by working backward and adding the daily average temperatures, for both the ambient and certified temperature, from the time of discovery until the sum of the temperatures equal the ADD. This equates to an approximate postmortem interval (Megyesi et al., 2005).

Many subsequent studies have utilized this quantitative approach with modifications for postmortem interval estimation. One such study was published in 2013 by Sutherland et al. The basic premise of this study closely followed that of Megyesi et al. but focused on the variable of body size. The decomposition of 15 small pigs and 15 large pigs was observed. It was found that the smaller pigs decomposed 2.82 times faster than the larger pigs. This shows that equations developed using total body scores to achieve the ADD must account for variables including body size (Sutherland et al., 2013). Other studies have focused on specific regions as their variables to account for environmental differences throughout the world such as Myburgh et al. (2013) whose study focused on the temperate region of South Africa and Suckling et al. (2016) who concentrated their study in central Texas.

Henceforth, it is unlikely that there can be a universal equation for postmortem interval estimation based on total body score and ADD. Rather, equations that are tailored for individual variables based on the circumstances of the death should be used. However, this can only be achieved through extensive research.

5. New and novel research methods

Despite the numerous methodologies of postmortem interval estimation mentioned throughout this chapter, there is yet to be a single method that can accurately predict the postmortem interval. Rather, a multitude of methods must be used together to achieve an approximate postmortem interval. Nonetheless, with the advancement of scientific knowledge regarding decomposition, new and novel methods of estimating the postmortem interval are continuously being researched. Many of these new methods focus on approaches that less affected by the variables that influence decomposition. Specifically, ribonucleic acid (RNA)/deoxyribonucleic acid (DNA) degradation and microbiomes have been of recent interest in the quest to find a more precise way of determining the time since death.

5.1 RNA/DNA degradation

In comparison to the other existing strategies for estimating the postmortem interval, molecular biological methods are a relatively new science. Molecular biological methods involve examining the levels of proteins and nucleic acids such as DNA and RNA remaining in the body following the death of an organism. After an organism dies, nucleases within the cell begin to degrade DNA and RNA, with the levels of these nucleic acids decreasing in a linear fashion over time (Bishop, 2015, pp. 1–26). Researchers can extract DNA and RNA from samples of these deceased organisms and quantify their concentrations through a variety of techniques such as electrophoresis, polymerase chain reactions, and computerized image analysis (El-Harouny et al., 2008). By determining the extent of degradation, the time since death can be estimated.

When these techniques for predicting the postmortem interval were first developed, scientists focused almost entirely on the degradation of DNA, not RNA (Hayman & Oxenham, 2020a, 2020b). This was due to the underlying belief that RNA was less stable and would degrade more rapidly, making this nucleic acid more challenging to analyze. Following the passage of time and the advancement of technology, research with RNA gained more popularity and its validity was tested. While results were not unanimously supportive across the board, several research studies garnered evidence for the method by demonstrating a correlation between RNA degradation and PMI when analyzing heart, liver, and brain tissue (Bauer et al., 2003; Sampaio-Silva et al., 2013).

Advancements in technology also furthered the understanding of how the species studied and the conditions the samples were exposed to influence results regarding genetic degradation. Early research utilized samples from small animals such as rats and conducted experiments in the laboratory setting with fixed conditions (Li et al., 2016). However, critics of this research questioned if these findings were truly representative of human tissues in a natural environment. The setting of a laboratory is extremely sterile compared to the natural world and lacks representative conditions in terms of temperature, pH, and humidity. More recent research has sought to overcome these issues by utilizing more relevant samples such as human fingernails and by exposing these samples to a variety of conditions for longer durations (Vass et al., 2013). This approach may be more time consuming and challenging to initiate but will likely be insightful in estimating the postmortem interval.

5.2 Microbiome

Another new approach for estimating the postmortem interval that researchers have been working on is evaluating the microbial communities associated with cadavers. Microbial communities, also referenced as microbiomes, are the combined genetic material of microorganisms in a particular environment. Researchers suggest that this method might be ideal for postmortem interval estimation because the types of microorganisms affecting decomposition are similar across all hosts and environments (Metcalf, 2019). With that being said, decomposition of mammals might have a predictable set of microbes that define different stages of decomposition. This eliminates the variability in decomposition among different species and climates meaning that this method has the potential to be universally applied to a variety of cases.

The studies that have assessed the practicality of microbial communities for postmortem interval estimation have evaluated samples from a variety of body sites including the skin, rectum, oral cavities, nose/ear, internal organs, and bone. From these studies, there are several fundamental concepts that must be recognized in order for the method to be justified. The first being that since microbiomes change after death, there is a difference between antemortem microbiomes and postmortem microbiomes. Furthermore, it must be recognized that postmortem microbiomes continuously change throughout decomposition. This is known as microbial succession. Lastly, the microbial succession that occurs after death happens in a predictable manner. This is what allows for microbiomes to be used in estimating the time since death (Hayman & Oxenham, 2020a, 2020b).

In order to use microbiomes as a means postmortem interval estimation, a regression model forms a microbial clock of death using postmortem microbial collection data with known postmortem intervals. On scene, a sample would be collected from the same region as the known data, and the microbes would be profiled from DNA sequencing. Machine learning is being used in this method due to the hundreds of thousands of DNA sequences these microbiome datasets have. Through this tool, patterns are being discovered in the complex datasets. Once the microbes are profiled, they can then be matched to a time on the microbial clock of death to determine the time since death. These models have made accurate postmortem interval estimates ± 2–3 days (Metcalf, 2019).

Although scholars have proved that this concept is effective in estimating the postmortem interval, it is important to note that there are some deficiencies in the research. Currently, there is little known about the timeframes in which the microbial clock is most exact, the environmental variables, and what sample types will prove most accurate for microbial succession. Overall, the appropriate methods and parameters for the machine leaning need to be better understood in order to produce the best models.

6. Limitations and application considerations

The postmortem interval has been of increasing interest to researchers for many years. Its applicability has clear benefits for death investigations and has proven to be a key factor in seeking justice. However, despite extensive research, a universally applicable postmortem interval method has yet to be attained. Every death investigation has a multitude of vastly different variables that influence the rate of decomposition and ultimately the investigative process. Many studies focus on one specific variable (i.e., body size, geographic region, temperature variance, etc.) and how those relate to the postmortem interval, but to effectively determine the time since death, all of the variables must be considered not just one. Additionally, the methods presented have limitations that influence their effectiveness.

Specifically, rigor mortis, livor mortis, and algor mortis have been thoroughly studied, but they lack practicality beyond the early stages of decomposition. Once rigor mortis dissipates, livor mortis fixes, and algor mortis reaches ambient temperatures, these methods are no longer useful for postmortem interval estimation. Similarly, postmortem muscle excitability is limited to the early postmortem interval as it is generally noted that muscles do not excite beyond 13 h postmortem (Madea, 1992). Furthermore, the postmortem muscle excitability method is not standardized in terms of mode of excitement and how the contractions are graded which inhibits the reliability of its use. Other methods such as the potassium concentration in the vitreous humor pose problems in that potassium levels vary from person to person.

Although there is a linear relationship between the potassium concentration levels in the vitreous humor and the time since death, the standard error also increases with the postmortem interval. This increasing standard error can alter the time since death determination by several days making it an inefficient method for cases of advanced decomposition.

New research studies, such as the RNA/DNA degradation and microbiome analysis, attempt to employ methods that are not as affected by variables of decomposition making them more applicable among a variety of cases. Although based on sound science and proven effective for postmortem interval estimation, these methods are costly and time consuming. They require lab processing, whereas previous methods can be utilized on scene by investigators. Many agencies do not have the financial capability to run lab work for every case nonetheless time to wait for lab results. These limitations affect the application of these novel methods.

The most practical method that can be used on scene by investigators and throughout the entire decomposition process is using total body score to achieve the ADD. A total body score can be determined from fresh to skeletonization and through established equations that score can then equate to ADD. The ADD are then used to establish the time since death. This method has many positive attributes, but it is not without limitations. For this method to be effective, a proper equation must be reached for the specific variables present. This requires extensive research accounting for a plethora of variables. Thus, this method is limited based on whether there are established equations that account for the variables present in the case.

Of all the numerous variables that affect the decomposition, temperature is widely regarded as the most influential. It is often a key factor for variability across most methods. Warmer temperatures speed up the rate of decomposition, while cooler temperature slows the rate of decomposition. This basic premise is essentially the foundation for determining the postmortem interval estimation. However, many studies utilize controlled temperatures which do not account for realworld temperature variance. This inhibits the effectiveness of the methods when employed in a real case.

For the studies that do account for temperature variances on scene, such as ones that utilize total body score and ADD, the limitation resides in the ability to determine scene temperature data for cases that are not near a certified weather station. The meteorological data are often pulled from the nearest airport or NOAA station; however, the crime scene may be miles away with different temperatures. To account for this difference, a method known as linear regression is often used. Linear regression is a validated statistical method that takes into account the differences between the certified temperature and crime scene temperature and develops an equation that allows for the differences to be adjusted. To do this, a temperature probe is placed at a crime scene for 5–7 days after a body has been found. This information is then compared to the nearest certified weather station, and a linear regression is preformed which emits an equation that allows for the temperatures to be corrected. The corrected crime scene temperature can then be used to establish the postmortem interval once the ADD have been determined. This extra step may appear as a nuisance, but a few degrees difference can considerably affect the accuracy of the postmortem interval, so it is necessary to account for any disparities.

Considering there are limitations and application considerations to every postmortem interval estimation methodology, it is recommended that a variety of methods are employed in order to achieve the most accurate postmortem interval estimation. By using several methods together, the standard error decreases and the postmortem interval estimation becomes more exact.

7. Conclusion

The postmortem interval estimation is of utmost importance in death investigations, and it cannot be overlooked. Its value extends to a variety of cases whether it be a recent homicide or a historic clandestine grave excavation. Clearly, there is an abundance of research on establishing the postmortem interval, but while many methods can reach an accurate estimation of the time since death in a controlled setting, when applied to real-world cases, the appropriate postmortem interval can be difficult to achieve. Especially since many methods are only applicable in the early postmortem period, remains older than 72 h can be challenging to classify. Despite this limitation, it is paramount that an accurate postmortem interval estimation is established so that death investigations can be properly assessed. Specifically, having an understanding of the time since death can assist investigators in confirming or repudiating suspect and witness statements as well as establishing the identity of a decedent. These factors are considerably crucial in cases where there is a lack of forensic evidence.

With advancements in our understanding of decomposition and the associated variables, future research must take a holistic approach to establishing a postmortem interval. This includes using a variety of methods that consider a multitude of variables. The more variables that are considered, the more likely a precise time since death estimation can be made. There also needs to be a primary focus on temperature, in that research is conducted with specificity to geographic regions. Since climate in the United States varies significantly across the country, regional climate differences need to be evaluated. For instance, if an equation using total body score and ADD to establish the postmortem interval is determined for the Southeast United States, it cannot be applied to a case on the West Coast because their climate, including temperature and precipitation, is entirely different meaning that the decomposition process will be altered as well. Similarly, seasonal variations in each region must also be acknowledged. Decomposition occurring in the Southeast during the summer will have a different process and timeframe than if it occurs in the winter. Accordingly, these are noteworthy variables that must be addressed. If research can move from using specific measures to a holistic approach and account for regional and seasonal climate differences, the likelihood of having a precise postmortem interval estimation can be greatly increased.

References

Adelson, L. (1952). Spontaneous human combustion and preternatural combustibility. *Journal of Criminal Law and Criminology, 42*, 793.

Amendt, J., Campobasso, C. P., Gaudry, E., Reiter, C., LeBlanc, H. N., & Hall, M. J. (2007). Best practice in forensic entomology—standards and guidelines. *International Journal of Legal Medicine, 121*(2), 90–104.

Baniak, N., Campos-Baniak, G., Mulla, A., & Kalra, J. (2015). Vitreous humor: A short review on post-mortem applications. *Journal of Clinical & Experimental Pathology, 4*(6), 1–7.

Bate-Smith, E. C., & Bendall, J. R. (1947). Rigor mortis and adenosine-triphosphate. *The Journal of Physiology, 106*(2), 177–185.

Bauer, M., Gramlich, I., Polzin, S., & Patzelt, D. (2003). Quantification of mRNA degradation as possible indicator of postmortem interval—a pilot study. *Legal Medicine, 5*(4), 220–227.

Benecke, M. (2001). A brief history of forensic entomology. *Forensic Science International, 120*(1–2), 2–14.

Benini, A., & Bonar, S. K. (1996). Andreas vesalius. *Spine, 21*(11), 1388–1393.

Bishop, C. P. (2015). *Estimating postmortem interval: A molecular approach.* Final Report. Morgantown: The US Department of Justice, Department of Biology, West Virginia University.

Byrd, J. H., & Tomberlin, J. K. (Eds.). (2019). *Forensic entomology: The utility of arthropods in legal investigations.* CRC press.

Capinera, J. L. (Ed.). (2008). *Encyclopedia of entomology.* Springer Science & Business Media.

Chandrakanth, H. V., Kanchan, T., Balaraj, B. M., Virupaksha, H. S., & Chandrashekar, T. N. (2013). Postmortem vitreous chemistry–an evaluation of sodium, potassium and chloride levels in estimation of time since death (during the first 36 h after death). *Journal of Forensic and Legal Medicine, 20*(4), 211–216.

Child, A. M. (1995). Towards and understanding of the microbial decomposition of archaeological bone in the burial environment. *Journal of Archaeological Science, 22*(2), 165–174.

Chin, G. (1998). The gender of buddhist truth: The female corpse in a group of Japanese paintings. *Japanese Journal of Religious Studies*, 277–317.

Choo, T. M., & Choi, Y. S. (2012). Historical development of forensic pathology in the United States. *Korean Journal of Legal Medicine, 36*(1), 15–21.

Coe, J. I. (1989). Vitreous potassium as a measure of the postmortem interval: An historical review and critical evaluation. *Forensic Science International, 42*(3), 201–213.

Cornaby, B. W. (1974). Carrion reduction by animals in contrasting tropical habitats. *Biotropica*, 51–63.

Dabbs, G. R., Connor, M., & Bytheway, J. A. (2016). Interobserver reliability of the total body score system for quantifying human decomposition. *Journal of Forensic Sciences, 61*(2), 445–451.

Davy, J. (1839). Observations on the temperature of the human body after death. In *Researches, physiological and anatomical* (pp. 228–248). Smith, Elder, and Co.

DiMaio, V., & DiMaio, D. (2001). Time of death. In *Forensic pathology.* CRC Press.

Dowler, B. (1846). Experimental researches on the post mortem contractility of the muscles, with observations on the reflex theory. *The Buffalo Medical Journal and Monthly Review of Medical and Surgical Science, 2*(3), 152–166. PMID: 35374611; PMCID: PMC7896923.

El-Harouny, M. A., El-Dakroory, S. A., Attalla, S. M., Hasan, N., & El-Nabi, S. E. H. (2008). The relationship between postmortem interval and DNA degradation in different tissues of drowned rats. *Mansoura Journal of Forensic Medicine and Clinical Toxicology, 16*(2), 45–61.

Finkbeiner, W. E., & Ursell, P. C. (2009). The Autopsy- past and present. In *Autopsy pathology: A manual and atlas*. Elsevier Health Sciences.

Fisher, B. A., & Fisher, D. R. (2012). Homicide investigations. In *Techniques of crime scene investigation*. CRC Press.

Galloway, A., Birkby, W. H., Jones, A. M., Henry, T. E., & Parks, B. O. (1989). Decay rates of human remains in an arid environment. *Journal of Forensic Sciences, 34*(3), 607–616.

Gelderman, H. T., Boer, L., Naujocks, T., IJzermans, A. C. M., & Duijst, W. L. J. M. (2018). The development of a post-mortem interval estimation for human remains found on land in The Netherlands. *International Journal of Legal Medicine, 132*(3), 863–873.

Hansson, L., Uotila, U., Lindfors, R., & Laiho, K. (1966). Potassium content of the vitreous body as an aid in determining the time of death. *Journal of Forensic Sciences, 11*(3), 390.

Hayman, J., & Oxenham, M. (2016a). Algor mortis and temperature-based methods of estimating the time since death. In *Human body decomposition*. Academic Press.

Hayman, J., & Oxenham, M. (2016b). Supravital reactions in the estimation of the time since death. In *Human body decomposition*. Academic Press.

Hayman, J., & Oxenham, M. (2020a). Biochemical methods of estimating time since death. In *Estimation of the time since death: Current research and future trends*. Academic Press.

Hayman, J., & Oxenham, M. (2020b). The importance of microbial communities in the estimation of the time since death. In *Estimation of the time since death: Current research and future trends*. Academic Press.

Henssge, C. (1988). Death time estimation in case work. I. The rectal temperature time of death nomogram. *Forensic Science International, 38*(3–4), 209–236.

Hughes, W. M. (1965). Levels of potassium in the vitreous humour after death. *Medicine, Science & the Law, 5*(3), 150–156.

Jaffe, F. A. (1962). Chemical postmortem changes in the intraocular fluid. *Journal of Forensic Sciences, 7*(231), e7.

Kaatsch, H. J., Schmidtke, E., & Nietsch, W. (1994). Photometric measurement of pressure-induced blanching of livor mortis as an aid to estimating time of death. *International Journal of Legal Medicine, 106*(4), 209–214.

Knight, B. (2002). Hypostatis and timing of death. In *Estimation of time since death in the early post-mortem period* (2nd ed.). Arnold.

Kori, S. (2018). Time since death from rigor mortis: Forensic prospective. *J Forensic Sci & Criminal Inves, 9*, 1–10.

Krompecher, T. (2016). Rigor mortis. In *Estimation of the time since death* (3rd ed.). CRC Press.

Kumara, T. K., Abu, H. A., & Bhupinder, S. (2017). Forensic entomology - insect development and temperature. *Journal of Forensic Sciences & Criminal Investigation, 4*(3).

Li, C., Wang, Q., Zhang, Y., Lin, H., Zhang, J., Huang, P., & Wang, Z. (2016). Research progress in the estimation of the postmortem interval by Chinese forensic scholars. *Forensic sciences research, 1*(1), 3–13.

Madea, B. (1992). Estimating time of death from measurement of the electrical excitability of skeletal muscle. *Journal of the Forensic Science Society, 32*(2), 117–129.

Madea, B. (2002). Post-mortem mechanical excitation of skeletal muscle. In *Estimation of time since death in the early post-mortem period* (2nd ed., pp. 206–208).

Madea, B. (Ed.). (2016a). Autolysis, putrefactive changes and postmortem chemistry. In *Estimation of the time since death* (3rd ed.). CRC Press.

Madea, B. (2016b). Methods for determining time of death. *Forensic Science, Medicine and Pathology, 12*(4), 451–485.

Madea, B. (Ed.). (2016c). Supravitality in tissues. *Estimation of the time since death* (3rd ed.). CRC Press.

Madea, B., & Henssge, C. (1990). Electrical excitability of skeletal muscle postmortem in casework. *Forensic Science International, 47*(3), 207–227.

Marshall, T. K., & Hoare, F. E. (1962). Estimating the time of death. The rectal cooling after death and its mathematical expression. *Journal of Forensic Sciences, 7*, 56–81.

Megyesi, M. S., Nawrocki, S. P., & Haskell, N. H. (2005). Using accumulated degree-days to estimate the postmortem interval from decomposed human remains. *Journal of Forensic Sciences, 50*(3), 618–626. PMID: 15932096.

Metcalf, J. L. (2019). Estimating the postmortem interval using microbes: Knowledge gaps and a path to technology adoption. *Forensic Science International: Genetics, 38*, 211–218.

Myburgh, J., L'Abbé, E. N., Steyn, M., & Becker, P. J. (2013). Estimating the postmortem interval (PMI) using accumulated degree-days (ADD) in a temperate region of South Africa. *Forensic Science International, 229*(1–3), 165.

Naumann, H. N. (1959). Postmortem chemistry of the vitreous body in man. *AMA Archives of Ophthalmology, 62*(3), 356–363.

Nawrocka, M., Frątczak, K., & Matuszewski, S. (2016). Inter-rater reliability of total body score—a scale for quantification of corpse decomposition. *Journal of Forensic Sciences, 61*(3), 798–802.

O'Malley, C. D. (1964). Pre-vesalian anatomy. In *Andreas vesalius of brussels* (pp. 1514–1564). Univ of California Press.

Prahlow, J. A. (2010). Postmortem changes and time of death. In *Forensic pathology for police, death investigators, attorneys, and forensic scientists*. Springer Science & Business Media.

Sampaio-Silva, F., Magalhães, T., Carvalho, F., Dinis-Oliveira, R. J., & Silvestre, R. (2013). Profiling of RNA degradation for estimation of post morterm interval. *PLoS One, 8*(2).

Spitz, W. U., Spitz, D. J., & Fisher, R. S. (Eds.). (2006). Time of death and changes after death. *Spitz and Fisher's medicolegal investigation of death: Guidelines for the application of pathology to crime investigation*. Charles C Thomas Publisher.

Suckling, J. K., Spradley, M. K., & Godde, K. (2016). A longitudinal study on human outdoor decomposition in Central Texas. *Journal of Forensic Sciences, 61*(1), 19–25.

Sutherland, A., Myburgh, J., Steyn, M., & Becker, P. J. (2013). The effect of body size on the rate of decomposition in a temperate region of South Africa. *Forensic Science International, 231*(1–3), 257–262.

Tz'u, S. (1981). *The washing away of wrongs: Forensic medicine in thirteenth-century China*. Center for Chinese Studies, the University of Michigan.

Usumoto, Y., Kudo, K., Tsuji, A., Ihama, Y., & Ikeda, N. (2019). Predictive equation for postmortem interval using spectrophotometric values of post-mortem lividity: A pilot study. *Forensic Science International, 297*, 47–55.

Vanezis, P., & Trujillo, O. (1996). Evaluation of hypostasis using a colorimeter measuring system and its application to assessment of the post-mortem interval (time of death). *Forensic Science International, 78*(1), 19–28.

Vass, A. A. (2001). Beyond the grave-understanding human decomposition. *Microbiology Today, 28*, 190–193.

Vass, A., Fleming, R., Harbison, S., Curran, J., & Williams, E. (2013). *Evaluating the use of DNA and RNA degradation for estimating the post-mortem interval.* Nat. Criminal Justice Ref. Service (ojp.gov). https://www.ojp.gov/pdffiles1/nij/grants/242113.pdf.

Warther, S., Sehner, S., Raupach, T., Püschel, K., & Anders, S. (2012). Estimation of the time since death: Post-mortem contractions of human skeletal muscles following mechanical stimulation (idiomuscular contraction). *International Journal of Legal Medicine, 126*(3), 399–405.

Zhou, C., & Byard, R. W. (2011). Factors and processes causing accelerated decomposition in human cadavers—an overview. *Journal of forensic and legal medicine, 18*(1), 6–9.

Further reading

Sturner, W. (1963). The vitreous humour: Postmortem potassium changes. *The lancet, 281*(7285), 807–808.

CHAPTER

Wildlife forensics: Osteology and DNA

5

Stephanie Hartley[1] and AnnMarie Clark[2]

[1]*SNA International Contractor Supporting the DPAA Mission, Alexandria, VA, United States;*
[2]*Maples Center for Forensic Medicine, University of Florida, Gainesville, FL, United States*

1. Introduction

When managing casework, forensic anthropologists must utilize a variety of techniques, such as comparative osteology (to include histology) and/or DNA analysis, in order to not only make an identification but to complete the proper reports required of them by forensic investigations. What, how, and when these techniques are applied can vary from one anthropologist to the next and from one case to the next, but a general workflow remains the same. When a specimen comes across a forensic anthropologists' desk, the first step is to determine if the specimen is osseous. A variety of different organic and inorganic materials can look similar to bone under the correct conditions (e.g., macroscopically charcoal fragments can look similar to small burned fragments of bone). Once the determination of osseous is made, the next step is to determine if the remains are human or faunal, which arguably is the more difficult task. The ability to make such determinations are directly associated with the training and available comparative material at the anthropologists' disposal. Additionally, a forensic anthropologist must be familiar with the faunal remains that are more prominent in their region, thus, making these determinations more efficiently.

The differences between human and faunal bone can be obvious or very subtle, depending on the faunal species or the amount of taphonomic alterations the bone has experienced (e.g., fragmentation, heat, erosion, etc.). Comparative osteology is one of the most common techniques that forensic anthropologists utilize in the determination of human versus faunal remains. Specifically, comparative osteology encompasses macroscopic analyses, such as gross morphology or osteometrics, as well as microscopic analyses, such as histomorphology and histomorphometry (e.g., Haversian canal diameter). Then, the macro and/or microscopic analyses are compared to known human and faunal reference materials in order to make an identification down to the genus and/or species level.

Forensic anthropologists may also utilize DNA analysis in order to determine if the osseous remains are human or faunal, especially in cases of extreme fragmentation where morphological and/or morphometric analysis is not clear. Advances in DNA analyses have continued to increase in the past few decades. And with this,

Methodological and Technological Advances in Death Investigations. https://doi.org/10.1016/B978-0-12-819394-5.00012-2

advances in human versus faunal differentiation have become increasing possible. DNA analysis looks at the nuclear and mitochondrial structure of the organism to determine the genus and species of an individual. Though, like in all sciences, limitations in DNA analysis still exist. Some limitations, which will be further discussed in this chapter, include degradation of material, heat exposure, or when genetic markers of speciation are unknown (e.g., the red snapper complex), or even just the overall cost of this type of analysis.

Comparative osteology and DNA analysis can be used sequentially or simultaneously. For example, a forensic anthropologist may use comparative osteology to determine the species of the osseous element and utilize DNA to validate their findings. Or DNA analysis may be used to identify an osseous element to a particular genus, and then comparative osteology allows an analyst to identify that element down to the species level. The first section of this chapter discusses the characteristics of human and faunal remains in relation to comparative osteology. The second section of this chapter discusses the uses of DNA analyses in identification. The last section of this chapter will give a few case study examples of how and when these various techniques can be used, with the overall goal of creating a better understanding of comparative osteological methods, and how and when DNA analysis is most useful.

2. Comparative osteology in identification

Prior to the development of DNA technology, morphological analysis via comparative osteology was the only scientific analysis available to identify species and individuals from evidence. While DNA technology has advanced in the past few decades, comparative osteology is still one of the more useful—and cost effective—tools in a forensic investigation of skeletal remains. There are two main categories of methodologies used in comparative osteology: (1) Macroscopic (i.e., gross morphology and osteometrics) and (2) microscopic (i.e., qualitative and quantitative histology). Analysts relying on osteological training, dichotomous keys, scientific literature, and/or a comparative collection can determine the species identification of a particular piece of evidence. Qualitative and quantitative osteological research has been relied on for centuries for comparative analysis and identification practices.

Overall, forensic anthropologists can utilize macro and microscopic morphology and osteometrics for the identification of skeletal elements. Gross morphology of bone is the qualitative characteristics of macroscopic size and shape of the element in question. One must remember that the skeletal element in question was once a living, dynamic tissue inside the body of a human or animal and continuously responding to the environment in which it lived. Thus, one of the major gross morphological differences between human and faunal remains is the result of its function and growth during life. Osteometrics is directly related to these same traits, but the manner in which the anthropologist conducts their analysis differs. Gross morphology uses terms such as "broad," "narrow," or "moderate," while osteometrics will determine a numeric associated with those qualitative categories (e.g., 47 mm). Microscopically, forensic anthropologists can conduct very similar examinations (i.e., qualitative and quantitative analyses) but on the structures that make up the skeletal element in question, such as the osteon and/or Haversian canal. In this section, broad-spectrum understandings of both macro and microscopic methodologies will be examined in regard to both human and faunal bone while also detailing examples of limitations in comparative osteological methodologies.

2.1 Macroscopic comparison of human versus faunal bone

Osteological training, gained from higher education and work experience, is the first tool in a forensic anthropologist's work belt. Understanding the biomechanics behind bone structure and bone physics helps an anthropologist understand and be able to identify skeletal landmarks with ease. Additionally, a baseline understanding of modern human physical variation and faunal variation is necessary to distinguish if the morphology is within or outside the range of possibility for bone from that species—considering age, sex, and pathological conditions that can alter bone, etc.

Scientific literature regarding human/faunal remains and dichotomous keys can be the next step in forensic analysis. Dichotomous keys are built upon observations to help the user classify and identify a species from a particular taxonomic group by taking the analyst through a series of detailed questions. Each question has a choice of answers with contrasting features (usually two, hence the term dichotomous) and by selecting the correct answer the analyst can classify the evidence from a broad classification (i.e., order, family) down to a specific identification (i.e., genus and species). A common pitfall with some dichotomous keys is that the key may not include all species from a genus. If the key is not a complete listing of all species in the genus, the analyst may conclude an improper species identification. A dichotomous key may lead the user to a false identification without knowing characteristics of other species are an option in the stepwise process of identification by dichotomous keys.

The most effective way for a forensic anthropologist to determine human or faunal remains is for the laboratory or institution to have an extensive comparative collection. Unlike literature or dichotomous keys, physical comparative collections allow the forensic anthropologist to look at the remains of known samples and compare them to the unknown sample in three dimensions and in real time. This allows for an analyst to look at the various features of the sample to find points of concordance and discordance (similarities and differences) between the known and unknown samples. These comparative collections should at minimum be comprised of the faunal remains most common in the region. For example, in south Louisiana hog, black bear, and deer should be among the comparative collections of those analysts, while dolphin and seal may be less necessary.

Almost all morphology-based analyses are class character-based analyses. Class characteristics are used to classify a specimen on a taxonomic level from order, family, genus, and ultimately, species if possible. The factors that are used for comparison for order, family, genus, and species identification determinations are often directly related to the function of those elements during life. Locomotive characteristics (to include musculoskeletal features) and developmental characteristics (age/sex-related changes) are the two main traits that can be analyzed in order to determine human versus faunal remains. Locomotive characteristics are some of the greatest anatomical indicators between human and faunal remains. For example, anatomically human bones represent a species that is bipedal and uses its forelimbs primarily to manipulate and carry other objects. Other faunal species may be quadrupedal (e.g., deer) and use its forelimbs for walking and balancing weight distributions or brachiators (e.g., monkeys) who use its forelimbs for swinging. The overall function of the bone is directly related to the amount of bone wear and remodeling needed for a particular region. Thus, when the function of the element differs, so will the macrostructure of the bone. While human and various faunal species may have the same bone types (e.g., humeri, radii, and ulnae), the overall size and shape of these elements are very distinct. For example, both human and deer ulnae decrease in size in the distal shaft compared to the proximal shaft, but the curvature of the shaft is distinct. Human ulnae are relatively straight (excluding any antemortem trauma or pathological conditions), while deer ulnae have a clear curvature to the bone. Additionally, the distal end of deer ulnae is overall smaller in size than most adult human ulnae.

During life, skeletal elements do not act alone; therefore, analysis of muscular attachments—or skeletal morphological indicators of muscle function—is another way to distinguish between human and faunal remains. For example, the size and shape of human crania differ from many other large faunal species. Specifically, the muscular attachments on the remains used for mastication are more gracile in humans than in other fauna such as a bear or hog. These types of macroscopically distinct functional variations can be seen throughout the body not just in the forelimbs and crania. For example, the transverse and spinous processes of human vertebrae are smaller in length than that of deer vertebrae. The knowledge of bone mechanics and skeletal landmarks helps a forensic anthropologist determine human or fauna from small fragments of remains that an untrained eye could not see.

Additionally, developmental characteristics can be very distinct between human and faunal remains, which can aid in specimen identification. It must be noted that neonatal or juvenile remains are morphologically different than their same species adult counterparts, which can obscure the identity of the element making it more difficult to classify (e.g., neonatal human femora can resemble adult turkey femora). In such instances, the morphology of the metaphases and epiphyses can help clarify if the element in question is juvenile or adult. While patterns of epiphyseal fusion vary between species, the morphology of a human epiphyseal plates clearly differs from faunal epiphyseal plates. Morphologically, human epiphyses are generally flat in appearance with microgrooves/structures across that surface. Unfused human epiphyseal surfaces are not intertwined with one another and are only held together in close proximity by the surrounding soft tissue. On the other end, faunal epiphyses also exhibit microgrooves/structures on the surface, but the general appearance is undulating (e.g., macro-ridges); this allows the epiphyseal plate to perfectly intertwine with the metaphysis, even prior to fusion. Fusion rates of the epiphyses also differ between species, which is why comparative collections should not only consist of various species, but also various ages of those species. Categories of fusion can also be used to help narrow down species. For example, while atypical of humans, it is very typical of certain faunal species (e.g., deer and horses) for the radius and ulna to be fused together.

In addition to skeletal function and developmental variations seen in skeletal remains, the sex of a specimen must also be taken into account for intraspecies variation. For example, biologically female and male humans can differ in pelvic morphologies, but they are both of the same species. Some faunal species have more sexual dimorphism than others; thus, comparative collections should also consist of specimens of both sexes. While some sexually dimorphic characteristics are easy to discern (e.g., antlers on male deer), others are more discrete (e.g., male black bears are larger in size than female black bears).

When the more *obvious* skeletal variations (stated above) are obscured by taphonomic alterations (such as fragmentation), differences in cortical thickness, relative density, and the presence of extensive trabecular bone in long bone elements can help determine if the specimen is human or faunal. In general, human bone is less dense in relation to its overall size, and the cortical bone is thinner than their faunal counterparts (e.g., ¼ vs. ½ of the total diameter). Extensive scientific literature is available for comparison of cortical bone thickness and overall density between known samples and the unknown specimen. Additionally, the general structuring of the medullary cavity of human versus faunal remains differs. Extensive webs of trabecule are present in human long bone, while in faunal long bone trabecule is mostly absent leaving a relatively smooth medullary surface. It must be noted though, that taphonomic alterations must be taken into account when examining the medullary surface. Trabecule is easily damaged and can be absent upon examination, even in human skeletal remains. Lastly, nonhuman bone can be distinguished by nutrient canals with medullary extensions. All of these traits can be analyzed radiographically as well, if extremely fragmented.

When general categorical descriptions cannot be used to determine human versus faunal remains, osteometrics may be a useful technique. More morphometric methodologies are currently being created and used within forensic anthropology. Morphometrics is the middle ground between geometry and biology. Morphometric methodologies use landmark data and various mathematical algorithms to analyze the overall form of an element. Morphometrics is especially useful for fragmented osseous material that has few to no distinguishable landmarks. Statistical analysis can be used to correctly determine if the material in question is human or faunal bone. For example, human humeri, femora, and tibiae can be distinguished with high accuracy from those elements of certain faunal species (e.g., sheep and pig), even when the unknown element is significantly fragmented with no identifiable morphological landmarks. Additionally, when a trained forensic anthropologist is not available for comparison (OsteoID), classification and regression decision trees are available for comparison of basic long bone and shoulder and pelvic girdle metrics to determine human versus faunal and potentially the species of the specimen.

Overall, macroscopic comparative osteology should be the first step, when possible, in forensic investigations. This type of analysis is nondestructive and can save time and resources that may be needed elsewhere in an investigation. In most forensic investigations, a determination of "not human" is sufficient. Species level determinations are an excellent way to effectively prove the conclusion of "not human" and can be used in specific casework to link faunal remains to a particular crime (e.g., illegal trafficking of endangered wildlife). Comparative osteological manuals and collections must be used to accurately visualize the macroscopic nuances of variation between distinct species. Trained comparative osteologists (i.e., most forensic anthropologists) are key in making this type of determination.

2.2 Microscopic comparison of human versus faunal bone

When macroscopic identifications cannot be made—usually due to taphonomic alterations such as extreme fragmentation—histomorphology (qualitative) and histomorphometric (quantitative) similarities and differences between human and faunal bone can aid in identification, even down to the species level. Just as human and faunal bone differ macroscopically due to general function and development, the microstructure of bone also reflects these differences.

Before detailing human and faunal bone microcharacteristics, one must first understand the aspects that make up bone. The following is a brief description of the microstructures of bone, but further details can be found in histological literature. Overall, the microstructure of bone is made up of three different types of bone (woven, lamellar, and/or fibrolamellar), and the relative amounts of these types of bone vary between taxonomic groups. Specialized software (e.g., scanning electron microscope) can be used to help detect variability in microscopic bone organization, size, and shape. The first of these bone types is woven bone, which is commonly seen in areas of osteogenesis where bone is laid down quickly. Osteogenesis can occur for a variety of reasons, but commonly, it is seen during trauma repair, fetal growth, and due to some pathological conditions (e.g., infections). Lamellar bone, on the other hand, is more organized and slower in production than woven bone. Within lamellar bone, there are primary and secondary osteons (including Haversian systems). Primary bone is created and laid down on an existing bone surface, while secondary bone is created and laid down where bone was resorbed. Haversian systems—neurovascular canals surrounded by layers of lamellae—are found within secondary bone. Lastly, fibrolamellar bone is a combination of alternating woven and lamellar bone layers. The alternating layering allows for this type of bone to be laid down in quick succession and thus, is seen more often in animals that have periods of rapid bone growth (e.g., birds). Fibrolamellar bone can also be further segregated into two factions: laminar and plexiform bone. Laminar bone has circumferential layers of lamellae, while plexiform bone has flat layers of lamellar and nonlamellar bone.

In order to distinguish between human and faunal bone, an analyst must look at all of these structures and compare them to known samples, both visually and statistically. One of the most common visually determined differences between human and faunal bone is the presence of plexiform bone. While both human and fauna can exhibit fibrolamellar bone (especially during early development), the organization of this type of bone differs. Fibrolamellar bone in humans may have a regular and organized structure, but it often does not have the appearance of plexiform bone. Plexiform bone is almost exclusively seen in faunal remains (with the exception of a rare amount in human fetal bone). Thus, if plexiform bone is seen in a large frequency, or in adult remains, then it can be concluded that the bone is not of human origin.

Another visually determined difference is the presence of secondary bone and Haversian systems. If the specimen in questions lacks these characteristics, then a conclusion of "not human" is valid. More specifically, it is known what specific infraclass fauna do not include such characteristics; therefore, not only could an analyst conclude "not human," but they could also narrow the faunal determination down to particular classes. It must be noted though that these characteristics are used to eliminate certain possibilities, not to negate the prior. For example, the presence of Haversian systems does not equate to human bone, but the lack of Haversian systems does equate to nonhuman. Many faunal remains also exhibit Haversian systems, such as fauna from the Orders Lagomorpha and Carnivora. Therefore, when there is the presence of Haversian systems, then other characteristics must be analyzed, such as the overall shape of these systems. Human Haversian systems are more irregular in shape than the circular osteons in faunal remains and/or vary in size. For example, if an unknown specimen exhibits cortical thickness consistent with that seen in human bone and the presence of Haversian systems, but the size is much smaller than typical human bone; then, it can be determined to be nonhuman. Though known quantitative differences should be used to back up these claims.

These quantitative differences—mircomorphometrics—are a useful tool to determine between human and faunal bone and can be used to determine genus/species. To use the example from above regarding Haversian systems: if Haversian systems are present, the amount, density, and size of them vary between taxonomic groups. It must be noted though that the most useful of these in the determination between human and faunal remains is Haversian canal size. In general, human Haverisan canals are larger in size than faunal Haversian canals. So, if the unknown specimen described above has a Haverisan canal diameter of 7.84 μm, then this number can be compared to known values for the various taxonomic groups, and it can be determined within the range of typical Haversian canal diameters for Rabbit femora. Reported values for these quantitative characteristics for various taxonomic groups and specific elements can be found in comparative histology literature. Therefore, an analyst must evaluate the micromorphometrics of their unknown specimen and compare it to known values for various taxonomic groups. Haversian systems are not the only variable that can distinguish between human and nonhuman. For example, osteon size and osteocyte lacunae size (cavity in which the osteocyte is found) have also been used to distinguish between human and pig bones. These types of morphometric methodologies have been increasing in popularity over the past few decades and continue to be re-evaluated to maintain field reliability standards.

While human versus faunal determination (and even potentially species determinations) are possible using histology, it is not without its limitations. For example, the use of histology is usually limited to when macroscopic analysis cannot determine what the bone is (e.g., too fragmented to determine the element), so the analyst has to consider that the specimen is from any part of the body of any species making comparison to known values more difficult. Age, sex, and pathological conditions can also obscure classifications, since comparative literature does not always include these variables. Additionally, taphonomic processes (e.g., heat, diagenesis, marine exposure) can cause changes in the microstructure of bone, distorting histological analyses. In such cases, alternate methodologies should be used for classification.

For the purpose of most forensic investigations though—as previously stated—the determination of "not human" for a particular specimen is all that is necessary for the investigation to proceed, which can consistently and reliably be determined using macro and microscopic comparative analysis. If an investigation specifically requests taxonomic level determinations outside of "not human," the examination and associated diagnostic notes should always follow the proper hierarchy of taxonomy starting from order down to the lowest possible taxonomic designation (genus and species, if possible). While these types of determinations are possible, it is more limited than just a determination of "not human" using traditional comparative osteology if the specimen is taphonomically altered. It is in this limitation that DNA analysis in species identification can be more useful.

Overall, when an analyst uses comparative osteology as the basis of their determinations, they should take detailed notes throughout the entire examination. Not only what reference samples were used, but the key characteristics used for identification, and the cited literature used to aid in the identification should be notated. Additionally, when documenting and analyzing submitted evidence, the type of material received, the condition of the evidence, and all morphological characters that were used for identification should be included in bench notes. The examiner should create forms and templates based on these analyses to streamline the analysis process and to ensure consistency on the collection of datapoints from the evidence being examined.

3. DNA analysis in identification

It may be necessary to resort to DNA when the bones are too fractured or weathered to make an identification based on their morphological characteristics. DNA is ubiquitous to all living creatures, and it persists after death for a very long time (Cherfas, 1991). DNA from mummies many thousands of years old has been successfully sequenced, and more recently, deceased King Richard III (1452–1485) was identified from his skeletal remains (King et al., 2014). The osteological clues were confirmed using DNA from the skeleton and contemporary living relatives. The mitochondrial DNA from the skeletal material was a perfect match to the DNA of a living direct-line female relative. DNA from skeletal material is more difficult to access than from tissue, and very old material can be very difficult. Bone that has been exposed to the elements or buried for long periods of time, especially in certain types of soils, is often severely compromised and does not yield useable DNA very readily. For these reasons, mitochondrial DNA is often the genomic DNA that is targeted for familial and species identification.

Cells within bones are captured within the bony structure and more difficult to access without also collecting calcium and other compromising compounds from the bones. In addition, the skeletal material may have been buried in soils that are high in humic acid or other compromising materials. These DNA extractions can be problematic and often require additional steps to access what DNA is still present. Methodology and techniques have been developed for extracting DNA from ancient bones and are usually quite successful (Rohland & Hofreiter, 2007). Needless to say, fresher bones are easier to work with than ancient bones and those that were marrow producing when live yield the best results. Once the DNA is extracted, the markers used for polymerase chain reaction (PCR) often need to target smaller segments of DNA due to degradation.

In general, the DNA targeted for human/nonhuman speciation is the mitochondrial DNA (mtDNA) (Fig. 5.1). The DNA that is sequestered in the mitochondria of a cell has been used for species identification since Kerry Mullis received the Nobel Peace Prize for his contributions to the discovery of PCR technology. Mitochondrial DNA is a relatively small (~16,000 bases), circular molecule of DNA contained within the mitochondria of the cell. There are typically anywhere from a few to many thousands of copies of mtDNA within the cytoplasm of each cell. It is maternally inherited and has been used to track the migration of humans across the world's landmasses. Its physical structure and the fact that there are many copies in a cell make the mtDNA especially resistant to degradation and available to PCR. While mtDNA cannot be used for individual identification, it is excellent for determining if skeletal material is human or "nonhuman" and if "nonhuman", what species the bone belongs to. Studies defining species and their populations have radically expanded the role of DNA in defining what is a species and how we can genetically identify those species. A bone too weathered or fragmented to identify based on morphological identification can yield its secret through the magic of PCR.

In cases were the bone is in better condition and more in-depth analyses can be attempted, the nuclear DNA (nDNA) can be accessed. Nuclear DNA is present in the nucleus of the cell. It is a single copy of double-stranded DNA with one copy from the mother and one from the father. During the process of meiosis (egg and sperm production) bits of homologous DNA are exchanged producing chromosomes that are unique from the parent chromosomes (Fig. 5.2). The random recombination of homologous DNA and the random joining of egg and sperm create an individual with unique DNA that can be used to identify individuals. PCR is used to identify

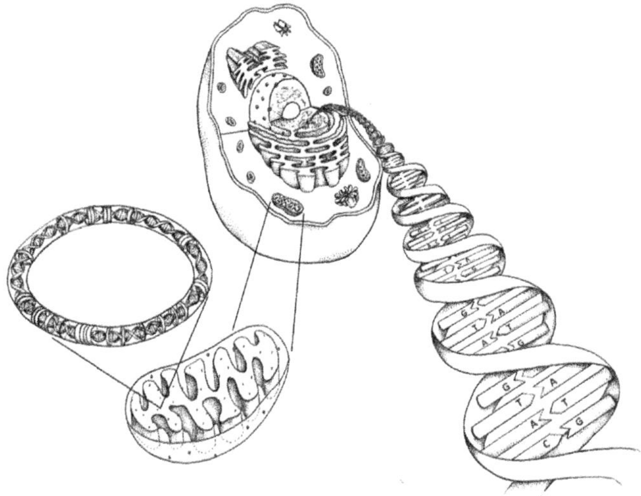

FIGURE 5.1

There are two types of DNA in every nucleated cell. Mitochondrial DNA (mtDNA, see left side), is contained within the mitochondria which are organelles floating in the cytoplasm of the cell. Each mitochondrion has its own DNA which is circular, about 16,500 bp in length, and nonrecombining. There are multiple mitochondria in each cell and they drive cellular respiration. Nuclear DNA (nDNA, see right side) is within the nucleus of the cell and its three billion nucleotides make up the chromosomes. nDNA is a double-stranded helix with one strand coming from the mother and the other strand coming from the father. It is packaged into chromosomes, the size and number of which are unique to each species. Random recombination during meiosis contributes to the unique DNA profile of each individual.

Illustration by Susan Underkoffler (2020).

individual genomic profiles; however, the markers used are specific to small areas of the genome that are informative. When the specific areas are combined, they form a genetic profile that is unique to the individual and for which a statistical likelihood can be calculated. nDNA is used when comparing evidence to determine if has all come from a single individual. Since nDNA is present in cells as a single copy, it is readily degraded so that it may not be available to a PCR query.

PCR is the technology that makes genetic identification of species a relatively easy task. Polymerase chain reaction (PCR) was described by Kerry Mullis in 1985. Scientists quickly saw the value of the technique and began to apply it to nonhuman species to genetically define what is a species and what is a population. PCR is a technique that targets a specific area of DNA within the whole genome of the organism, nuclear, and mitochondrial and then makes many copies of that segment to make analyses easier. During replication of the DNA within a cell, the DNA becomes single stranded, and the enzyme that drives the replication, Taq

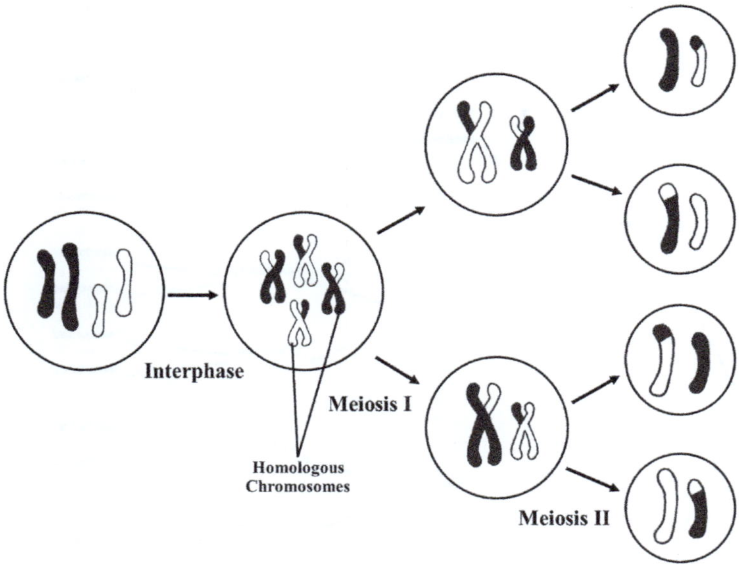

FIGURE 5.2

Meiosis is the process by which nDNA is replicated for gamete production. During meiosis I the strands of DNA separate and bits of homologous chromosome DNA are randomly swapped between the strands creating new and different strands to be passed along in the eggs and sperm. Meiosis II is the phase of gamete production where the new chromosomes are replicated and the single strands are sequestered into four eggs or four sperm.

Illustration by Susan Underkoffler (2020).

polymerase, starts at one end of the DNA strand and runs to the opposite end creating a complimentary strand. The other single strand of DNA is replicated in the same manner but with the Taq running in the opposite direction.

PCR takes advantage of this natural process using primers, which are short strands of manufactured DNA that are designed to be complimentary to the strands of DNA with the target between the primers (Fig. 5.3). Prior knowledge of the nucleotide sequence surrounding the target DNA is required. The primers are rather like bookends in that they are just outside the targeted DNA and face each other. The DNA of interest is between the primers and can be amplified (copied) to make analysis of the nucleotide sequence possible. A DNA molecule is double stranded, with the strands being complimentary and directional. When the DNA becomes single stranded for replication, the primer that is complimentary to the specific strand will attach and the Taq will start at the primer and replicated that strand. After two rounds of PCR, the targeted DNA is a strand with the primer at each end, and there is a geometric increase of that target yielding many millions of copies of the

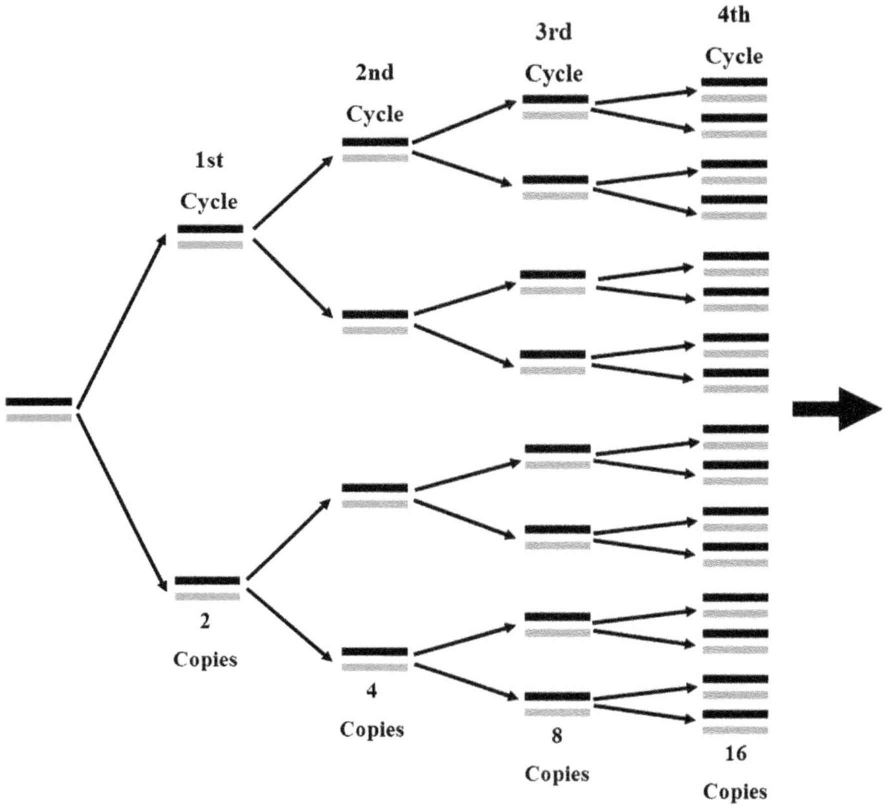

FIGURE 5.3

PCR is a chemical replication of a targeted section of DNA. It is a geometric progression after the second cycle in a thermocycler. Primers are 20 +/− nucleotides of synthesized known sequence DNA designed to have 3′ and 5′ ends so they can anneal to the DNA strands in sense and antisense orientation to replicate the DNA between the primers. This orientation causes the primers to face each other, like bookends, so that the targeted DNA between them is amplified. The first cycle of PCR establishes the defined DNA fragment of interest and the subsequent cycles increase the number of fragments in the reaction in a geometric fashion ending with millions of copies that can be analyzed for the content.

Illustration by Susan Underkoffler (2020).

target. It is now possible to determine the order of the nucleotides, the sequence, to identify the species that the DNA originated from.

Once primers are designed, they produce a consistent product that is reliable and repeatable in all laboratories. This means that a species identification of a bone fragment using a PCR assay should have the same result regardless of what laboratory or technician runs the assay. This is vitally important when the determination between human or nonhuman is being applied to a criminal case.

Once a successful PCR reaction has produced a product, that product can be prepared for sequencing. This entails removing any leftover primers and other reagents used for the PCR reaction leaving only the millions of copies of the targeted double-stranded DNA. This can then be sequenced so the order of the nucleotides can be determined. This sequence can then be compared to other sequences in various databases to determine the species of the sample. One of the largest databases used is GenBank, which is a publicly available database of sequences of most species at most areas of their genomes. It is maintained by the National Institutes of Health and searchable using BLAST, an algorithm designed for comparisons of sequences. The result generated is the closest match to the query sequence that was submitted for comparison.

A "match" in GenBank is based on a comparison of the sequence of the nucleotides between the submitted query and the sequences in the database. The first 100 closest aligned sequences are displayed along with the statistical information on the reliability of the match. It is not necessarily the correct answer as GenBank does not make comparisons within a specific species unless that parameter has been defined before the search begins. If a limited number of sequences of specific species are present in the database, then is it likely that the associated alignments will not be strong. It is, however, a good starting point for determining the species of an unknown bone fragment. Multiple primer sets can be used to help validate a species identification.

3.1 Case studies

When skeletal remains are found, a forensic anthropologist or pathologist can aid in the identification of that specimen. Then, when determined to be faunal remains they are often discarded appropriately if a determination of "nonhuman" is sufficient for the law enforcement requirements. However, in some instances, "nonhuman" is only the first request of law enforcement, and they wish to know the genus/species of the specimen to further their investigation. The following three case studies are good examples of how DNA analysis can be used to aid in identification of species, when law enforcement requests more details than just the determination of "nonhuman."

3.1.1 Case 1

Sometimes, it can be difficult to look at bones and determine if they are human or nonhuman. But once the unknown specimen is determined to be nonhuman, the question then becomes, "has a crime been committed by possession or take of the animal." The wildlife officer involved in this case determined that the bones he was collecting were not human but did not know what animal they belonged to. He suspected poaching, but the bones did not appear to belong to a deer. He also seized a roast sized piece of meat from a freezer on the assumption that it might have come from the same animal. The bones were examined by a forensic pathologist who determined that they were a humerus and left femur, likely from *Ursus americanus*, a black bear (Fig. 5.4). The meat could not be identified as to species,

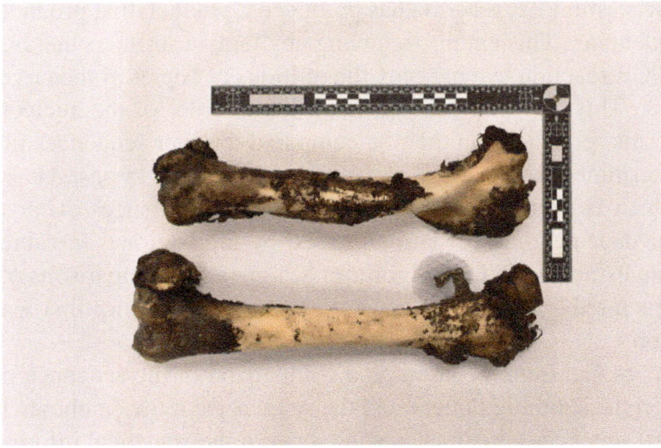

FIGURE 5.4

These long bones were morphologically identified as being a femur and a humerus from a bear, but the officer wanted genetic confirmation. DNA analysis did confirm that the bones were from an *Ursus americanus*, a black bear.

although the size of the roast indicated that it came from a large animal. DNA was extracted from the bones and the meat and amplified with a universal primer that targets a portion of the mtDNA commonly used for species determination. Subsequent comparisons of the sequences generated by PCR to sequences in GenBank confirmed that the bones did indeed come from a bear. The meat, however, had come from *Sus scrofa*, a hog.

3.1.2 Case 2

In a related case, 20+ bones were recovered from a burial pit geographically close to where the black bear bones from the first case were found. The bones were apparently from a variety of different species. Some bones appeared to be consistent with more bear bones. Other bones appeared to be from other small species. DNA extracted from the bones revealed that they were from bear, hog, and white tail deer, *Odocoileus virginianus* (Fig. 5.5). Because of the large number of bear bones that appeared to be present, the officers wanted to know if all the bear bones were from a single animal or multiple animals. Several bones were randomly selected and the DNA extracted. Primers that are used for individual identification and specific to bears were used in a PCR amplification. The genetic profiles were then compared, and it was determined that several bears were represented by multiple bones. This supported the contention by the officers that the site was a long-term burial site for a variety of poached animals. This was eventually confirmed by the defendant. As he poached animals, he used the same area to dispose of skeletal remains in shallow pits.

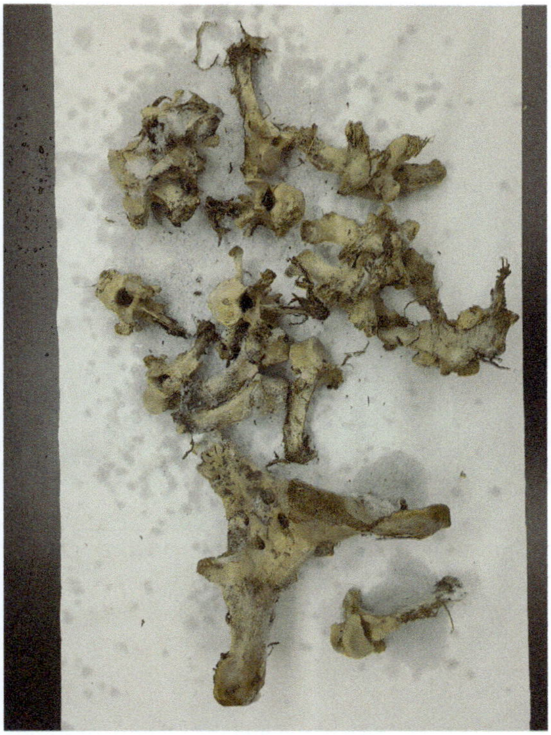

FIGURE 5.5

These vertebrae and coccyx were morphologically identified as belonging to a bear. The request for this case was to determine if all the bones were from the same animal or multiple animals. DNA analysis revealed that the bones were from multiple bears.

3.1.3 Case 3

Santeria is an Afro-Caribbean religion which has its origins in the West African practice of Yoruba and the Roman Catholic forms of Christianity and spiritualism. As part of the worship, there is often a metal pot on an alter with a variety of items contained within. The items include bits of metal, stones, twigs, bones, and feathers, among other things. Sacrifice of animals is common as is a human skull, which becomes covered in wax as candles burn on it during the ceremonies. The skulls used are generally from very old graves and not contemporary. The bones in the pots can be from a variety of animals, although the sacrificial animal is generally a goat or chicken (Fig. 5.6). A small cast iron pot with a chain around it was found partially buried in the Florida Everglades. It was identified as a ceremonial Santeria vessel. The vessel contained the usual variety of bones, feathers, bits of metal, glass, and stones, sticks, and a human skull covered in candle wax. The skull was determined to be from an historical grave and not contemporary. The contents of the pot were

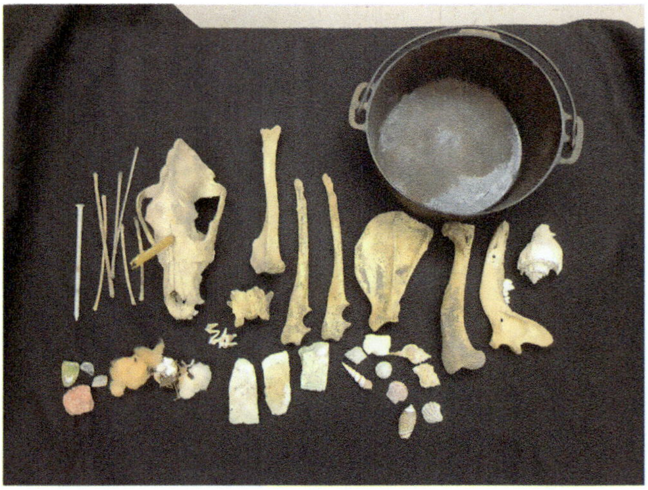

FIGURE 5.6

Santeria pots are often made of cast iron and filled with a variety of items that are important to the shaman who maintains the pot. It is often filled with bones, metal, glass, shells, candles, and other items. Blood sacrifices are not unusual and DNA has revealed that small animals such as goat kids and lambs, and birds, especially chickens, are the most common species that are sacrificed.

covered in what appeared to be fresh blood and the identity of some of the bones was in question. It was unknown if the bones were from the endangered key deer or another animal such as a goat or sheep. Since the morphological identification of the bones was unclear, DNA was requested. DNA revealed that the blood was from *Gallus gallus*, or domestic chicken, and the bones were from goats.

4. Conclusions

Within forensic investigations, a variety of species may be brought in as potential evidence. It is the responsibility of forensic anthropologists to use a variety of techniques and resources to be able to identify if the specimen is human or faunal. These forensic investigations can use both comparative osteology and DNA analysis in order to make these determinations. While DNA analysis is most useful for cases of extreme fragmentation and degradation, the most common and efficient technique is often comparative osteology when there is sufficient material to work with. There are many limitations to both of these techniques and thus, not all species can be positively identified whether due to deficits in publicly accessible databases, or to the lacking numbers available in those databases or material too degraded or fragmented for osteological identification. However, in most forensic investigations, a determination of "not human" is sufficient. In this manner, comparative osteology (macro and microscopic analyses) should be the primary tool for identification. If a determination of "not human" cannot be reliably determined or species-specific determinations are required, then analysts can turn to DNA analysis. Regardless of the technique used, continued collections of both osteological and DNA data are imperative in order to further advance the science of identification within forensic investigations and to bolster statistical databases.

References

Cherfas, J. (1991). Ancient DNA: still busy after death. *Science, 253*, 1354.

King, T. E., Fortes, G. G., Balaresque, P., Thomas, M. G., Balding, D., Maisano Delser, P., Neumann, R., Parson, W., Knapp, M., Walsh, S., Tonasso, L., Holt, J., Kayser, M., Appleby, J., Forster, P., Ekserdjian, D., Hofreiter, M., Schürer, K., et al. (2014). Identification of the remains of King Richard III. *Nature Communications, 5*, 5631. https://doi.org/10.1038/ncomms6631

Rohland, N., & Hofreiter, M. (2007). Ancient DNA extraction from bones and teeth. *Nature Protocols, 2*(7), 1756–1762. https://doi.org/10.1038/nprot.2007.247

Further reading

Adams, B. (2011). In B. Adams, & P. Crabtree (Eds.), *Comparative osteology: A laboratory and field guide of common North American animals*. Academic Press.

Bernt, M., Braband, A., Schierwater, B., & Stadler, P. F. (2013). Genetic aspects of mitochondrial genome evolution. *Molecular Phylogenetics and Evolution, 69*(2), 328–338.

Boore, J. (1999). Animal mitochondrial genomes. *Nucleic Acids Research, 27*(8), 1767–1780.

Crowder, C. (2012). In C. Crowder, & S. Stout (Eds.), *Bone histology: An anthropological perspective*. CRC Press.

Cuijpers, A. G. F. M. (2009). The application of bone histology for species identification in archaeology; with a photo catalogue. *Geoarcheology.*

France, D. L. (2021). *Human and nonhuman bone identification: A color atlas*. CRC Press.

Funk, C. W., Caminer, M., & Ron, S. R. (2011). High levels of cryptic species diversity uncovered in Amazonian frogs. *Proceedings of the Royal Society B, 279*(1734). https://doi.org/10.1098/rspb.2011.1653

Pereira, S. L. (2000). Mitochondrial genome organization and vertebrate phylogenetics. *Genetics and Molecular Biology, 23*(4). https://doi.org/10.1590/S1415-47572000000400008

Pfenninger, M., & Schwenk, K. (2007). Cryptic animal species are homogeneously distributed among taxa and biogeographical regions. *BMC Evolutionary Biology, 7*(121). https://doi.org/10.1186/1471-2148-7-121

CHAPTER

6 Unmanned aerial systems for the search and documentation of clandestine human remains

Daniel J. Wescott[1], Gene Robinson[2], Derek T. Anderson[3] and Bryce Murray[3]

[1]*Texas State University, Department of Anthropology, Forensic Anthropology Center at Texas State, San Marcos, TX, United States;* [2]*Gene Robinson Consulting, Wimberley, TX, United States;* [3]*Department of Electrical Engineering and Computer Science, University of Missouri, Columbia, MO, United States*

List of abbreviations

ACE adaptive coherence estimator
AFTER Australian Facility for Taphonomic Experimental Research
CDI cadaver decomposition island
CNN convolutional neural networks
COA certificate of authorization
EM electromagnetic
GSD ground sampling distance
IR infrared
LWIR long wave infrared
NDVI Normalized Difference Vegetation Index
NIR near infrared
PMI postmortem interval
RGB red, green, blue
SfM Structure from Motion
SIFT scale invariant feature transforms
SLAM simultaneous localization and mapping
SWIR shortwave infrared
UAS unmanned aerial systems
VNIR visible and near infrared

Clandestine human remains are often discovered during medicolegal death investigations using witness information and/or traditional search methods such as pedestrian survey, human remains detection dogs, and/or geophysical prospecting in high probability areas (France et al., 1992, 1997; Killam, 2004). However, traditional

Methodological and Technological Advances in Death Investigations. https://doi.org/10.1016/B978-0-12-819394-5.00003-1

methods for locating the clandestine remains of deceased individuals are often time- and resource-consuming, have suboptimal success, and can lead to accidental alterations of the scene before it is fully documented. The use of unmanned aerial systems (UAS), also referred to as sensor equipped drones, has the potential for obtaining nondestructive, accurate, reliable, and high-resolution spatial and spectral output for locating and documenting potential scenes containing human remains, especially when searching large remote geographical areas. The UAS can be used to detect the body itself or environmental anomalies (e.g., the cadaver decomposition island, grave mound, or vegetation differences) caused by the presence of the decomposing body, which will aid investigators in the search.

Unmanned aerial systems are increasingly being used by the civil services (e.g., law enforcement, border patrol, firefighters) for search and rescue, crime and traffic accident scene reconstruction, emergency disaster response, observing hazardous spills or fires, and monitoring crowds (Police Executive Research Forum, 2020). These agencies have found that the use of UAS can minimize the amount of personnel and expense (e.g., compared to manned aircraft or on-ground personnel) that would otherwise be required for many situations (Police Executive Research Forum, 2020; Valdovinos et al., 2016). A number of papers have been published recently on the use of drones in the civil services (American Red Cross Measure, 2015; Police Executive Research Forum, 2020; Valdovinos et al., 2016; Eftychidis et al.). For example, a recent document by the Police Executive Research Forum (Police Executive Research Forum, 2020) provides information on the uses of UAS in law enforcement, how to establish a drone program, and the potential malicious use of drones.

Over the next decades the use of UAS will also be increasingly used by anthropological, law enforcement, and civilian search teams to aid in locating clandestine human remains, conducting preprocessing assessment, and documenting scenes. However, the use of UAS to search for clandestine remains and document potential scenes requires an understanding of the technological and operational capabilities and constraints of the systems, the strategies for processing and interpreting spatial, spectral, and temporal data, as well as the legal issues associated with over-flight (Slonecker et al., 2016). This chapter reviews UAS and remote sensor technology and its potential use in locating and documenting scenes containing human remains. We first review technical aspects of UAS, sensors, and algorithms. We then discuss how UAS technology can be used for detecting surface and buried human remains and documenting outdoor scenes. Here, the primary focus will be on the search for single bodies by local investigators since several recent papers have been devoted to the search for mass graves using remote sensing, especially for human rights cases (Blau et al., 2018; Kalacska & Bell, 2006; Kalacska et al., 2009).

1. Unmanned aerial systems/vehicles and regulations

In general, UAS are small, lightweight fixed-wing or multirotor aircraft that can be operated manually, semi-autonomously, or fully autonomously. UAS carry sensors or camera payloads, which send video or still images to the operator/pilot.

The term UAS typically includes all the necessary components including the aircraft (unmanned aerial vehicle or drone), remote control, and sensor. The advantage of UAS for search and documentation of outdoor crime scenes is that they can be flown at relatively low altitudes, over large search areas, and over numerous terrain types to locate potential sites that can be further investigated. In other words, the UAS can be preprogrammed to fly a specific path and help to search large areas systematically and safely, and their data can be processed by a computer or involve a human in the process.

There are two major types of UAS. Fixed-wing aircraft are generally used to overfly large areas or areas that require multiple passes necessitating long flight times. Due to their availability and ease of use, multirotor aircraft are more frequently utilized. While multirotor aircraft (Fig. 6.1) do have a reduced flight-time compared to the fixed wing, advantages include smaller launch sites and increased maneuverability. Maneuverability is important because it impacts sensing factors like look-angle and ground sampling distance, for example, which in return affect algorithmic processing (e.g., 3D reconstruction), especially during documentation.

Once the scene is located, the UAS can also be used to conduct preprocessing assessment and nondestructive documentation of the scene (Davenport, 2001; Murray et al., 2018a, 2018b). The images collected by the on-board sensor provide an overall aerial view or survey to assess the search area (e.g., determine the boundaries of the scene and the location and taphonomic state of the human remains as well as document spatial relationships between the remains and other evidence)

FIGURE 6.1

Multirotor unmanned aerial system (UAS) flying at low altitude at the forensic anthropology research facility at Texas State University with enlarged view of UAS.

Credit: Forensic Anthropology Center at Texas State.

FIGURE 6.2

Overview aerial survey of a body placed at the forensic anthropology research facility at Texas State University showing tire tracks, vultures, and other objects that can be used to determine the boundaries of the scene and the type of evidence that may need to be collected during the investigation.

Credit: Gene Robinson.

and assist in recovery planning prior to inadvertent disturbance caused by personnel entering the scene (Fig. 6.2).

There is a need for search and recovery teams to follow local, state, and federal laws when using UAS to search for clandestine remains and to be aware of privacy issues that may arise. The Federal Aviation Administrations (FAA) has numerous directives associated with the use of UAS (FAA.gov/uas). The current FAA regulation is the 14 CFR Part 107 that addresses specific uses and limitations to UAS. An agency may operate UAS under either a Part 107 Operator's Certificate or an FAA Certificate of Authorization (COA), but not both. If a COA is used, the agency must follow it exactly as written and approved. For Part 107, the operator is restricted to the Part 107 regulation. However, in some cases, it may be necessary to fly outside the limitations of the Part 107. In these cases, the FAA's Special Government Interest process allows for exceptions in areas of emergency for first responders. If the agency operates under the commercial Part 107 section, they may request waivers for any subsection that may be required (e.g., flights at night or beyond the visual line of sight or above an altitude of 400 feet). A waiver for FAA Part 107.29 (daylight only operations), for example, allows the use of UAS for nighttime operations utilizing thermal vision when temperature differentials would be conducive to detecting the heat of decomposition.

In summary, there are different types and sizes of UAS that can be used for detecting and documenting outdoor scenes containing human remains. The specific UAS used will be dependent on the specific needs of the case and the overall mission of the program. Pilots must be aware of the operational uses and limitations of the UAS and follow local, state, and federal regulations.

2. Remote sensing

The search for clandestine human remains using UAS is a form of remote sensing or collecting data on an object without physically contacting it. The sensor mounted on the UAS records emitted and reflected electromagnetic (EM) radiation. The electromagnetic spectrum can be divided based on the wavelength. The wavelengths visible to the human eye is only a narrow range (400–700 nm) of the electromagnetic spectrum, but in recent years, numerous different sensors have become commercially available as UAS payload that can detect surface or obscured evidence, including human remains, outside the range of human vision. In this section, we briefly review the types of sensors and methods for processing and interpreting the imagery collected.

2.1 Sensor types

Sensors are either active or passive. Passive sensing records reflected or radiated energy from an object, with the sun being the energy source, whereas, in active sensing, the sensor emits a signal and records its reflection from the object. For example, taking a selfie without flash is passive sensing but if a flash is used it is active sensing. Common passive sensors include thermal cameras, RGB (red, green, blue bands in the visible spectrum or color) cameras, and hyperspectral sensors. Common active sensors include LiDAR, sonar, and radar. LiDAR, for example, emits a laser and records the relative distance of an object to the sensor, which is practical when building 3D reconstructions.

The most used passive UAS sensor is RGB that captures spatial still images or video. These sensors are relatively inexpensive and are ideal to see the ground surface realistically. The near-infrared (NIR) band is adjacent to the visible in electromagnetic spectrum. The visible and near-infrared (VNIR) has been extensively used for looking at plant stress because it is highly indicative of the presence of chlorophyll, allowing the investigator to detect differences between healthy and unhealthy plants, which can be useful for the search of clandestine graves (discussed below). Specifically, the normalized difference vegetation index (NDVI) is an index that measures the relationship between the red and near infrared bands (Glenn et al., 2008). Near infrared is also ideal for detecting organically rich soils (Chen et al., 2005) that occur when organic materials are purged from the body during decomposition (discussed below). The long wave infrared detects thermal radiation, giving a heatmap of an area. Infrared detectors can be used to detect clandestine remains if they are warmer or cooler than the surrounding area. Human remains can emit heat as either internal heat or as reflected heat, and thermal imaging cameras can detect patterns of heat variation across the terrain that can be effectively used to locate potential surface remains during search missions. However, thermal sensors can be sensitive to atmospheric conditions which cause inaccuracies in recording the absolute temperature, so they typically produce relative heat differences (Ammer & Ring, 2005). Fortunately, when using infrared to search for clandestine remains, we are not necessarily concerned with measuring the actual temperatures but rather the relative temperature differences between objects in the sensor's field of view. One advantage to using long wave infrared sensors is that they can be used in day-time or night-time conditions, whereas an RGB camera cannot be effectively used at night (Glenn et al., 2008).

There are also multi- and hyperspectral sensors, which allow for the simultaneous collection of light intensity (radiance) across the EM spectrum. The multi- and hyper- describe the number of bands, not the range of the electromagnetic spectrum. Typically, multispectral cameras detect 4–10 bands, while hyperspectral sensors can detect hundreds of narrow bands, where each band covers a portion of the EM spectrum.

Hyperspectral sensors allow one to select the spectral bands of the EM spectrum (ultraviolet, visible, near-infrared, mid-infrared, and thermal infrared) that provides the greatest contrast and most appropriate fingerprint for detecting human remains depending on the coverage area, type of scene (burial or surface), environmental conditions, geographical features, and postmortem interval (Kalacska et al., 2009; Snirer, 2013). One goal of hyperspectral sensors is to distinguish between different objects by examining their spectral signature. Some chemicals may have very similar spectral properties; however, if the hyperspectral sensor has high spectral resolution, the chemicals can be correctly identified. Until recently, hyperspectral sensors were only flown on manned aircraft and satellites due to their cost, size, weight, and power requirements. However, several companies are now manufacturing hyperspectral cameras for small UAS.

2.2 Structure from motion

Structure from motion (SfM) can be a useful tool for not only detecting clandestine remains and graves but also for documenting outdoor crime scenes. Structure from motion is a photogrammetric ranging method for approximating 3D structure from sources like 2D imagery and/or motion data. Developing a 3D scene reconstruction has many benefits. When documenting a scene, it is important to have accurate measurements. Plant height, leaf area, and light exposure can be estimated from 3D data (Shafiekhani et al., 2017). Another benefit is once a 3D reconstruction is built, other sensor data can be registered or aligned with these data. Without registering each sensor, there will not be a pixel-to-pixel mapping, and each sensor would have to be studied independently. Furthermore, 3D reconstructions are also potentially useful for detection of real-world features to identified burial mounds, for example.

Structure from motion is related to, but not the same as Simultaneous Localization and Mapping (SLAM) and Multi-View Stereo (MVS) (Bailer et al., 2012; Shan et al., 2014). Approaches range from incremental structure from motion (i.e., add one image at a time to grow a reconstruction) to global, which utilizes more/all data for reconstruction. In general, global methods have been shown to provide better accuracy over incremental SfM (Jiang et al., 2013; Moulon et al., 2013; Wilson & Snavely, 2014). Approaches can also be organized with respect to sparse modeling (i.e., fewer 3D data points generated) via SfM and dense (more 3D samples) modeling via MVS. The reader can refer to Ozyesil (Ozyesil et al., 2017) for a recent review of state-of-the-art in SfM. A number of commercial solutions exist for structure from motion (e.g., AgiSoft and Pix4D). However, there are a number of open source solutions for researchers such as OpenSFM (https://opensfm.org), OpenDroneMap (https:/www.opendronemap.org), COLMAP (https://demuc.de/colmap/), and VisualSFM (https://ccwu.me/vsfm/).

Almost all structure from motion processing occur offline after the UAS has collected data. See DenseSLAM (http://www.i3s.unice.fr/robotvision/index.php/portfolio/162-denseslam) and OrbSLAM (https://webdiis.unizar.es/~raulmur/orbslam/) for details regarding real-time construction of 3D scenes. It is well known that SfM algorithms are sensitive to data quality. The point is SfM needs to identify enough unique key points or tie points across imagery to calculate a 3D reconstruction. As a result, a number of rules of thumb have arose such as flights that ensure 80% or more overlap between consecutive imagery, flying at altitudes in line with the focal distance of the camera/lens, flying at a proper speed to minimize the impact motion blur, time of day to maximize radiance, and others (https://www.i3.unice.fr/robotvision/index.php/portfolio/162-denseslam, https://webdiis.unizar.es/~raulmur/orbslam).

2.3 Image processing and interpretation

While understanding the data collection process and developing procedures and protocols is critical, it is only one piece of the puzzle. Algorithms must be identified or developed to appropriately analyze the data to provide insights to a user for documentation and detection. Meaning, since a vast amount of data are produced by a UAS, efficient processing and effectively reporting (e.g., visualization and user interfaces) is required for meaningful and actionable insights. The above SfM section detailed one set of image processing algorithms for 3D reconstruction, which enables both detection and documentation. In this section, we briefly review algorithms related to detection from sensor data.

Generally speaking, sensor modality determines algorithm relevance. For example, RGB imagery (also known as three band multi spectral) is usually not processed the same as hyperspectral data. Each pixel in a hyperspectral camera tells a story. That is, it is a highly detailed signature/feature that informs us about radiance/reflectance characteristics over hundreds of bands for a material of interest (clothing, blood, plants, soil, etc.). As such, many hyperspectral algorithms operate at the pixel level (e.g., RX detector for anomaly detection and ACE for classification). However, numerous hyperspectral algorithms have been proposed that operate on a combination of hyperspectral (pixel-level spectral) and spatial (e.g., 2D pixel-2-pixel or 3D) information (Ghamisi et al., 2017). On the other hand, RGB, even if radiometrically calibrated, is usually not a unique feature. For example, if a pixel is "red," is that red for a shirt, car, blood, etc.? While RGB has been used locally for tasks like anomaly detection (e.g., does this pixel color look different from other pixels in some user specified region of interest?), most successful algorithms in image processing and computer vision (e.g., the scale invariant feature transform and convolutional neural networks) operate the same, if not more robust, on grayscale (no color) for tasks like object detection, face recognition, and beyond. Biologically speaking, this is not shocking as the majority of visual elements in the human visual system are rods versus cones. Next, unique multispectral sensors like the MicaSense RedEdge are five banded (red, green, blue, red edge, near infrared) and designed for precise algorithms like NDVI (approximation to the state of plant health). The reader can refer to SPIE, remote sensing, IEEE TGARS, IEEE JSTARS, and other journals for spectrum specialized algorithms to process infrared (e.g., ratios of infrared bands for identification of disturbed earth). However, object detection and automatic target detection in infrared are generally solved as a monochromatic image problem using methods like convolutional neural networks.

The last factor considered herein is image processing algorithm needs. The point is, many powerful tools exist today to accomplish tasks in detection and documentation. Some of these methods are based on physics (e.g., NDVI), while others do not have parameters (e.g., the RX detector). However, the majority of algorithms to date that relate to detection are made up of parameters. In the case of adaptive coherence estimator (ACE), for example, a user is expected to provide a measurement for the material of interest (e.g., the color of blue jeans so the sensor can detect it). However, convolutional neural networks, which process a combination of spatial, spectral, and temporal data, require training data. The question is, where do these data come from for forensics? Furthermore, do the training data have sufficient statistical power with respect to environmental variation (e.g., geographic, seasonal, etc.)? While the community has produced a number of ways to combat these factors (e.g., data augmentation and transfer learning), this is a big consideration related to the detection of clandestine human remains.

An example of the algorithms that are available is contained in one commercial product that does pixel level scans in the RGB bands called Loc8 (www.usri.ca). This software offers users the ability to scan a large number of images, and the algorithm allows the user to specify a midline range of RGB values in all channels to allow for hue and saturation, then specify a range both above and below the midline to include in the scan. Automation functions allow for locking channels such as the primary in RGB and scanning either up or down from the locked channel based upon the environment operated in.

In summary, there are numerous sensors/cameras available that can be mounted on a UAS. The sensor can be passive (use the sun as the source of energy) or active (senor generates it own source of energy) that can detect specific bands of electromagnetic energy. The optimal sensor for the mission will depend on factors such as the landscape, postmortem interval, season of search, and weather conditions at the time of search. The collection of data from the sensor, however, is only part of the process. The images must be processed and analyzed to successfully locate and document the human remains. Fortunately, numerous methods have been developed in other fields and commercially and open source software is often already available.

3. Detection of surface human remains

In some locations, clandestine remains are likely to be found on the ground surface rather than buried due to perpetrator time constraints and geological features. Due to the presence of the body on the surface, several methods can be used to detect the human remains and/or environmental disturbances caused by the decomposition processes. The optimal type of sensor is dependent on numerous factors including geographical features, depositional environment, the taphonomic conditions of the remains, postmortem interval (PMI), season of death and search, and weather conditions (e.g., cloud cover) during the search. Regarding the body, visible spectrum cameras may be ideal for locating the human remains themselves, especially when in a fresh state or clothed. Likewise, human remains can emit heat as either internal heat or as reflected heat, and thermal imaging cameras can detect patterns of heat variation across the terrain that can be effectively used to locate potential surface remains during search missions. After death the body begins to cool until it reaches ambient temperature. However, decomposition processes such as the activity of bacteria and insects can generate heat that is detectable with thermal imaging, especially when the ambient temperature is between 10 and 35°C (DesMarais, 2014). Amendt and colleagues (Amendt et al., 2017) used helicopter mounted infrared to monitor pig cadavers over a 21-day period. The results demonstrate there is a great enough thermal difference between the decomposing body and the surrounding environment to detect the carcasses for several weeks. They (Amendt et al., 2017) argue that the thermal difference is primarily related to the decomposition process including maggot activity. However, recent research at Texas State University has found that desiccated skin and other tissues and the organic fluids forming the cadaver decomposition island absorb solar radiation differently than the surrounding terrain and can be detected much longer than 21 days. Depending on the weather conditions (e.g., cloud cover) and time of day, the body may emit more or less heat than the surrounding environment (Fig. 6.3). Using thermal imaging, for example, the desiccated bodies are detectable due to the difference in thermal energy emitted (Fig. 6.4). The skin of the desiccated body will heat up due to infrared waves from the sunlight causing it to become hotter than the surrounding environment similar to the surface of a car in the summer. The differences in thermal energy can be used to detect the human remains visually or using machine learning algorithms. This method can be used if the body retains desiccated skin but is likely most useful on sunny days when there is more intense ultraviolet radiation from the sun.

Previous research has also demonstrated the potential of active sensing using ultraviolet to detect bones on the ground surface and underwater (Brown, 1998; Christensen et al., 2014; Swaraldahab & Cristensen, 2016). Under ultraviolet light (~490 nm) bone proteins in the collagen will fluoresce (Swaraldahab & Cristensen, 2016). However, these studies have not explored the effects of vegetation and soil covering the bones. Likewise, no attempt has been made to date to put an alternative light source on a UAS that is powerful enough to luminate bone from the altitude of the UAS.

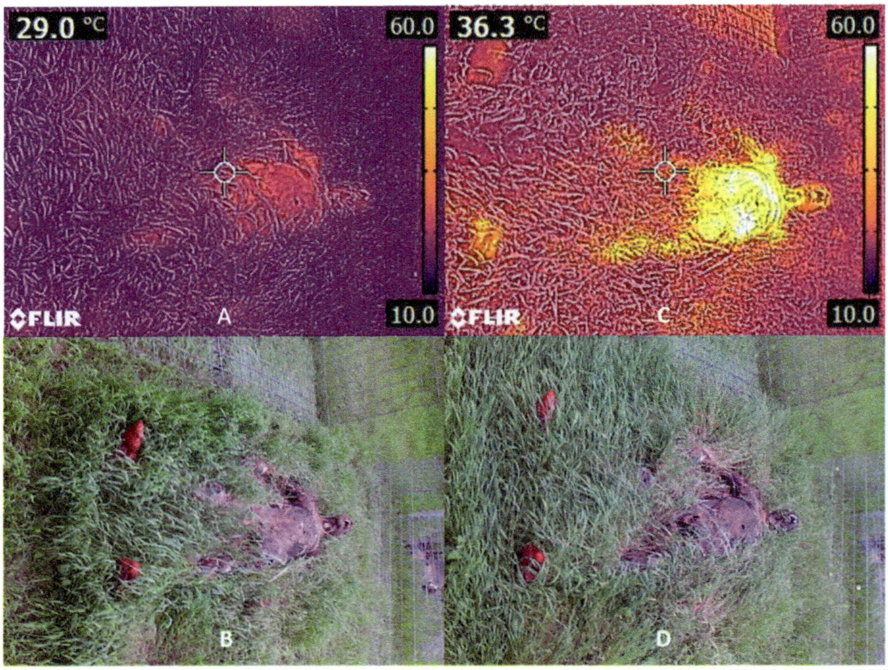

FIGURE 6.3

Ground-level thermal and color photographs of one desiccated individual at the forensic anthropology research facility at Texas State illustrating reflected heat on a cloudy (a and b) and sunny day (c and d) in late spring with similar ambient temperatures.

Credit: Daniel Wescott.

In many cases, especially when the body is in advanced decomposition, skeletonized, or grievously scavenged, the detection of environmental disturbances may prove more successful using remote sensing than the body itself. Human remains left to decompose on the ground surface undergo a dynamic process which temporarily alters the soil and vegetation below and immediately surrounding the body. Fluids purged from the body during decomposition result in a cadaver decomposition island which can be detectable for years (Benninger et al., 2008; Isaacks). Initially, as the organic materials from the body seep into the soil, nearby plants will die and the soil will darken in an approximate oval around the body (Fig. 6.5). The size of the cadaver decomposition island is dependent on the time of year, presence of scavengers, and the body mass of the decedent (Carter et al., 2007; Towne, 2000). The cadaver decomposition island soils generally contain higher levels of inorganic nitrogen and phosphorus and have a lower pH than soils outside the cadaver decomposition island (Towne, 2000). Additionally, Aitkenhead-Peterson et al. (Aitkenhead-Peterson) discovered that organic carbon, dissolved organic nitrogen, nitrate, calcium, and potassium are also in greater abundance in

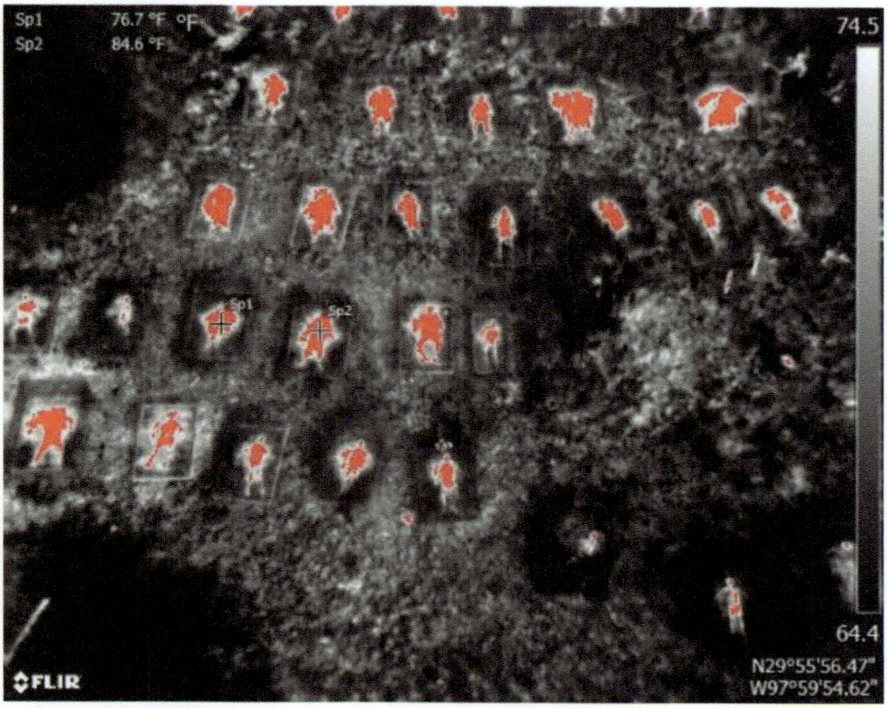

FIGURE 6.4

Aerial thermal photograph of human cadavers at the forensic anthropology research facility at Texas State.

Credit: Daniel Wescott.

the cadaver decomposition island than surrounding soils, which may be detectable with hyperspectral and near infrared sensors. Eventually opportunistic plants will utilize the increased organic materials in the soil and grow at an intensified rate in the area surrounding the cadaver decomposition island (Carter et al., 2007). As time progresses, the richness and diversity of the plant species at the cadaver decomposition island increase as a result of the influx of opportunistic flora (Towne, 2000).

Isaacks (Isaacks), for example, demonstrated the cadaver decomposition island could be detected for several years using near infrared whether the body was present or not. She found that the greater inorganic solids, organic matter, and water in the CDI soil has a different reflectance than the surrounding soil. Likewise, the reflectance of flora near and in the cadaver decomposition island frequently differ from the surrounding vegetation, especially in the spring and early summer. Isaacks (Isaacks) showed that cadaver decomposition islands have a unique near infrared signature and that the signature changed over time (Fig. 6.6). During the early postmortem interval, the cadaver decomposition island in the grayscale near infrared image appears as a dark area in the image due to the increased organic material in the

FIGURE 6.5

Cadaver at the forensic anthropology Research facility at Texas State University illustrating the cadaver decomposition island and destruction of flora around the body.

Credit: Daniel Wescott.

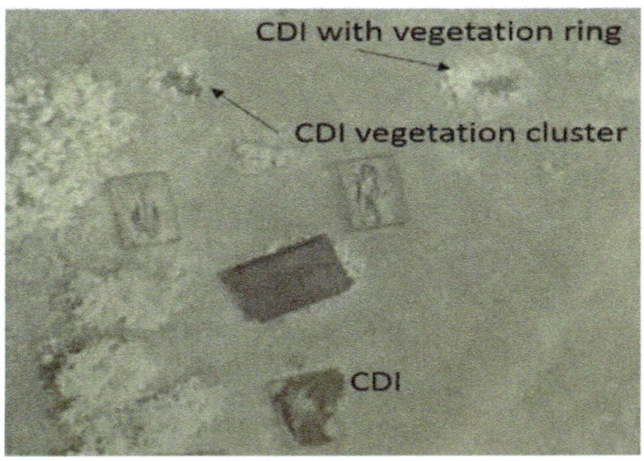

FIGURE 6.6

Unmanned aerial system (UAS) aerial photo at the forensic anthropology research facility at Texas State University showing changes in the cadaver decomposition island (CDI) over time.

Credit: Gene Robinson.

soil. During advanced decomposition, the cadaver decomposition island is best detected by an area of low reflectance surrounded by a dense area of high reflectance caused by the ring of growing vegetation around the cadaver decomposition island (Fig. 6.6). Once the body was skeletonized, the signature was primarily a dense area of high reflectance as plants grew in the cadaver decomposition island soil.

In summary, for human remains on the ground surface, remote sensing can be used to detect the body/clothing or environmental anomalies using a variety of sensors. The most appropriate type of sensor used will depend on the PMI and the condition of the remains. If the body itself is not visible, environmental anomalies such as the cadaver decomposition island can be used as a starting point to search for the cadaver.

4. Detection of buried human remains

The search for clandestine graves is focused primarily on the identification of environmental anomalies (e.g., bare ground, soil elevation, new vegetation, tire tracks, etc.) which will change over time. Differences in the compaction, moisture, and mineralogical properties associated with burial soils (grave soils) can be used to detect subtle differences in the soil between disturbed and unaffected soils. The properties of the soil control the shape of the spectral curve and wavelength specific absorption. Buried human remains may also be detected using thermal imagery because the burial area reacts differently to heat dissipation. As a result, thermal imaging surveys may be most productive when conducted just before sunrise or just after sunset since the soil within the grave heats and cools at a different rate than the surrounding earth (Davenport, 2001; Larson et al., 2011).

Vegetation can also be used to detect buried human remains because the buried carcass has an effect on the surrounding plant community (Caccianiga et al., 2012; Watson & Forbes, 2008). Compared to surrounding soils, vegetation has higher reflectance in the visible and near infrared range and lower reflectance of the red light because of chlorophyll absorption in the red wavelength. Mechanical disturbance caused initially by excavation of the grave initially results in burial sites devoid of plants, which can often be detected with an RGB sensor. Later, nutrient balance alterations can influence the plant community. The mechanical disturbance of the soil destroys established plants and provides a seedbed for the establishment of new plant species, especially herbaceous weed species (Blau et al., 2018; Caccianiga et al., 2012; Killam, 2004; Ward, 2013; Watson & Forbes, 2008). In addition, surrounding plants can become stressed by changes in soil nutrients. Once revegetation occurs, the herbaceous plants growing in the grave soil will differ, at least temporarily, from the surrounding vegetation in species diversity and later in lushness (France et al., 1992, 1997). Pioneer weed plants become established first and more abundant in the grave soils than the surrounding landscape. Hyperspectral imaging may be useful for identifying these unusual patches of vegetation. In addition, vegetation growing in recently disturbed soil may be younger than the surrounding

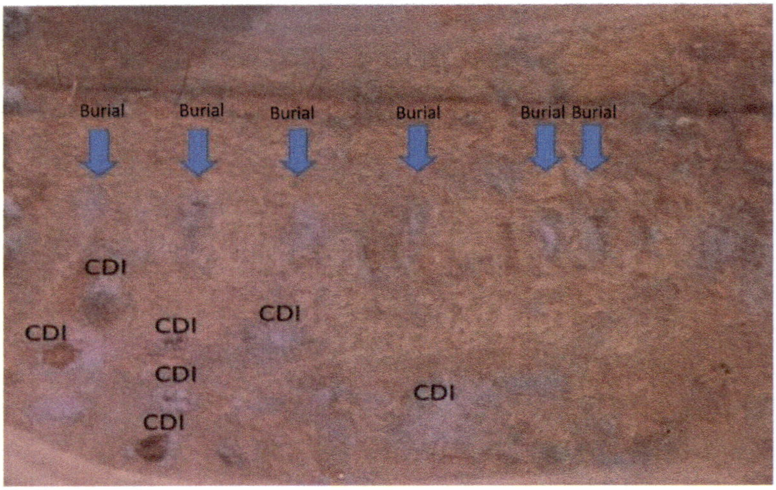

FIGURE 6.7

Near infrared aerial image of burials at the forensic anthropology research facility at Texas State University. Graves to the far left were placed in the beginning of 2013 and recorded in the spring of 2019. The graves are detectable due to differences in the vegetation. Note that control graves to the left of the graves with bodies are not detectable.

Credit: Gene Robinson.

plants depending on the time of year and can be detected in the ultraviolet and near infrared ranges (Ruffell & McKinley, 2008). Recent work in central Texas has discovered that graves as old as 7 years containing human remains can be detected using near infrared because of slight differences in the reflectance of the vegetation on the grave (Fig. 6.6). Control graves, of the same age, however are not detectable (Fig. 6.7).

Research on the detection of graves using remote sensing has long been an interest in forensic science, but most studies have focused on ground penetrating radar, electrical resistivity, or imagery from satellite, helicopter, or airplanes and often using animals as surrogates (Kalacska & Bell, 2006; Kalacska et al., 2009; Leblanc et al., 2014; Novo et al., 2011; Pringle et al., 2012; Ravmond et al., 2014; Schultz et al., 2006; Snires, 2013). For example, Kakacska and colleagues (Kalacska et al., 2009) explored the use of airborne hyperspectral imaging to detect an experimental mass grave of cattle in Costa Rica. They discovered a clear advantage of using near infrared and short-wave infrared imaging over visible spectrum to detect mass graves and to differentiate the mass graves from control grave soils. More recently, LeBlanc et al. (Leblanc et al., 2014) demonstrated with a blind-test the effectiveness of airborne hyperspectral imaging to locate a single burial in a semi-urban area in Canada.

Blau and colleagues (Blau et al., 2018) constructed six experimental graves containing from zero to six cadavers in an eucalypt woodland area at the Australian

Facility for Taphonomic Experimental Research (AFTER). The graves were monitored with temperature and moisture loggers, time-lapse imagery, and aerial multispectral imagery (RGB, red edge, and NIR) via a UAS at 40 m above ground level. In addition, they conducted botanical surveys and soil chemistry analysis. After approximately 1 year a LiDAR survey was conducted, which was able to detect all the mass graves but not the single burial. At this time final results of the work at AFTER have not been published.

Unfortunately, there is currently no established criminalistic protocol for using a UAS with sensing capabilities for outdoor scenes containing human remains. Therefore, there is a need for evidence-based best practices and protocols for search and recovery teams to use for detecting and documenting outdoor crime scenes using UAS remote sensing depending on the geographical location they are working. Currently, the authors are conducting research funded through the National Institute of Justice (2019-DU-BX-0027) to develop best practices and protocols as well as algorithms that will increase success in locating and documenting human remains using UAS remote sensing. The purpose of the project is to collect, analyze, and process data to develop flexible best practices and protocols to search for and document outdoor human remains scenes for search teams that will maximize success of detection and/or documentation. Another goal is to evaluate state-of-the-art tools, identify gaps, and determine where/how algorithms can assist an expert. Algorithms will enhance UAS productivity for identifying clandestine human remains sites. Evidence-based research has the potential to greatly impact criminal justice policy and practice, especially when it is conducted in collaboration with end users or practitioners.

5. Conclusions

UAS are a potentially valuable tool for civilian and law enforcement search teams to locate clandestine human remains and then conduct nondestructive documentation prior to personnel entering the potential scene. However, the most appropriate sensor (visible, near-infrared, infrared, hyperspectral, multispectral) used can be dependent on numerous factors (e.g., whether the body is on the surface or buried, landscape, postmortem interval, season of search, weather conditions at time of search). As a result, there is a need for evidence-based best practices and protocols for search and recovery teams to use for detecting and documenting outdoor crime scenes using UAS remote sensing and for basic research on its applications. For UAS to be successful in detecting and documenting clandestine remains, pilots need to have a clear understanding of the technical and operational capabilities of the UAS and how to process and interpret the output data. Furthermore, it is essential that pilots follow local, state, and federal laws and protect the privacy of the public when conducting missions. Finally, pilots need to be aware of the environmental anomalies that may increase detection. Working in conjunction with anthropologists and law enforcement can aid in the success.

References

Aitkenhead-Peterson.

Amendt, J., Rodner, S., Schuch, C., Sprenger, H., Weidlich, L., & Reckel, F. (2017). Helicopter thermal imaging for detecting insect infested cadavers. *Science & Justice, 57*, 366–372.

American Red Cross Measure. (2015). *Drones for disaster response and relief operations.* https://www.issuelab.org/resources/21683/21683.pdf.

Ammer, K., & Ring, E. F. (2005). Influence of the field of view on temperature readings from thermal imaging. *Themology International, 15*(3), 99–103.

Bailer, C., Finckh, M., & Lensch, H. P. (2012). Scale robust multi view stereo. ECCV(III). *LNCS, 7574*, 398–411.

Benninger, L. A., Carter, D. O., & Forbes, S. L. (2008). The biochemical alteration of soil beneath a decomposing carcass. *Forensic Science International, 180*, 70–75.

Blau, S., Sterenberg, J., Weeden, P., Urzedo, F., Wright, R., & Watson, C. (2018). Exploring non-invasive approaches in the detection of clandestine human burials: Developing a way forward. *Forensic Science Research, 3*(4), 304–326.

Brown, T. E. (1998). *Combining A line search with an alternative light source when searching for skeletal remains.* thesis. Dept Forensic Science, George Mason University.

Caccianiga, M., Bottacin, S., & Cattaneo, C. (2012). Vegetation dynamics as a tool for detecting clandestine graves. *Journal of Forensic Sciences, 57*(4), 983–988.

Carter, D. O., Yellowlee, D., & Tibbett, M. (2007). Cadaver decomposition in terrestrial ecosystems. *Naturwissenschaften, 94*, 12–24.

Chen, F., Kissel, D. E., West, L. T., Rickman, D., Luvall, J. C., & Adkins, W. (2005). Mapping surface soil organic carbon for crop fields with remote sensing. *Journal of Soil and Water Conservation, 60*, 51–57.

Christensen, A., Horn, K., & Smith, V. (2014). The use of alternative light source for detecting bones underwater. *Journal of Forensic Sciences, 90*(4), 1046–1048.

Davenport, G. C. (2001). Remote sensing application in forensic investigations. *Historical Archaeology, 35*, 87–100.

DesMarais, A. M. (2014). Detection of cadaveric remains by thermal imaging camera. *Journal of Forensic Identification, 64*(5), 489–512.

Eftychidis, G., Gkotsis, I., Kolios, P., & Peleties, C. UAV and their use in servicing the community. In G. Leventakis, & M. R. Haberfeld (Eds.), Community-oriented policing and technological innovations. SpringerBriefs in criminology (pp. 119-131).

France, D. L., Griffin, T. J., Swanburg, J. G., Lindemann, J. W., Davenport, G. C., Trammel, V., Armbrust, C. T., Kondrateiff, B., Nelson, A., Castellano, K., & Hopkins, D. (1992). A multidisciplinary approach to the detection of clandestine graves. *Journal of Forensic Sciences, 37*(6), 1445–1458.

France, D. L., Griffin, T. J., Swanburg, J. G., Lindemann, J. W., Davenport, G. C., Trammell, V., Travis, C. T., Kondrateiff, B., Nelson, A., Castellano, K., Hopkins, D., & Adair, T. (1997). Necrosearch revisited: Further multidisciplinary approaches to the detection of clandestine graves. In W. D. Haglund, & M. H. Sorg (Eds.), *Forensic taphonomy: The postmortem fate of human remains* (pp. 497–509). Boca Raton: CRC Press.

Ghamisi, P., Hoffle, B., & Zhu, X. X. (2017). Hyperspectral and LiDAR data fusion using extinction profiles and deep convolutional neural network. *Ieee Journal of Selected Topics in Applied Earth Observations and Remote Sensing, 10*(6), 3011–3024.

Glenn, E. P., Huete, A. R., & Nagler, P. L. (2008). Relationship between remotely-sensed vegetation indices, canopy attributes and plant physiological processes: What vegetation indices can and cannot tell us about the landscape. *Sensors, 8*(4), 2136–2160.

Isaacks, M. E. R. The use of near-infrared remote sensing in the detection of clandestine human remains [thesis]. Dept Anthropology, Texas State University.

Jiang, N., Cui, Z., & Tan, P. A. (2013). Global linear method for camera pose registration. In *International conference on computer vision*. https://doi.org/10.1109/ICCV.2013.66

Kalacska, M., & Bell, L. S. (2006). Remote sensing as a tool for detection of clandestine mass graves. *Canadian Society of Forensic Science Journal, 39*, 1–13.

Kalacska, M. E., Bell, L. S., Sanchez-Azofeifa, G. A., et al. (2009). The application of remote sensing for detecting mass graves: An experimental animal case study from Costa Rica. *Journal of Forensic Sciences, 54*, 159–166.

Killam, E. W. (2004). *The detection of human remains* (1st ed.). Springfield, IL: Charles C. Publisher.

Larson, D. O., Vass, A. A., & Wise, M. (2011). Advanced scientific methods and procedures in the forensic investigation of clandestine graves. *Journal of Contemporary Criminal Justice, 27*(2), 149–182.

Leblanc, G., Kalacska, M., & Soffer, R. (2014). Detection of single graves by airborne hyperspectral imaging. *Forensic Science International, 245*, 17–23.

Moulon, P., Monasse, P., & Marlet, R. (2013). Global fusion of relative motion for robust, accurate and scalable structure from motion. In *International conference on computer vision (ICCV)*.

Murray, B., Anderson, D. T., Wescott, D. J., Moorhead, R., & Anderson, M. F. (2018). Survey and insights into unmanned aerial-vehicle-based detection and documentation of clandestine graves and human remains. *Human Biology, 90*(1), 45–61.

Murray, B., Wescott, D. J., Anderson, D. T., & Moorhead, R. (2018). *A forensic anthropology user interface for automating search using remotely sensed data from unmanned aerial vehicles: Preliminary findings*. Austin, TX: American Association of Physical Anthropologists, 2018.

Novo, A., Lorenzo, H., Rial, F. I., & Solla, M. (2011). 3D GPR in forensics: Fining a clandestine grave in a mountainous environment. *Forensic Science International, 204*, 134–138.

Ozyesil, O., Voroninski, V., Basri, R., & Singer, A. (2017). *A survey of structure from motion*. arXiv, 1701.08493.

Police Executive Research Forum. (2020). *Drones: A report on the use of drones by public safety agencies - and a wake-up call about the threats of malicious drone attacks*. Washington, DC: Office of Community Oriented Policing Services.

Pringle, J. K., Holland, C., Szkornik, K., & Harrison, M. (2012). Establishing forensic search methodologies and geophysical surveying for the detection of clandestine graves in coastal beach environments. *Forensic Science International, 219*, e29–e36.

Ravmond, N. A., Card, B. L., & Baker, I. L. (2014). A new forensics: Developing standard remote sensing methodologies to detect and document mass atrocities. *Genocide Studies and Prevention: International Journal, 8*(3), 33–48.

Ruffell, A., & McKinley, J. (2008). *Geoforensics*. New York: Wiley.

Schultz, J. J., Collins, M. E., & Falsetti, A. B. (2006). Sequential monitoring of burials containing large pig cadavers using ground-penetrating radar. *Journal of Forensic Sciences, 51*(3), 607–616.

Shafiekhani, A., Kadam, S., Fritschi, F. B., & DeSouza, G. (2017). Vinobot and vinoculer: Two robotic platforms for high-throughput field phenotyping. *Sensors, 17*(1), 214.

Shan, Q., Curless, B., Furukawa, Y., Hernandez, C., & Seitz, S. M. (2014). Occluding contours for multi-view stereo. In *The IEEE conference on computer vision and pattern recognition (CVPR)* (pp. 4002–4009).

Slonecker, E. T., Allen, D. W., & Resmini, R. G. (2016). Towards establishing compact imaging spectrometer standards. *International Journal of Experimental Spectroscopic Techniques, 1*(1), 1–6.

Snirer, E. (2013). *Hyperspectral remote sensing of individual gravesites - exploring the effects of cadaver decomposition on vegetation and soil spectra.* thesis. Montreal: McGill University.

Snires, E. (2013). *Hyperspectral remote sensing of individual gravesites – exploring the effects of cadaver decomposition on vegetation and soil spectra.* thesis. Montreal: Department of Geography, McGrill University.

Swaraldahab, A. H., & Cristensen, A. M. (2016). The effect of time on bone fluorescence: Implications for using alternative light sources to search for skeletal remains. *Journal of Forensic Sciences, 61*(2), 442–444.

Towne, E. G. (2000). Prairie vegetation and soil nutrients responses to ungulate carcasses. *Oecologia, 122*, 232–239.

Valdovinos, M., Specht, J., & Zeunik, J. (2016). *Law enforcement and unmanned aircraft systems (UAS): Guidelines to enhance community trust.* Washington, DC: Office of Community Oriented Policing Services.

Ward, J. S. (2013). *Using vegetation to date clandestine graves.* Forensic Magazine (May).

Watson, C. J., & Forbes, S. L. (2008). An investigation of the vegetation associated with grave sites in southern Ontario. *Canadian Society of Forensic Sciences, 41*(4), 199–207.

Wilson, K., & Snavely, N. (2014). Robust global translation with 1DSfM. In *European conference on computer vision.*

CHAPTER

The use of GIS for cases of comingling

7

Sarah Voeller[1,2]

[1]*North Carolina State University, CCSI, International Association for Identification, Raleigh, NC, United States;* [2]*Cambridge Regional College, Cambridge, England, United Kingdom*

1. Introduction

A mass grave investigation is not straightforward, and challenges are often present. After victims are interred in mass graves, the taphonomic processes that follow can confound investigations. These processes include environmental conditions, animal activity, and human activity (Ubelaker, 1997). While anthropologists can determine the effects of environment and animal activity, changes due to human activity are more problematic. Offenders may attempt to burn or disarticulate victims in order to prevent identification. Also, graves are often relocated or combined in an effort to keep evidence hidden (Haglund & Sorg, 1997).

These activities typically cause commingling or the mixing together of individuals. Commingling poses problems for identification, collection of evidence for criminal prosecution, and timely repatriation (Ubelaker, 2008, pp. 1–6). The less complete a body, the less information the anthropologist has for identification and crime analysis. There are various methods available to address this problem including morphological techniques, mathematical and statistical models, radiographs, fluorescence, molecular analysis, and chemical analysis (Snow & Folk, 1970; Eyman, 1965; McKern, 1958; Fulton et al., 1986; Finnegan & Chauduri, 1990). However, the most commonly employed are DNA or morphological methods that detect size, shape, age, sex, and similarities or differences among bilateral elements (Holland et al., 1993; Buikstra & Gordon, 1980; Adams & Konigsberg, 2004; Byrd & Adams, 2003; L'Abbe, 2005; Owsley et al., 1995). While these techniques are effective, DNA analysis is considered costly, and most other methods are time consuming. Fortunately, in our fast-evolving world, DNA analysis is becoming more accessible and cost effective. For example, the International Commission on Missing Persons (ICMP) has developed it's own DNA laboratory and created databases of mitochondrial DNA from relatives of missing people in order to run their own samples. This is imperative in combatting the cost of using a private laboratory and backlog of requests for private laboratories (ICMP, 2019).

A recent study investigated the efficacy of reassociating commingled body parts with spatial analysis (Tuller et al., 2008). In this project, the provenience of every body part in the grave was mapped with a total station. These data were then used to

Methodological and Technological Advances in Death Investigations. https://doi.org/10.1016/B978-0-12-819394-5.00011-0

reassociate body parts based on proximity. This approach resulted in an 88% success rate when applied to a mass grave composed of primary and secondary interments. While this study showed the utility of spatial analysis in a mass grave setting, further exploration of this method will serve to delineate the scenarios when this method will be most useful, assess error rates, and create a replicable protocol.

The purpose of this research is to present a method for reassociating commingled remains that is low-cost and time efficient. Under the assumption that objects that are close to each other in space are most likely related, this research tested the hypothesis that a disarticulated skeletal element in closest proximity to a corresponding element is most likely associated with that element. A mass grave scenario was reproduced using domestic pigs. The provenience of elements was taken with a total station and a prism. Spatial analysis was used as the primary tool for reassociation of individuals. The study served to develop a protocol for spatial analysis, delineate the appropriate application, and assess the potential error of the method. A secondary goal of this research was to illustrate the utility of GIS databases for documenting and analyzing crime scenes in general.

2. Materials and methods

2.1 Using pigs as a proxy for humans

A mass grave commingling was recreated using domestic pigs (*Sus scrofa*). Pigs have proven to be an acceptable analog for human subjects (Byrd & Castner, 2009; Catts, 1992). Ten pigs were used for this project ranging in development from infant to adult both male and female to represent the common demographic found in a mass grave related to genocide, a situation in which individuals of a specific ethnic group are harmed indiscriminate of age and sex (OSAPG, 2014). Notable examples of mass graves resulting from genocide include those recovered in Rwanda and Srebrenica, Bosnia (Caplan, 2007; Maxwell & Ross, 2011; Neuffer, 1999; Stover & Peress, 1998). Pig sizes ranged from 4 to 150 lb. Specifically, two fetal, two 50 lb., two 70 lb., two 90 lb., and two pigs between 100 and 150 lb., were used. This aided in the project control, which included distinguishing pigs based on bone size differences.

The pigs were obtained from the North Carolina State University (NCSU) swine farm according to NCSU REG 10.10.01, the Animal Care and Use Procedures. Eight of the pigs were humanly euthanized by captive bolt pistol at the swine farm. The fetal pigs were not euthanized as they died of natural causes during birth. The pigs were euthanized a few hours prior to the study. Swine farm employees transported the pigs to the Lake Wheeler Field Site and placed them in the grave.

2.2 The research field site

The study was conducted on land owned by NCSU in the Lake Wheeler area. The grave site was located behind a cornfield just in front of a heavily wooded area. The soil consisted of clay-loam according to a Munsell color chart, which categorizes soil types by color and texture (Munsell & Color, 2000). The grave site consisted of an open pit that measured 10′24" (312 cm) by 8′53" (260 cm) in length and width and 6′ 4" (195 cm) in depth. The pit was excavated by the NCSU Lake Wheeler field crew in 2012 when it was initially used for another decomposition study (Honeycutt, 2012). To allow water drainage during rainstorms, a pipe was installed running from the bottom of the grave underground to an area of lower elevation. A wire screen was placed in front of the drainage hole to prevent clogging or loss of bones. The pit was cleaned and reutilized for the present study.

On July 17, 2014, the pigs were placed in the grave. The pigs were arranged close together so that limbs were overlapping to encourage commingling. Care was taken to place pigs of the same size on opposite sides of the grave to aid in overall control. A total station was used to record the initial position of the pigs. The total station was placed 1 m away from the corner of the grave. A benchmark, back site, and second fixed point were created so that the same coordinate system could be used during the excavation. Points were taken on the head, thorax, and backside of each pig to capture orientation (Fig. 7.1).

After the pigs were placed in the grave and recorded with the total station, a metal cage was constructed around the grave to keep out animal scavengers

FIGURE 7.1

Total station points referenced to a vertical photograph.

FIGURE 7.2

Cage built to protect the remains from scavengers.

(Fig. 7.2). An opening to the grave was created on the front side of the cage. This allowed for internal maintenance when needed. A scale made of 4 m sticks sitting on top of cinder blocks was placed in the corner of the grave. This was included so all photographs taken of the grave would have a scale.

2.3 Time lapse photography and aerial photographs

Part of the control for this study is the measurement of movement from vertical photographs using time lapse photography. A Cannon Rebel XS, which is a digital SLR camera, was used. Time lapse functions were made possible with a time-lapse intervalometer, which is a remote control timer. This device was plugged into the camera and programmed to take a photograph every hour. The camera took hourly photographs, only during daylight hours due to battery life. Batteries in the camera were changed each day. In order to leave the camera outside all day, a weatherproof camera container was created with an ammunition box. A small camera lens–sized hole was cut in the bottom of the ammunition box. A circular piece of plexiglass was placed in the hole and sealed with glue. The camera, with the lens placed over the glass, and the remote control were secured in the ammunition box protecting the devices from the weather. The camera was placed over the grave on a sliding rack system so it could be removed daily. The photographic process was facilitated by Forensic Photographer Gary Knight.

2.4 Excavation

The pigs were allowed to decompose and commingle over the course of 3 months. On October 16, 2014, the cage was removed, but the camera was left in place in order to take pictures during the excavation. The excavation began on October 17, 2014. Fig. 7.3 shows the state of the commingled remains on October, 16, 2014.

FIGURE 7.3

Commingled remains on October, 16, 2014.

During each total station set up, the back site was measured so that it could be compared to the initial back site measurement. If error was high (over 1 cm), the total station was checked and reset-up. On average, the back site was no more than 2 mm off.

Four letter codes were used to identify bones in the total station. These codes correspond to bone type and the location on the bone. Areas of articulation were mapped so that disarticulated bones could be reassociated with the closest missing elements. Both proximal and distal ends of long bones were mapped so that orientation would be accounted for in the reassociation process. For example, a proximal ulna should be reassociated with the closest distal humerus; this is differentiated from a proximal humerus. Codes did not include sides or differentiation between carpals and tarsals, vertebrae types, rib types, and front and hind metapodials (equivalent to human metacarpals) and phalanges. This was done in an effort to save time. Bone side and specific type were determined post excavation. Codes are presented in Table 7.1. Once a bone was mapped, it was placed in a paper bag with the total station id number, code, and coordinates written on it. In order to reduce the number of bags used, different types of bones were placed in the same bag. This allowed every bone to stay associated with its total station id number and provenience. This information was also manually recorded in a coordinate log to create a backup set of data in case of any error with the total station. Evidence bags from each day were sealed in a cardboard box with the date and stored in a cool dry location. Between work days, the grave was covered with chicken wire that was secured to the ground with metal stakes.

Because the pigs were juveniles, bones consisted of unfused elements. Vertebrae were often in two or three pieces, and long bone epiphyses were unfused. In the north half of the grave every bone, epiphysis and unfused element was recorded. In the south half, only full bones and essential portions of unfused elements were mapped. For example, only the vertebral arcs were mapped, while the bodies were omitted. This was done in order to compare the time it would take to map all elements versus just the essential elements. The two strategies can also be

Table 7.1 Bone codes.

BASI—cranium, taken on the middle of the basilar area	**PFEM**—proximal femur, taken at proximal articular surface
OCCR—cranium, taken on the right occipital condyle	**DFEM**—distal femur, taken at distal articular surface
OCCL—cranium, taken on the left occipital condyle	**PATL**—patella, taken at middle of exposed bone
VERT—vertebrae, taken at middle of exposed bone	**PTIB**—proximal tibia, taken at proximal articular surface
SCAP—scapula, taken at middle of glenoid fossa	**DTIB**—distal tibia, taken at distal articular surface
RIBH—rib, point taken at costal facet, or head	**PFIB**—proximal fibula, taken at proximal articular surface
RIBS—rib, point taken and sternal end	**DFIB**—distal fibula, taken at distal articular surface
PHUM—proximal humerus, taken at middle of proximal articular surface	**TALU**—talus, taken at middle of exposed bone
DHUM—distal humerus, taken at middle of distal articular humerus	**CALC**—calcaneus, taken as close to articular surface as possible
PRAD—proximal radius, taken at middle of proximal articular surface	**OCX1**—os coxa, taken at middle of sacro-iliac joint
DRAD—distal radius, taken at middle of distal articular surface	**OCX2**—os coxa, taken at mid-acetabulum
PULN—proximal ulna, taken at proximal articular surface	**OCX3**—os coxa, taken at middle of pubic symphysis
DULN—distal ulna, taken at distal articular surface	**OCX4**—os coxa, taken at middle of unfused surface
DMET—distal metapodial, taken at distal articular surface	**MANL**—mandible, taken on left mandibular condyle
PMET- proximal metapodial, taken at proximal articular surface	**MANR**—mandible, taken on right mandibular condyle
PHAL—phalanx, taken from center of exposed bone	**EPIP**—epiphyses, taken in the middle of exposed bone
CARP—for both carpals and tarsals, taken and middle of exposed bone	**STER**—sternum, taken from middle of exposed bone

considered the difference between highly fragmented assemblages versus unfragmented assemblages containing adults with fully fused elements. It should also be noted that some fetal bones were not found. These bones moved a great deal within the grave and were too small to track through time-lapse photography. Some small bones were either covered with mud or washed through the drain during storms.

The excavation took a total of 2 weeks of working days to complete. The first half of the excavation was completed with four to five people, and the second half was completed with two people. While four is the ideal number of people, two is the minimum that can be used, and it significantly slows down the process. The excavation was completed on December, 20, 2014.

2.5 Reassociation using GIS

2.5.1 Near 3D analysis

ArcMap 10.2, a program in the ArcGIS suite, was used to make reassociations based on spatial relationships. Data were transferred from the total station to the computer as a text file. The text file was then converted to an Excel worksheet that is compatible with ArcGIS. Side, measurement, and age information were then collected from the bones and added to the Excel sheet in separate columns. These data were loaded into ArcMap. Near 3D, a tool in the ArcGIS suite for 3D data, was used to complete the spatial analysis. This tool calculates the three-dimensional distances from one set of data to the closest feature in another set of data based on xyz coordinates. For example, a group of left distal femora was compared with a group of left proximal tibiae. In order to use Near 3D, the data were split into separate feature classes representing left and right and proximal and distal portions of bones. The bones included in the analysis were scapulae, humeri, radii, ulnae, ilia, femora, tibiae, fibulae, tali, and calcanei as they could be confidently identified and sided. The closest missing elements for each group were found using Near 3D. Results were exported to Excel worksheets where they were checked for accuracy using the control methods. If the first closest match was incorrect, the next closest element was searched until the correct match was found. This was done by separating the incorrectly reassociated bone into its own feature class in ArcMap and comparing it to the entire group of closest missing elements, so a distance was calculated for every bone. Small bones such as ribs, vertebrae, carpals, metapodials, and phalanges could not be sided with confidence. However, associated clusters of ribs and vertebrae were identified using spatial statistics.

2.5.2 Hot Spot Analysis

Hot Spot Analysis, another tool in ArcGIS, was used to identify associated clusters of bones. This analysis calculates the Getis-Ord (GI*) statistic for every feature in the dataset. This statistic measures the degree of clustering and identifies high or low (hot or cold) levels of clustering in cells (Ord & Getis, 1995). In order to do this, points were converted to polygons by spatially joining a grid with the data points. The cell size chosen for the grid was 0.05 m as it captured spatial patterns the best. After the spatial join, each grid cell became a polygon containing a given number of points where each point is a bone. *Z*-scores and *P*-values were calculated for each cell, which determined hot and cold areas. Each cell's point count was compared with the point count in its neighboring cell. The sum for a cell and its neighbors (local sum) was compared to the sum of all the other cells in the grid. A high *z-score* resulted when the local sum was much higher than the expected sum indicating a hot spot. A spot can be hot or cold at a 90%, 95%, or 99% confidence level, which is indicated by the *P-values*. The inputs for this tool include the conceptualization of spatial relationships parameter, distance method, and the fixed distance band value. "Fixed Distance Band," which is recommended for point data, was used for the conceptualization of spatial parameters. This means a distance band that determines which cells will influence other cells must be set. The distance method was set to "Euclidean Distance", a straight line between two points. The value used for the distance band, when working with vertebrae, was 0.207 m. This value is three times the standard deviation of the average distance between vertebrae that was computed with Near 3D using vertebrae as both the input and near feature. Anything further away was considered a spatial outlier. A distance band of 0.103 m was used for ribs. Ribs are composed of two points: the head and sternal end of the rib. Only one point was chosen to represent the group. The rib head was chosen because it is articulated to a vertebra and likely to have undergone less movement than the sternal end that is only attached to cartilage.

2.6 Methods for control

2.6.1 Osteometric sorting

Osteometric sorting is an accepted, commonly used method for sorting commingled remains in a forensic setting (Byrd & Adams, 2003). This method relies on size and shape differences between individuals that allow bones to be segregated. Osteometric sorting is most appropriate when there are various body sizes in the sample as is the case in this project. The null hypothesis is that the two bones being compared are from the same person. The goal is to segregate the bones by rejecting the null hypothesis. Regression is used to quantify the linear relationship between individual bones from a reference sample. Regression formulas are created to predict the measurement of the dependent variable. This value and other regression parameters are used to derive a t-value. P-values are then calculated using a two-tailed t-distribution. A 90% prediction interval and an alpha of 0.1 are used for sorting. This is suggested by Byrd and Adams (2003) as it offers the most acceptable results.

A reference sample is needed to create regression formulas. Such samples exist for human remains (i.e., the Forensic Databank). However, for this project, a reference sample of pig measurements was created. The sample ranged from fetal to adult and came from three sources. One pig skeleton from NCSU, one from the North Carolina Museum of Sciences and 22 from the Smithsonian Institution were used. Many of these were partial skeletons, and no skulls were measured. Therefore, only certain bones can be controlled for using this method. Some pig bones were difficult to identify and were not included in osteometric sorting. Crania, vertebrae, phalanges, metapodials, ribs, carpals, and tarsals were not included. Vertebra were unfused and usually in multiple pieces. While it is possible with human remains, it is difficult to distinguish between frontal and hind phalanges and metapodials in pigs. It is also difficult to side them. These bones look very similar in the pig due to quadrupedal locomotion (Hillson, 1999, p. 46). Of the tarsals, only the talus and calcaneus were used as they are easily identifiable.

Byrd and Adams (2003) found that taking both length and breadth measurements of a bone captured more information. Both length and breadth measurements were taken for each element. Bones were measured according to standards for animal bones outlined by Von Den Driesch (1976). Measurement tools included an osteometric board and sliding and spreading calipers. The measurements for each element were transformed into a single variable by adding them together and taking the natural logarithm. This captured both shape and size and made the values easier to work with. This was done for both the reference sample and the unknown elements. Statistical analysis was completed in SAS 9.4. The SAS proc reg procedure was used (Freud & Littell, 2000). Regression formulas were created for pairs of each type of bone, for a total of eight formulas.

Calculation of t and P-values from the regression parameters was done in Excel. T-values were derived using a formula modified by Byrd (2008, pp. 199–220):

$$t = |\hat{y} - yi| / \left[(\text{S.E.}) \times \sqrt{\left[1 + (1/N) + (xi - x)^2/(N \times Sx^2)\right]}\,\right].$$

In this equation, ŷ is the predicted value from the regression model, y*i* is the dependent variable, S.E. is the standard error of the regression model, N is the sample size used to calculate the regression model, x*i* is the independent variable, x is the reference sample mean of the independent variable, and Sx is the reference sample standard deviation of the independent variable. P-values were calculated in Excel using the two-tailed Student's t-distribution. Every possible match was assessed and compared to the spatial analysis results. Bones were segregated when the P-value was below 0.1. However, a P-value above 0.1 does not mean the two bones belong together. This only indicates that there is above a 10% probability that the variation, between the two bones resulted from chance.

2.6.2 Visual pair matching

Visual pair matching is a method in which bilateral bones are compared based on robusticity, muscle markings, epiphyseal shape, bilateral expression, pathology, and general symmetry (Adams & Konigsberg, 2004). This was used to confirm the associations made using Near 3D that were also controlled with osteometric sorting. All paired elements were visually matched using this method. Adams and Konigsberg (2004) indicate it is feasible to sort between elements when there is a small group of individuals that vary significantly in size, which is the case in the current project. Associations were made between elements by seriating the paired elements by size and then grouping them by size, taphonomy, and morphology. One pig was covered in clay due to its placement in the grave. Another pig had significant periosteal reaction on most bones (See Fig. 7.4).

2.6.3 Time lapse photography

Time-lapse photography was used to track the location and movement over time of all bones large enough to be visible in the picture. A time-lapse video was created from the hourly photographs taken every day. Visual tracking worked well for all bones except phalanges, carpals, and metapodials. When osteometric sorting and

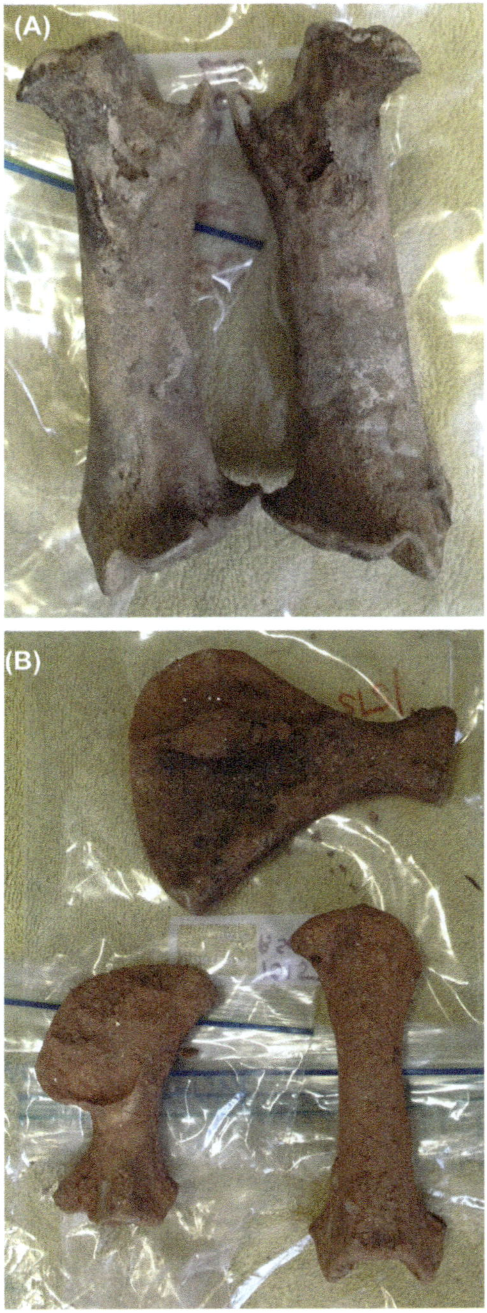

FIGURE 7.4

Visual matching based on morphological similarities. Bilateral periosteal reactions are shown on the left (a) and taphonomic similarities, clay staining, are shown on the right (b).

visual pair matching did not agree, the time-lapse footage was referenced to assess the movement and final location of specific bones. Ribs, vertebrae, crania, and mandibles were segregated by referencing the video and comparing the final photograph with the total station points.

2.7 Results for reassociation using GIS

2.7.1 Near 3D analysis

Elements were correctly reassociated with the first closest match in 136 out of 148 cases (91.89%) using Near 3D. The second closest element was correct in 11 cases (7.43%), and the fifth closest match was correct in one case (0.67%). Of the 12 incorrect reassociations, 8 (66.7%) were due to a mismatch between adult and fetal bone. The remains of the fetal pigs moved the most out of all of the subjects most likely due to their small size and light weight. The fetal pigs also decomposed quicker than juvenile pigs, which is consistent with taphonomy literature showing that size is a factor in decomposition (Hale & Ross, 2015). Bones tended to move toward the SE corner of the grave. This is due to a slight drop in gradient in the SE corner to facilitate drainage of rainwater. Fetal and other smaller bones such as phalanges shifted toward the SE corner during storms when the grave filled with water. On average, the closest missing element was 10.82 cm away. The closest matching pair was 1.53 cm away from each other. The most distant matching pair was 108.1 cm away from each other. This was a left fetal humerus and scapula. Maps of the grave in which elements are individuated are presented in Figs. 7.5 and 7.6. Fig. 7.5 includes only the points, while Fig. 7.6 includes the points and a referenced photo. The initial locations of the pigs are included in both maps to visualize the overall movement of elements. The direction of movement toward the SE corner of the grave can also be seen.

For illustrative purposes, the results for the reassociation of left humeri and radii are presented in Table 7.2. The first column titled "Number" shows the number assigned to the bone in ArcMap. The column titled "LN" is the natural logarithm of the summed measurements of the dependent variable; in this case, that would be the humerus. The column titled "Xi" is the natural logarithm of the summed measurements of the independent variable; in this case, that would be the radius. The column titled "predicted" contains a formula from the regression model of radius on humerus. The values in this column are the predicted values from the formula. The column titled "Formula 1" contains the first part of Byrd's *t*-value formula; = ABS (Predicted—LN). The column titled "Formula 2" contains the second part of the formula = 0.10,275*SQRT(1+(1/37)+(Xi-5.0,176,245)^2/(37*0.469,441^2)). The column titled "T-value" is Formula 1/Formula 2. The column titled "*P*-value" contains = T.DIST.2T (*t*-value, 36) with 36 degrees of freedom. This is the two-tailed *t*-distribution. The columns titled "642," "826," "880," and so on are the numbers for each radius tested with each humerus. Each match was tested by imputing the ln of each radius in the "Xi" column and copying the resulting *P*-values to the appropriate radius column. *P*-values lower than 0.1 indicate that the bones do not

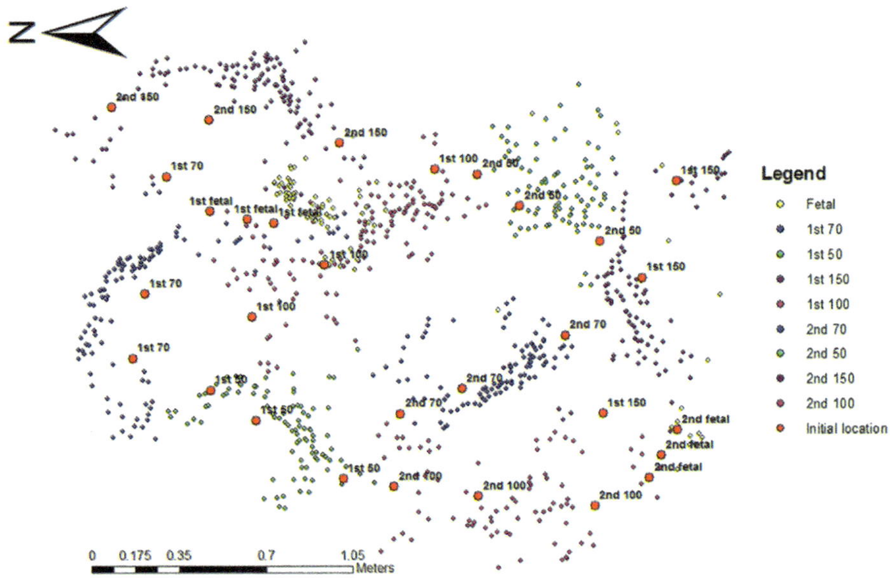

FIGURE 7.5

Individuated skeletal elements.

FIGURE 7.6

Individuated skeletal elements referenced to a photo.

Table 7.2 Results for the spatial reassociation of left humeri and radii.

Right Humerus and Right Radius																					
Number	LN	Age	Xi	Predicted	Formula 1	Formula 2	T-Value	P-Value	Rad 642	Rad 826	Rad 880	Rad 1026	Rad 1255	Rad 1457	Rad 1526	Rad 1681	Rad 1895	Distance	Match	OS
Hum 377	5.0575		4.80648	5.092917	0.0354167	0.1044061	0.339221	0.7364	0.0263	0.5280	0.0000	0.0293	0.8239	0.4742	0.0620	0.0102	0.7364	0.3344	1st	6
Hum 627	5.2807		4.80648	5.092917	0.1877833	0.1044061	1.798586	0.0805	0.8628	0.1481	0.0000	0.8999	0.0860	0.1652	0.8298	0.5727	0.0805	0.2211	1st	4
Hum 655	4.1667	Fetal	4.80648	5.092917	0.9262467	0.1044061	8.871579	0.0000	0.0000	0.0000	0.9718	0.0000	0.0000	0.0000	0.0000	0.0000	0.0000	0.3136	2nd	9
Hum 1015	5.1896		4.80648	5.092917	0.0967033	0.1044061	0.926223	0.3605	0.3013	0.5333	0.0000	0.3233	0.3048	0.5903	0.5148	0.1574	0.3605	0.1150	1st	2
Hum 1220	5.0454		4.80648	5.092917	0.0475567	0.1044061	0.455497	0.6515	0.0200	0.4560	0.0000	0.0224	0.7356	0.4067	0.0484	0.0076	0.6515	0.0731	1st	6
Hum 1461	5.0370		4.80648	5.092917	0.0559667	0.1044061	0.536048	0.5952	0.0165	0.4096	0.0000	0.0185	0.6763	0.3636	0.0406	0.0062	0.5952	0.0603	1st	6
Hum 1478	5.2439		4.80648	5.092917	0.1509433	0.1044061	1.445733	0.1569	0.7009	0.2582	0.0000	0.6338	0.1274	0.2947	0.8917	0.3621	0.1569	0.0676	1st	2
Hum 1685	5.2852		4.80648	5.092917	0.1923133	0.1044061	1.841974	0.0737	0.8969	0.1310	0.0000	0.9341	0.0582	0.1530	0.7963	0.6023	0.0737	0.0891	1st	5
Hum 1806	5.0239		4.80648	5.092917	0.0690367	0.1044061	0.661233	0.5127	0.0122	0.3437	0.0000	0.0137	0.5884	0.3027	0.0807	0.0044	0.5127	0.0581	1st	7

Table 7.3 Overall results.

Reassociations			
Articulated elements	**Number of queries**	**Correct**	**Incorrect**
Humerus/radius	18	16	2
Humerus/ulna	19	15	4
Scapula/humerus	20	18	2
Femur/tibia	19	18	1
Tibia/fibula	19	18	1
Talus/calcaneus	16	16	0
Tibia/talus	19	19	0
Femur/ilium	18	16	2
Total	148	136	12
Percentage	100%	91.89%	8.11%

match. Cells highlighted in yellow indicate a correct match based on proximity. Cells highlighted in red indicate an incorrect match based on proximity. The cells highlighted in light blue indicate the true match if a match was incorrect. The overall results are presented in Table 7.3.

2.7.2 Hot Spot Analysis

Only the results for the Hot Spot Analysis of ribs and vertebrae will be discussed here. The carpals, phalanges, and metapodials could not be controlled for. Seven vertebrae clusters composed of 452 significant cells were identified. Eight rib clusters composed of 199 significant cells were identified. Fig. 7.7 shows the legend used to interpret the Hot Spot Analysis results. Figs. 7.8 and 7.9 show the results for vertebrae and ribs. Accuracy of Hot Spot Analysis for identifying individuals was calculated by quantifying the number of vertebrae or ribs captured in significant cells of clusters. Results show that 73.75% of vertebrae and 76.69% of ribs were spatially clustered (Tables 7.4 and 7.5).

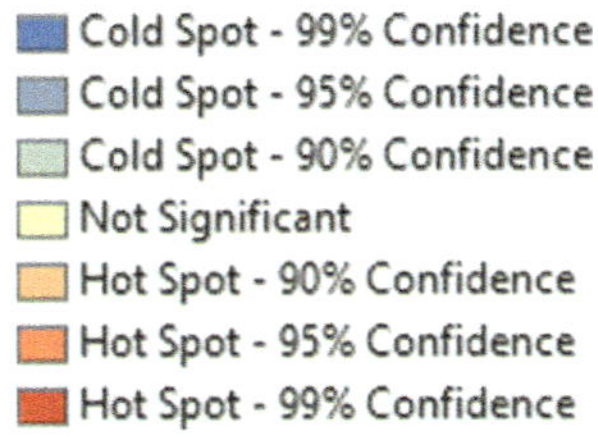

FIGURE 7.7

Colors that represent hot and cold cells.

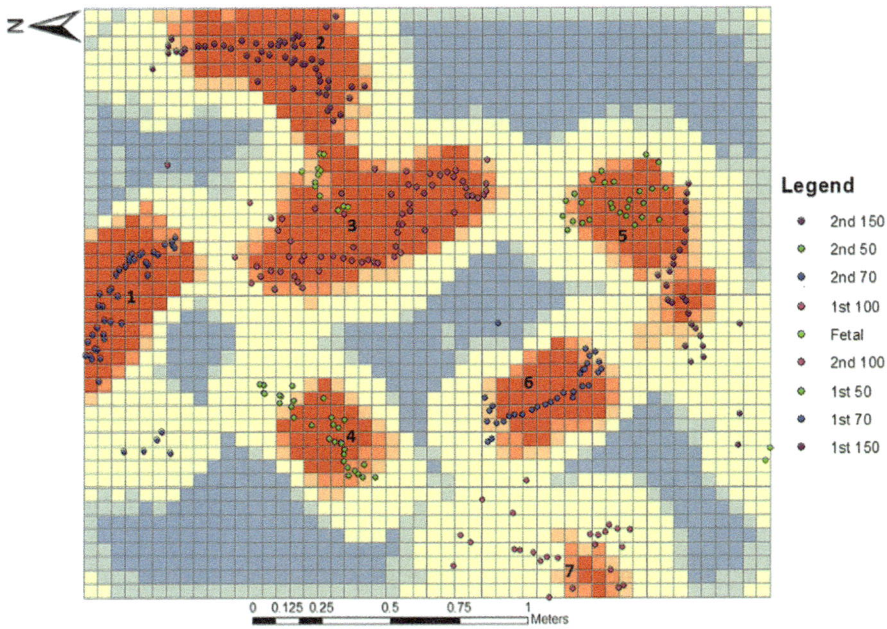

FIGURE 7.8

Hot Spot Analysis of vertebrae.

2.8 Discussion

2.8.1 Reassociations made with GIS

2.8.1.1 Near 3D analysis

Reassociation using spatial analysis should be considered as one of many techniques used to reassociate commingled remains. While the Near 3D analysis resulted in a 91.89% success rate, it cannot confirm, with statistical confidence, each match made based on proximity. Osteometric sorting produces results with statistical confidence levels and visual pair matching permits visual inspection of overall morphology and taphonomic changes. While these methods are useful in situations of small scale commingling they become less useful when the number of individuals increases

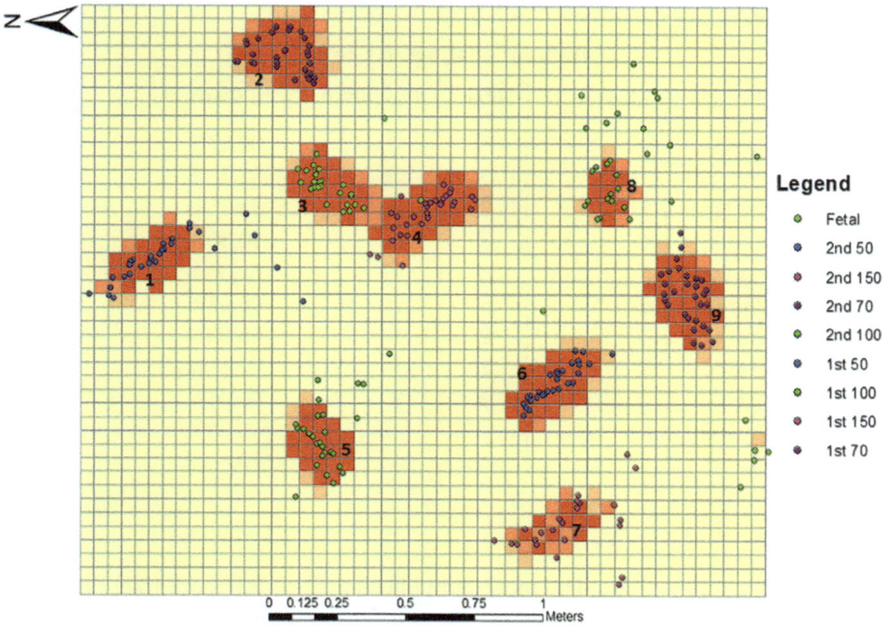

FIGURE 7.9

Hot Spot Analysis of ribs.

Table 7.4 Results for Hot Spot Analysis of vertebrae.

Hotspot analysis of vertebrae				
Pig	**Cluster**	**Vertebrae**	**#In cluster**	**% Correct**
1st 70	1	45	40	88.89%
2nd 150	2	52	47	90.38%
1st 100	3	64	59	92.19%
1st fetal	3	12	10	83.33%
1st 50	4	31	20	64.52%
2nd 50	5	27	22	81.48%
1st 150	5	27	14	51.85%
2nd 70	6	32	20	62.50%
2nd 100	7	28	4	14.29%
2nd fetal	No cluster	2	0	0.00%
Overall		320	236	73.75%

Table 7.5 Results for Hot Spot Analysis of ribs.

Hotspot analysis of ribs				
Pig	**Cluster**	**Ribs**	**#In cluster**	**% Correct**
1st 70	1	30	20	66.67%
2nd 150	2	30	28	93.33%
1st fetal	3	29	26	89.66%
1s 100	4	32	29	90.63%
1st 50	5	27	17	62.96%
2nd 70	6	30	29	96.67%
2nd 100	7	24	14	58.33%
2nd 50	8	26	11	42.31%
1st 150	9	33	30	90.91%
2nd fetal	No cluster	5	0	0.00%
Overall		266	204	76.69%

(Byrd, 2008, pp. 199–220). The more individuals present the more likely it is that there will be persons with bones of similar size and morphology. For best results in both small and large-scale commingling, a method such as Near 3D should be employed in combination with these methods. Used as a first approach, spatial analysis matches skeletal elements based on proximity, which will decrease the number of comparisons that need to be made using osteometric sorting and/or visual pair matching. Each match can be confirmed with the other methods. If a match is rejected, the second closest element will be compared and so on. Once a match is accepted, one can move on to the next reassociation.

2.8.1.2 Hot Spot Analysis

Vertebrae and ribs were controlled for using time-lapse photography. Seven vertebrae clusters were identified. Because every unfused element was mapped in the north portion of the grave, the map indicates that clusters in the north portion of the grave have more than 27 (average number of vertebrae in a pig) vertebrae per cluster. Vertebral bodies and arches were mostly unfused and were mapped separately. Therefore, the clusters in the north are more numerous but still compose one pig. In the south portion of the grave, only representative portions (the vertebral arcs) of the vertebrae were mapped, so there are an anatomically correct number of vertebrae representing a pig. After segregating vertebrae, it was discovered that some vertebrae in cluster three were from the first fetal pig; therefore, this cluster represents two pigs. Cluster five contains the vertebrae of two pigs; the second 50 lb. pig and the second 150 lb. pig. From the map in Fig. 7.8 and Tables 7.4, it is clear that not all of the vertebrae from the second fetal were found to create a cluster. A total of 73.75% of vertebrae were included in the clusters. The remaining vertebrae are in close proximity but are not included in cells with significant *P*-values.

Nine rib clusters were identified. These clusters leave out more elements than the vertebral clusters but are more accurate in identifying individual pigs. Depending on the interpretation of the analyst, clusters 3 and 4 may be combined. However, accounting for the correct number of ribs in the body can assist in determining if the clusters should be separated. In this case, it is known that the clusters should be separated as the grouping contains two pigs. Again, not enough ribs from the second fetal pig were found to create a cluster of significant cells; however, an association was identified by 1 cell indicating moderate clustering. A total of 76.69% of ribs were included in clusters. Ribs not included in clusters were more dispersed compared to the vertebrae.

While some interpretation is necessary, clusters represented individual pigs well. Of most importance, the Hot Spot Analysis produces results based on statistical computations that can be considered quantitative and objective. It addresses the smaller bones that are largely ignored by other reassociation methods. Lastly, because clusters tended to represent individual pigs, Hot Spot Analysis can aid in estimating the minimum number of individuals present.

2.9 The mapping process

The overall amount of time taken to map the grave was 14 days. The grave measured approximately 10 x 8 ½ ft. and contained 10 individuals. This is a rather small endeavor in comparison to a mass grave measuring 82 x 8 ft. containing 289 individuals (Tuller et al., 2008). Translating this method to a mass grave of this size and capacity may not seem practical; however; for this project, the number of people helping ranged from two to six. More than half of the time only two people were available to map. If four people (the ideal number to employ the mapping process) were available every day, the process would have been much quicker. Two different mapping strategies were employed. In the north portion of the grave, every element was mapped. This included epiphysis, fragments, and sesamoid bones as well as unfused portions. This lengthened the process substantially. In the south portion of the grave, these elements were omitted, which would be more comparable to a mass grave containing fewer juveniles with little fragmentation. In this study, every coordinate taken was read aloud and manually recorded. This was done to account for potential user error. The total station records every point, but the user must press "Record." In the present study, this was important because most users were inexperienced. A number of points had to be corrected using the manual bone log due to user errors with the machine. This also protects against the possibility that the machine is damaged and information is lost. While mapping a site with a total station is much quicker than using traditional hand measurements, the strategy can be improved further. For the most efficient process, it is suggested that four to five people be employed to map the grave in its entirety, extraneous elements are not mapped and coordinates are recorded only with the total station. Another way to speed up the process would be using an external keyboard with the total station, so codes can be quickly typed in and recorded.

Typically, the user must scroll through a list of codes saved in the total station every time a different point is recorded.

Not all the codes used in this analysis were found to be of use for reassociation. It is suggested that these codes be excluded when implementing this method in a real scenario. Only one measurement should be taken on the cranium, mandible, and portions of the os coxa. Codes EPIP, OCX4, OCCR, OCCL, EPIP, and MANL or MANR were extraneous and should be removed. If types of vertebrae can be identified in the field quickly it would be helpful to record them with a separate code, for example, CERV for cervical vertebrae. This would help to confirm the associations for clusters of vertebrae found in the hotspot analysis. If metacarpals and metatarsals can be differentiated, they should also receive their own code. If bones can be sided quickly in the field, this should also be included in the code or recorded separately as it saves time during post-processing.

Since this project was completed, new technology has become available to speed up the mapping process. 3D scanners, which were considered far too expensive in the past, have become affordable and are an option for some agencies. A 3D scanner, such as a FARO laser scanner, can be quickly set up to scan the surrounding area in a matter of minutes. This scanner collects a cloud of data points. Multiple scans can be taken from different angles and depths as the grave is excavated and then merged together in a computer program. Additional research is needed to see exactly how this analysis could be done with a 3D scanner.

2.10 Limitations

This method associates left and right sides separately; therefore, other measures must be taken to reassociate left and right sides. The method tested in this study focused on reassociating previously articulated elements. Due to the maturity of the pigs, many bones were unfused. This was not a problem for easily identifiable elements such as long bones or portions of the os coxae; however, specific vertebrae, especially when fragmentary, could not be identified. This prevented certain skeletal elements from being reassociated. For example, the first cervical vertebra articulates with the cranium. Because first cervical vertebrae were not identified, they could not be reassociated with crania. Bones must be accurately identified in order to reassociate them with the correct element. It is because of this that Hot Spot Analysis, instead of Near 3D, was used to identify spatially associated clusters of vertebrae and ribs. In a previous study, crania were reassociated with the superior points of full vertebral columns (Tuller et al., 2008). This is recommended when articulated vertebral columns are present and first cervical vertebrae can be identified.

The skeletal commingling created for this study represented surface scatter. Buried remains take months or even years to decompose depending on the environment (Ubelaker, 1997). The time frame for this study did not allow the time needed for buried remains to decompose and commingle. Placing the pigs on the ground surface permitted time for decomposition as well as natural processes to take place which moved the bones. While perpetrators frequently bury victims in order to hide their crimes, surface scatter of remains occurs as well. For example, Physicians for Human Rights conducted an investigation of surface scatter and buried remains at Kibuye Catholic Church after the Rwandan Genocide (Haglund et al., 2001). The present study serves to demonstrate the protocol for applying spatial analysis to a commingled assemblage of remains that have been found in situ. In order to employ the method, remains must be mapped in their original context, be it surface scatter or excavated burial.

Another limitation to consider is the use of proprietary software. ArcGIS has a licensing cost that may be prohibitive. However, spatial analysis can be conducted in a number of GIS programs. It is appropriate to highlight an open source program that is capable of conducting the analysis and presenting the data. GRASS is an open source GIS program that can even be used without an internet connection. In order to conduct the analysis in GRASS the total station points must be saved as a CSV file. The CSV file can be uploaded into GRASS using the v.in.ascii command. Coordinate types (e.g., left distal humerus) must be separated in different vector files, or groups. The command v.distance locates the nearest elements in a "to" vector map for elements in a "from" vector map. For example the "to" vector map would be left distal humerus and the "from" vector map would be left proximal radius. This is similar to Near 3D in ArcGIS.

While ArcMap is limited, both GRASS and ArcScene, another program in the ArcGIS suite, are useful for working with and displaying 3d vector data. The data can be rotated around and viewed from any angle. Animations can be made to illustrate relationships among certain points in 3D.

3. Conclusion

The findings of this research show that spatial analysis should be one of the techniques used to reassociate commingled remains. It is most useful when employed first and then followed by other methods. Using spatial analysis first will reduce the number of comparisons that need to be made with osteometric sorting or visual pair matching, which will hasten the reassociation process. It has the potential to be particularly useful in a large scale commingling when metric and visual methods are more difficult to employ and in commingling situations where DNA comparisons are not an option. A method such as Hot Spot Analysis should be employed for the commingling of highly fragmented assemblages or small skeletal elements that are not addressed by other methods.

Reassociations made with the Near 3D analysis were correct in 91.89% of cases. Hot Spot Analysis succeeded in identifying clusters of vertebrae and ribs that contained individual pigs. While interpretation of the clusters requires a human element such as knowledge of human osteology, on average, 75.22% of vertebrae and ribs were spatially clustered. Both spatial analysis methods used in this study are quantitative and objective and display high accuracy rates. This is important as the methods used by the scientific community should be tested and have known error rates.

A practical implementation of this method should involve mapping the remains in situ using a device such as a total station. To map with minimal error, the operator of the total station should be experienced especially if the project requires numerous machine set-ups. Articular areas of bones should be recorded, using either the codes in this study or codes developed with another specific purpose. The use of an external keyboard is encouraged if using a total station. Points should be downloaded from the total station to an Excel file on the computer and then uploaded to ArcGIS, GRASS or another available GIS program. Articular categories such as left proximal humerus should be separated. A function such as Near 3D or v.distance should be used to query the distance of one set of elements to its set of counterpart elements. The output from this function will indicate the closest missing elements for each set.

Beyond the reassociation of commingled remains, spatial data can be used to recreate any aspect of the crime scene. If buildings, trees, and artifacts, etc. are also mapped, spatial relationships between the surrounding areas, pieces of evidence, and remains can be assessed. Maps that are precisely to scale can be created to represent the crime scene. This is useful to investigators if they need to recreate a crime scene in court months or even years in the future. The method can also be employed in a bioarcheological setting. Mapping remains and artifacts in context is not only useful for reassociating commingled skeletal elements but also for site interpretation as well as preservation once the site has been destroyed.

References

Adams, B. J., & Konigsberg, L. W. (2004). Estimation of the most likely number of individuals from commingled human skeletal remains. *American Journal of Physical Anthropology, 125*(2), 138–151.

Buikstra, J. E., & Gordon, C. C. (1980). Individuation in forensic science study: Decapitation. *Journal of Forensic Sciences, 25*(1), 246–259.

Byrd, J. E. (2008). *Models and methods for osteometric sorting. Recovery, analysis, and identification of commingled human remains*. Springer.

Byrd, John E., & Adams, Bradley J. (2003). Osteometric sorting of commingled human remains. *Journal of Forensic Sciences, 48*(4), 0022–1198, 717 pp.

Byrd, J. H., & Castner, J. L. (2009). *Forensic entomology: The utility of arthropods in legal investigations*. CRC press.

Caplan, P. (2007). Never again?: Genocide memorials in Rwanda. *Anthropology Today, 23*(1), 20–22. https://doi.org/10.1111/j.1467-8322.2007.00486.x

Catts, E. (1992). Problems in estimating the postmortem interval in death investigations. *Journal of Agricultural Entomology, 9*(4), 245–255.

Eyman, C. E. (1965). Ultraviolet fluorescence as a means of skeletal identification. *American Antiquity, 31*(1), 109–112. Retrieved from http://www.jstor.org.prox.lib.ncsu.edu/stable/2694031.

Finnegan, M., & Chaudhuri, S. (1990). Identification of commingled skeletal remains using isotopic strontium. In *42nd annual meeting of the American Academy of Forensic Science, Cincinnati, OH.*

Freud, R. J., & Littell, R. C. (2000). *SAS system for regression.* Sas Institute.

Fulton, B. A., Meloan, C. E., & Finnegan, M. (1986). Reassembling scattered and mixed human bones by trace element ratios. *Journal of Forensic Sciences, 31*(4), 1455–1462.

Haglund, W. D., Connor, M., & Scott, D. D. (2001). The Archaeology of Contemporary mass graves. *Historical Archaeology, 35*(1), 57–69. Archaeologists as Forensic Investigators: Defining the Role.

Haglund, W. D., & Sorg, M. H. (Eds.). (1997). *Forensic taphonomy: The postmortem fate of human remains.* CRC Press.

Hale, A. R., & Ross, A. H. (February 2015). *An innovative analysis of the postmortem interval and its role in juvenile decomposition.* Orlando, FL: Poster presented at the American Academy of Forensic Science.

Hillson, S. (1999). *Mammal bones and teeth: An introductory guide to methods of identification Institute of Archaeology.*

Holland, M. M., Fisher, D. L., Mitchell, L. G., Rodriquez, W. C., Canik, J. J., Merril, C. R., & Weedn, V. W. (1993). Mitochondrial DNA sequence analysis of human skeletal remains: Identification of remains from the vietnam war. *Journal of Forensic Sciences, 38*(3), 542–553.

Honeycutt, Kenda K. (2012). *Fracture patterns and taphonomic processes in a mass grave environment: A quantitative analysis.*

ICMP. (August 15, 2019). *Standing capacity.* Retrieved from https://www.icmp.int/what-we-do/technical-assistance/standing-capacity/.

L'Abbe, E. N. (2005). A case of commingled remains from rural South Africa. *Forensic Science International, 151*(2–3), 201–206.

Maxwell, A., & Ross, A. H. (2011). Epidemiology of genocide: An example from the former yugoslavia. *Forensic Science Policy & Management: International Journal, 2*(2), 94–102.

McKern, T. W. (1958). *The use of short wave ultra-violet rays for the segregation of commingled skeletal remains.*

Munsell, A. H., & Color, M. (2000). *Munsell soil color charts Munsell Color.*

Neuffer, E. (1999). Mass graves. *Nieman Reports, 53*(2), 9.

Office of the UN Special Advisor on the Prevention of Genocide (OSAPG).(2014). https://www.un.org/en/preventgenocide/adviser/pdf/osapg_analysis_framework.pdf.

Ord, J. K., & Getis, A. (1995). Local spatial autocorrelation statistics: Distributional issues and an application. *Geographical Analysis, 27*(4), 286–306.

Owsley, D. W., Ubelaker, D. H., Houck, M. M., Sandness, K. L., Grant, W. E., Craig, E. A., Woltanski, T. J., & Peerwani, N. (1995). The role of forensic anthropology in the recovery and analysis of Branch Davidian Compound victims: Techniques of analysis. *Journal of Forensic Sciences, 40*(3), 341–348.

Snow, C. C., & Folk, E. D. (1970). Statistical assessment of commingled skeletal remains. *American Journal of Physical Anthropology, 32*(3), 423–427.

Stover, E., & Peress, G. (1998). *The graves: Srebrenica and vukovar.* Scalo Verlag Ac.

Tuller, H., Hofmeister, U., & Daley, S. (2008). Spatial analysis of mass grave mapping data to assist in the re-association of disarticulated and commingled human remains. In *Recovery, analysis, and identification of commingled human remains* (pp. 7–29). Humana Press.

Ubelaker, D. H. (1997). Taphonomic applications in forensic anthropology. In D. Hagelund, & M. Sorg (Eds.), *Forensic taphonomy: The postmortem fate of human remains.*

Ubelaker, D. H. (2008). *Methodology in commingling analysis: An historical overview. Recovery, analysis, and identification of commingled human remains*. Springer.

Von Den Driesch, A. (1976). *A guide to the measurement of animal bones from archaeological sites: As developed by the institut für palaeoanatomie, domestikationsforschung und geschichte der tiermedizin of the university of munich Peabody Museum Press.*

CHAPTER

Unidentified decedent investigation protocols

8

Ann H. Ross[1] and Nicholas V. Passalacqua[2]

[1]*Department of Biological Sciences, North Carolina State University, Raleigh, NC, United States;*
[2]*Western Carolina University, Cullowhee, NC, United States*

1. Introduction

The investigation of unidentified decedents is a multidisciplinary endeavor, requiring communication and collaboration between numerous individuals, organizations, and oftentimes, databases. The death investigation system of the United States is highly variable with cities, counties, states, etc., being covered by different forms of law enforcement agencies (e.g., sheriffs, local police, state police, federal bureau of investigation, etc.), as well as different forms of medicolegal authorities (e.g., coroner, medical examiner, deputy medical examiner, justice of the peace, etc.) (Hanzlick, 2014). Because of this variability in jurisdictional coverage, the United States lacks unified or consistent protocols for death investigations. This lack of consistency in death investigation offices results in a lack of consistency in the roles of the medicolegal authority (Thomas, 2014), qualifications for death investigation, professionals (Hanzlick & Fudenberg, 2014), pay for death investigation personnel (Kemp, 2014; Passalacqua et al., 2020), and availability/usage of death investigation experts in support roles (i.e., forensic anthropologists, forensic entomologists) (Christensen et al., 2015).

As the death investigation system of the United States is quite varied, so are the jurisdictional definitions of what constitutes a cold case (Adcock & Stein, 2015); however, typically a cold case is one where all investigative leads have been exhausted. Traditionally, we think of cold case investigations as a reinvestigation of evidence and remains from 20 or more years previous, but for decomposed unidentified decedents, these cases may start "cold" and only get "colder" as time goes on (that is, evidence may deteriorate over time or become more difficult to find comparisons for). In terms of death investigations, cold cases typically represent those in which the identity of a set of remains is unable to be established. For decomposed unidentified decedents, these cases may start "cold," with little evidence from which to base an investigation. If a set of remains is unable to be identified, they may be curated at the office of the medicolegal authority indefinitely or buried as an unknown in a pauper cemetery. In other instances, some portions of the remains may be resected and retained for future investigative use, and the rest of the remains cremated (e.g., California Senate Bill 1066).

Methodological and Technological Advances in Death Investigations. https://doi.org/10.1016/B978-0-12-819394-5.00004-3

The goal of this chapter is to present a novel approach to forensic anthropology consultation with medical examiner offices in order to resolve unidentified decedent cases, with a focus on cold cases. The authors developed and piloted this approach in North Carolina, as the model of forensic anthropology consultation in this state is common in many others. That is, in North Carolina, there are certified forensic anthropologists working as educators in various locations in the state, but there are no forensic anthropologists employed at any of the regional pathology centers. This lack of full-time forensic anthropological expertise at medical examiner offices is common, in part due to funding deficiencies in the medicolegal death investigation system overall but also due to variance in office caseloads (Christensen et al., 2015; Hanzlick, 2014; Pilloud et al., 2022).

This chapter presents a pilot-initiative for generating a North Carolina-wide forensic anthropology partnership between North Carolina State University and Western Carolina University, two institutions located on either side of the state, both having certified forensic anthropologists in leadership roles of academic forensic anthropology programs. The goal of this pilot project was to investigate unidentified missing-person cold cases via forensic anthropological, isotopic (for geolocation) investigations, and forensic genealogical analyses. This project focused on unidentified cases from the Office of the Chief Medical Examiner, located in Raleigh, NC, and the Mecklenburg County Medical Examiner's office located in Charlotte, NC.

2. Role of forensic anthropology in the identification process

The use of forensic science in death investigations is a multidisciplinary endeavor involving such disciplines as forensic-anthropology, archeology, biology, botany, chemistry (i.e., toxicology), entomology, odontology, law enforcement, and pathology. In terms of death investigations, medical examiners/forensic pathologists can be considered experts at examining soft tissues to determine the cause and manner of death (via autopsies). However, in cases where the soft tissues may be decomposed or altered by taphonomic modifications, such as dismemberment or burning, the utility of forensic pathology and traditional autopsy may be reduced. In such cases, forensic anthropology is a valuable investigative tool.

Forensic anthropologists are experts in outdoor search and recovery of evidence, including human remains (i.e., forensic archeology), as well as laboratory analysis of the skeleton (which includes the bones, dentition, and cartilage). Thus, forensic anthropologists contribute to death investigations by: performing systematic searches of areas to locate scenes containing human remains and associated evidence; performing recovery operations of a scene to maximize outdoor evidence collection, including contextual and spatial data; determining the forensic or medicolegal significance of questioned material (e.g., is this bone from a human?);

sorting remains of commingling assemblages into individuals; analyzing unidentified human remains to develop a biological profile for an individual (i.e., estimating age-at-death, population affinity, sex, and stature); contributing to the medical examiner's determination of the cause of death by examining the remains for trauma as well as taphonomic modifications (i.e., damage that may have occurred after death); and by performing an identification, usually by comparing postmortem radiographs of the unidentified remains to antemortem radiographs of a known individual.

The expertise of forensic anthropologists is in the recovery, sorting, analysis, and identification of remains, and therefore, forensic anthropologists are routinely called upon by various law enforcement or death investigation agencies to assist in forensic casework. However, rather than being full-time investigative staff, the majority of forensic anthropologists are employed at colleges and universities and consult with law enforcement and medical examiners as needed (Passalacqua et al., 2020; Berryman & Lanfear, 2012). Because of this, the use of forensic anthropology in casework varies based on jurisdiction, accessibility, and familiarity with the utility of forensic anthropology (Christensen et al., 2015). Additionally, the types of cases analyzed by forensic anthropologists also vary by jurisdiction, for example approximately 80% of the forensic anthropology reports written at the Western Michigan University Homer Stryker M.D. School of Medicine in Kalamazoo, Michigan, are radiographic identifications (Jered Cornelison Pers Com. Feb 2021), while other offices write much fewer identification reports, but many more reports focusing solely on age estimation or trauma analysis (Passalacqua et al., 2021; Pilloud et al., 2022).

3. Unidentified decedents in North Carolina

Referred to as the "silent mass disaster" (Ritter, 2007), according to the FBI's National Crime Information Center (NCIC) missing person and unidentified person files, as of December 31, 2021, there were 93,718 active missing person records and 8415 unidentified persons records. Of the 8415 records, 892 were entered in 2021 of which 575 or 64% are deceased unidentified records; six or 1% are unidentified catastrophe victims; and 311 or 35% are living unidentified persons (NCIC Missing Person and Unidentified Person Statistics, 2021). Many of those in the missing persons records are thought to be deceased, but their remains have not yet been located or identified. Experts estimate that there are approximately 40,000 to 50,000 unidentified dead in the US (109th Congress, Second Session, page 7), most of which are thought to be victims of homicides. This means that only 2.4% of the unidentified dead are accounted for by the NCIC database. This crisis has led to the development of the National Missing and Unidentified System (NamUs), which is currently sponsored by the National Institute of Justice and the Department of Justice.

According to the National Missing and Unidentified Persons System (NAMUS), there are presently 145 sets of unidentified remains in North Carolina (as of February 2023). However, it is currently unclear exactly how many sets of unidentified human remains are being curated in North Carolina medical examiner offices, as they may not have all been entered into NamUs. Additionally, while most, if not all, of these individuals have been examined by a forensic pathologist, it is unclear how many of these individuals particularly the older cold cases have been examined by a forensic anthropologist or other medicolegal experts.

Death investigation in North Carolina is performed by a statewide medical examiner system. The initial investigation is performed by local medical examiners who are appointed to work in one or more of the 100 counties in the state. Most, but not all, of the individuals performing this duty have advanced medical training. Cases that require detailed examination (e.g., internal autopsies) are sent to one of nine regional pathology centers located throughout the state. While there are a handful of forensic anthropologists certified by the American Board of Forensic Anthropology (ABFA) located in North Carolina, none of them are employed at any of the regional pathology centers. Instead, forensic anthropology casework in NC is initiated either by law enforcement or medical examiners on a case by case basis by contacting the forensic anthropologists in the state who are employed at institutions of higher learning.

Until our pilot project was funded by a University of North Carolina (UNC) Inter-instituitional grant, there was no standardized protocol for the investigation of decomposed or skeletonized remains in North Carolina. Due to a lack of well-preserved soft tissue in these cases, autopsies are largely ineffective, often producing inconclusive results. Because of this, regional pathologists use different experts with varying levels of experience for consultation and identification. In addition, there is little communication between the regional offices and the Office of the Chief Medical Examiner (the central office, located in Raleigh, NC) concerning unidentified cases. This lack of standardized investigative protocols and communication created an issue of generating an increasingly large backlog of unidentified cases needing additional analysis and investigation.

The inability to identify a set of human remains may occur for many reasons. From an organizational standpoint, there must be staff investigating the case, to begin with. As many offices are understaffed/underfunded, many sets of remains likely remain unidentified simply because there are not sufficient resources to perform the investigation. From an evidentiary standpoint, the most important (and most obvious) factors affecting the ability to reach an identification are (1) having some evidence of who the unidentified decedent *could* be and (2) having antemortem records of sufficient quality to compare to the unidentified remains. In cases where human skeletal remains are recovered with no associated evidence, it is much more difficult to generate a reasonable list of missing individuals to compare the unidentified remains to make an identification. Additionally, without comparative antemortem records from the known, missing individual, such as dental radiographs; medical radiographs, or other medical records; or a DNA reference sample, even if there is evidence suggestive of an identity for an unknown set of remains, an actual identification may not be possible.

There are of course many other possible contributing factors that may prevent, or delay, an identification from being made, including: the decedent not being reported missing; lack of interagency communication (i.e., lack of communication/use of databases); lack of access/use of proper experts (i.e., lack of funding to pay for required professional analysis); incorrect analytical conclusions leading investigators to rule out the actual missing individual; and structural violence against marginalized groups (i.e., investigators not putting in enough effort to reach an identification because of someone's perceived identity, as has been documented for sex workers and BIPOC individuals in the United States (Goad, 2020).

4. A unified approach to the investigation of unidentified remains using forensic anthropology

The majority of effort in cold case investigations falls upon law enforcement, which may or may not have some type of cold case investigation team (Adcock & Stein, 2015). However, here we will be focusing on the scientific components of a cold case investigation, in particular, scientific approaches to making an identification of an unknown set of remains. There is a growing call for more innovative and collaborative approaches to cold case investigations (Chapman et al., 2020; Chattopadhyay et al., 2013; Fox et al., 2020; Goad, 2020; Zubanska & Knut, 2018). As part of this call, Goad (2020), recently encouraged forensic anthropologists to become more involved in the humanitarian crisis of the unidentified in the United States particularly because so many of these unidentified individuals come from marginalized populations, and anthropology is rooted in understanding structural violence and advocating for the marginalized. Forensic anthropologists are often considered to be the most qualified professionals when it comes to the identification of unknown decedents, not just regarding their general anthropological education (Goad, 2020), but also in terms of their understanding of human biological diversity and its relationship to individualizing characteristics (de Boer et al., 2019; Kahana & Hiss, 2009). As such, it is not uncommon for forensic anthropologists to have leadership roles in large projects attempting to identify unknown decedents. Typically, such projects are the result of some form of disaster, either natural (e.g., landslides, earthquakes, tsunamis), accidental (e.g., building collapses, plane crashes), or resulting from violence (e.g., genocide in Srebrenica, Bosnia, and Herzegovina, the 9/11 terrorist attack in the United States). However, as others have argued (Ritter, 2007), mounting numbers of unidentified individuals could also be considered a disaster or at least a problem that could lead to a disaster-like scenario.

The authors (NVP and AHR, both ABFA-certified forensic anthropologists) recently began a pilot project in North Carolina in an attempt to directly address unidentified cold cases in the state. This project was started to unify and standardize the practice of forensic anthropology in North Carolina, within the larger context of identifying unknown cold cases in the state as a proof of concept. As part of this forensic anthropology partnership, the forensic anthropology programs at North Carolina State University (NCSU) and Western Carolina University (WCU) synchronized their standard operating procedures (SOPs); created a template for forensic anthropology reporting and peer review; established routine communications between program faculty and students in regard to casework analysis, review, and training using collaboration software (in this case, Smartsheet); and began to generate a network of communication between the NCSU, WCU, the North Carolina medical examiner system, and various law enforcement agencies.

5. The importance of reanalyzing cold cases

While basic analyses were available for some of the North Carolina cold cases, many of these biological profiles (i.e., estimates of age, population affinity, sex, and stature) were suspect as they were performed by inexperienced osteologists (not certified forensic anthropologists) using outdated methods. Additionally, the authors were concerned that other, potentially individualizing skeletal information may have been overlooked in these older, more superficial analyses. Further, not all of these cases had been added to the NamUs unidentified database, nor did they all have DNA reference samples submitted to NamUS. Thus, this project worked with staff at the State Medical Examiner office to rectify these issues in NamUS, creating and submitting updated biological profiles, collating individualizing information, and collecting and submitting DNA samples.

In addition to the forensic anthropological reanalysis, and data entry/updating of NamUS, this project utilized forensic genealogy. Forensic genealogy, also referred to as Investigative Genetic Genealogy (IGG), involves the use of genetic information from unknown individuals typically being compared to large databases of known genetic information produced from direct-to-consumer genetic testing, paired with family tree information (Kling et al., 2021). Unlike national DNA databases, which typically include 16–22 autosomal STRs, and thus only provide possible links to close genetic relatives (e.g., siblings, parents, cousins, aunts, uncles), direct-to-consumer genetic tests provide 600,000 SNPs, which allows for much greater potential in making genetic links (Kling et al., 2021). The pairing of this high-resolution genetic data with family tree information thus allows for the possible connection of an unknown individual to distant genetic relatives. The forensic genealogist can then narrow down the list of potential matches even further based on additional information, such as: the context of the case; the biological profile; individualizing characteristics; isotopic data; etc. Currently, the most famous case that utilized forensic genealogy is that of the Golden State Killer (Phillips, 2018; Wickenheiser, 2019). However, the identification of skeletal remains found in a cave in 1979 and 1991 as Joseph Henry Loveless, an outlaw last seen in 1916, is also an excellent example of the extent to which distant relatives and circumstantial evidence may result in an identification (Thompson, 2020).

6. Cold case re-evaluation example

Our pilot initiative resulted in the formation of a multidisciplinary/multiagency team that included forensic anthropology (including isotopic analyses), medical examiners, law enforcement investigations, and forensic genealogy. This proof-of-concept project succeeded in identifying six unidentified decedents to date, with death years ranging from 1976 to 2019 using our collaborative multipronged approach.

6.1 Michael Joe Wesley Baker—year of discovery 2005

This case is an example of the advantage of reanalyzing cold cases using a multidisciplinary approach, which is presented to demonstrate the broader benefit of this project. On November 11, 2005 incomplete, unidentified skeletal remains were discovered in an abandoned burned-out house by children playing in Harnett County, North Carolina. According to the fire marshall, the abandoned house had burned in December 2003, but the debris was never cleared.

6.2 Forensic anthropological analysis

As part of the protocols described above, the remains found in 2005 were reanalyzed. Our team began systematically re-examining the skeletal remains housed by the Office of the Chief Medical Examiner in an effort to clear some of the backlog of unidentified human remains in North Carolina.

6.2.1 Taphonomic alteration

The skeleton was represented by approximately 52% of the skeletal elements. Charring was exhibited on ~6%, and ~22% of the recovered skeletal material exhibited calcination. Fig. 8.1 diagrams the carbonization and calcination burn patterns. The thermal alteration includes: the destruction of the knee (i.e., distal femora, patellae, and proximal tibiae) and left elbow (i.e., distal humerus and proximal ulnae and radii). The range of carbonization to calcination of the face suggests that the decedent was most likely in a flexed position with the posterior structures protected from the thermal source with the lower limbs and distal upper limbs exposed to high temperatures based on the amount of calcination in that area.

6.2.2 Biological profile

Using standard forensic anthropological methods, the remains were estimated to belong to a European American male between the ages of 24 and 35 years of age with a mean stature of 5 feet 11.3 inches. Because the remains had significant thermal alteration ante- and perimortem trauma was not observable on the fragmented remains.

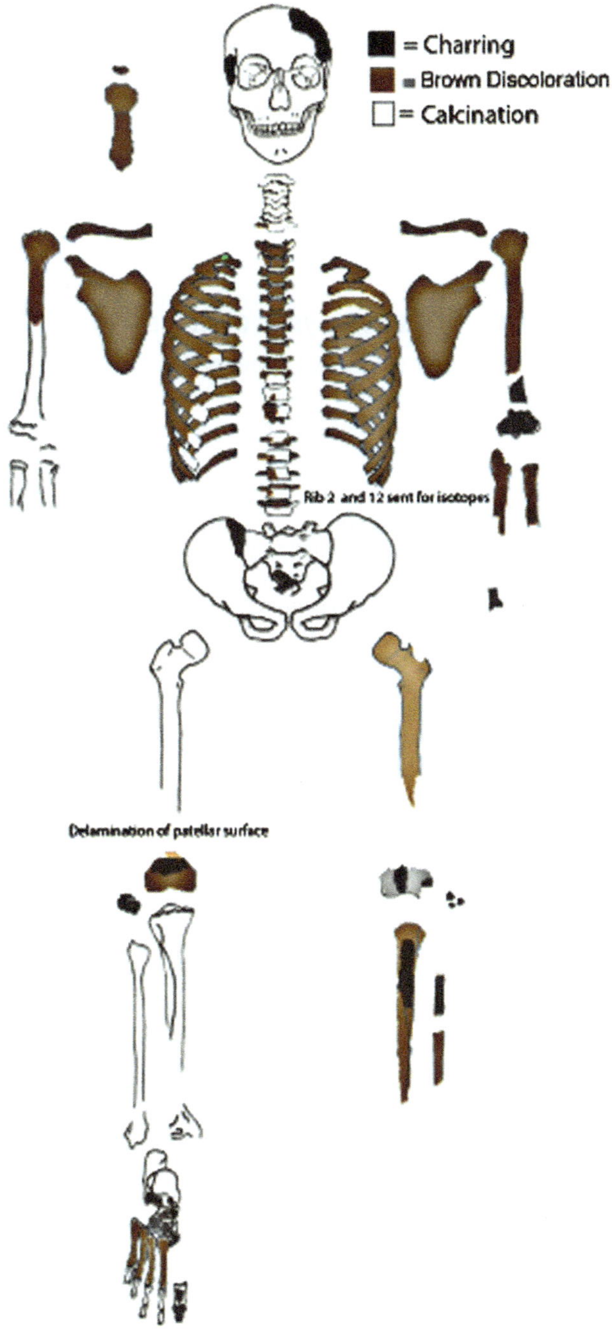

FIGURE 8.1

Taphonomic diagram showing absent structures, calcination is present in white, blue-gray, and black indicate charring and carbonization, respectively. Other discoloration not related to thermal alteration is in brown.

Credit: Ann Ross.

6.2.3 Isotopic analysis

To elucidate whether the remains were native to North Carolina, the continental US, or foreign-born individual, a right maxillary molar and the left second rib were sent out for stable and heavy isotope analysis including Carbon (δ13C), oxygen (δ18O), strontium (87Sr/86Sr), and lead (206Pb/204 Pb 207Pb/204 Pb, 208Pb/204 Pb). Because permanent teeth once formed do not remodel during the lifespan, these teeth provide a reference to childhood residency. Bone on the other hand remodels throughout the lifespan, depending on the skeletal element sampled, it can provide information regarding where a decedent spent their recent years and provide useful information whether the decedent was local or not with regards to a geographic region (please see Chapter 9 by Ammer and colleagues for detailed information). Based on the results of the analysis and the isotopic signatures it suggested that the decedent was born in the US and spent their childhood in the southern region of the US such as central to east Texas or central to south Florida and did not reside in North Carolina for an extended period prior to death.

6.3 Forensic genetic genealogy

As part of the new unidentified human remains protocol cases were selected for IGG that met the criteria of having forensic anthropology reexamination and sufficient investigative evidence. Part of this protocol also includes entering case information into NamUS, and samples were sent in for DNA analysis. Another bone sample (left femoral fragment) was submitted for additional DNA as no results were obtained from the original sample entered in CODIS. IGG requires a single nucleotide polymorphism (SNP) profile that can generate up to hundreds of thousands of SNPs, while CODIS uses short-tandem repeat or STR (Sorrell et al., 2022). FGG differs from familial DNA searching in that IGG is referenced against private genealogy databases of both close and distant relatives while familial DNA searches CODIS for biological relatives (Sorrell et al., 2022).

6.4 Identification and case resolution

It is important to utilize this multipronged approach as forensic anthropological estimation including isotopic analysis and investigations inform the forensic genealogists while building the family trees (Fig. 8.2).

Through this process a full biological sibling was found to our unidentified decedent, who was then able to be identified as Michael Joe Wesley Baker. Michael Joe Wesley Baker was 24 years old when he was last seen alive in 2003 (DOB February 15, 1979), was born in Bexar Texas, and had only moved to North Carolina a year or two before his death.

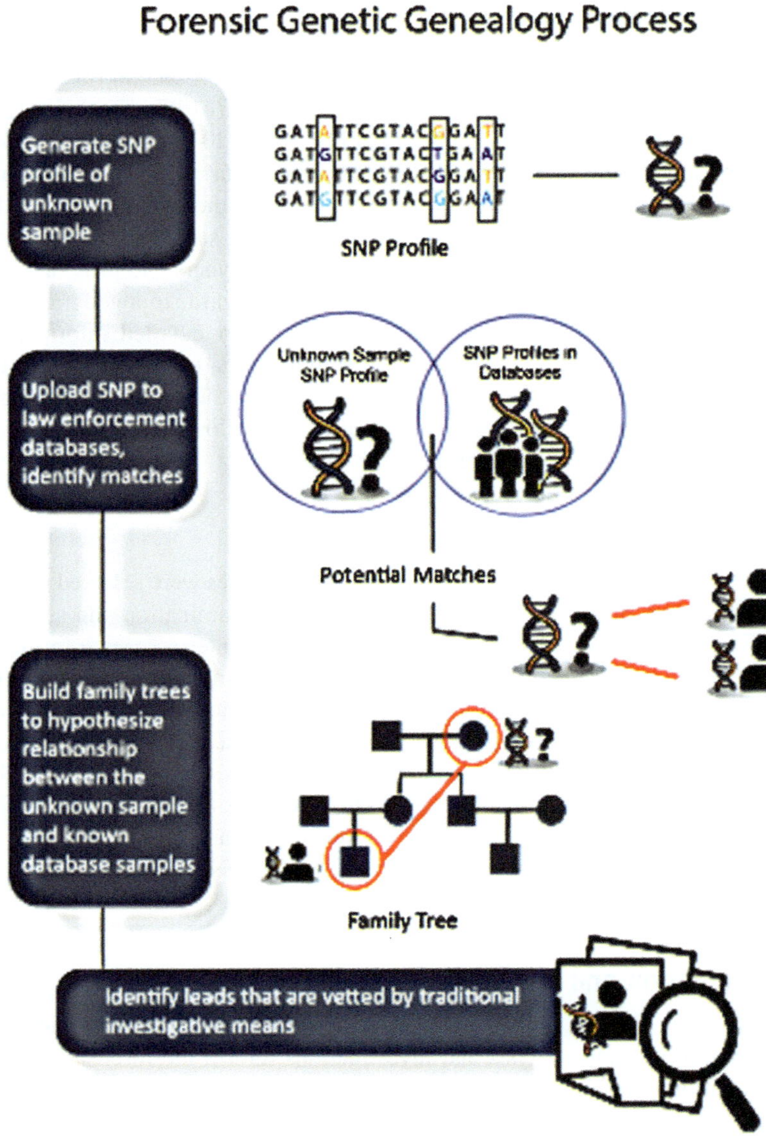

FIGURE 8.2

Forensic genetic genealogy (FGG) steps.

Credit: Public Domain-All material appearing in this publication is in the public domain and may be reproduced or copied without permission from the U.S. Department of Justice (DOJ).

6.5 Investigation

The investigation by Harnett County Sherriff's Department revealed that Michael Joe Wesley Baker left his girlfriend's house in November 2003, which was a close distance from the burned-out building where his remains were found in 2005, and 2 weeks prior had received a speeding ticket. His sister did not submit a missing person's report until 2007 as the family was estranged.

Acknowledgments

Thanks to the University of North Carolina system for supporting this work through a 2019 Interinstitutional Planning Grant. Additional thanks to the North Carolina Office of the Chief Medical Examiner and to Clyde Gibbs for his assistance with facilitating the cold case analyses.

References

Adcock, J. M., & Stein, S. L. (2015). *Cold cases: Evaluation models with follow-up strategies for investigators*. Boca Raton: CRC Press.

Berryman, Hugh E., & Lanfear, Alicja K. (2012). Forensic anthropologists in medical examiner's and Coroner's offices: A history. In D. Dirkmaat (Ed.), *A companion to forensic anthropology*. Malden, MA: John Wiley & Sons, Ltd.

de Boer, H. H., Blau, S., Delabarde, T., & Hackman, L. (2019). The role of forensic anthropology in disaster victim identification (DVI): Recent developments and future prospects. *Forensic Sciences Research, 4*(4), 303–315.

Chapman, B., Keatley, D., Oatley, G., Coumbaros, J., & Maker, G. (2020). A review and recommendation for the integration of forensic expertise within police cold case reviews. *Journal of Criminal Psychology, 10*(2), 79–91.

Chattopadhyay, S., Shee, B., & Sukul, B. (2013). Unidentified bodies at autopsy – a disaster in disguise. *Egyptian Journal of Food Science, 3*, 112–115.

Christensen, A. M., Passalacqua, N. V., Schmunk, G. A., Fudenberg, J., Hartnett, K., Mitchell, R. A., Love, J. C., deJong, J., & Petaros, A. (2015). The value and availability of forensic anthropological consultation in medicolegal death investigations. *Forensic Science, Medicine and Pathology, 11*(3), 438–441, 2015.

Fox, B., Miley, L. N., Allen, S., Boness, J., Dodge, C., Khachatryan, N., Lyle, M., McKinley, S., Peake, J., & Rozo, M. (2020). Law enforcement and academics working together on cold case investigations: Lessons learned and paths forward. *Journal of Criminal Psychology, 10*(2), 93–111.

Goad, G. (2020). Expanding humanitarian forensic action: An approach to U.S. cold cases. *Forensic Anthropology, 3*(1), 50–58.

Hanzlick, R. L. (2014). A perspective on medicolegal death investigation in the United States: 2013. *Academic Forensic Pathology, 4*(1), 2–9.

Hanzlick, R. L., & Fudenberg, J. (2014). Coroner versus medical examiner systems: Can we end the debate? *Academic Forensic Pathology, 4*(1), 10–17.

Kahana, T., & Hiss, J. (2009). The role of forensic anthropology in mass fatality incidents management. *Forensic Science Policy & Management: International Journal, 1*(3), 144–149.

Kemp, W. L. (2014). Forensic pathologist salaries in the United States: The results of internet data collection. *Academic Forensic Pathology, 4*, 505–513.

Kling, D., Phillips, C., Kennett, D., & Tillmar, A. (2021). Investigative genetic genealogy: Current methods, knowledge and practice. *Forensic Science International: Genetics, 52*, 1–23.

NCIC Missing Person and Unidentified Person Statistics. (2021). https://www.fbi.gov/file-repository/2021-ncic-missing-person-and-unidentified-personstatistics.pdf/view.

Passalacqua, N. V., Chu, E. Y., & Pilloud, M. A. (2020). Salaries in forensic anthropology and academic anthropology. *Forensic Anthropology, 3*(2), 120–131.

Passalacqua, N. V., Pilloud, M. A., & Philbin, C. S. (2021). Caseloads in forensic anthropology. In *Presented at the American academy of forensic sciences 73rd annual meeting* (Houston, TX).

Phillips, C. (2018). The Golden State Killer investigation and the nascent field of forensic genealogy. *Forensic Science International: Genetics, 36*, 186–188.

Pilloud, M. A., Passalacqua, N. V., & Philbin, C. S. (2022). Caseloads in forensic anthropology. *American Journal of Biological Anthropology, 177*, 556–565.

Ritter, N. (2007). *Missing persons and unidentified remains: The nation's silent mass disaster* (Vol. 256, pp. 2–7). National Institute of Justice Journal.

Sorrell, Cody, Rodriguez, Ashley, Shute, Rebecca, Shannon, Krauss, & Melton, Patricia (September 2022). An introduction to forensic genetic genealogy technology for forensic science service providers. In *Forensic technology center of excellence*. U.S. Department of Justice, National Institute of Justice, Office of Investigative and Forensic Sciences.

Thomas, L. C. (2014). Coroner duties that differ from typical medical examiner duties. *Academic Forensic Pathology, 4*(1), 11–23.

Thompson, N. (2020). *DNA detectives are using new tools to solve decades-old cold cases*. Wired Magazine. https://www.wired.co.uk/article/forensic-genealogy-dna-cold-cases.

Wickenheiser, R. A. (2019). Forensic genealogy, bioethics, and the golden state killer case. *Forensic Science International: Synergy, 1*, 114–125.

Zubanska, M., & Knut, P. (2018). Cold cases from the past, modern forensic tools and police cold case units, or crimen grave non potest esse impunible – Part II. *Issues of Forensic Science, 299*(1), 61–71.

CHAPTER

9 Forensic isotope provenancing for undocumented border crosser human remains: Application, overview, and case studies

Saskia Ammer[1], Robyn Kramer[2], Eric Bartelink[3]

[1]*University of Coimbra, Coimbra, Portugal;* [2]*University of Otago, Dunedin, New Zealand;* [3]*California State University, Chico, Chico, CA, United States*

1. Introduction

One major role of forensic anthropology is the identification of human remains, primarily focusing on establishing a biological profile for the deceased individual in question. The biological profile consists of age, ancestry, sex, stature, as well as other identifying aspects such as antemortem trauma, pathological conditions, and other individualizing characteristics. Often, establishing a biological profile can be a tedious task as the remains may be significantly fragmented, degraded, or missing due to environmental and taphonomic processes. Furthermore, as the world is becoming more and more globalized, it is becoming increasingly difficult to determine the ancestry or the potential place of origin of an unidentified individual. Consequently, much of the difficulty associated with identifying the dead, and undocumented border crossers (UBCs) in particular, stems from an inability to narrow down the search criteria for missing persons' reports. Therefore, investigators and forensic anthropologists need sophisticated tools to aid identification efforts, which most recently have involved the use of biomolecular and biogeochemical sciences into their approaches.

Thus far, the "Holy Grail" in identification efforts has been DNA typing. While DNA is the most prominent method of establishing the identity of an individual, it is oftentimes not possible. DNA typing is often too expensive or ineffective when remains are too degraded for DNA extraction. Furthermore, familial reference DNA samples may not be available in the federal Combined DNA Index System (CODIS) database and therefore cannot be compared with the forensic samples collected from the deceased individual. This, especially, is a challenge when dealing with the identification of UBCs whose families may be hesitant to submit their DNA as a

Methodological and Technological Advances in Death Investigations. https://doi.org/10.1016/B978-0-12-819394-5.00013-4

reference sample for fear of deportation. Forensic anthropologists and nongovernmental organizations, like Colibrí Center for Human Rights (www.colibricenter.org), South Texas Human Rights Center (www.southtexashumanrights.org), and the Argentine Forensic Anthropology Team (www.EAAF.org) work with the public to provide a safe environment to submit missing person reports and DNA reference samples. However, even if these familial DNA samples are collected, they still cannot be uploaded into CODIS since they were not collected by the approved law enforcement authorities.

Isotope analysis has proven to be a useful and reliable tool for aiding identification. The isotopic compositions of human bones, teeth, and hair are useful biomarkers for reconstructing the likely locations and movements of individuals (Bartelink et al., 2018a; Ehleringer et al., 2008). Isotope data can assist the identification effort for unidentified individuals by predicting the geographic region-of-origin and adding the criteria of "location of residence" to biological profiles and supporting case files. This can allow for the filtering of missing person reports that do not fit the criteria for the unidentified individual. For example, a family from Guatemala searching for their lost loved one could filter out the cases that indicate isotopic residential histories that are inconsistent with Guatemala. Even though various disciplines have employed isotope analysis for research, forensic anthropologists have only recently begun to utilize these methods in actual casework. To the authors' knowledge, combining forensic anthropology with cutting-edge techniques in chemistry to resolve large-scale humanitarian identification efforts is rare.

1.1 The humanitarian issue at hand

In 1948, the United Nations established the Declaration of Human Rights (Universal Declaration of Human Rights (217 [III] A), 1948). Among the many enumerated rights, the declaration established that it is a human right to be treated with dignity and that "everyone has the right to recognition everywhere as a person before the law" Rights (United Nations General Assembly 1948: Article 6). Though not explicitly stated by the United Nations, these rights are granted during life and remain in effect after death. Therefore, every person, living or dead, has the right to be recognized and treated with dignity and respect.

Between 1998 and 2017, at least 7216 people lost their lives attempting to cross the border from Mexico into the United States (Colibrí Center for Human Rights, 2018). The total number of recorded migrant deaths by the Human Borders' "Arizona Open GIS Initiative for Deceased Migrants" is 3205 (Fig. 9.1). It is important to note that these numbers only represent the deaths recorded in Arizona and not the deaths in the other three border states of California, New Mexico, and Texas. Furthermore, the dark number of migrant deaths along the Mexico-U.S. border is likely significantly higher because many missing (and likely deceased) are never found. In 2016, 170 cases were recorded, and in 2019,163 cases were documented by the initiative (Figs. 9.2 and 9.3). During the years of 2017 and 2018, the numbers were lower, at slightly above 130 per year. It is predicted that the border will only

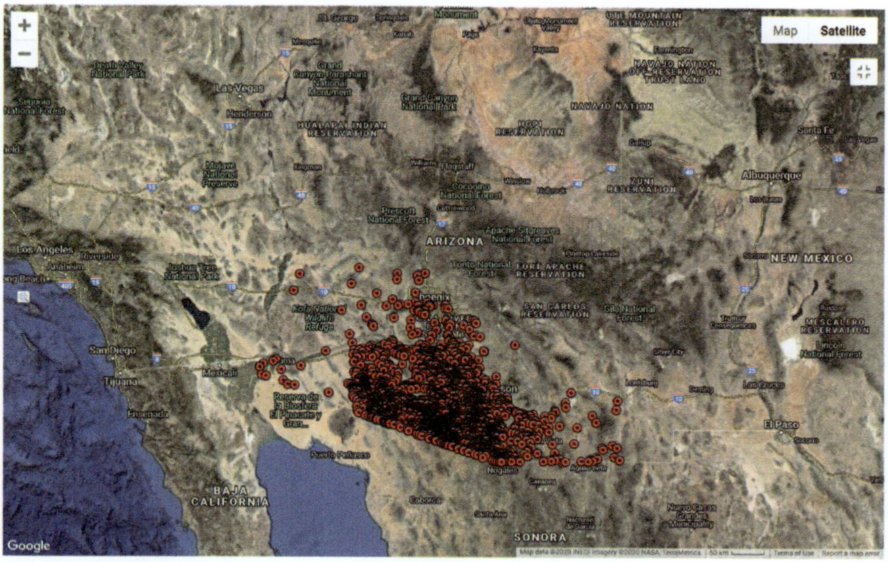

FIGURE 9.1

Map of migrant mortality in Arizona—all recorded migrant deaths since 1981 (Humane Borders Inc., 2020).

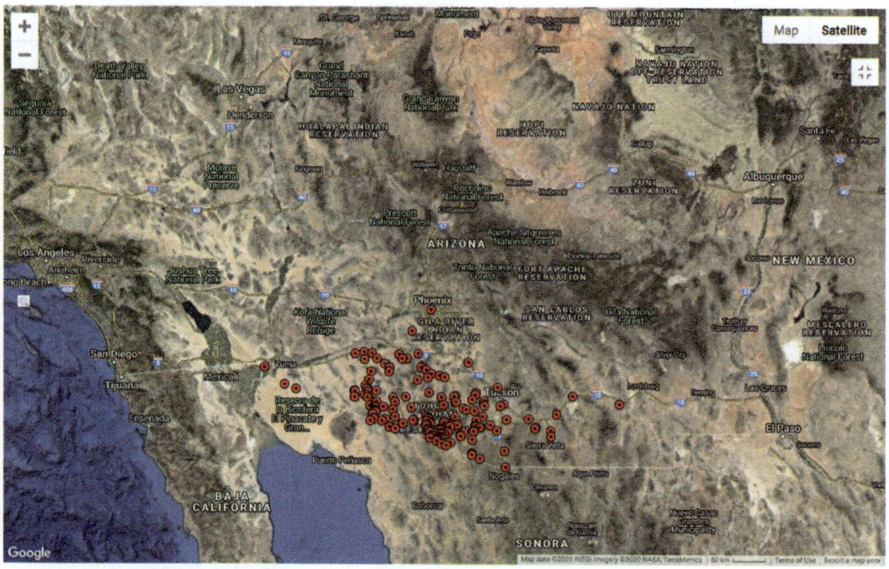

FIGURE 9.2

Map of migrant mortality in Arizona—recorded migrant deaths of 2016 (Humane Borders Inc., 2020).

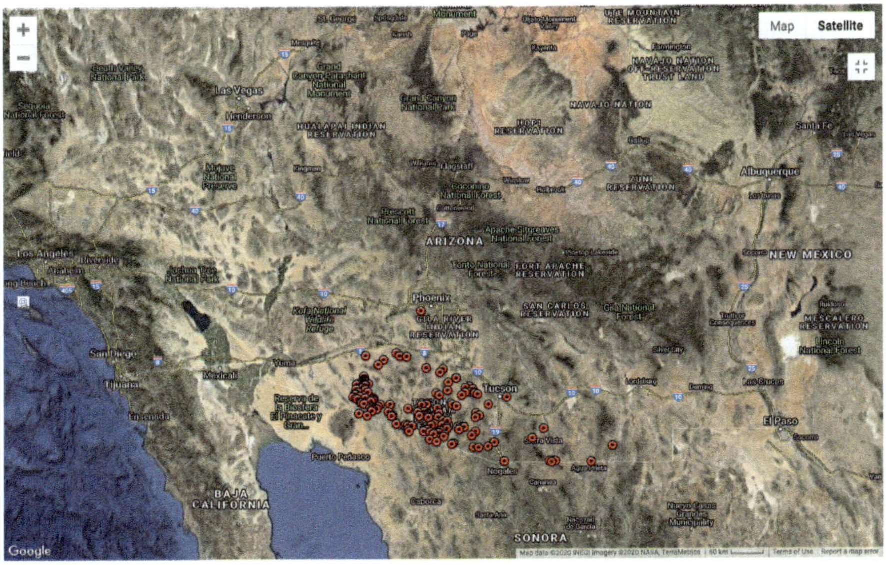

FIGURE 9.3

Map of migrant mortality in Arizona—recorded migrant deaths of 2019 (Humane Borders Inc., 2020).

become more deadly. Recently, a volunteer for the organization *No More Deaths/No Mas Muertes* was standing retrial for harboring charges, following a previous mistrial, after aiding two migrants at the organization's medical camp (arrested in January 2018, on trial and retrial in 2019). The volunteer ended up not being found not guilty. Nonetheless, it is expected that this trial will have a negative impact on humanitarian aid and is seen as an intimidation strategy by the United States government. John Fife, one of the founders of *No More Deaths*, commented that:

> *Since 2013, the Tucson sector of the Border Patrol has had a written agreement with* No More Deaths *(NMD) that they will respect the NMD camp as a medical facility under the international Red Cross standards, which prohibit government interference with humanitarian aid centers. That agreement now has been violated by the Border Patrol under the most suspicious circumstances. The Border Patrol acknowledged that they tracked a group for 18 miles, but only after the migrants sought medical treatment did the Border Patrol try to arrest them. The choice to interdict these people only after they entered the No More Deaths' camp is direct evidence that this was a direct attack on humanitarian aid. At the same time, the weather forecast is for record-setting deadly temperatures.*
>
> **No More Deaths/No Mas Muertes (2017).**

Hundreds of unidentified deceased migrants are found within the United States along the Mexico-U.S. border each year and the number has increased over the past decade. To understand the complexity of the issue at hand, it is important to comprehend why the border has become so dangerous and deadly. The deaths and disappearance of thousands of migrants are a direct result of border security measures and economic agreements. The Clinton Administration signed the North American Free Trade Agreement (NAFTA), a free trade agreement between Canada, the United States, and Mexico, that went into effect January 1, 1994. NAFTA was presented as an initiative to reduce the unauthorized immigration at the Mexico-U.S. border by creating jobs in Mexico. Instead, the implementation of NAFTA had disastrous effects on the economy of Mexico and culminated in the loss of millions of jobs (de León, 2015). As the rate of illegal immigration across the border elevated, the U.S. Border Patrol increased their border security and enforcement policies through initiatives such as Operation Gatekeeper in San Diego, California; Operation Safeguard in southern Arizona; Operation Hold the Line in El Paso, Texas; and Operation Rio Grande in south Texas (de León, 2015).

Enforcement of increased border security was centralized to larger communities and cities, which created a "funnel effect" for migrants seeking to cross the Mexico-U.S. border. Instead of crossing into the safe territories of the border, like San Diego or El Paso, the border-crossing movement was funneled into the remote, uninhabited desert. This is a policy now referred to as "prevention through deterrence" (de León, 2015; Spradley et al., 2019) where the harsh desert environment acts as a natural deterrent and, supposedly prevents border crossings. However, again, the policies had adverse effects. Worsening economic conditions and high rates of violence have provided individuals with little choice than to risk crossing the Mexico-U.S. border in search for economic opportunities or asylum (Illingworth, 2015). Due to the increased border security enforcement and militarization of the urban ports of entry, the number of migrant deaths in the Sonoran desert of Arizona increased from an annual average of 12 deaths to 170 each year (Illingworth, 2015). De León (2015) argues that the U.S. immigration policies and enforcement practices are a form of structural violence because they inflict both physical and emotional trauma and target a particular group of people, in this case migrants from Mexico and Central America. The structural violence is inflicted indirectly as it is cloaked behind a curtain of federal policies and border security "operations" ensuring that the trauma and deaths of thousands of migrants appear to be the result of natural and unavoidable circumstances (de León, 2015).

The funneling of migrants into high-risk regions of the Mexico-U.S. border has resulted in a tremendous increase in the number of deaths in the deserts and mountainous regions of border-states. In the poorer counties of southern Texas, human remains recovered along the border were often buried without autopsies, formal investigations, or even attempts at scientific identification until recently. These small counties (e.g., Brooks County, Starr County, etc.) often lack medical examiners, forensically trained coroners, and funds to implement identification efforts. In Arizona, however, migrant deaths are investigated thoroughly, and as of 2019, two forensic anthropologists are employed by the Pima County Office of the Medical Examiner (PCOME) in Tucson to focus on unidentified migrant cases.

Several organizations and institutions, such as the Colibrí Center for Human Rights (CCHR), Texas State University's Operation Identification (OpID), the PCOME, and the Forensic Border Coalition aid the identification efforts of deceased migrants with hopes of returning the remains of the deceased to their next of kin. The efforts to repatriate the remains to their families are primarily hindered by the inability to restrict the search area to smaller, manageable, and more probable locations.

Previous research has found that a migrant's place of origin can play a major role in the unauthorized crossing experience. For instance, 86% of all identified decedents recovered in Arizona and identified by PCOME are Mexican nationals. Among those positively identified, migrants from central Mexico (24%) were the most prevalent, followed by those from southern Mexico (20%), west-central Mexico (16%), and northern Mexico (14%) (Anderson & Parks, 2008; Martinez et al., 2015; Massey et al., 2002). In contrast, Texas State University's Operation Identification (OpID) reports that more individuals with Central American nationalities are recovered in southern Texas than Mexican nationals (Kramer, 2018; Spradley et al., 2019).

While this chapter focuses on the humanitarian crises along the Mexico–U.S. border, there are many other crises in which isotope analysis for potential region of origin determination could be helpful. According to the United Nations High Commissioner for Refugees (2019), 70.8 million people are currently being forcibly displaced worldwide. As one example, around 18,000 people have been reported missing or deceased between 2014 and 2018 on the Mediterranean route to Europe. It is important to note that this only includes the Mediterranean route and does not include the Baltic route, which is known to be just as deadly during the winter months. Furthermore, it can be expected that the number of deaths is much higher than what is reported by the UN Refugee Agency as many missing persons cases are never reported (to the correct authorities) and will, therefore, remain unaccounted for.

Unfortunately, those two highlighted cases of displacement and forced migration are not the only ones. Many others exist and highlight how dire the situations have become for millions around the world, for example in the Democratic Republic of Congo, Nigeria, South Sudan, Venezuela, Central African Republic, Syria, Yemen, Afghanistan, the millions of Rohingya fleeing Myanmar, and the general emergency situation in Central America. Forced displacement and violence lead to thousands of unidentified deceased migrants within certain regions and countries. For instance, Mexico and Central American countries are not only faced with missing (and unidentified) undocumented border crossers but also with "forced missing" within countries that experience violence associated with cartels and gang activity. This issue has caught the attention of the world through the case of the abducted and still missing 43 students from a college in Ayotzinapa (Guerrero) (Wilkinson, 2018). Similarly, Brazil faces some of the highest murder rates in the world. According to the United Nations Office on Drugs and Crime (2019), about 1.2 million people died as a result of intentional homicide in Brazil between the years of 1991 and 2017, many of whom have not been identified.

While current humanitarian crises around the world deserve attention from scientists and forensic investigations, there are also past conflicts that have left thousands missing and unidentified. Many families are still waiting for information on their loved ones lost during past wars. The Defense POW/MIA Accounting Agency (DPAA) aims to identify and account for the missing personnel and have government-funded laboratories in Hawaii and Nebraska. The DPAA has recently started to employ isotopic analysis to aid the identification of missing soldiers (Bartelink et al., 2014).

1.2 Pima County office of the medical examiner (PCOME) and Operation Identification (OpID): Aiding the humanitarian crisis at the Mexico—U.S. Border

The PCOME is a Medical Examiner and Forensic Science Center that provides death investigation services for Pima County, Arizona. The PCOME provides services for four additional counties aside from Pima County, stretching over the entirety of the Arizona—Mexico border. Consequently, this medical examiner's office covers approximately 95% of all reported undocumented migrant deaths in Arizona.

Dr. Bruce Anderson, a forensic anthropologist at PCOME, has been working for over a decade on identifying deceased UBCs in conjunction with cultural anthropologists. This collaboration, headed by Dr. Robin Reineke, led to the founding of the Colibrí Center for Human Rights. Colibrí is a not-for-profit, nongovernmental organization dedicated to ending the loss of life and suffering of undocumented migrants on the Mexico—U.S. border. Colibrí is a family advocacy organization that collects missing persons' reports and DNA samples from relatives of missing migrants in an attempt to match data, build a community, and help raise consciousness about this human rights crisis (Colibrí Center for Human Rights, 2018; Illingworth, 2015).

In Texas, Dr. Kate Spradley is the director of Operation Identification (OpID), an organization nested within the Forensic Anthropology Center at Texas State University. The major objective of OpID is to identify and repatriate the skeletal remains of undocumented deceased Latin American migrants recovered in south Texas. Since 2013, OpID has performed numerous exhumations of deceased Latin American migrants that were buried as unidentified remains in cemeteries within Brooks, Starr, and Cameron counties in south Texas. Skeletal remains recovered during these exhumations are collected, analyzed, and temporarily stored at Texas State University until they are identified and repatriated to their families. The forensic anthropological data derived from the skeletal analyses are used to construct "Unidentified Persons" profiles on the National Missing and Unidentified Persons (NamUs) database (https://www.namus.gov/UnidentifiedPersons/Search). Friends and families of missing persons can search through missing persons, unidentified, and unclaimed case reports in the NamUs database to search for their loved ones. NamUs is a free and secure online database that is open to the public and offers free forensic services nationwide to aid in the identification of unidentified human remains (see Chapter 8 for a discussion on unidentified human skeletal remains protocols established in North Carolina).

These organizations and many others (Argentine Forensic Anthropology Team, South Texas Human Rights Center, etc.) have joined together in an agreement to share information concerning migrant deaths with the goal of increasing the number of positive identifications and to better understand the scope and impact of migrant deaths (Anderson & Spradley, 2016; Spradley, 2014).

1.3 Issues with DNA typing

As mentioned above, DNA typing is often too expensive, too time intensive or ineffective when remains are too degraded for DNA extraction. Furthermore, DNA typing and comparison is often not possible in investigations of UBCs for various reasons. The University of North Texas Center for Human Identification (UNTCHI) is a federally funded and accredited forensic laboratory that has handled many of the unidentified and missing persons samples in the United States (University of North Texas Center for Human Identification, 2019). In Texas, the Criminal Code of Procedures explains that all unidentified forensic cases require a formal investigation with DNA samples taken and sent to a state lab (UNTCHI) for analysis and inclusion in the federal DNA databases (Spradley et al., 2019).

Laws concerning unidentified human remains vary by state and, frequently, local investigators do not collect DNA samples because there has been a lack of awareness of the law by small, poorly equipped county law enforcement agencies, and if the person found is a presumed migrant, they may not be considered a priority. Moreover, DNA databases present a significant issue. When DNA is collected, it is submitted to the CODIS, a genetic database run by U.S. Federal Bureau of Investigation (FBI) (Federal Bureau of Investigation, 2020a, 2020b). CODIS has two databases: (1) a criminal database containing genetic information for offenders and DNA collected at crime scenes and (2) a database containing DNA samples from missing persons and unidentified human remains. These databases are kept separate to ensure that a person submitting a familial DNA sample is not at risk of arrest if they left their DNA at a crime scene (Federal Bureau of Investigation, 2020a, 2020b). However, many people fear a breach of conduct, wish to maintain their autonomy, and thus refrain from submitting their DNA into the federal database to protect their privacy and their families. Not only are people apprehensive about submitting a familial DNA samples, they oftentimes do not live in the United States and are therefore not able to submit a DNA sample or do not even know that their loved one is missing. Therefore, CODIS will not necessarily have genetic reference data that will assist identification efforts for many deceased and missing migrants.

Furthermore, CODIS is not easily cross-referenced with international genetic databases, which means that DNA submitted by families in another country is difficult to compare with the U.S. database. Lastly, and most importantly, for migrant-related cases, families of missing persons may reside in the U.S. already and fear deportation if their names and their genetic information are submitted into a federal repository (Spradley et al., 2019). For these reasons, many nongovernmental organizations and human rights groups are essential to migrant identification efforts because they provide a safe environment for families to report loved ones missing and provide reference DNA samples that will not be included in the federal system.

Previously, the use of isotope analysis to UBCs has only been applied after all other avenues for evidence collection have failed to produce a positive identification. Instead of using isotope analysis as a last resort, we believe isotope analysis should be incorporated into the standard tissue sampling protocols for unidentified migrant cases. This means that the isotopic data can provide another important line of evidence (i.e., diet composition, country of residence, and migration history) to aid in the identification of the individual. Below, the principles of isotope analysis and its application to forensic science are discussed in further detail to illustrate its contribution to the deceased migrant identification efforts.

2. Isotope principles and basics explained

Stable isotope techniques were first developed in the 1950s to gain an understanding of how different earth elements are chemically altered in kinetic and equilibrium reactions. Later, in the 1970s, they were implemented to reconstruct diet and migration patterns of both living and extinct animals. Isotopic variation in nature results from a phenomenon called fractionation that explains why different food and water sources vary in isotopic composition. Plants and animals record these isotopic variations (which occur due to biological, geological, and environmental processes) in their tissues. Isotopes are thus useful for reconstructing past environments for various fields of research, such as archeology and paleoclimatology, and have recently been used in modern contexts in fields like conservation, ecology, food forensics, and forensic anthropology. Before using isotopes to estimate the geographic origin of unidentified human remains, it is necessary to understand the basic principles of isotopes: what they are and how they are measured.

Isotopes are the name given to a single chemical element, such as oxygen or carbon, that have many naturally occurring forms that vary at the atomic level by the number of protons to neutrons present (Fry, 2006; Hoefs, 2015; Katzenberg, 2007; McMurry & Fay, 2004; Schoeninger & Moore, 1992). The number of neutrons and protons contribute to the overall mass of the atom. Although the isotopes—and their masses—may vary for any element, they retain similar chemical properties to one another because they maintain the same number of protons and electrons (Schoeninger & Moore, 1992; Schwarcz & Schoeninger, 1991). One widely recognized isotope in archeology, ^{14}C, is used in radiocarbon dating to determine the approximate age of organic materials by measuring the amount of ^{14}C present. The so-called carbon-14 isotope is a "heavy" isotope of carbon that differs from the most abundant isotope,

^{12}C, because it has six protons and eight neutrons as opposed to six protons and six neutrons; the ^{13}C isotope has six protons and seven neutrons.

In addition to varying numbers of neutrons, isotopes can be divided into two key groups: stable and unstable (Fry, 2006). Stable isotopes retain their nuclear configuration, while unstable isotopes decay (change their nuclear configuration) over time; ^{14}C is an unstable isotope of carbon while both ^{12}C and ^{13}C are stable isotopes. Stable isotopes are found in all bio-elements (e.g., oxygen, hydrogen, carbon, nitrogen, and sulfur), which are the basic building blocks of matter.

Isotopes are measured as ratios that compare heavy isotopes to light isotopes for an individual element using mass spectrometry (Katzenberg, 2007; Schoeninger & Moore, 1992). For example, oxygen isotope ratios are calculated based on the ratio of the heavy to light stable isotopes $(\boldsymbol{\delta}^{18}O = {}^{18}O/{}^{16}O)$ as compared to an international standard. All isotope ratios have a special notation, delta ($\boldsymbol{\delta}$), that "denote[s] a difference measurement made relative to standards during the actual analysis" (Fry, 2006). The equation below shows the method used to calculate the values for isotopes, in this case, oxygen (Fry, 2006).

$$\delta^{18}O = \left[\left(\left({}^{18}O / {}^{16}O\right)\ \text{sample} / \left({}^{18}O / {}^{16}O\right)\ \text{standard}\right) - 1\right]$$

As the ratio-of-ratios calculated is typically small, $\boldsymbol{\delta}$ values are presented in "per mil," denoted by the ‰ symbol. Calculations using this equation can produce negative or positive values. Computing a negative $\boldsymbol{\delta}$ value means that less of the heavy isotope remains in the standard than the material being measured. Conversely, a positive $\boldsymbol{\delta}$ value means that the sample is enriched in the heavy isotope relative to the standard (Fry, 2006).

2.1 Isotopic variation and fractionation

Stable isotopes of the elements are not uniformly distributed globally. Various isotopes, such as oxygen, find themselves in a state of constant partitioning that results in one isotope of oxygen existing more prevalently compared to another in materials. This process is referred to as fractionation (Hoefs, 2015).

Generally speaking, there are two different types of isotopic fractionation, one occurring in biochemical processes and the other occurring during physio-chemical processes. Both describe processes that affect the relative abundance of isotopes. The fractionation occurring during biochemical processes is influenced by the reduced mass of a system, primary bond strength (energy), and bond length, resulting in the breakage or formation in the rate-determining step of the reaction for the atom or its isotope. The effects associated with this kind of fractionation are called primary or kinetic isotope effects since the degree of fractionation is dependent on the reaction kinetics of the particular chemical reaction (Meier-Augenstein, 2011). Isotopic fractionation during physio-chemical processes refers to fractionation events occurring during diffusion, evaporation, two-phase partitioning, and molecular spectroscopy. This one is influenced by the reduced mass of a system such as different velocities of isotopic molecules of the same compound in the gas phase or difference in absorption of energy (Meier-Augenstein, 2011). The isotopic effects of this kind of fractionation are called secondary or dynamic isotope effects as the chemical bonds are not broken or formed.

A classic example of isotopic fractionation, called the Rayleigh distillation, describes the diminishing presence of heavy isotopes, such as ^{18}O, along with increasing latitudes and altitudes, such as mountainous landscapes (Bentley & Knipper, 2005). Therefore, heavy isotopes of oxygen and hydrogen should be more prevalent near coastal regions that receive the first precipitation events and become gradually depleted as the rain clouds move inland (i.e., the continentality effect). Lighter isotopes are retained in the atmosphere longer and released as rain clouds and storm systems move farther inland, commonly referred to as isotopic depletion (Fry, 2006). Additionally, Brettell et al. (2012) have shown that boiled water is isotopically heavier due to preferential loss of ^{16}O to steam as it evaporates off the initial water sample.

Therefore, the $\delta^{18}O$ values derived from skeletal remains should reflect the diet and water intake of the individual after fractionation events occur during evaporation, condensation, and precipitation (Bentley & Knipper, 2005; Bösl et al., 2006).

Isotopic signatures are not only influenced by nature but are altered in living tissues due to physiological factors. For example, diet, metabolism, nutritional stress, body size, and heat loss mechanisms may also have significant fractionation effects (Daniel Bryant & Froelich, 1995; Kohn et al., 1996). Furthermore, stable isotope analysis is sensitive to any changes in diet, deviations from physiological homeostasis, and metabolic disorders such as osteoporosis, diabetes, or protein stress (Reitsema, 2013, 2015). Furthermore, the "nursing effect" can influence the isotopic signature of humans and other mammals in early forming dental tissue. The metabolic fractionation that occurs within a nursing mother's body leads to a 0.7‰ enrichment in the $\delta^{18}O$ values of breastmilk above the mother's isotopic signature (White et al., 2011; Wright & Schwarcz, 1998, 1999). This enrichment in ^{18}O is then incorporated into the mineralizing teeth of the infant during the nursing period. This phenomenon is especially prominent in the permanent incisors, canines, and first molars and should be taken into consideration when examining these teeth for isotopic signatures.

Generally speaking, the phrase "you are what you eat" summarizes what effect the nutritional influences have on human bodies (Tykot, 2004). The isotopic composition of food sources ingested and water imbibed will be incorporated into the bodily fluids and tissues of an organism. Longinelli (1984) demonstrated that a linear relationship exists ($R = 0.98$) between the isotopic composition of ingested water from the diet and body water. Thus, it is important to consider the time of formation and the rate of remodeling for tissues that will be sampled for isotope analysis to avoid inherent biases with the interpretation of the results.

In the following section, we present overviews for dietary isotopes (carbon, nitrogen, and sulfur), geolocation isotopes (strontium, oxygen, hydrogen, and lead), and an isotope that has potential use in forensic provenancing research (neodymium). Further discussion of isotope fractionation can be found throughout the isotope-related literature (Fry, 2006; Schoeller, 1999; Van Klinken et al., 2002).

2.2 Overview of dietary, geolocation, and novel isotopes

First, the isotopes most commonly known as "dietary isotopes" are discussed which include carbon, nitrogen, and sulfur. Dietary isotopes are well established and have been used extensively in ecological and archeological studies. Then, isotopes that are commonly used for geolocation research (hydrogen, oxygen, strontium, and lead) are reviewed because they are particularly useful for region of origin predictions and assignments. Lastly, a novel isotope, neodymium, is discussed because of its potential contribution to future geolocation research.

2.2.1 Dietary isotopes

2.2.1.1 Carbon (C)

Carbon has 15 known isotopes, of which two are stable and have relative abundances of 98.89% and 1.11% on Earth, respectively (Craig, 1953; Wagner et al., 2018). Carbon isotopes vary in plants as a product of the three different photosynthetic pathways: C_3, C_4, and CAM (Table 9.1). C_3 plants discriminate more against the heavier isotope of carbon (^{13}C) when incorporating CO_2 into their tissues, resulting in more negative $\delta^{13}C$ values than C_4 plants (White et al., 2011). C_3 plants comprise approximately 95% of the earth's plants and include fruits, vegetables, and grains such as wheat and rice (Reitsema, 2015). C_4 plants, on the other hand, do not discriminate as much against ^{13}C when incorporating CO_2 into their tissues, resulting in less negative $\delta^{13}C$ values (White et al., 2011). C_4 plants include corn (maize), sugarcane, amaranth, millet, and sorghum (Reitsema, 2015). The third photosynthetic pathway, crassulacean acid metabolism (CAM), includes plants that can utilize either the C_3 or C_4 pathways depending on environmental factors; CAM plants include pineapples, succulents, and cacti (Reitsema, 2015; Schoeninger & Moore, 1992) and are not typically major components of the human diet.

Studies have shown that in control-fed animals, dietary protein is the primary contributor to bone collagen, whereas products of the entire diet are represented in bone bioiapatite and tooth enamel (Ambrose & Norr, 1993; Tieszen & Fagre, 1993). In humans, an estimated fractionation of 9.5‰ to as much as 11‰ or 12‰ in $\delta^{13}C$ values between diet and bone apatite has been found (Ambrose & Norr, 1993; Hedges, 2003).

Table 9.1 Plant classifications according to their produced stable carbon isotope ranges.

Plant type	$\delta^{13}C$ values	Food examples
C_3 plants	Low $\delta^{13}C$ values	Including fruits, vegetables, and some grains such as wheat and rice
C_4 plants	High $\delta^{13}C$ values	Including corn (maize), sugarcane, millet, sorghum, amaranth
Crassulacean acid metabolism (CAM) plants	Intermediate and overlapping $\delta^{13}C$ values	Pineapple, succulents, and cacti

Adapted from Reitsema (2015).

The differences in photosynthetic pathways of C_3 and C_4 plants and its isotopic effect on skeletal tissues have been outlined by Tykot (2006).

Marine fish, terrestrial animals, and freshwater fish typically display high, intermediate, and low $\delta^{13}C$ values, respectively, owing to fluctuations in atmospheric and aquatic carbon sources (Reitsema, 2015).

2.2.1.2 Nitrogen (N)

Nitrogen is an element that exists as two stable isotopes (^{14}N and ^{15}N) and 14 radioisotopes (Cartigny & Busigny, 2018). The $\delta^{15}N$ isotope values are useful for interpreting and understanding the sources of animal protein that a person consumes during life. Moving up the food chain, $\delta^{15}N$ values become higher due to fractionation during nitrogen metabolism (Meier-Augenstein, 2011; O'Connell et al., 2012; Reitsema, 2015; Steele & Daniel, 1978). Organisms that do not consume animal protein are located on the lower tiers of the food chain and exhibit lower $\delta^{15}N$ values (depleted in ^{15}N), while carnivorous animals are higher in the food chain and exhibit higher $\delta^{15}N$ values (Deniro & Epstein, 1981). Additionally, $\delta^{15}N$ values can provide information about the presence of fertilizers used in agricultural products. For example, organic produce typically displays higher $\delta^{15}N$ values (Meier-Augenstein, 2011). Other factors that can lead to elevated $\delta^{15}N$ values include environmental factors such as aridity as well as metabolic factors such as starvation and wasting due to illness or disease.

Culture and social structures, like social status or gender, can play a major role in how food resources (i.e., diet, specifically meat resources) are distributed within a society. In other words, $\delta^{15}N$ values can be used to make predictions about the influence of cultural phenomenon on the human body (Agarwal & Glencross, 2011). Bender et al. (2015) demonstrate that $\delta^{15}N$ values can reflect differences in low versus high socioeconomic status groups using hair from living humans from Cali Colombia. Furthermore, nitrogen isotopes can be used to differentiate coastal-dwelling populations from inland, terrestrial-dwelling populations. The consumption of marine proteins results in higher $\delta^{15}N$ values of tissues compared to organisms subsisting on terrestrial food sources (Deniro & Epstein, 1981; White et al., 2011).

2.2.1.3 Sulfur (S)

Sulfur has four naturally occurring stable isotopes (^{32}S (95.018%), ^{33}S (0.75%), ^{34}S (4.215%), and ^{36}S (0.017%)) as well as one cosmogenic isotope (^{35}S) (Farquhar, 2018).

Sulfur isotopes have traditionally been used to establish the geological chronology of sediment stratigraphy (Rickard, 2012). Sulfur isotopes vary with the underlying bedrock lithology, microbial activity in the soil, and other environmental factors (Richards et al., 2003). Stable sulfur isotope ratios ($\delta^{34}S$) can reflect diet and geographic residence because $\delta^{34}S$ values in plants vary with the isotopic values of underlying bedrock, and fractionation is essentially nonexistent (Meier-Augenstein, 2011; Richards et al., 2003; Valenzuela et al., 2011).

Higher $\delta^{34}S$ values are representative of marine water, intermediate $\delta^{34}S$ values are illustrative of terrestrial water, and low $\delta^{34}S$ values are seen in freshwater (Reitsema, 2015). However, it is important to note that the "sea spray effect" can influence coastal $\delta^{34}S$ values to mimic marine water signatures (Wadleigh et al., 1994). A more recent study by Valenzuela et al. (2011) created a sulfur "isotopic landscape" (isoscape) of North America by sampling human hair from 73 cities across the United States. The isoscape model identified geospatial patterning in $\delta^{34}S$ ratios, with considerably lower values occurring in the Great Plains region of the United States with higher $\delta^{34}S$ values occurring near the eastern, western, and southern coasts (Valenzuela et al., 2011). Therefore, lower $\delta^{34}S$ values are found among inland terrestrial ecosystems, while higher $\delta^{34}S$ values are indicative of marine and coastal ecosystems.

2.2.2 Geolocation isotopes

2.2.2.1 Oxygen (O)

Oxygen is an element that exists in three stable isotope forms (^{16}O, ^{17}O, and ^{18}O) (Bao et al., 2016) and is used for isotope analysis because there is a strong linear relationship between the oxygen composition of body tissue and that of the water ingested during the time of that tissue's formation. Furthermore, 60% percent of the human body is composed of oxygen and hydrogen (Emsley, 2011). Oxygen isotope ($\delta^{18}O$) values reflect the water that an individual takes into their system during life. Dietary $\delta^{18}O$ is a proxy for environmental $\delta^{18}O$ and is influenced by evaporation, condensation, and precipitation (Bentley & Knipper, 2005; Knudson et al., 2009). The geological signal that is taken up in liquid form through the water is transferred to various tissues, internal and external (Ehleringer et al., 2010). Therefore, $\delta^{18}O$ values are an indicator of climate and diet, meaning that probable regions of origin can be predicted for individuals based on their measured isotope ratios.

In 2008, Ehleringer and colleagues published an article demonstrating a predictive model that employs hydrogen ($\delta^{2}H$) and $\delta^{18}O$ in hair to predict region-of-origin for humans from 65 cities in the United States (Ehleringer et al., 2008). The $\delta^{18}O$ and $\delta^{2}H$ isoscapes were created using tap-water collected across the continent. The authors concluded that the model explained more than 85% of the isotopic variation observed in hair samples, and they noted that the unexplained variation may be due to the "continental supermarket" producing nonlocal signatures in the samples (Ehleringer et al., 2008).

2.2.2.2 Hydrogen (H)

Hydrogen has three naturally occurring isotopes, of which two are stable (^{1}H and ^{2}H) and one is radioactive (^{3}H). ^{1}H is the most abundant on Earth (Schimmelmann & Sauer, 2018).

Depending on the latitude, altitude, temperature, and distance to the ocean, precipitation (meteoric), $\delta^{2}H$ water values can range from −230 to +20‰ (Meier-

Augenstein, 2011). Hydrogen isotope values in human hair correlate with geography (Ehleringer et al., 2008) and are useful for predicting residence patterns in medico-legal contexts over the course of weeks to months prior to death, the time frame dependent on the length of the hair.

As discussed in the section concerning oxygen isotopes, hydrogen isotopes are also representative of climatic patterns and proximity to the oceans. The precipitation patterns that were explained above apply to hydrogen as well, given than oxygen and hydrogen are strongly correlated and form a global meteoric water line. Humans derive their hydrogen values from drinking water (including water used to prepare food), water stored in food (representing the food's place of origin), and the bonded hydrogen within the chemical structures of food resources (Meier-Augenstein, 2011).

2.2.2.3 Strontium (Sr)

Strontium has four naturally occurring stable isotopes (^{84}Sr (0.56%), ^{86}Sr (9.86%), ^{87}Sr (7.0%), and ^{88}Sr (82.58%)) (Ropp, 2013) and is a naturally occurring alkaline earth metal (Group IIA) with an atomic mass of 87.62 ± 0.01 u (Faure & Powell, 1972). ^{87}Sr is formed by the decay of rubidium (Rb), a naturally occurring substance in geologic materials, and the quantity of Sr varies based on the age of a mineral (Beard & Johnson, 2000; Bentley, 2006; Faure & Powell, 1972). Rb and Sr naturally occur in igneous, metamorphic, and sedimentary rock (Faure & Powell, 1972). Strontium closely resembles calcium (Ca) and readily substitutes for Ca in the inorganic component of bones and teeth, hydroxyapatite, due to their similar atomic structuring. In provenancing research, the ratio of ^{87}Sr to ^{86}Sr is measured in tissues. For the geo/trace-elements of strontium and lead (as opposed to bio-elements that make up most of organic matter), raw ratios are used because they are meaningful to several decimal places. ^{87}Sr/^{86}Sr ratios vary based on the age of the rock, given that ^{87}Sr is a decay product of ^{87}Rb; however, it is not radioactive (it is radiogenic, thus produced by radioactivity instead). Lower ^{87}Sr/^{86}Sr ratios are associated with younger rocks, while higher ratios indicate older geological formations. The ratio of ^{87}Sr/^{86}Sr is used because of their similar relative abundances (Capo et al., 1998).

The ^{87}Sr/^{86}Sr ratio of an organism's tissues reflects the intake of environmental ^{87}Sr/^{86}Sr values during the time of tissue formation and can be used as an indicator of residency and to track migration (Fig. 9.4; Beard & Johnson, 2000; Bentley & Knipper, 2005; Alexander Bentley, 2006; Lee-Thorp, 2008) because there is little to no mass-dependent fractionation occurring during ecological, chemical, or biological processes (Capo et al., 1998; Åberg, 1995).

In herbivores, the ^{87}Sr/^{86}Sr ratios represent an average of the plant material that is ingested from the local landscape. Migration studies using strontium isotopes have been conducted for many regions around the world, such as Europe (Bentley & Knipper, 2005; Alexander Bentley et al., 2004; Bol et al., 2007; Kootker et al., 2016; Schweissing & Grupe, 2003), Africa (Sealy et al., 1991; Sillen et al., 1995),

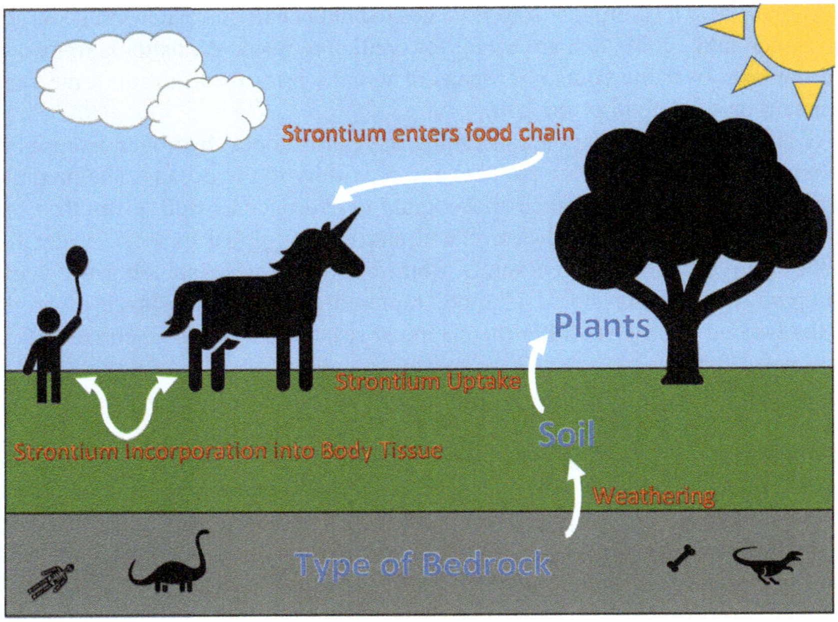

FIGURE 9.4

Incorporation of strontium into the human skeleton.

Central America (Bataille et al., 2012; Freiwald, 2011; Knudson & Buikstra, 2007; Laffoon et al., 2017; Price et al., 2000, 2008, 2015; Thornton, 2011; Warner et al., 2018; White et al., 2007; Wright, 2005, 2012), South America (Knudson & Buikstra, 2007; Knudson et al., 2005, 2009), North America (Ezzo et al., 1997; Price et al., 1994), and Asia (Regan, 2006).

Research using $^{87}Sr/^{86}Sr$ ratios in forensic settings has increased steadily and has been applied to provenancing unidentified individuals in a variety of contexts (Bartelink et al., 2016; Beard & Johnson, 2000; Benson et al., 2006; Juarez, 2008). Recent contributions to the field by Kramer et al. (2020) have provided the forensic anthropological community with a preliminary strontium isoscape for Mexico and Central America derived from a compilation of previously published isotopic data. Furthermore, Ammer's doctoral thesis developed a $^{87}Sr/^{86}Sr$ isoscape from human hair samples collected throughout Mexico. Given the amount of ongoing research, an isoscape representing $^{87}Sr/^{86}Sr$ values in tap water across Mexico and North America will eventually be developed.

2.2.2.4 Lead (pb)

Lead has four isotopes that occur naturally: ^{204}Pb, ^{206}Pb, ^{207}Pb, and ^{208}Pb. Like strontium isotopes, lead isotope variations in nature are dependent on the local geology (Chen et al., 2002, pp. 40–42) and are incorporated into biological tissues with little to no fractionation (Stille & Shields, 1997). Lead isotopes are representative of the anthropogenic influences in a region such as industrial mining, transport, waste dumping and incineration, leaded gasoline, and heating through coal combustion (Åberg, 1995; Lehn & Graw, 2014). Essentially, lead isotope ratios reflect anthropogenic lead contamination. Despite the issues of contamination, lead isotopes are still useful for provenancing research (Kamenov & Gulson, 2014). For example, Regan (2006) showed differences in the carbon, oxygen, strontium, and lead isotopic compositions of remains from deceased U.S. soldiers and local residents of various Asian countries.

2.2.3 Other isotopes

The above-mentioned elements (H, C, N, O, S, Sr, and Pb) are relatively well-established methods of isotope analysis in archeology and forensic anthropology. However, neodymium (Nd) shows great potential for use in isotope research because, like strontium isotopes, it reflects underlying geological formations (Plomp et al., 2019; Pye, 2004). Furthermore, the potential is seen in the elements of boron, lithium, and molybdenum (Bartelink & Chesson, 2019). All three are ingested through dietary sources and have a distinct signatures in the human body. However, these have thus far not been used in forensic research, and therefore, no baselines, references, or methodologies tailored to forensic anthropology regarding instrumentation exist.

2.2.3.1 Neodymium (Nd)

Neodymium has five stable (^{142}Nd, ^{143}Nd, ^{145}Nd, ^{146}Nd, and ^{148}Nd) and two radiogenic isotopes (^{144}Nd and ^{150}Nd) (National Center for Biotechnology Information, 2019). Of the isotopes, a ratio of ^{143}Nd to ^{144}Nd seems to be most useful for provenancing studies. Neodymium elemental concentrations and isotopes have been used previously to provenance sediment depositions (Vroon et al., 1995), but their application to unidentified human remains is still in the early stages of development. Recently, Plomp et al. (2019) explored the use of both neodymium and strontium isotopes for provenancing human dental enamel and found that the isotope values correlated with local geology for 83% of their test samples. Neodymium isotopes are not influenced by the "sea spray effect" because of their relatively low concentration in ocean water (Tachikawa et al., 1999). This could make neodymium isotopes especially useful for human provenancing in coastal regions.

3. Skeletal elements commonly used for isotope analysis, turnover rates, and diagenesis

Theoretically, any biological tissue or bodily fluid can be used for isotopic analysis, such as blood, muscle, or nails. However, in forensic anthropology bones, teeth, and hair are most commonly used because they are very durable and do not decompose easily compared to other human tissues. The isotope ratios derived from human bone, dental enamel, and hair (as well as nails) create a thorough representation of geological residence throughout the life of the individual because each tissue shows a different timeframe of life history.

Tissue remodeling is a cyclical process of resorption and deposition (White et al., 2011). Remodeling rates and growth times vary within an organism. According to Ortner (2003), a healthy adult may resorb and replace approximately three million new bone remodeling units, also called basic multicellular units, each one taking 3–4 months from activation to completion in a single year (Frost, 1999). The standard turnover rate of bone consists of a balancing act between the destructive action of the osteoclasts and the production capability of the osteoblasts. Osteoclasts resorb bone at a rate of about 3 weeks per site, whereas osteoblasts need three to 4 months per site for bone deposition (Martin, 2000; Martin et al., 2015; Ortner, 2003).

Isotope analysis typically focuses on individual molecular compounds and requires a basic comprehension of the compositional differences between biological tissues. Human bones, teeth, hair, and nails are great candidates for isotope analysis due to their particular makeup. A brief overview of these tissues and their structures is provided below.

3.1 Bone structure, composition, and remodeling

There are 206 bones in the average adult skeleton that are differentiated by type: long, short, irregular, flat, and sesamoid (bone embedded within muscle or tendon). Bone functions to provide support and protection of organs, to produce red and white blood cells within the bone marrow, to store minerals, to provide structure and support for the body, and to enable mobility.

Bone is a composite material that is formed of organic proteins (collagen) and inorganic minerals (primarily calcium phosphate minerals, i.e., hydroxyapatite). These components make up approximately 30% and 70% of the dry bone weight, respectively (Martin et al., 2015). Collagen is the main structural protein in the extracellular space in the various connective tissues in the human body. It is the most abundant protein in mammals and is mostly found in fibrous tissues, such as tendons, ligaments, and skin. It can also be found in bones, corneas, cartilage, blood vessels, intervertebral discs, the gut, and dentin (Ortner, 2003). The crystals of hydroxyapatite, or bioapatite, infiltrate the collagen matrix, giving the bone its hardness and rigidity (White et al., 2011). Isotopically speaking, the collagen will primarily reflect dietary protein intake, while the bioapatite is representative of the whole diet, including carbohydrates, fats, and proteins not used in tissue synthesis (Ambrose & Norr, 1993; Tykot, 2006; Tieszen & Fagre, 1993).

Bone remodeling is needed to provide the body with calcium and phosphate that is locked within the structure of bone (Martin, 2000; Ortner, 2003) and occurs continuously throughout the lifespan of an individual. Even though human bone is a highly durable material, the human body continually replaces damaged or fatigued osseous tissue with new, structurally sound tissue through remodeling (White et al.,

2011). Bones that consist predominantly of cancellous bone (such as ribs, vertebrae, and the iliac crest) have more rapid remodeling rates, while bones that have denser compact bone exhibit slower remodeling rates. Compact bone can store information for up to 50 years (Hedges et al., 2007; Lehn & Graw, 2014; Rummel et al., 2007). The faster remodeling rate (~25%) of cancellous bone is associated with the support of mineral homeostasis, which is necessary for the maintenance of certain physiological functions (Ortner, 2003). During childhood and adolescence, remodeling rates can be 2 to 5 times higher than in fully developed bones. Middle-aged adult skeletons contain about 50% of the deposited information from their youth (Lehn & Graw, 2014). The mineral component and collagen of bone have similar remodeling rates and integration times (Wild et al., 2000; Young Shin et al., 2004), making it elementally stable and ideal for isotope analysis.

3.2 Tooth enamel structure, composition, and remodeling

Humans develop two sets of teeth during their lifetime: deciduous and permanent teeth. The deciduous teeth begin mineralizing in utero and erupt from the alveolar process of the mandible and maxilla during early infancy through early childhood. The permanent tooth crowns start calcification at birth and continue forming until approximately 10 years of age (Hillson, 1996; Nelson, 2014; Smith, 1991).

Tooth enamel is composed of ~97% inorganic minerals (hydroxyapatite), ~1% organic protein (amelogenin), and ~2% water (He & Swain, 2007; Hillson, 1996). The organic portion of tooth enamel is primarily composed of the protein, amelogenin, which has a similar function as collagen in bone, thus providing a structural matrix for the deposition of inorganic minerals (Hillson, 1996). The inorganic mineral portion of tooth enamel functions similarly to bone but consists of larger crystals and contains a superior structural organizational matrix that allows for fewer ionic substitutions than bone (Ross & Pawlina, 2010). The inorganic material consists predominantly of calcium phosphate in the form of hydroxyapatite crystals, which are carbonated or fluoridated (Gwinnett, 1992; Hueb De Menezes Oliveira et al., 2010; ten Cate & Featherstone, 1991).

The enamel microstructure is composed of crystals arranged in prisms or rods that run roughly perpendicular from the dentin-enamel junction toward the surface of the tooth (Fava et al., 1997; Ortner, 2003; ten Cate & Featherstone, 1991). The interfacial area between prisms is called interprismatic enamel and is protein-rich (Fejerskov et al., 1984). In the prismless enamel layer, the hydroxyapatite crystals are arranged parallel to one another and perpendicular to the surface of the enamel (Fava et al., 1997; Hueb De Menezes Oliveira et al., 2010; Stack, 1967). Because of its high mineral content, enamel is the hardest tissue in the human body. Furthermore, unlike bone and dentin, enamel does not experience turnover, meaning that once deposited it remains unchanged throughout life (Hillson, 1996; Ortner, 2003). Since teeth do not remodel, they maintain their elemental signature throughout the lifetime of an individual. This means teeth are elementally stable and make perfect biomaterial for isotope analysis (Lee-Thorp, 2002).

3.3 Hair structure, composition, and remodeling

Human scalp hair starts growing from follicles, which are little "pockets" in the skin. Blood vessels around these follicles create new cells, allowing the hair to grow. There are 80,000 to 150,000 follicles located on the scalp (Krause & Foitzik, 2006). Hair is the only organ in the mammalian organism that undergoes life-long cycles of rapid growth, regression, and resting periods, referred to as anagen, catagen, and telogen, respectively (Krause & Foitzik, 2006). According to Font and collegues (2012), human hair is made of keratin, which is a tough structural fibrous protein that comprises of 50% carbon, 21% nitrogen, 17.5% hydrogen, 6.5% oxygen, and 5% sulfur. Trace elements of metals, such as strontium and lead, can be integrated into hair through diet and exposure to exogenous sources such as air and water.

Once hair exits the skin, the exposed portion dies and ceases to take in nutrients. Human scalp hair grows on average of 1.1 cm per month, and since the elemental exchange between hair and blood ceases when it dies, it retains the biogenic and dietary information (Font et al., 2012; Krause & Foitzik, 2006). It is important to note, however, that not all hair grows at the same rate and it is essential to choose hair wisely when it is not analyzed as a bulk sample but rather used to acquire information from a certain time period (Mekota et al., 2006). This method of using human scalp hair strands to chronologically reconstruct changes in diet or residence patterns has been demonstrated on modern individuals as well as for archeological casework (Chesson et al., 2018; Lehn et al., 2019; Hülsemann et al., 2015; Santamaria-Fernandez et al., 2009).

3.4 Diagenesis and forensic material

Diagenesis refers to any physical, chemical, or biological alteration of sediments or biological remains following initial deposition (Meier-Augenstein, 2011). Causes, mechanisms, and effects vary widely depending on the material (Darwent & Lyman, 2001). No tissue is completely immune to diagenetic processes, but the dense makeup of tooth enamel is very resilient to postmortem alteration. Bone is a porous tissue and is understandably more prone to diagenesis. For burials, the extent of diagenetic alteration to bone largely depends on the chemistry of the burial context and material culture associated with the body. A clothed individual buried in a cairn on the ground surface will not exhibit the same diagenetic patterns as someone in similar clothing buried underground. Furthermore, Hedges (2002) cites several intrinsic factors that may determine the diagenetic influences, such as size, shape, condition, and age of the bone.

Decomposition facilities, colloquially termed "body farms", around the world seek to explore the extrinsic factors (e.g., temperature, aridity, microbial activity, scavenging, etc.) that contribute to differential decomposition rates in hopes of better estimating the postmortem interval for forensic cases.

When performing isotope analysis, it is crucial to understand inherent biases such as diagenesis that may influence results, especially if the material is from a medicolegal setting and subject to the Daubert criteria (Christensen & Crowder, 2009). Overall, in most modern forensic anthropology cases, diagenesis will not have a negative effect on the isotopic results unless the remains have been buried or exposed to the elements for long periods of time (longer than months) (Bartelink & Chesson, 2019).

Hair and nails are most prone to changes due to diagenesis. It has been shown that, potentially, extrinsic signatures can be incorporated into hair structures (Kempson & Lombi, 2011). Specifically, bathing water can influence strontium isotope values of hair and nail incorporated after it has exited the skin (Tipple et al., 2018; Mancuso & Ehleringer, 2018). Therefore, it is plausible that precipitation water (e.g., during the rainy season in the Arizona desert lands) or decomposition fluids interacting with the environment could alter isotopic signatures of hair. An example of the potential extrinsic influence on the results of $^{87}Sr/^{86}Sr$ values in hair can be seen in the UBC cases from the PCOME. The values are all elevated compared to the other $^{87}Sr/^{86}Sr$ isotopic signatures found within all the individuals (Fig. 9.5). However, none of these potential extrinsic factors have been thoroughly explored and baseline research is needed.

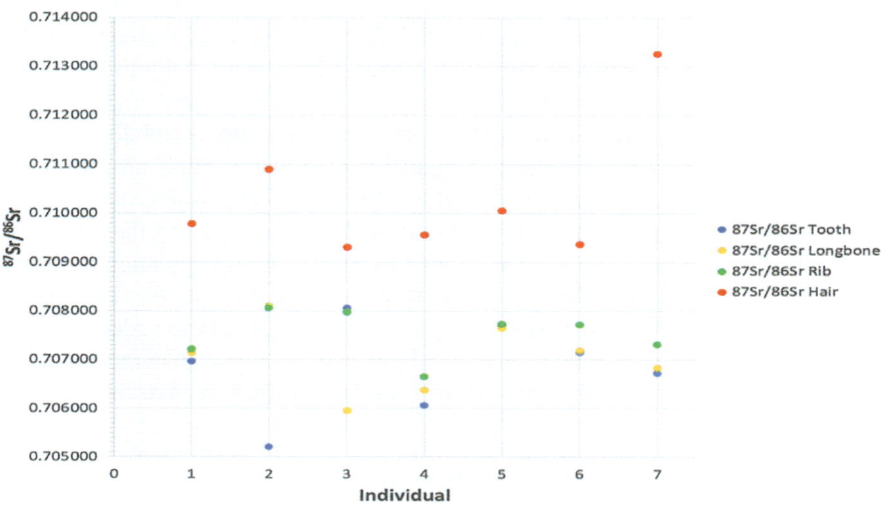

FIGURE 9.5

Elevated $^{87}Sr/^{86}Sr$ values in hair were found in UBC cases from the Pima county office of the medical examiner. Hair samples were analyzed in bulk. Bataille and Bowen (2012) isoscape based on the bedrock age model of Beard and Johnson (2000) mostly estimates $^{87}Sr/^{86}Sr$ values of 0.711–0.713 along the Arizona border.

4. Isoscapes

According to Bowen (2010), West et al. (2010), the distribution of spatio-temporal isotopes can be mapped and predicted across space and time using "isoscapes" or isotopic landscapes. Isoscapes represent spatially explicit predictions of isotope ratios by interpolating natural spatial isotopic distributions to global-scale patterns. These are produced by using process-level models of elemental isotope fractions or distribution in a geographic information system (GIS) (Bowen, 2010a). Isoscapes are created by sampling an environmental source, such as soil, plants, water, or local bedrock as well as biological materials like bones, teeth, hair, ceramics, trees, fruits, or vegetables to characterize the isotope baseline value for a local region.

Using geostatistical methods, isotope values for untested sites can be predicted or inferred using interpolation (Bowen, 2010a, 2010b). Interpolation should be employed cautiously because it may not consider the additional sources that contribute to the bioavailability of an isotope, such as the atmosphere, climate, and distribution of soil and bedrock (Bataille & Bowen, 2012). The analysis of isoscapes and the comparison of the isoscape predictions with observational data have been used for various purposes, such as to test biogeochemical models, calculate aerially integrated biogeochemical fluxes based on isotope mass balance, and determine spatial connectivity in biogeochemical, ecological, and anthropogenic systems (Bowen, 2010a, 2010b).

In 2000, Beard and Johnson constructed a geological isoscape displaying the isotopic variation for $^{87}Sr/^{86}Sr$ within the continental U.S. The strength of the isoscape relied on the "isotopic distinctiveness" of different geographic regions and the knowledge of local bio available strontium composition (Beard & Johnson, 2000). The methods and application of the isoscape created by Beard and Johnson (2000) can be applied to all isotopes that depict geospatial patterns and distributions and are not limited to strontium alone. A limitation of current isotopic provenancing research concerning Latin American migrants is that the existing isotope data are not representative of all regions of Central America and Mexico, meaning that region of origin estimations will rely on coarse-grained isoscapes and interpolation for areas lacking information. This is the case for most regions of the world. As new isotope data are collected from the environment (e.g., plants, water, soil) and added to open-access isotope repositories, the accuracy and precision of provenancing should increase and become more useful for sourcing unidentified human remains.

4.1 ArcGIS and R software for building isoscapes

Various analytical and computational tools are used to build isoscapes using computer programs, such as ArcGIS and R-Studio (Environmental Systems Research Institute (ESRI), 2018; R Core Team, 2020). R-Studio has a steeper learning curve and requires using the R programming language and software available for free online (www.r-project.org). R-Studio is an optional interface for the R program, which makes software navigation more user-friendly. If funding is not an issue, ArcGIS offers a user-friendly "point and click" interface that rarely requires knowledge of coding languages. Many companies and universities have licenses from ArcGIS, and students and researchers can request access key codes for free from their institution. Within the field, you will see researchers using one program over the other or some researchers utilizing functions on both programs. When performing tasks like interpolation mentioned above, ArcGIS provides a "geostatistical wizard" that walks the user through each step of the process (Environmental Systems Research Institute (ESRI), 2018). For R, many public libraries with interpolation scripts and codes are available online for free and only require a quick search engine check to find and download.

Essentially, choosing the software to perform interpolation depends on the goals of the research and the "intellectual" investment the scientist wants to make. ArcGIS is a fast and straightforward approach once familiar with the interface. It is sufficient for simple kriging interpolation jobs that do not involve covariates (such as temperature, elevation, bedrock, soil pH, etc.). Making advanced models in ArcGIS may prove difficult because the interface becomes less user-friendly as more covariates are incorporated into the model framework, and ArcGIS lacks a large support network for asking questions and solving model construction dilemmas.

On the contrary, R uses a programming language that the researcher must learn, which takes some serious commitment and patience. While the introductory phase is much longer than with ArcGIS, it gives the researcher much more control over the model (for example, adjusting the sill, range, and nugget to create the variogram; adjusting the number of points used in the prediction, etc.) and the desired outcomes. Of course, this can also lead to some undesired results, such as when too many cuts are introduced to the colorRamp (Fig. 9.6). When constructing isoscapes, R allows for easy consideration of covariates like the random forest modeling framework. The

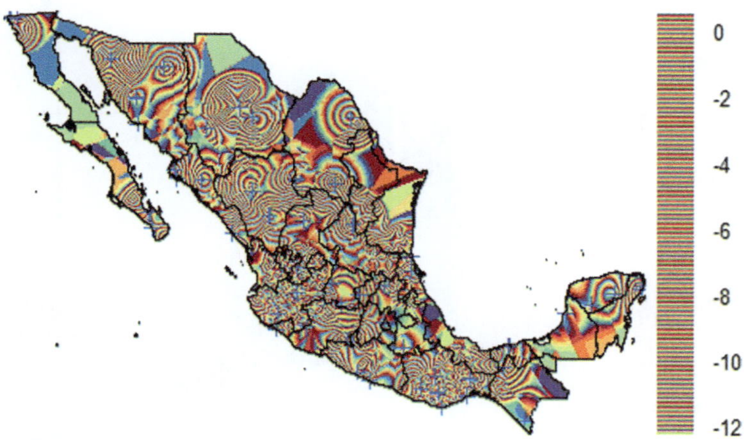

FIGURE 9.6

The programming language R allows for more control over the model, which can lead to some unwanted results—even psychedelic results.

resulting isoscapes will be much more sophisticated and will consider more information. Furthermore, the support community is tremendous and truly promotes the open-access movement by publicly providing code, packages, and coding assistance in papers, on GitHub, and/or Stack Overflow.

Overall, deciding between those two options will depend on the preferences and needs of the researcher. If the isoscape is supposed to present a spatial overview of the isotopic values without a lot of added information, using ArcGIS will be the most efficient option (Fig. 9.7). If the isoscape should incorporate covariates, then using the R programming language will yield the most success (Fig. 9.8).

Isoscapes can be constructed using a plethora of methods from process-based models to sample-dependent models that rely on interpolation to predict nonsampled regions. The most commonly employed interpolation method used for isoscapes is kriging using a Gaussian regression process to interpolate, which provides the best linear prediction of the intermediate values while remaining unbiased. Some researchers also use a Spline with Barriers approach (e.g., Laffoon et al., 2017), which interpolates from points employing a minimum curvature spline technique. This interpolation technique uses barriers, which can be beneficial for certain areas of the world depending on the shape of the region to be interpolated.

Bataille et al. (2018) published a machine-learning method that combines environmental covariate variables, bioavailable $^{87}Sr/^{86}Sr$ data, and a process-based bedrock $^{87}Sr/^{86}Sr$ model in a random forest regression framework to produce an isoscape. The R-script for the model construction is publicly available through *PLOS ONE* online and sources for the environmental variables used as covariates in the

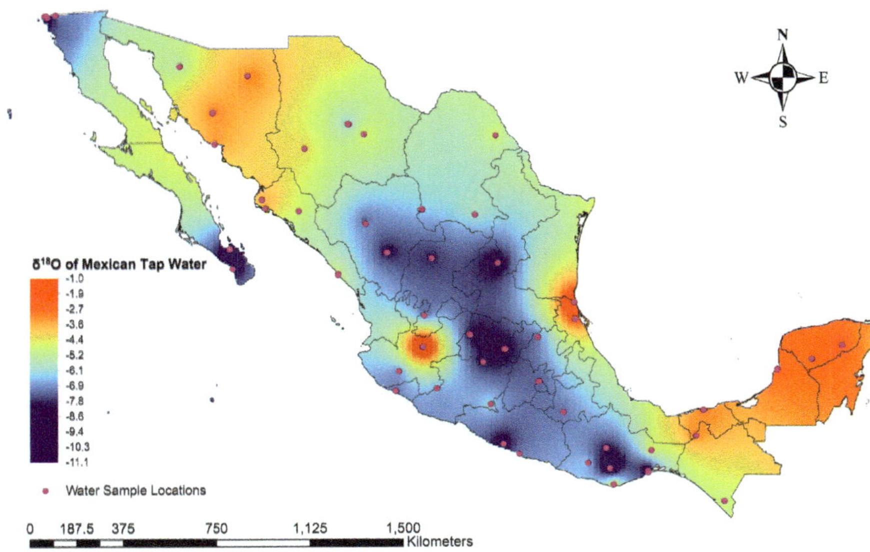

FIGURE 9.7

$\delta^{18}O$ isoscape of Mexican tap water using ArcGIS and ordinary kriging.

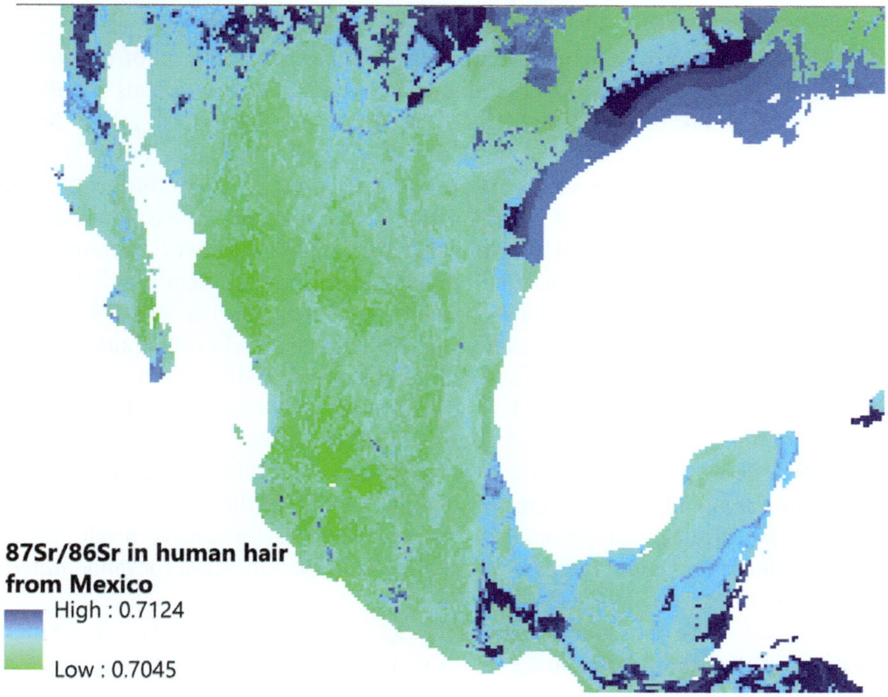

FIGURE 9.8

Preliminary $^{87}Sr/^{86}Sr$ isoscape of human hair from Mexico using an adjusted Bataille et al. (2018) coding script.

regression are listed in Table 9.2 of the article (Bataille et al., 2018). This R code script was adjusted to create an $^{87}Sr/^{86}Sr$ isoscape representing human hair collected throughout Mexico.

Table 9.2 $^{87}Sr/^{86}Sr$ and $\delta^{18}O$ data for OpID forensic cases[a].

OpID case	Tooth selected	$^{87}Sr/^{86}Sr$	$^{87}Sr/^{86}Sr$ SE	$\delta^{18}O_c$ (VPDB)	$\delta^{18}O_c$ SE
OpID-0395	Maxillary premolar (#4)	0.71721	0.00001	−2.95	0.179
OpID-0415	Mandibular premolar (#29)	0.70591	0.00008	−4.80	0.181
OpID-0608	Maxillary premolar (#5)	0.70595	0.00001	−5.04	0.181

SE, *standard error*; $_c$, *carbonate.*

[a] *Data collected during Kramer's Master's research (2018) with permission from Operation Identification.*

4.2 Isotope analysis and region-of-origin predictions

Isotope analysis has proven to be a useful method for predicting region-of-origin and tracking changing residence patterns among individuals during various stages of their lives (Bartelink et al., 2014, 2016, 2018b; Bartelink & Chesson, 2019; Beard & Johnson, 2000; Benson et al., 2006; Kramer et al., 2020; Regan, 2006; Warner et al., 2018). As isotopes are incorporated into the hard (i.e., bones and teeth) and soft tissues (i.e., skin, hair, nails) of organisms, the tissues reflect the isotopic signatures of food and water ingested while that particular tissue was forming. For example, teeth record a signature of childhood diet because the dentition is formed during infancy and childhood and does not remodel throughout life (Hillson, 2013). Bones, on the other hand, are constantly remodeling and should reflect the last 1-2 decades of dietary intake based on which bone is sampled (Hill & Orth, 1998). Isotopes derived from soft tissues, like hair and fingernails, have been used to track diet and migration months and even weeks before death (Ehleringer et al., 2008; Tipple, 2015). By targeting different tissues, investigators can infer diet and predict residential location for an individual during specific time periods of their life prior to death. Therefore, performing isotope analysis can provide investigators with additional lines of evidence that could increase the likelihood of identification for unidentified forensic cases.

As stressed above, a migrant's region-of-origin is a crucial piece of evidence that aids the identification process and plays a major role in shaping their reasons for migration, how and where they attempt to cross the Mexico-U.S. border, and their desired final destinations. For example, the majority of deceased migrants recovered in southern Texas and identified by OpID originate from the Central American countries of El Salvador, Honduras, and Guatemala, the so-called Northern Triangle countries (Kramer et al., 2020). On the other hand, the PCOME in Arizona experiences a larger portion of Mexican nationals among their identified deceased migrant cases (Martinez et al., 2015; Anderson & Parks, 2008; Massey et al., 2002). It is important to understand the nationality profiles of recovered deceased migrants because they can be used to better understand the scope of the issue and potentially bring awareness to the events affecting migration and the humanitarian crisis at the border. Isotope analysis provides a novel approach for predicting country-of-origin for deceased unidentified Latin American migrants and may prove useful in humanitarian crises around the world.

4.3 Case studies using isoscapes for provenancing unidentified human remains

Similar to the creation of isoscapes, there are varying approaches to establish region-of-origin assignments. The first approach is the rather simple conditional correlation assignment, which sets boundaries around the recorded tissue value and shows all regions where this value range is represented. The second method to visualize the region-of-origin assignment for unidentified human remains is the maximum likelihood assignment, which does not exclude or include any particular region but shows the probability percentage of an individual to be from a certain region on a continuous color scale. The latter is a more sophisticated approach and is expected to be used in the future, especially in combination with isoscapes created in with the R programming language.

4.3.1 Conditional correlation assignment method: Region-of-origin assignment using a newly developed oxygen tap water isoscape for Mexico

A successful application of an isoscape for the region-of-origin assignment has been demonstrated by Ammer and collegues (2020), proving that the tap water data and its consequently developed isoscape can give valuable information regarding region-of-origin prediction. One of the individuals used for this study was found in 2016, in the Sonoran Desert in Pima County, Arizona.

First, the analyzed $\delta^{18}O$ value of the tooth enamel of this individual was converted from calibrated VPDB standard to the VSMOW standard (used for isotopic water analyses) using the following formulae.

1. Tooth bioapatite $\delta^{18}O$ (VPDBcarbonate)– > tooth bioapatite $\delta^{18}O$ (VSMOW-carbonate) 1.03,091 * $\delta^{18}O$ (VPDBcarbonate) + 30.91 = $\delta^{18}O$ (VSMOWcarbonate) (Coplen, 1988)
2. Tooth bioapatite $\delta^{18}O$ (VSMOWcarbonate)– > tooth bioapatite $\delta^{18}O$ (VSMOWphosphate) 0.98 * $\delta^{18}O$ (VSMOWcarbonate) - 8.5 = $\delta^{18}O$ (VSMOWphosphate) (Iacumin et al., 1996)
3. Tooth bioapatite (VSMOWphosphate)– > predicted water (VSMOWphosphate) 1.54 * $\delta^{18}O$ (VSMOWphosphate) - 33.72 = $\delta^{18}O$ (VSMOWphosphate)

Using the developed $\delta^{18}O$ isoscape from tap water, the raster calculator in ArcGIS 10.6 (Environmental Systems Research Institute (ESRI), 2018) was used to create a conditional correlation map representing the possible regions of origins based on the $\delta^{18}O$ value derived from the human tooth mentioned above. The resulting map is shown below (Fig. 9.9). As this individual was recently identified, it was possible to validate the assignment prediction (green dot on the predictive map).

4.3.2 Maximum likelihood estimation assignment method: A dual-isotope approach to identifying deceased Latin Americans recovered in southern Texas

Much of the difficulty in identification and the return of deceased migrants to their families results from an inability to restrict the search range to more probable options. Kramer et al. (2020) recently published promising results of their attempt to define region-of-origin for deceased undocumented Latin American migrants recovered in

FIGURE 9.9

Conditional $\delta^{18}O$ correlation map indicating possible regions of origin. The birthplace of the recently identified individual is marked with the green dot (as published in Ammer et al. (2020).

southern Texas using strontium ($^{87}Sr/^{86}Sr$) and oxygen ($\delta^{18}O$) isotopes derived from dental enamel (Fig. 9.10). The authors found that utilizing the dual-isotope approach and a maximum likelihood assignment model produced a quantifiable region of childhood residence predictions and accurately estimated the nationality of one of the two cases (Kramer et al., 2020).

Here, we provide the region of childhood residence assignments for three additional migrant cases that were not included in Kramer and colleague's previous publication. Table 9.2 provides a summary of the isotopic data and the sampled teeth obtained from each case. Fig. 9.10 displays the probability density maps produced by the assignment model for three deceased migrants recovered in southern Texas using isotopes derived from their tooth enamel.

Of the three OpID forensic cases, an identification has been made for one case as of July 2019. OpID-0608 has been identified as an adult male of Guatemalan nationality, and the assignment model strongly plots him into the Sierra Madre Mountain range of Honduras and Guatemala (Fig. 9.10), meaning the model was successful at predicting region of childhood residence. The other two cases remain unidentified and the accuracy of their assignments cannot be quantified. However, the model can be used to filter out missing person reports that may match the biological profile for the individual but are not congruent with the isotopic provenancing evidence and residential history for the person.

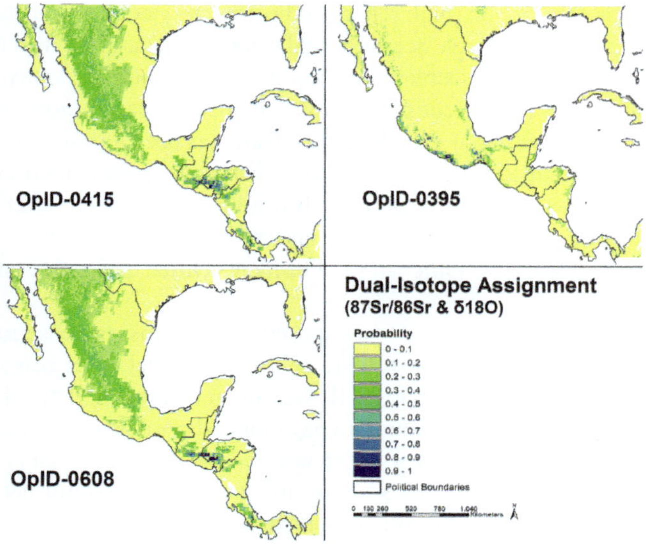

FIGURE 9.10

Dual-isotope assignments for three OpID cases. Results displayed as probability densities with dark blue representing the most probable regions of childhood residence.

By utilizing these isotope assignment methodologies, isotope analysis can assist with identification efforts by reducing the potential matches for unknown cases within the NamUs database by providing evidence of residential history and potential nationalities for the decedents. Nonetheless, more isotope baseline sampling must be completed to assess the accuracy and precision of these models and to improve the current models to further narrow down potential regions of origin. Since isotope analysis in a forensic context is still relatively novel, many research questions are left to be answered to establish best practices and standards. Furthermore, in regards to the humanitarian aspect of isotope analysis, the exploration of altered isotope values in cases of starvation and malnutrition should also be explored (Neuberger et al., 2013). The implications of this could be tremendous as it could potentially be useful in the conviction of torture, war crimes, and other crimes against humanity.

5. Open access data and the future of isotope research in forensic anthropology

The past decade has seen a major push toward "big data" and open access repositories for storing massive compilations of data, such as the National Health and Nutrition Examination Survey and the World Health Organization's Global Database on Child Growth and Malnutrition. Access to these large-scale databases provides larger sample sizes and, therefore, more statistically significant results. There is also a greater potential to impact the public (high school and community college students, the general public, etc.) when they have access to real scientific data. If the data are not hidden behind a pay-wall such as a required subscription to a journal, it may shorten the timeline for publishing new scientific research and, ideally, lead to more collaborative research through the sharing of data. Recently, there has been a push toward publicly available data, highlighted by the Obama administration's policy memorandum that directed Federal agencies with more than 100 million dollars in R&D funding to make the results of their research publicly and freely available within 1 year of the initial publication (Executive Office of the President- Office of Science and Technology Policy, 2013).

The pros of open access data are juxtaposed by the cons: increase in derivative research, creating a "race to publish first," and the fear that other researchers will steal your data. Many open access journals lack the reputation and prestige of traditional journals and require the author(s) to pay hundreds or even thousands of dollars in publishing fees to make their work open access. Additionally, open access to scientific data removes the researcher's ability to ensure that the information is used ethically. For example, pharmaceutical companies and private firms representing oil companies can skew data and draw biased conclusions to reflect the needs of their companies.

Generally, the earth sciences have been pioneers in establishing open access data repositories that give credit to the researchers and their collected samples (e.g., International Geo Sample Number on geosamples.org, National Oceanic and Atmospheric Administration, International Atomic Energy Agency, etc.). Another example of a successful large-scale database is WaterIsotopes.org, a repository of oxygen and hydrogen isotopic values in various bodies of water, such as tap water, precipitation, and river water. It is not only possible to search and pull data from this database but also to contribute new research data to the repository. For example, the tap water data for Mexico collected by Ammer during her Ph.D. research are publicly available on this database (Project ID 198- MEX Water). Two up and coming data sharing isotope tools worth mentioning are IsoBank and assignR, one aiming to compile data from various fields of isotopic research and the other developing an R package to use for region-of-origin assignments by comparison to known data. To ensure "good" comparisons, it is pertinent that the methods and methodologies for sample preparation and analysis are comparable (preferably ensured through interlab comparisons).

As the successful research projects completed by the authors illustrate, it is pertinent to push toward large-scale isotope databases and provide an incentive for researchers to make their results publicly available. This goal can only be achieved by also pushing toward standardization of methods, which has generally been lacking in forensic anthropology and forensic isotope analysis.

In the near future, researchers will likely be required to publish their workflow, including their data and software. Publishing the baseline data of scientific research will enable others to check the methodologies for validity and give more credit (and citations) to the scientists who create new methods, publish r-scripts and codes, or simply publish their data (Piwowar et al., 2007). There are many ways to make research publicly available with open access journals or public organized repositories, like WaterIsotopes.org. Nonetheless, the forensic sciences (in particular forensic anthropology) are in many ways lacking those data-sharing networks. Unless the home university has agreements with publishers, peer-reviewed open access publishing can cost several thousand dollars, money that most researchers do not have. Furthermore, forensic anthropology has yet to establish a culture of data sharing and to establish common data repositories.

It is practically impossible to find a standardized overview of skeletal data collection methods used around the world which highlights this issue. Until the sharing of data is widely accepted in forensic sciences and anthropology, websites such as figshare.com can provide a solution for ambitious pioneer scientists. On this website, researchers can publish posters, code, figures, papers, null and negative results, as well as datasets. As an added benefit, the service also provides DOIs for the shared content, enabling the researcher to get citations for their work as well as track how the data are being used.

It is expected that the sciences will develop rapidly once more data are publicly available because, oftentimes, the data can be used for various research projects and scientific fields. For example, tap water data can be used for region-of-origin assignments of undocumented borders crossers but also in hydrology, for example, in water management agencies. One set of data can be explored by many scientific fields, but if it is not publicly available, some questions may never be answered or even asked. Furthermore, the region-of-origin assignments will only be as good as the available data. A person cannot be assigned to regions from where there are no reliable isotopic data available. Open-access data are essential to the advancement of all scientific fields of inquiry. Forensic anthropology must be ready to align its trajectory with the future of science and move away from the traditional practice of data hoarding.

6. Conclusion and future directions

The primary impetus of this chapter was to introduce the reader to the humanitarian crisis along the southern border of the U.S. and show how isotope research can aid in the identification efforts of deceased undocumented border crossers. We hope we were able to achieve these main goals by presenting case studies from Arizona and Texas to illustrate the application of isotopes and forensic anthropology for aiding this identification effort. Additionally, we hope to inspire other researchers to push for publicly available data in forensic anthropology and isotope research to further aid the humanitarian catastrophes happening all over the world.

In the near future, several large-scale isotope research projects will be conducted that have the potential to achieve the goal of resolving and preventing the crisis of missing people around the world. Ammer aims to develop strontium and oxygen isoscapes for tap water and hair across North America, not only with the data from her

Ph.D. research but also from public data repositories and the aid from other collaborators who will make their data available for this research project.

Furthermore, the International Committee of the Red Cross has initiated a focus group consisting of several isotope experts from various scientific fields to create isotopic coverage of the entire continent of Africa. The project aims to drastically reduce the number of unidentified remains and persons considered missing by assigning probable regions-of-origins to the unidentified human remains.

Of course, the outcomes of these research projects will not only provide new investigative leads for the identification of human remains but will also apply to many other areas of scientific research. An example of how broadly applicable isotopic research is applied to Kramer who has helped to construct an $^{87}Sr/^{86}Sr$ isoscape for New Zealand. The model will be used by a New Zealand governmental agency, the Ministry of Primary Industries, to predict the region-of-origin of foreign pests found at international ports of entry into the country. The model will also be available for use in research fields, like ecological conservation, food science, forensics, and archeology. This illustrates why open-access research data and method transparency can lead to collaborative research within the field of forensic anthropology and science in general.

To accomplish the goal of more publicly available data and data repositories (for isotope analysis) in forensic anthropology, it is essential that preparation and analytical methods of human remains are standardized and validated by independent entities to ensure best practice (national and international Standard Operating Procedures). Furthermore, it is important that training in chemistry is offered to forensic anthropologists and their students. This is especially important because many isotope laboratories lack experience with modern human remains and lack knowledge of the chemical compositions of skeletal elements. Therefore, problems arise with isotope analyses and the interpretation of the resulting data. This chapter provided a brief, but not all-encompassing, overview of biological tissues used for isotope analysis and isotopes that are commonly used for provenancing unidentified human remains to be used as a starting point for early career researchers and students interested in pursuing isotope-related research.

7. Funding

Funding was awarded to Ammer by the Humanitarian and Human Rights Research Center, with the financial support of the American Academy of Forensic Sciences and the National Institute of Justice. Funding for Kramer was awarded by the Graduate College at Texas State University, the Grady Early Endowment Fellowship, and the Forensic Anthropology Center at Texas State. Both Ammer and Kramer attended the NSF-ITCE SPATIAL Short-course at the University of Utah, which was and is an invaluable resource for the research conducted. We would like to especially thank Lesley Chesson for her input and editing of this chapter.

References

Åberg, G. (1995). The use of natural strontium isotopes as tracers in environmental studies. *Water, Air, & Soil Pollution, 79*(1–4), 309–322. https://doi.org/10.1007/BF01100444

Agarwal, S. C., & Glencross, B. A. (2011). Building a social bioarchaeology. In S. C. Agarwal, & B. A. Glencross (Eds.), *Social bioarchaeology*. https://doi.org/10.1002/9781444390537.ch1

Ambrose, S. H., & Norr, L. (1993). Experimental evidence for the relationship of the carbon isotope ratios of whole diet and dietary protein to those of bone collagen and carbonate. In J. B. Lambert, & G. Grupe (Eds.), *Prehistoric human bone- archaeology at the molecular level* (pp. 1–37). Springer Berlin Heidelberg. https://doi.org/10.1007/978-3-662-02894-0_1

Ammer, S. T. M., Bartelink, E. J., Vollner, J. M., Anderson, B. E., & Cunha, E. M. (2020). Spatial distributions of oxygen stable isotope ratios in tap water from Mexico for region of origin predictions of unidentified border crossers. *Journal of Forensic Sciences, 65*(4), 1049–1055. https://doi.org/10.1111/1556-4029.14283

Anderson, B. E., & Parks, B. O. (2008). Symposium on border crossing deaths: Introduction. *Journal of Forensic Sciences, 53*(1), 6–7. https://doi.org/10.1111/j.1556-4029.2007.00608.x.

Anderson, B. E., & Spradley, M. K. (2016). The role of the anthropologist in the identification of migrant remains in the American southwest. *Academic Forensic Pathology, 6*(3), 432–438. https://doi.org/10.23907/2016.044

Bao, H., Cao, X., & Hayles, J. A. (2016). Triple oxygen isotopes: Fundamental relationships and applications. *Annual Review of Earth and Planetary Sciences, 44*(1), 463–492. https://doi.org/10.1146/annurev-earth-060115-012340

Bartelink, E. J., Berg, G. E., Beasley, M. M., & Chesson, L. A. (2014). Application of stable isotope forensics for predicting region of origin of human remains from past wars and conflicts. *Annals of Anthropological Practice, 38*(1), 124–136. https://doi.org/10.1111/napa.12047

Bartelink, E. J., Berg, G. E., Chesson, L. A., Tipple, B. J., Beasley, M. M., Prince-Buitenhuys, J. R., MacInnes, H., MacKinnon, A. T., & Latham, K. E. (2018a). Applications of stable isotope forensics for geolocating unidentified human remains from past conflict situations and large-scale humanitarian efforts. In *New perspectives in forensic human skeletal identification* (pp. 175–184). Elsevier. https://doi.org/10.1016/b978-0-12-805429-1.00015-6

Bartelink, E. J., Berg, G. E., Chesson, L. A., Tipple, B. J., Beasley, M. M., Prince-Buitenhuys, J. R., MacInnes, H., MacKinnon, A. T., & Latham, K. E. (2018b). Applications of stable isotope forensics for geolocating unidentified human remains from past conflict situations and large-scale humanitarian efforts. In K. E. Latham, E. J. Bartelink, & M. Finnegan (Eds.), *New perspectives in forensic human skeletal identification* (pp. 175–184). Academic Press. https://doi.org/10.1016/b978-0-12-805429-1.00015-6

Bartelink, E., Berry, R., & Chesson, L. (2014). Stable isotopes and human provenancing. In *Advances in forensic human identification* (pp. 165–192). Taylor and Francis. https://doi.org/10.1201/b16509

Bartelink, E. J., & Chesson, L. A. (2019). Recent applications of isotope analysis to forensic anthropology. *Forensic Sciences Research, 4*(1), 29–44. https://doi.org/10.1080/20961790.2018.1549527

Bartelink, E. J., Mackinnon, A. T., Prince-Buitenhuys, J. R., Tipple, B. J., & Chesson, L. A. (2016). Stable isotope forensics as an investigative tool in missing persons investigations. In S. Morewitz, & C. Sturdy Colls (Eds.), *Handbook of missing persons* (pp. 443–462). Springer International Publishing. https://doi.org/10.1007/978-3-319-40199-7_29

Bataille, C. P., & Bowen, G. J. (2012). Mapping 87Sr/86Sr variations in bedrock and water for large scale provenance studies. *Chemical Geology, 304–305*, 39–52. https://doi.org/10.1016/j.chemgeo.2012.01.028

Bataille, Clement P., Laffoon, J., & Bowen, G. J. (2012). Mapping multiple source effects on the strontium isotopic signatures of ecosystems from the circum-Caribbean region. *Ecosphere, 3*(12), 1–24. https://doi.org/10.1890/es12-00155.1

Bataille, Clement P., von Holstein, I. C. C., Laffoon, J. E., Willmes, M., Liu, X. M., & Davies, G. R. (2018). A bioavailable strontium isoscape for western Europe: A machine learning approach. *PLoS One, 13*(5), e0197386. https://doi.org/10.1371/journal.pone.0197386

Beard, B. L., & Johnson, C. M. (2000). Strontium isotope composition of skeletal material can determine the birth place and geographic mobility of humans and animals. *Journal of Forensic Sciences, 45*(5), 14829J. https://doi.org/10.1520/jfs14829j

Bender, R. L., Dufour, D. L., Valenzuela, L. O., Cerling, T. E., Sponheimer, M., Reina, J. C., & Ehleringer, J. R. (2015). Stable isotopes (carbon, nitrogen, sulfur), diet, and anthropometry in urban Colombian women: Investigating socioeconomic differences. *American Journal of Human Biology, 27*(2), 207–218. https://doi.org/10.1002/ajhb.22640

Benson, S., Lennard, C., Maynard, P., & Roux, C. (2006). Forensic applications of isotope ratio mass spectrometry - a review. *Forensic Science International, 157*(1), 1–22. https://doi.org/10.1016/j.forsciint.2005.03.012

Bentley, R. Alexander (2006). Strontium isotopes from the earth to the archaeological skeleton: A review. *Journal of Archaeological Method and Theory, 13*(3), 135–187. https://doi.org/10.1007/s10816-006-9009-x

Bentley, R. A., & Knipper, C. (2005). Geographical patterns in biologically available strontium, carbon and oxygen isotope signatures in prehistoric SW Germany. *Archaeometry, 47*(3), 629–644. https://doi.org/10.1111/j.1475-4754.2005.00223.x

Bentley, R. Alexander, Price, T. D., & Stephan, E. (2004). Determining the "local" 87Sr/86Sr range for archaeological skeletons: A case study from neolithic Europe. *Journal of Archaeological Science, 31*(4), 365–375. https://doi.org/10.1016/j.jas.2003.09.003

Bol, R., Marsh, J., & Heaton, T. H. E. (2007). Multiple stable isotope (18O, 13C, 15N and 34S) analysis of human hair to identify the recent migrants in a rural community in SW England. *Rapid Communications in Mass Spectrometry, 21*(18), 2951–2954. https://doi.org/10.1002/rcm.3168

Bösl, C., Grupe, G., & Peters, J. (2006). A late neolithic vertebrate food web based on stable isotope analyses. *International Journal of Osteoarchaeology, 14*(4), 296–315. https://doi.org/10.1002/oa.834

Bowen, G. J. (2010a). Isoscapes: Spatial pattern in isotopic biogeochemistry. *Annual Review of Earth and Planetary Sciences, 38*(1), 161–187. https://doi.org/10.1146/annurev-earth-040809-152429

Bowen, G. J. (2010b). Statistical and geostatistical mapping of precipitation water isotope ratios. In *Isoscapes: Understanding movement, pattern, and process on Earth through isotope mapping*. https://doi.org/10.1007/978-90-481-3354-3_7

Brettell, R., Montgomery, J., & Evans, J. (2012). Brewing and stewing: The effect of culturally mediated behaviour on the oxygen isotope composition of ingested fluids and the implications for human provenance studies. *Journal of Analytical Atomic Spectrometry, 27*(5), 778–785. https://doi.org/10.1039/c2ja10335d

Capo, R. C., Stewart, B. W., & Chadwick, O. A. (1998). Strontium isotopes as tracers of ecosystem processes: Theory and methods. *Geoderma, 82*(1–3), 197–225. https://doi.org/10.1016/S0016-7061(97)00102-X

Cartigny, P., & Busigny, V. (2018). Nitrogen isotopes. In William M. White (Ed.), *Encyclopedia of geochemistry: A comprehensive reference source on the chemistry of the earth* (pp. 991–1003). Springer International Publishing. https://doi.org/10.1007/978-3-319-39312-4_197

ten Cate, J. M., & Featherstone, J. D. B. (1991). Mechanistic aspects of the interactions between fluoride and dental enamel. *Critical Reviews in Oral Biology & Medicine, 2*(2), 283–296. https://doi.org/10.1177/10454411910020030101

Chen, D., Yang, C., Huang, Z., & Wang, X. (2002). *Using lead isotope ratios to distinguish between samples of the traditional Chinese medicine dan-shen*. Agilent Technologies.

Chesson, L. A., Tipple, B. J., Youmans, L. V., O'Brien, M. A., & Harmon, M. M. (2018). Forensic identification of human skeletal remains using isotopes: A brief history of applications from archaeological dig sites to modern crime scenes. In K. E. Latham, & E. J. Bartelink (Eds.), *New perspectives in forensic human skeletal identification* (pp. 157–173). Elsevier.

Christensen, A. M., & Crowder, C. M. (2009). Evidentiary standards for forensic anthropology. *Journal of Forensic Sciences, 54*(6), 1211–1216. https://doi.org/10.1111/j.1556-4029.2009.01176.x

Colibrı́ center for human rights. (2018). Press Kit. https://www.colibricenter.org/press-kit-pdf-download/.

Coplen, T. B. (1988). Normalization of oxygen and hydrogen isotope data. *Chemical Geology: Isotope Geoscience section, 72*(4), 293–297. https://doi.org/10.1016/0168-9622(88)90042-5

Craig, H. (1953). The geochemistry of the stable carbon isotopes. *Geochimica et Cosmochimica Acta, 3*(2–3), 53–92. https://doi.org/10.1016/0016-7037(53)90001-5

Daniel Bryant, J., & Froelich, P. N. (1995). A model of oxygen isotope fractionation in body water of large mammals. *Geochimica et Cosmochimica Acta, 59*(21), 4523–4537. https://doi.org/10.1016/0016-7037(95)00250-4

Darwent, C., & Lyman, R. (2001). Detecting the postburial fragmentation of carpals, tarsals, and phalanges. In W. D. Haglund, & M. H. Sorg (Eds.), *Advances in forensic taphonomy* (pp. 355–377). https://doi.org/10.1201/9781420058352-24, 355-377.

Deniro, M. J., & Epstein, S. (1981). Influence of diet on the distribution of nitrogen isotopes in animals. *Geochimica et Cosmochimica Acta, 45*(3), 341–351. https://doi.org/10.1016/0016-7037(81)90244-1

Ehleringer, J. R., Bowen, G. J., Chesson, L. A., West, A. G., Podlesak, D. W., & Cerling, T. E. (2008). Hydrogen and oxygen isotope ratios in human hair are related to geography. *Proceedings of the National Academy of Sciences of the United States of America, 105*(8), 2788–2793. https://doi.org/10.1073/pnas.0712228105

Ehleringer, J. R., Thompson, A. H., Podlesak, D. W., Bowen, G. J., Chesson, L. A., Cerling, T. E., Park, T., Dostie, P., & Schwarcz, H. (2010). A framework for the incorporation of isotopes and isoscapes in geospatial forensic investigations. In *Isoscapes: Understanding movement, pattern, and process on Earth through isotope mapping* (pp. 357–387). https://doi.org/10.1007/978-90-481-3354-3_17

Emsley, J. (2011). *Nature's building blocks: An A-Z guide to the elements*. Oxford University Press.

Environmental Systems Research Institute (ESRI). (2018). *ArcGIS desktop release 10.6.1* (10.6.1.).

Executive Office of the President- Office of Science and Technology Policy. (2013). *Memorandum for the heads of executive departments and agencies- increasing access to the results of federally funded scientific research.*

Ezzo, J. A., Johnson, C. M., & Price, T. D. (1997). Analytical perspectives on prehistoric migration: A case study from east-central Arizona. *Journal of Archaeological Science, 24*(5), 447–466. https://doi.org/10.1006/jasc.1996.0129

Farquhar, J. (2018). Sulfur isotopes. In William M. White (Ed.), *Encyclopedia of geochemistry: A comprehensive reference source on the chemistry of the earth* (pp. 1402–1409). Springer International Publishing. https://doi.org/10.1007/978-3-319-39312-4_74

Faure, G., & Powell, J. L. (1972). Strontium isotope geology. In *Strontium isotope geology.* Springer Berlin Heidelberg. https://doi.org/10.1007/978-3-642-65367-4

Fava, M., Watanabe, I.-S., Fava-de-Moraes, F., & Costa, L. (1997). Prismless enamel in human non-erupted deciduous molar teeth: A scanning electron microscopic study. *Revista de Odontologia Da Universidade de São Paulo, 11*(4), 239–243. https://doi.org/10.1590/s0103-06631997000400003

Federal Bureau of Investigation. (2020a). *Combined DNA Index system (CODIS)*. https://www.fbi.gov/services/laboratory/biometric-analysis/codis.

Federal Bureau of Investigation. (2020b). *Frequently asked questions on CODIS and NDIS*. https://www.fbi.gov/services/laboratory/biometric-analysis/codis/codis-and-ndis-fact-sheet.

Fejerskov, O., Josephsen, K., & Nyvad, B. (1984). Surface ultrastructure of unerupted mature human enamel. *Caries Research, 18*(4), 302–314. https://doi.org/10.1159/000260781

Font, L., Van Der Peijl, G., Van Wetten, I., Vroon, P., Van Der Wagt, B., & Davies, G. (2012). Strontium and lead isotope ratios in human hair: Investigating a potential tool for determining recent human geographical movements. *Journal of Analytical Atomic Spectrometry, 27*(5), 719–732. https://doi.org/10.1039/c2ja10361c

Freiwald, C. (2011). *Maya migration networks: Reconstructing population movement in the Belize river valley during the late and terminal classic*. University of Wisconsin-Madison.

Frost, H. M. (1999). On the estrogen-bone relationship and postmenopausal bone loss: A new model. *Journal of Bone and Mineral Research, 14*(9), 1473–1477. https://doi.org/10.1359/jbmr.1999.14.9.1473

Fry, B. (2006). Stable isotope ecology. In *Stable isotope ecology.* New York: Springer.

Gwinnett, A. J. (1992). Structure and composition of enamel. In *Operative dentistry.*

Hedges, R. E. M. (2002). Bone diagenesis: An overview of processes. *Archaeometry, 44*(3), 319–328. https://doi.org/10.1111/1475-4754.00064

Hedges, Robert E. M. (2003). On bone collagen - apatite-carbonate isotopic relationships. *International Journal of Osteoarchaeology, 13*(1–2), 66–79. https://doi.org/10.1002/oa.660

Hedges, Robert E. M., Clement, J. G., Thomas, C. D. L., & O'Connell, T. C. (2007). Collagen turnover in the adult femoral mid-shaft: Modeled from anthropogenic radiocarbon tracer measurements. *American Journal of Physical Anthropology, 133*(2), 808–816. https://doi.org/10.1002/ajpa.20598

He, L. H., & Swain, M. V. (2007). Enamel-A "metallic-like" deformable biocomposite. *Journal of Dentistry, 35*(5), 431–437. https://doi.org/10.1016/j.jdent.2006.12.002

Hill, P. A., & Orth, M. (1998). Bone remodelling. *British Journal of Orthodontics, 25*, 101–107. https://doi.org/10.1093/ortho/25.2.101

Hillson, S. (1996). Dental anthropology. In *Dental anthropology*. Cambridge University Press. https://doi.org/10.1017/cbo9781139170697

Hillson, S. (2013). Tooth development in human evolution and bioarchaeology. In *Tooth development in human evolution and bioarchaeology*. https://doi.org/10.1017/CBO9780511894916

Hoefs, J. (2015). Stable isotope geochemistry: Seventh edition. In *Stable isotope geochemistry* (6th ed.). Springer Science & Business Media. https://doi.org/10.1007/978-3-540-70708-0

Hueb De Menezes Oliveira, M. A., Torres, C. P., Gomes-Silva, J. M., Chinelatti, M. A., Hueb De Menezes, F. C., Palma-Dibb, R. G., & Borsatto, M. C. (2010). Microstructure and mineral composition of dental enamel of permanent and deciduous teeth. *Microscopy Research and Technique, 73*(5), 572–577. https://doi.org/10.1002/jemt.20796

Hülsemann, F., Lehn, C., Schneider, S., Jackson, G., Hill, S., Rossmann, A., Scheid, N., Dunn, P. J. H., Flenker, U., & Schänzer, W. (2015). Global spatial distributions of nitrogen and carbon stable isotope ratios of modern human hair. *Rapid Communications in Mass Spectrometry, 29*(22), 2111–2121. https://doi.org/10.1002/rcm.7370

Humane Borders Inc. (2020). *Arizona open GIS initiative for deceased migrants*.

Iacumin, P., Bocherens, H., Mariotti, A., & Longinelli, A. (1996). Oxygen isotope analyses of co-existing carbonate and phosphate in biogenic apatite: A way to monitor diagenetic alteration of bone phosphate? *Earth and Planetary Science Letters, 142*(1–2), 1–6. https://doi.org/10.1016/0012-821x(96)00093-3

Illingworth, S. (August 4, 2015). *Identifying the bodies of border crossers*. The Huffington Post. http://www.huffingtonpost.com/sarah-illingworth/identifying-the-bodies-of-border-crossers_b_7023596.html.

Juarez, C. A. (2008). Strontium and geolocation, the pathway to identification for deceased undocumented Mexican border-crossers: A preliminary report. *Journal of Forensic Sciences, 53*(1), 46–49. https://doi.org/10.1111/j.1556-4029.2007.00610.x

Kamenov, G. D., & Gulson, B. L. (2014). The Pb isotopic record of historical to modern human lead exposure. *Science of the Total Environment, 490*, 861–870. https://doi.org/10.1016/j.scitotenv.2014.05.085

Katzenberg, M. A. (2007). Stable isotope analysis: A tool for studying past diet, demography, and life history. In M. A. Katzenberg, & S. R. Saunders (Eds.), *Biological anthropology of the human skeleton: Second edition* (2nd ed.). John Wiley & Sons, Inc. https://doi.org/10.1002/9780470245842.ch13

Kempson, I. M., & Lombi, E. (2011). Hair analysis as a biomonitor for toxicology, disease and health status. *Chemical Society Reviews, 40*(7), 3915–3940. https://doi.org/10.1039/c1cs15021a

Knudson, K. J., & Buikstra, J. E. (2007). Residential mobility and resource use in the Chiribaya polity of southern Peru: Strontium isotope analysis of Archaeological tooth enamel and bone. *International Journal of Osteoarchaeology, 17*(6), 563–580. https://doi.org/10.1002/oa.916

Knudson, K. J., Tung, T. A., Nystrom, K. C., Price, T. D., & Fullagar, P. D. (2005). The origin of the Juch'uypampa Cave mummies: Strontium isotope analysis of archaeological human remains from Bolivia. *Journal of Archaeological Science, 32*(6), 903–913. https://doi.org/10.1016/j.jas.2005.01.007

Knudson, K. J., Williams, S. R., Osborn, R., Forgey, K., & Williams, P. R. (2009). The geographic origins of Nasca trophy heads using strontium, oxygen, and carbon isotope data. *Journal of Anthropological Archaeology, 28*(2), 244–257. https://doi.org/10.1016/j.jaa.2008.10.006

Kohn, M. J., Schoeninger, M. J., & Valley, J. W. (1996). Herbivore tooth oxygen isotope compositions: Effects of diet and physiology. *Geochimica et Cosmochimica Acta, 60*(20), 3889–3896. https://doi.org/10.1016/0016-7037(96)00248-7

Kootker, L. M., van Lanen, R. J., Kars, H., & Davies, G. R. (2016). Strontium isoscapes in The Netherlands. Spatial variations in 87Sr/86Sr as a proxy for palaeomobility. *Journal of Archaeological Science: Report, 6*, 1–13. https://doi.org/10.1016/j.jasrep.2016.01.015

Kramer, R. T. (2018). *Application of stable isotopes and geostatistics to predict region of geographic origin for deceased migrants recovered in southern Texas*. San Marcos: Texas State University.

Kramer, R., Bartelink, E., Herrmann, N., Spradley, M., & Bataille, C. (2020). Application of stable isotopes and geostatistics to infer region of geographic origin for deceased unidentified Latin American migrants. Chapter submitted. In R. C. Parra, S. C. Zapico, & D. H. Ubelaker (Eds.), *Humanitarian forensic science: Interacting with the dead and the living*. Wiley & Sons, Inc.

Krause, K., & Foitzik, K. (2006). Biology of the hair follicle: The basics. *Seminars in Cutaneous Medicine and Surgery, 25*, 2–10. https://doi.org/10.1016/j.sder.2006.01.002

Laffoon, J. E., Sonnemann, T. F., Shafie, T., Hofman, C. L., Brandes, U., & Davies, G. R. (2017). Investigating human geographic origins using dual-isotope (87 Sr/86 Sr, ä18 O) assignment approaches. *PLoS One, 12*(2). https://doi.org/10.1371/journal.pone.0172562

Lee-Thorp, J. (2002). Two decades of progress towards understanding fossilization processes and isotopic signals in calcified tissue minerals. *Archaeometry, 44*(3), 435–446. https://doi.org/10.1111/1475-4754.t01-1-00076

Lee-Thorp, J. A. (2008). On isotopes and old bones. *Archaeometry, 50*(6), 925–950. https://doi.org/10.1111/j.1475-4754.2008.00441.x

Lehn, C., & Graw, M. (2014). Stabilisotopenanalysen an Körpergeweben von unbekannten Personen: Grundlagen, Probennahme, Analysen, Interpretation. *Rechtsmedizin, 24*(2), 129–143. https://doi.org/10.1007/s00194-014-0946-5

Lehn, Christine, Kalbhenn, E. M., Rossmann, A., & Graw, M. (2019). Revealing details of stays abroad by sequential stable isotope analyses along human hair strands. *International Journal of Legal Medicine, 133*(3), 935–947. https://doi.org/10.1007/s00414-018-1866-9

de León, J. (2015). The land of open graves: Living and dying on the migrant trail. In *The land of open graves*. University of Califrornia Press. https://doi.org/10.1111/ciso.12122

Longinelli, A. (1984). Oxygen isotopes in mammal bone phosphate: A new tool for paleohydrological and paleoclimatological research? *Geochimica et Cosmochimica Acta, 48*(2), 385–390. https://doi.org/10.1016/0016-7037(84)90259-X

Mancuso, C. J., & Ehleringer, J. R. (2018). Strontium isotope ratios (87Sr/86Sr) of human fingernail clippings reveal multiple location signals. *Rapid Communications in Mass Spectrometry, 32*(22), 1922–1930. https://doi.org/10.1002/rcm.8270

Martin, R. B. (2000). Toward a unifying theory of bone remodeling. *Bone, 26*(1), 1–6. https://doi.org/10.1016/S8756-3282(99)00241-0

Martin, R. Bruce, Burr, D. B., Sharkey, N. A., & Fyhrie, D. P. (2015). *Skeletal tissue mechanics* (2nd ed.). Springer New York. https://doi.org/10.1007/978-1-4939-3002-9

Martinez, D. E., Reineke, R., Rubio-Goldsmith, R., Anderson, B. E., Hess, G. L., & Parks, B. O. (2015). A continued humanitarian crisis at the border: Undocumented border crosser deaths recorded by the Pima county office of the medical examiner, 1990-2012. *SSRN Electronic Journal*. https://doi.org/10.2139/ssrn.2633209

Massey, D. S., Durand, J., & Malone, N. J. (2002). *Beyond smoke and mirrors: Mexican immigration in an era of economic integration*. Russell Sage Foundation. https://doi.org/10.7758/9781610443821

McMurry, J., & Fay, R. (2004). Hydrogen, oxygen and water. In K. P. Hamann (Ed.), *Chemistry* (4th ed., pp. 575–599). Pearson Education.

Meier-Augenstein, W. (2011). Stable isotope forensics: An introduction to the forensic application of stable isotope analysis. In *Stable isotope forensics: An introduction to the forensic application of stable isotope analysis* (1st ed.). John Wiley and Sons. https://doi.org/10.1002/9780470688762

Mekota, A. M., Grupe, G., Ufer, S., & Cuntz, U. (2006). Serial analysis of stable nitrogen and carbon isotopes in hair: Monitoring starvation and recovery phases of patients suffering from anorexia nervosa. *Rapid Communications in Mass Spectrometry, 20*(10), 1604–1610. https://doi.org/10.1002/rcm.2477

National Center for Biotechnology Information. (2019). *PubChem database. Neodymium*. CID=23934.

Nelson, S. (2014). *Wheeler's dental anatomy, physiology and occlusion* (10th ed.). Elsevier.

Neuberger, F. M., Jopp, E., Graw, M., Püschel, K., & Grupe, G. (2013). Signs of malnutrition and starvation-Reconstruction of nutritional life histories by serial isotopic analyses of hair. *Forensic Science International, 226*(1–3), 22–32. https://doi.org/10.1016/j.forsciint.2012.10.037

No More Deaths/No Mas Muertes. (June 16, 2017). *Border Patrol raids humanitarian-aid camp in targeted attack*. https://nomoredeaths.org/border-patrol-raids-humanitarian-aid-camp-in-targeted-attack/.

O'Connell, T. C., Kneale, C. J., Tasevska, N., & Kuhnle, G. G. C. (2012). The diet-body offset in human nitrogen isotopic values: A controlled dietary study. *American Journal of Physical Anthropology, 149*(3), 426–434. https://doi.org/10.1002/ajpa.22140

Ortner, D. J. (2003). Identification of pathological conditions in human skeletal remains. In D. J. Ortner (Ed.), *Identification of pathological conditions in human skeletal remains*. Elsevier Inc. https://doi.org/10.1016/B978-0-12-528628-2.X5037-6

Piwowar, H. A., Day, R. S., & Fridsma, D. B. (2007). Sharing detailed research data is associated with increased citation rate. *PLoS One, 2*(3). https://doi.org/10.1371/journal.pone.0000308

Plomp, E., von Holstein, I. C. C., Koornneef, J. M., Smeets, R. J., Baart, J. A., Forouzanfar, T., & Davies, G. R. (2019). Evaluation of neodymium isotope analysis of human dental enamel as a provenance indicator using 10 13 Ω amplifiers (TIMS). *Science & Justice, 59*(3), 322–331. https://doi.org/10.1016/j.scijus.2019.02.001

Price, T. D., Burton, J. H., Fullagar, P. D., Wright, L. E., Buikstra, J. E., & Tiesler, V. (2008). Strontium isotopes and the study of human mobility in ancient Mesoamerica. *Latin American Antiquity, 19*(2), 167–180. https://doi.org/10.1017/S1045663500007781

Price, T. D., Burton, J. H., Fullagar, P. D., Wright, L. E., Buikstra, J. E., & Tiesler, V. (2015). Strontium isotopes and the study of human mobility among the ancient maya. In *Archaeology and bioarchaeology of population movement among the prehispanic maya* (pp. 119–132). https://doi.org/10.1007/978-3-319-10858-2_11

Price, T. D., Johnson, C. M., Ezzo, J. A., Ericson, J., & Burton, J. H. (1994). Residential mobility in the prehistoric southwest United States: A preliminary study using strontium isotope analysis. *Journal of Archaeological Science, 21*(3), 315–330. https://doi.org/10.1006/jasc.1994.1031

Price, T. D., Manzanilla, L., & Middleton, W. D. (2000). Immigration and the ancient city of teotihuacan in Mexico: A study using strontium isotope ratios in human bone and teeth. *Journal of Archaeological Science, 27*(10), 903–913. https://doi.org/10.1006/jasc.1999.0504

Pye, K. (2004). Isotope and trace element analysis of human teeth and bones for forensic purposes. *Geological Society - Special Publications, 232*, 215–236. https://doi.org/10.1144/GSL.SP.2004.232.01.20

R Core Team. (2020). *The R: A language and environment for statistical computing*. Vienna, Austria: R Foundation for Statistical Computing. http://r-project.org/.

Regan, L. A. (2006). *Isotopic determination of region of origin in modern people: Applications for identification of US war-dead from the Vietnam Conflict*. Gainesville: Florida University.

Reitsema, L. J. (2013). Beyond diet reconstruction: Stable isotope applications to human physiology, health, and nutrition. *American Journal of Human Biology, 25*(4), 445–456. https://doi.org/10.1002/ajhb.22398

Reitsema, L. J. (2015). Laboratory and field methods for stable isotope analysis in human biology. *American Journal of Human Biology, 27*(5), 593–604. https://doi.org/10.1002/ajhb.22754

Richards, M. P., Fuller, B. T., Sponheimer, M., Robinson, T., & Ayliffe, L. (2003). Sulphur isotopes in palaeodietary studies: A review and results from a controlled feeding experiment. *International Journal of Osteoarchaeology, Special Issue: Bone Chemistry*, 37–45. https://doi.org/10.1002/oa.654

Rickard, D. (2012). Sedimentary sulfur isotope biogeochemistry. In *Developments in sedimentology* (pp. 419–473). https://doi.org/10.1016/B978-0-444-52989-3.00011-8

Ropp, R. C. (2013). The alkaline earths as metals. In *Encyclopedia of the alkaline earth compounds*. https://doi.org/10.1016/b978-0-444-59550-8.00001-6

Ross, M. H., & Pawlina, W. (2010). *Histology: A text and atlas* (6th ed.). Lippincott Williams & Wilkins.

Rummel, S., Hölzl, S., & Horn, P. (2007). Isotopensignaturen von Bio- und Geo-Elementen in der Forensik. In B. Herrmann, & K.-S. Saternus (Eds.), *Biologische spurenkunde, band 1: Kriminalbiologie* (pp. 381–407). Springer Berlin Heidelberg. https://doi.org/10.1007/978-3-540-71111-7_18

Santamaria-Fernandez, R., Giner Martínez-Sierra, J., Marchante-Gayón, J. M., García-Alonso, J. I., & Hearn, R. (2009). Measurement of longitudinal sulfur isotopic variations by laser ablation MC-ICP-MS in single human hair strands. *Analytical and Bioanalytical Chemistry, 394*(1), 225–233. https://doi.org/10.1007/s00216-009-2615-1

Schimmelmann, A., & Sauer, P. E. (2018). Hydrogen isotopes. In W. M. White (Ed.), *Encyclopedia of geochemistry. Encyclopedia of earth sciences series*. Cham: Springer. https://doi.org/10.1007/978-3-319-39312-4_326

Schoeller, D. A. (1999). Isotope fractionation: Why aren't we what we eat? *Journal of Archaeological Science, 26*(6), 667–673. https://doi.org/10.1006/jasc.1998.0391

Schoeninger, M. J., & Moore, K. (1992). Bone stable isotope studies in archaeology. *Journal of World PreHistory, 6*(2), 247–296. https://doi.org/10.1007/BF00975551

Schwarcz, H. P., & Schoeninger, M. J. (1991). Stable isotope analyses in human nutritional ecology. *American Journal of Physical Anthropology, 34*(13S), 283–321. https://doi.org/10.1002/ajpa.1330340613

Schweissing, M. M., & Grupe, G. (2003). Stable strontium isotopes in human teeth and bone: A key to migration events of the late roman period in bavaria. *Journal of Archaeological Science, 30*(11), 1373–1383. https://doi.org/10.1016/S0305-4403(03)00025-6

Sealy, J. C., van der Merwe, N. J., Sillen, A., Kruger, F. J., & Krueger, H. W. (1991). 87Sr86Sr as a dietary indicator in modern and archaeological bone. *Journal of Archaeological Science, 18*(3), 399–416. https://doi.org/10.1016/0305-4403(91)90074-Y

Sillen, A., Hall, G., & Armstrong, R. (1995). Strontium calcium ratios (Sr/Ca) and strontium isotopic ratios (87Sr/86Sr) of Australopithecus robustus and Homo sp. from Swartkrans. *Journal of Human Evolution, 28*(3), 277–285. https://doi.org/10.1006/jhev.1995.1020

Smith, B. H. (1991). Standards of human tooth formation and dental age assessment. In M. A. Kelley, & C. S. Larsen (Eds.), *Advances in dental anthropology* (pp. 143–168). John Wiley and Sons Ltd. https://doi.org/10.1002/ajhb.1310030624

Spradley, M. K. (2014). Toward estimating geographic origin of migrant remains along the United States-Mexico border. *Annals of Anthropological Practice, 38*(1), 101–110. https://doi.org/10.1111/napa.12045

Spradley, M. K., Herrmann, N. P., Siegert, C. B., & McDaneld, C. P. (2019). Identifying migrant remains in southsouth Texas: Policy and practice. *Forensic Sciences Research, 4*(1), 60–68. https://doi.org/10.1080/20961790.2018.1497437

Stack, M. V. (1967). Chemical organization of the organic matrix of enamel: Volume 2. In A. E. W. Miles, & J. H. Allan (Eds.), *Structural and chemical organization of teeth* (pp. 317–346). Academic Press.

Steele, K. W., & Daniel, R. M. (1978). Fractionation of nitrogen isotopes by animals: A further complication to the use of variations in the natural abundance of 15N for tracer studies. *The Journal of Agricultural Science, 90*(1), 7–9. https://doi.org/10.1017/S002185960004853X

Stille, P., & Shields, G. (1997). Radiogenic isotope geochemistry of sedimentary and aquatic systems. In *Radiogenic isotope geochemistry of sedimentary and aquatic systems*. https://doi.org/10.1007/bfb0117747

Tachikawa, K., Jeandel, C., & Roy-Barman, M. (1999). A new approach to the Nd residence time in the ocean: The role of atmospheric inputs. *Earth and Planetary Science Letters, 170*(4), 433–446. https://doi.org/10.1016/S0012-821X(99)00127-2

Thornton, E. K. (2011). Reconstructing ancient Maya animal trade through strontium isotope (87Sr/86Sr) analysis. *Journal of Archaeological Science, 38*(12), 3254–3263. https://doi.org/10.1016/j.jas.2011.06.035

Tieszen, L. L., & Fagre, T. (1993). Effect of diet quality and composition on the isotopic composition of respiratory CO2, bone collagen, bioapatite, and soft tissues. In Joseph B. Lambert, & G. Grupe (Eds.), *Prehistoric human bone* (pp. 121–155). Springer Berlin Heidelberg. https://doi.org/10.1007/978-3-662-02894-0_5

Tipple, B. J. (2015). *Isotope analyses of hair as a trace evidence tool to reconstruct human movements: Combining strontium isotope with hydrogen/oxygen isotope data* (pp. 1–50).

Tipple, Brett J., Valenzuela, L. O., & Ehleringer, J. R. (2018). Strontium isotope ratios of human hair record intra-city variations in tap water source. *Scientific Reports, 8*(1), 3334. https://doi.org/10.1038/s41598-018-21359-0

Tykot, R. H. (2004). *Stable isotopes and diet: You are what you eat.* International School of Physics "Enrico Fermi" Course.

Tykot, Robert H. (2006). Isotope analyses and the histories of maize. In J. E. Staller, R. H. Tykot, & B. F. Benz (Eds.), *Histories of maize: Multidisciplinary approaches to the prehistory, linguistics, biogeography, domestication, and evolution of maize* (1st ed., pp. 131–142). Elsevier Academic Press. https://doi.org/10.1016/b978-012369364-8/50262-x

United Nations High Commissioner for Refugees. (2019). *Global trends: Forced displacement in.*

United Nations Office on Drugs and Crime. (2019). *Global Study on Homicide- Homicide trends, patterns and criminal justice response.* https://www.unodc.org/documents/data-and-analysis/gsh/Booklet2.pdf.

Universal declaration of human rights (217 [III] A).(1948). http://www.un.org/en/universal-declaration-human-rights/.

University of North Texas Center for Human Identification. (2019). *No Title.* https://www.untchi.org.

Valenzuela, L. O., Chesson, L. A., O'Grady, S. P., Cerling, T. E., & Ehleringer, J. R. (2011). Spatial distributions of carbon, nitrogen and sulfur isotope ratios in human hair across the central United States. *Rapid Communications in Mass Spectrometry, 25*(7), 861–868. https://doi.org/10.1002/rcm.4934

Van Klinken, G. J., Richards, M. P., & Hedges, B. E. M. (2002). An overview of causes for stable isotopic variations in past European human populations: Environmental, ecophysiological, and cultural effects. In *Biogeochemical approaches to paleodietary analysis* (pp. 39–63). https://doi.org/10.1007/0-306-47194-9_3

Vroon, P. Z., van Bergen, M. J., Klaver, G. J., & White, W. M. (1995). Strontium, neodymium, and lead isotopic and trace-element signatures of the east Indonesian sediments: Provenance and implications for banda arc magma genesis. *Geochimica et Cosmochimica Acta, 59*(12), 2573–2598. https://doi.org/10.1016/0016-7037(95)00151-4

Wadleigh, M. A., Schwarcz, H. P., & Kramer, J. R. (1994). Sulphur isotope tests of seasalt correction factors in precipitation: Nova Scotia, Canada. *Water, Air, & Soil Pollution, 77*(1–2), 1–6. https://doi.org/10.1007/BF00483047

Wagner, T., Magill, C. R., & Herrle, J. O. (2018). Carbon isotopes. In William M. White (Ed.), *Encyclopedia of geochemistry: A comprehensive reference source on the chemistry of the earth* (pp. 194–204). Springer International Publishing. https://doi.org/10.1007/978-3-319-39312-4_176

Warner, M. M., Plemons, A. M., Herrmann, N. P., & Regan, L. A. (2018). Refining stable oxygen and hydrogen isoscapes for the identification of human remains in Mississippi. *Journal of Forensic Sciences, 63*(2), 395–402. https://doi.org/10.1111/1556-4029.13575

West, J. B., Bowen, G. J., Dawson, T. E., & Tu, K. P. (2010). Isoscapes: Understanding movement, pattern, and process on earth through isotope mapping. In *Isoscapes: Understanding movement, pattern, and process on earth through isotope mapping.* https://doi.org/10.1007/978-90-481-3354-3

White, T. D., Black, M. T., & Folkens, P. A. (2011). Human osteology: Third edition. In *Human osteology: Third edition* (3rd ed.). Academic Press.

White, C. D., Price, T. D., & Longstaffec, F. J. (2007). Residential histories of the human sacrifices at the Moon Pyramid, Teotihuacan: Evidence from oxygen and strontium isotopes. *Ancient Mesoamerica, 18*(1), 159–172. https://doi.org/10.1017/S0956536107000119

Wild, E. M., Arlamovsky, K. A., Golser, R., Kutschera, W., Priller, A., Puchegger, S., Rom, W., Steier, P., & Vycudilik, W. (2000). 14C dating with the bomb peak: An application to forensic medicine. *Nuclear Instruments and Methods in Physics Research, Section B: Beam Interactions with Materials and Atoms, 172*(1–4), 944–950. https://doi.org/10.1016/S0168-583X(00)00227-5

Wilkinson, D. (November 26, 2018). *Mexico: Forced disappearance, an ongoing crime*. Human Rights Watch, El Universal. https://www.hrw.org/news/2018/11/26/mexico-forced-disappearance-ongoing-crime.

Wright, L. E. (2005). Identifying immigrants to Tikal, Guatemala: Defining local variability in strontium isotope ratios of human tooth enamel. *Journal of Archaeological Science, 32*(4), 555–566. https://doi.org/10.1016/j.jas.2004.11.011

Wright, L. E. (2012). Immigration to Tikal, Guatemala: Evidence from stable strontium and oxygen isotopes. *Journal of Anthropological Archaeology, 31*(3), 334–352. https://doi.org/10.1016/j.jaa.2012.02.001

Wright, L. E., & Schwarcz, H. P. (1998). Stable carbon and oxygen isotopes in human tooth enamel: Identifying breastfeeding and weaning in prehistory. *American Journal of Physical Anthropology, 106*(1), 1–18. https://doi.org/10.1002/(SICI)1096-8644(199805)106:1<1::AID-AJPA1>3.0.CO;2-W

Wright, L. E., & Schwarcz, H. P. (1999). Correspondence between stable carbon, oxygen and nitrogen isotopes in human tooth enamel and dentine: Infant diets at Kaminaljuyu. *Journal of Archaeological Science, 26*(9), 1159–1170. https://doi.org/10.1006/jasc.1998.0351

Young Shin, J., O'Connell, T., Black, S., & Hedges, R. (2004). Differentiating bone osteonal turnover rates by density fractionation; validation using the bomb 14 C atmospheric pulse. *Radiocarbon, 46*(2), 853–861. https://doi.org/10.1017/s0033822200035888

CHAPTER

Mass fatalities and Rapid DNA

10

Kim Gin

Sacramento County Coroner, Retired Kim Gin Professional Solutions, LLC - Owner/CEO, Fairhope, AL, United States

1. Introduction

When a mass fatality event occurs, identifying disaster victims is of the utmost importance for a variety of reasons. Bringing closure to family and friends of the decedents is ultimately the number one goal as this will aid them in the grieving process, but there are also secondary goals with achieving identification that can range from legal issues for insurance purposes, obtaining FEMA reimbursement to help with the loss of property and paying for funeral arrangements, to establishing identity of the decedent, so the cause and manner are also properly assigned. The last reason may not make sense, after all, the decedents are involved in a mass fatality event and are considered mass fatality victims, but it is not unheard of that someone may commit suicide rather than face whatever event is occurring or a homicide may occur during the event timeline, and establishing the victim's identity may be necessary to establish the correct cause and manner. No matter the reason for making positive identification, identifying disaster victims is a priority.

Mass fatality events are usually defined as any single event that overwhelms the emergency system and can range from earthquakes, fires, tornadoes, hurricanes, train derailments, and plane crashes, to criminal and terrorist events such as bombings or mass shootings. With any type of event, the aftermath can create different kinds of barriers for recovery, such as location of the remains and instability of the incident site(s), which can further challenge the recovery of disaster victim remains. For example, drowning victims after a flood may take time to locate before recovery can occur with protracted time spent in the water or fire victims may be left at an incident site for an extended period of time while first responders work to put out fires, and then, once the area is deemed safe enough for search and recovery efforts, the site itself may require specialized teams working together to actually identify human remains from debris. This extended time frame after death until recovery can further increase the degradation of remains and make the postmortem identification a much harder task.

Traditional methods of identification used in day-to-day operations, such as fingerprints and dental comparison, are still utilized to make postmortem disaster victim identification (DVI), but just on a much larger scale. Until recently, DVI

Methodological and Technological Advances in Death Investigations. https://doi.org/10.1016/B978-0-12-819394-5.00009-2

technologies have not changed much at all. The use of fingerprints, dental comparison and conventional DNA analysis has remained the standards for identification up until the last few years in the U.S. Medicolegal death field. The significant change was due to the introduction of Rapid DNA technology (Tan et al., 2013; Turingan et al., 2019, 2020; Turnigan et al., 2016), which was first utilized in the camp fire and then months later in the conception dive boat fire, both of which will be discussed in more detail later in this chapter. This introduction of the new technology cemented the use of Rapid DNA in this arena and shortened a once arduous and lengthy identification process.

Often these mass events, particularly fires, bombings, and aviation accidents are so devastating that the results of the incident negate or severely minimize the use of fingerprints, visual identification, hardware identification and, in some instances, dental comparison. The results of these events ravage the human body making DVI so difficult that turning to DNA evidence is the only option. Mass incidents involving fire, chemicals, water, and explosions may prove detrimental to most identifying features even if found quickly after death, but DNA evidence can survive extremes of weather, fires, devastation from bombings, and even some chemicals, making DNA analysis ideal for identification following a mass fatality event. DNA identification or DNA typing has become a valuable tool in DVI for over 20 years with DNA analysis being used in such events as the 9/11 World Trade Center bombing, Hurricane Katrina, and other incidents (Biesecker et al., 2005; Brenner & Weir, 2003; Deng et al., 2005; Donkervoort et al., 2008; Hartman et al., 2011; Hsu et al., 1999; Leclair et al., 2001; McEntire et al., 2012; Sudoyo et al., 2008).

Unfortunately, not all disaster victims are identified in a timely manner. In December of 2004, a 9.1 magnitude earthquake in the seabed off the Sumatra Coast triggered a massive Tsunami that hit 14 countries, flattening resorts and villages in its wake. There were an estimated 230,000 victims and approximately 10% remain unidentified, with many buried in unmarked graves (Morgan et al., 2006; CBS News 22, 2014).

2. The future of disaster victim identification

In the past, conventional DNA analysis for identification has relied upon sophisticated equipment in a laboratory setting where technical personnel process the samples, analyze the resulting DNA data, and perform kinship analysis. This process is laborious and time-consuming, with time spent packaging forensic evidence samples at the scene or in a morgue setting, transporting samples, and then performing DNA analysis. Since many Coroner and Medical Examiner Offices do not employ lab personnel, they do not have the sophisticated DNA lab equipment necessary to make identifications by traditional means and must rely on outside labs to do the work. Unfortunately, even a relatively small disaster can overwhelm local forensic laboratories, and these labs are already stretched thin with their processing of evidentiary samples for criminal cases. Another issue is that the laboratory near the disaster may be rendered unusable by the event itself and another outside lab would have to be located to analyze samples, further delaying identifications. Taken together, the result is that laboratory-based DNA identification of disaster victims typically requires years and is, in many cases, never even attempted.

The recent introduction of Rapid DNA for DVI has allowed the entire process to be compressed, and identifications relying on DNA identification can be made much more quickly than conventional DNA analysis—typically in hours to days. The term "Rapid DNA" refers to the automated system of generating a short tandem repeat (STR) profile (also known as a DNA profile or DNA ID) in 2 hours, typically performed in the field by nontechnical users. The ability to deploy Rapid DNA systems at disaster sites, morgues, hospitals, police stations, and office buildings is dramatically changing the paradigm for integrating DNA into DVI—DNA is becoming a primary identification modality that is more accurate than any other and can determine kinship, unlike any other.

2.1 Rapid DNA: Privacy and advantages in DVI

A common question about Rapid DNA analysis concerns privacy. A DNA ID—whether performed using Rapid DNA or conventional lab techniques—reports the sizes of 27 STR regions scattered throughout the chromosome. These regions vary from person to person but do not contain genes—they were chosen specifically because they do not contain any information of the donor's past, current, or future medical condition, behavior, appearance, age, or ethnicity. DNA IDs are incredibly valuable for identifying an individual and their genetic relationship with close family members—but they contain no other information.

DNA has additional advantages over other biometric modalities. Teeth and fingerprint evidence can change over the years. Teeth change from childhood to adulthood with even more marked changes on the teeth themselves throughout the lifetime which can make DVI difficult if not impossible even if antemortem records are located. Fingerprints, although very hardy, can also be altered even minutely by injuries, burns, and other influences that can further challenge the DVI process. DNA, in contrast, cannot be altered and a profile can be generated with a surprisingly small amount of sample making DNA evidence well-suited for DVI (Fig. 10.1).

2.2 The basics of Rapid DNA

Rapid DNA is a fully automated process that can be completed, from start to finish, in less than 2 hours (see Fig. 10.2). In the camp fire, it was decided that using the ANDE Rapid DNA instrument was the best course of action. This was due to the highly degraded state of the remains and the concomitant lack of ability to successfully use other modalities. The sheer number of victims made using traditional DNA analysis impractical and the long-time frame unacceptable. This Rapid DNA instrument was ideal because it can be operated by nontechnical personnel outside of a laboratory setting and can run up to five samples at one time. Running multiple

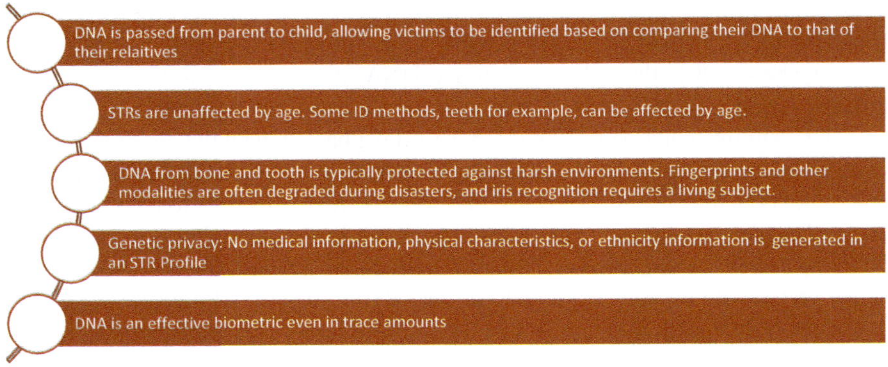

FIGURE 10.1

Why DNA and short tandem repeat (STR) markers are good biometrics in disaster victim identification.

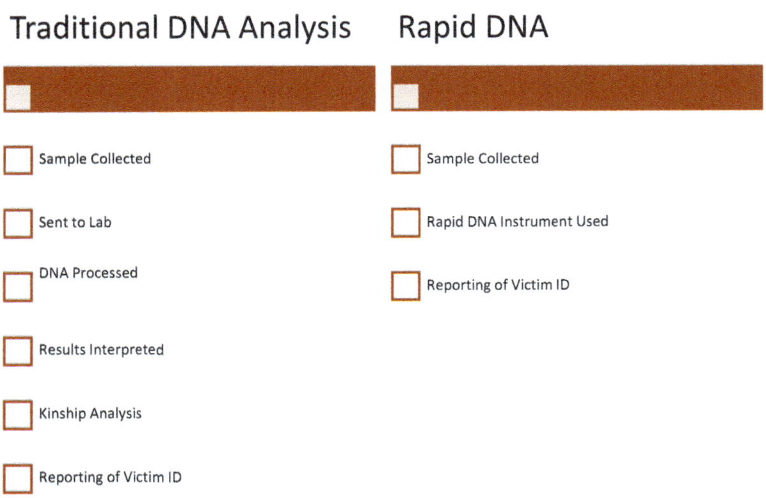

FIGURE 10.2

Traditional DNA analysis steps versus Rapid DNA.

samples simultaneously makes the entire DVI process more efficient, especially when running the highly degraded samples that are characteristic of most mass fatality events. During the wildfire, Rapid DNA instruments were located in a rented RV and at an abandoned retail store.

The benefits of quickly and efficiently identifying mass fatality victims can be shared by law enforcement agencies, medicolegal death agencies, and families to name just a few. The family benefits were touched on above, but the ability to receive confirmation of a loved ones death in hours versus months, frees the family and friends to move through the stages of grief rather than remaining in limbo every day wondering if their loved one is still alive, referred to as "ambiguous loss" (Boss et al., 2003). The financial benefit is also a tremendous benefit as families can initiate the reimbursement process much sooner with Rapid DNA than has been possible historically. On the law enforcement and medicolegal death agency side, identifying disaster victims quickly and efficiently frees personnel to move on to more challenging identification scenarios and the multitude of other tasks that must be completed in mass fatality management. The inclusion of Rapid DNA is truly a game changer in DVI.

2.3 Sampling for DNA analysis

When using Rapid DNA, the samples that can be tested are the same types of samples used in conventional laboratory DNA analysis. Sample types may include bone, saliva, soft tissue, blood, and organs. All of these sample options are important as the flexibility optimizes success across a wide range of disaster scenarios. For example, a cheek swab may be appropriate for a relatively intact victim recovered from a collapsed building or shooting soon after the event, whereas a bone fragment may be best suited for a set of highly degraded remains following a fire.

Genomic DNA typing of soft tissue of some of these victims may be impossible due to autolysis or destruction of the tissue, microbial contamination, or environmental factors, but the DNA present in bone, particularly dense cortical bone, and teeth, may remain intact for an extended period from years to millennia (Green et al., 2006; Latham et al., 2013) and will still be viable for DNA analysis. In many cases, the degradation of disaster victim samples may be such that bone or teeth are all that is available of the victim to analyze. The ability to analyze bone makes Rapid DNA a good option for speedy, accurate identification of the most degraded samples commonly found with mass fatality victims. The Rapid DNA system will also analyze, in circumstances when no biological family are known or available (in some adoption cases, for example), antemortem biological samples (samples taken prior to death from victims, such as surgical samples). Rapid DNA IDs generated from evidence acquired from known victim sources, such as toothbrushes and hair from hairbrushes, can be analyzed as well to aid in identification.

2.4 Disaster victim identification and the Santa Barbara Dive Boat Fire

Rapid DNA technology was used in the 2018 Camp Fire in Butte County California, discussed in detail later in this chapter, to help with the identifications for most of the 85 victims of that horrific wildfire. Rapid DNA was used again in September 2019 to identify all 34 victims in the Santa Barbara Conception Dive Boat Fire. The Conception was sailing with 33 passengers and six crew members on a Labor Day diving excursion when a fire started in the passenger quarters in the early morning hours. One crew member was down below and perished along with the passengers.

The remaining five crew members were rescued, and the dive boat sank in the deep waters after catching fire. In that incident, the Sacramento County Coroner's Office agreed to assist the Santa Barbara County Sheriff's Office in the identification process via Rapid DNA. This method of identification was chosen due to the state of the victims once recovered where fingerprint evidence was not available in many of the victims, visual confirmation was impossible, and antemortem dental records were difficult to obtain due to the victims living outside the area and the country in some instances. Rapid DNA was a fast, accurate solution.

The two agencies, along with assistance from multiple other state and federal agencies, were successful in identifying all 34 of the boat fire victims that were found in the waters near the Santa Cruz Islands. The 34 identifications were completed in 10 days, with the majority of the victims identified within 1 day of being located in the water, and all the victims had a completed DNA profile within 1 day of recovery. The last victim was found on day 10 following the incident and was identified the very same day. Fingerprint identification was completed on all of the victims, that could be successfully fingerprinted, but due to the state of the remains that would have been an impossible avenue for all of the victims of this event. This was an unprecedented achievement in mass fatality identification all due to the implementation of Rapid DNA (Photos 1 and 2).

PHOTO 1

Temporary morgue set up outside of Santa Barbara County Sheriff's Office.

PHOTO 2

Los Angeles county refrigerated trucks.

3. Rapid DNA and disaster management

Effectively incorporating Rapid DNA into disaster management requires a change in the traditional steps of biological sampling. Prior to the advent of Rapid DNA in DVI, obtaining samples for DNA occurred after autopsy at the morgue, either temporary or permanent, and after representatives of all the other necessary disciplines completed their examinations. DNA sampling has traditionally been the last step in the process when all other avenues of identification have been exhausted, making traditional DNA profiling ultimately the very last resort in DVI. Rapid DNA makes this established process in the steps of fatality management no longer necessary or advisable. Rapid DNA should be front and center in the process along with the other disciplines and, in many cases, before even attempting the other biometric modalities. Integrating Rapid DNA into the mass fatality management steps depends on the state of the remains. The more degraded the remains, the more likely that DNA analysis will be the only avenue for DVI.

4. Disciplines used in disaster victim identification

Depending on the type of mass fatality event, various disciplines can be involved in helping with cause of death, manner of death, and identification of victims. There are some events that may use only some of the disciplines, for example, disaster victims from floods may still be intact so forensic anthropology may not be needed or victims from a mass shooting may be able to be identified by fingerprints so disciplines other than pathology/medicolegal may not be needed. Some mass fatality events are going to require the use of all the disciplines, wildfires are a good example where every discipline might be used. The most common disciplines in mass fatality management identification are Forensic Odontology, Forensic Anthropology, Forensic Pathology, and Medicolegal Death Investigation and DNA analysis (Fig. 10.3).

4.1 Defining the world of medicolegal death investigation

To better understand the process of mass fatality management and successful DVI management, one must first understand the world of medicolegal death investigation. Medicolegal death investigation varies in the United States, and even disciplines that work closely with the death investigation agencies may not completely understand it. The term "Forensic Pathology" can be used in general for the examination process in the mass fatality management steps, but to help define the discipline further, a forensic pathologist is titled as such in offices that are not run by a medical examiner.

A forensic pathologist can be referred to as a forensic pathologist in any system or a medical examiner and a forensic pathologist in a medical examiner system. A pathologist and a forensic pathologist differ in that a forensic pathologist completes a forensic pathology fellowship program and passes the necessary exams to become a forensic pathologist. Some offices use both pathologists and forensic pathologists for examinations, but most use forensic pathologists for forensic or criminal cases at the minimum. The shortage of these much-coveted doctors has left most agencies shorthanded and dependent on other specialties to assist in what are deemed nonforensic cases. The nation is comprised of various types of medicolegal death investigation agencies that

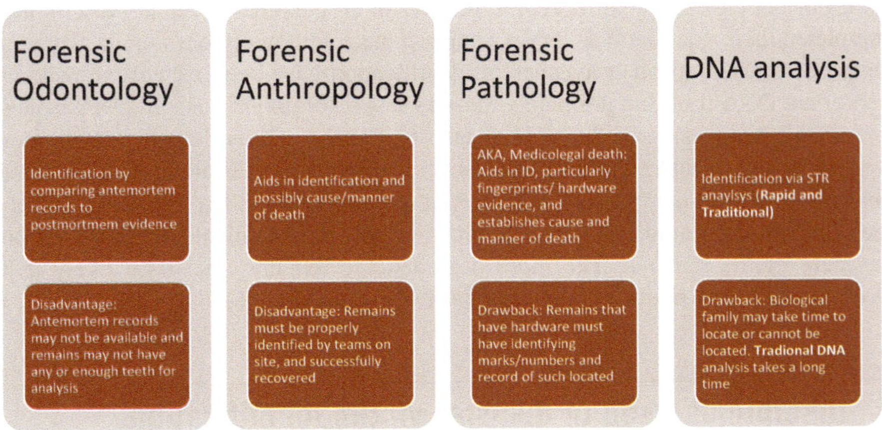

FIGURE 10.3

Common disciplines in disaster victim identification (DVI).

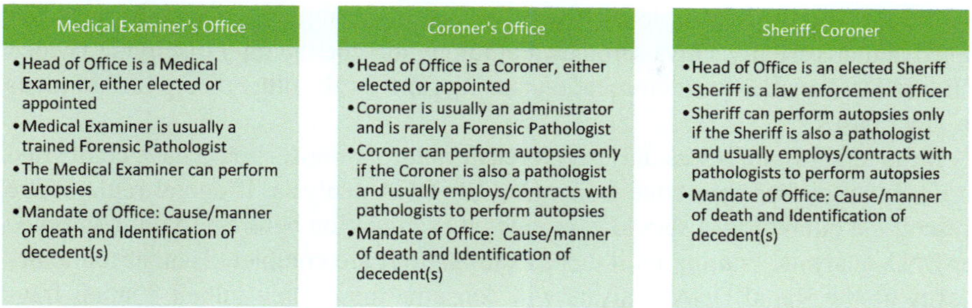

FIGURE 10.4

Three of the most common types of medicolegal death offices in the U.S. Not all types of offices/mandates are included.

can be called Coroner, Medical Examiner, Sheriff-Coroner, or a combination of Medical Examiner-Coroner, just to list the most common titles (Fig. 10.4).

The agencies generally operate the same way, no matter the name, with pathologists conducting exams, and the cause and manner of death, and identification of the deceased, being the office's main mandates. These offices can be privately operated in some States offering pathology services to government agencies or more commonly, government run completely, in a county or state system, or a combination of county/state services. The offices often work very closely with forensic odontologists, dentists that have been trained to identify decedents based on comparison of antemortem (before death) and postmortem (after death) evidence, and forensic anthropologists to help with identification in both day-to-day operations and DVI.

5. The steps surrounding disaster victim identification

With the addition of Rapid DNA into the mass fatality identification process, pathology or medicolegal death investigation agencies can directly identify disaster victims instead of waiting until all other disciplines have attempted to identify the victim. Sending samples to a forensic DNA laboratory for conventional processing once all other avenues of identification have failed is no longer a reasonable approach. Rapid DNA can be used much sooner in the process and will often make identifications quicker than the other methods. For bodies that are sufficiently intact such that sampling of bodily fluids is possible without damaging other evidence, samples such as blood can be taken anytime in the process and usually is taken right away with pathologist permission and often guidance. Blood can be sampled directly from the body or from dried blood on Flinders Technology Associates (FTA) cards, specially treated cotton fiber paper that can be used for blood sample preservation.

Tissue or organ sampling may also occur right away with pathologist permission or guidance depending upon the condition of the remains. Utilizing blood, tissue, or organ samples for Rapid DNA processing, the identification can be made even before the autopsy is completed if family reference samples (FRS) have been obtained and are usually saliva samples. Pathology may be the only discipline needed if Rapid DNA makes the identification, saving time for the other disciplines to focus on other cases.

If the remains are bones only, the forensic anthropologist should have completed an examination before a bone is sampled for DNA analysis. If dental remains are present, the odontologist should complete an examination before a tooth is sampled for DNA analysis. Waiting until these examinations are complete is an absolute necessity as the Rapid DNA analysis will consume the sample (albeit a small fragment). Managing the process of obtaining samples and examinations is extremely important, so that the steps are taken in the proper order, especially when the disaster victim remains have been reduced to skeletal remains (Fig. 10.5).

5.1 Temporary versus permanent morgue sites

The words temporary and permanent morgue sites were mentioned above. It is not unusual to have more than one morgue functioning at the same time depending on the mass fatality event. A temporary morgue site may be set up due to a variety of reasons including, but not exclusive to, distance of the permanent morgue from the incident site, destruction or damage of the permanent morgue, necessity of storage/examination while recovery efforts are conducted, and the wait for transport and staffing issues with operating recovery effort while managing a permanent morgue. A temporary morgue site can be established with exams and sample collection performed at the temporary location if needed. A temporary morgue site was set up in the camp fire simply to aid in proper storage of victims until they could be transported to the permanent morgue site. The Rapid DNA instrument can be set up at the temporary

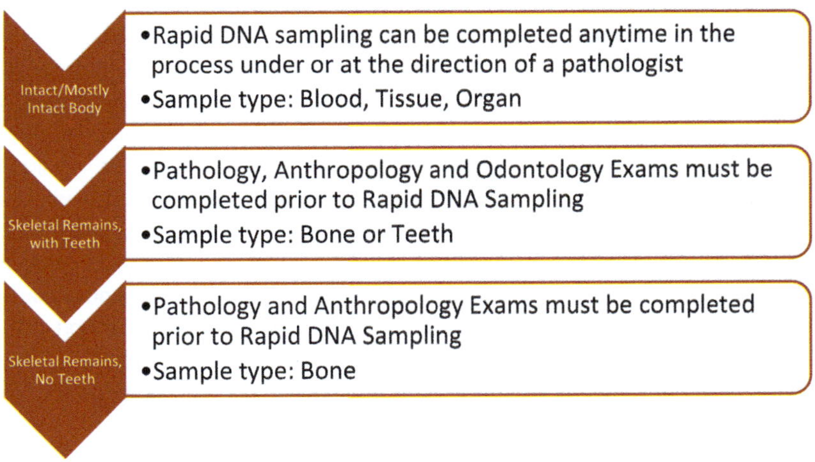

FIGURE 10.5

Diagram of inclusion of Rapid DNA in disaster victim identification steps.

site to run samples right away before remains are transported to the permanent morgue or to the final resting place for the deceased. This was not done in the camp fire because the fire was not controlled for weeks, and the site was not ideal for running samples due to the danger of wildfire. However, if a temporary morgue site is necessary for whatever reason, it may be that running samples in the location may be an option for quicker turnaround time in DVI.

6. Utilizing a Family Assistance Center

If more than one Rapid DNA instrument is available, an instrument can also be placed in the Family Assistance Center (FAC) if one is activated. Some incidents do not require an FAC activation, but most events will require this crucial step as it provides a variety of much needed services. FAC resources include transportation services, clerical services, daycare, and crisis intervention specialists for the family and friends of the victims and also serve as a central location for collection DNA samples (buccal swabs) from biological family members. It is not recommended to have the victim samples transported to the FAC for analysis, but rather the family reference samples (FRS) taken from and analyzed within the FAC and compared to victim samples analyzed at the morgue or another location that has been set up to run the Rapid DNA instrument. This reduces travel time and makes identification even quicker.

There are some privacy considerations that should be addressed when operating a Rapid DNA instrument in the FAC. The location should be isolated within the FAC with limited access. A dedicated station should be maintained within the FAC for staff to take biological samples from the family members. There are forms that must be completed by the family and interview questions to understand and document the precise relationship between the FRS donor and the victim. Privacy must be a priority for the staff and families within the location, so the proper samples are taken. It is not uncommon for a family member to not understand genetics and try to give a sample when they are not biologically connected to the victim such as in adoptions. Staff elected to take these samples must understand what questions to ask from the beginning of the event so time is not wasted in taking samples that are of no use in DNA analysis. Parent–child samples and sibling samples are the best samples to obtain for analysis. In some cases, half-sibling and aunt/uncle siblings can work for analysis. Cousins and beyond rarely work. When taking sibling/half-sibling samples and aunt/uncle samples without parental samples, the more sibling samples obtained, the better for analysis. Staff should be made aware of the potential for multiple samples needed in these cases (Photo 3).

Even if a second instrument is unavailable, setting up an FAC is not only crucial to getting information and services to families but also is very beneficial to obtaining FRS in one central location then transporting them to the site where the Rapid DNA instrument is set up for analysis. As samples are collected, one or more instruments may be reassigned from analyzing victim samples to analyzing FRS, depending on

PHOTO 3

ANDE Rapid DNA instrument in Family Assistance Center.

the number of available samples and instruments. For example, in the Conception Dive Boat Fire, all the victim samples were completed quickly from time of recovery, with the profiles generated within 1 day of being located. The FRS took longer because most of the families lived outside of the area. Since it was taking longer to acquire the FRS, once all victim profiles were obtained, the instrument designated for victims was eventually used as an additional FRS instrument so the FRS analysis could be completed more quickly (Fig. 10.6).

7. Case study: Camp Fire, Butte County California

The ANDE Rapid DNA technology was implemented in the November 2018 Camp Fire that occurred in Butte County, California. This massive wildfire burned hot and fast leaving a decimated Butte County in its wake. As of 2022, it was the most destructive wildfire in the State's history, consuming 153,336 acres and killing 85 people (CAL Fire, 2019; The Washington Post, 2018). Eighty-four victims were located on scene, and one died much later in the hospital from wildfire-related injuries. Numerous agencies responded to help with containing the fire and ongoing

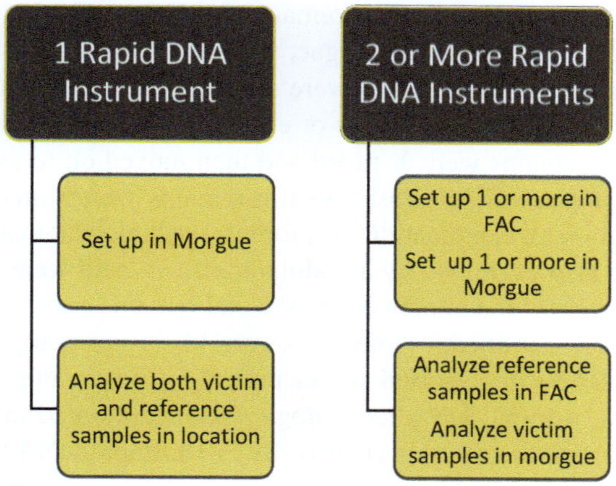

FIGURE 10.6

Distribution of Rapid DNA instruments for optimal identification. As more instruments are added, other options for optimal distribution can be considered.

search and rescue efforts, and more agencies were added when the response changed to a search and recovery effort. The agencies varied from fire and law to medicolegal agencies to anthropology teams.

The camp fire started on November 8, 2018, and was not the only incident California was experiencing when it started. The day before the camp fire broke out, the deadly Borderline Bar and Grill shooting in Ventura County had occurred where a gunman had killed 13 people including an officer (VC Star – Part of the USA Today Network, 2018) and another fire, the Woolsey Fire (National Park Service (NPS), 2018), had broken out in Los Angeles and Ventura Counties. The combination of the two wildfires, and the deadly mass shooting severely stretched the emergency services in California.

The Butte County Sheriff's Office was the agency of jurisdiction for the camp fire and was tasked with coordinating the response effort to the camp fire along with cause and manner of death and DVI. This involved collaboration with a multitude of agencies including the California's Office of Emergency Services (CAL OES), CAL Fire, the National Guard, California Highway Patrol, medicolegal death investigators throughout California, various search-and-rescue teams from agencies throughout the state and other agencies that offered their help. In addition to the fire and law requests, the Butte County Sheriff's Office requested the assistance of forensic anthropology teams from California and Nevada. The Butte County Sheriff's Office through CAL OES requested assistance from the Sacramento County Coroner's Office. The request was twofold, assist Butte County Sheriff's Office by determining the cause of death and identifying the camp fire victims.

A temporary morgue site consisting of a refrigerated truck was set up in Butte County for storage of Unidentified Human Remains (UHR). This ensured that further degradation was not caused by the elements and postmortem decomposition was slowed. At the end of each day, the remains were transported to the Sacramento County Morgue. Upon arrival at the morgue, each victim was processed. If the UHR could be fingerprinted, the fingerprints were scanned via a live scan instrument stationed in the morgue, then any property or evidence was cataloged, photographed, and packaged. The remains were X-rayed and then moved on to examination. If it was after hours for exams, the disaster victim remains were stored in the morgue refrigeration unit until an examination by a forensic pathologist could be conducted. The remains were also examined by an odontologist, if teeth were available, and a forensic anthropologist if the remains were skeletal remains only. It quickly became clear that traditional identification methods were likely not going to work for the bulk of the 84 victims transported to Sacramento County, due to the severely degraded remains, so Rapid DNA technology was incorporated into the workflow for the identification of the disaster victims. By 2018, Rapid DNA had been proven for use in law enforcement and military applications, but this was the first time it had been attempted in DVI (although the ANDE system had been tested at a number of DVI exercises organized by the Department of Homeland Security) (Photo 5).

7.1 Recovery stage

The recovery of human remains was conducted by forensic anthropology teams that were built for efficiency and comprised of California State University, Chico (CSU, CHICO) anthropology faculty, alumni, and students, experts from UC Santa Cruz, the University of Nevada, Reno, the University of Nevada, Las Vegas, and the Clark County Medical Examiner's Office in Las Vegas. These teams were outfitted with other personnel to respond to areas in the cities of Concow, Paradise, and Magalia, between November 10–28, 2018, with three additional search days

PHOTO 4

Typical remains brought in, the items on the right side of the photo are actually building materials.

PHOTO 5

Refrigerated truck used for storage and transportation during camp fire.

conducted in December and then again in January of 2019, in order to search for additional remains.

One of the obstacles noted early on was that the teams were largely comprised of agencies that had little to no death investigation experience. Their help, although crucial, was an obstacle when specific information was needed such as the need for time of death for death certification or the ability to distinguish degraded victim remains from degraded building material. The teams were quickly educated and an anthropologist was either assigned to each team or performed necessary reviews of a location if remains were suspected to be present. The teams used the missing persons lists that were updated each day to help guide the search and recovery efforts. In major disasters, it is not uncommon to have inflated missing persons' lists that are reconciled over time as the confusion of the incident tapers off. This was the case in the camp fire where the actual final number of 84 missing, was much higher at the beginning of the search and recovery effort, originally in the thousands, that slowly reconciled to possibly 150 missing then narrowed down to the final reconciliation. The displacement of residents from the evacuated area and multiple reports of missing people with various versions of a name were two of the major reasons for the confusion.

Many of the remains were burned and degraded and clearly identifiable as bodies or portions of bodies, but some potential remains were harder to determine. The forensic anthropology teams examined these types of potential remains on scene and determined whether the potential remains were in fact human remains. The teams used search patterns that started with a perimeter walk around any buildings or other structures in question, then moved on to a foot survey that was a minimally invasive walk, as much as possible, through the ruined structures. Finally, the teams used small hand tools to conduct a thorough search. The tools used to carefully excavate the scenes were sieves and hand trowels with other small hands tools used as needed. Carefully excavating with the small tools allowed the team to make a more thorough recovery of remains. The teams were extremely careful due to the possibility of fragmentary teeth and dental appliances (Blau & Briggs, 2011) that might be located within the remains.

The areas with visible bone were fully excavated, and 1 meter around the location was also excavated, leading to the recovery of pacemakers, teeth, and dental appliances. The teams used paper evidence bags to store the items located and these items were transported in paper evidence bags that were stored inside body bags. In the morgue, the forensic anthropologists used anthropologic methods (Buikstra & Ubelaker, 1994; Moore-Jansen et al., 1994, pp. 1–78) to aid in identifications. Age, sex, stature, and sometimes medical history such as osteoporosis, were determined, if the thermal damage to the remains was minor enough to still examine the remains. Unfortunately, very few of the disaster victim remains fell into that category. Once the remains were sent to the morgue, a forensic anthropologist would examine the remains again and remove anything that was not human (Photo 4).

8. Identifying the camp fire disaster victims

8.1 Radiographic features and hardware

Prior to autopsy, all the victims were X-rayed per standard DVI protocol. The purpose of x-raying disaster victims is primarily to assist with identification. The X-ray can identify hardware or antemortem injuries. If evidence of an antemortem injury is located, medical records can sometimes be obtained to help with identification. The same was true for surgical hardware. Any hardware placed in a human body for longer than 1 year must have identifying numbers on the device. One of the obstacles of using this method for identification is that the identifying numbers on the hardware must be compared with some type of antemortem information such as medical records.

Unfortunately, the state of the remains made locating antemortem injuries almost nonexistent due to the badly burned remains located, many of which were not even intact bones. Out of all the disaster victims x-rayed during the identification process, only 12 sets of remains had hardware that was also recovered such as pacemakers, a shoulder implant, and knee hardware. Most of the hardware located were so burned that interrogating pacemakers or reading identifying markings on hardware was impossible. However, in two cases, an artificial shoulder and knee were thoroughly cleaned of soot and debris, and identifying numbers were located on both.

The locations where the two implants were found yielded tentative identifications or possible names of the victims; however, no one could give information as to where to locate medical records for these two individuals so quickly obtaining the records was problematic. The medical offices in the area were severely damaged and the local hospital survived the fire, but the medical records department was severely damaged. To help with this issue, a massive search for medical records was initiated by multiple agencies, the Butte County Sheriff's Office, the Sacramento County Coroner's Office, and the California Department of Justice, Missing and Unidentified Unit, worked together to locate records by looking at various places the two individuals lived as adults and calling offices that might have seen them. Both individuals had served in the military, which helped hone the search. The effort took 67 days for one set of records to be obtained and 87 days for the second set to be obtained for comparison. It was a long, arduous search that involved substantial staff time and an extended period to receive the records, but the efforts paid off and the two victims were positively identified by hardware.

8.2 Forensic odontology

Forensic odontology is a valuable tool in both day-to-day identification and DVI. Forensic odontologists can make identifications using antemortem records on very degraded teeth, even fire damaged, simply because teeth are very strong and will hold up quite well to fire. One of the most common problems in using this method is usually the inability to locate antemortem records to make a comparison. This was a major issue in the camp fire due to the sheer number of structures that burned, many of them medical and dental offices. Some of the dental offices had electronic records that were stored in the cloud, but many either had electronic records that had to be accessed in their office, which could not be accessed or were still using paper files. Despite the destruction of antemortem records or inability to access these records, 16 of the disaster victims were identified by odontologists, making it the second highest identification modality used to identify victims in the camp fire.

8.3 Fingerprint analysis

Due to the destruction of the wildfire, only five disaster victims out of the 84 recovered had fingerprints that could be obtained. Four of the victims were positively identified at the Sacramento County Coroner's Morgue using the Livescan fingerprint database. This database is a statewide database that is maintained by the California Department of Justice. A fifth victim was identified by the casting of a thumbprint that was submitted to the California Department of Justice, Latent Prints Unit. The Butte County Sheriff's Department located a possible victim known to live at the address where the remains were found. This potential victim's fingerprints were pinpointed as a tentative identification. This casting was compared to the tentative identification and the identification was completed. No other camp fire victims could be identified with this method.

8.4 Rapid DNA identification

Out of 84 victims processed by the Sacramento County Coroner's Office, only 23 could be identified by conventional methods. Some of the identifications that were completed required a tremendous amount of work by multiple agencies to find antemortem evidence just to make the identifications. Due to the low number of identifications made by conventional means, it left the bulk of the identifications, DNA was the last remaining modality that had any chance to positively identify these remaining victims.

The problem, as discussed earlier in this chapter, with using conventional laboratory DNA methods is the length of time it would take to make these identifications. With so many victims requiring DNA analysis and only one identification able to be made using traditional methods, the Sacramento County Coroner's Office, and the Butte County Sheriff's Office, looked to Rapid DNA on the fourth day after the first set of victim remains were recovered to analyze these samples and attempt to identify the victims quickly.

The Rapid DNA instruments supplied by ANDE were set up in a standard size RV at the FAC in Butte County and in a similar RV at the Sacramento County Morgue. The Butte County RV was stationed as such to assist in obtaining family reference samples. The morgue RV was set up to run unidentified human remains. The instruments were extremely easy to set up, requiring only an electrical source and no need for calibration before operating.

The instrument uses two types of disposable chips. The A-chip can process up to five buccal swab samples in one run, and the I-chip processes up to four DVI samples per run. The A-chip is primarily used for FRS and the I-chip is primarily used for unidentified human remains (and for other crime scene samples). The ability to run multiple samples at one time means a much faster turnaround time for identification and is ideal for DVI (Fig. 10.7).

Rapid DNA identification using the ANDE system was performed on a total of 69 sets of remains and of the 69, 62, or 89.9% generated DNA profiles or IDs all within hours of sample receipt. This high percentage that was achieved is extraordinary in

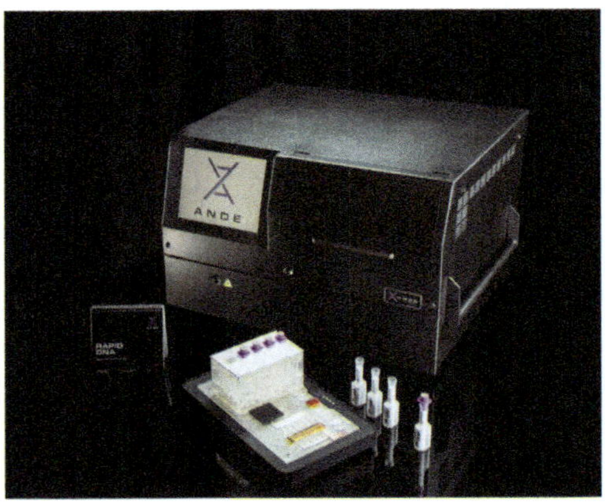

FIGURE 10.7

ANDE Rapid DNA operating system, instrument, chip, and swabs.

Courtesy of ANDE, www.ande.com.

this event because the remains in most cases were so heavily degraded. These victim DNA IDs were then used for familial searching although the available FRS were limited initially. Because of the almost immediate availability of victim profiles, the Butte County Sheriff's Office conducted an aggressive campaign to find biological family members from the missing persons list with much success, leading to a total of 255 DNA IDs generated from FRS being placed into the ANDE system 2018 Camp Fire DNA database. Of the 255, 219 were processed in the ANDE System including two profiles generated from antemortem tissue block samples and the remaining 36 were generated by a traditional laboratory using conventional methods. From the 62 sets of remains that had Rapid DNA profiles generated, 60 victims were positively identified with the initial identifications made on the fourth day of the recovery of the first victims, and most identifications were made within 2 weeks, well before the devastating wildfire was even brought under control.

8.5 Camp fire case summary

The introduction of Rapid DNA into the camp fire victim identification process cemented Rapid DNA's role in a mass fatality event. The camp fire victims were severely burned with many of the remains reduced to a handful of bones making Rapid DNA the most successful of the identification modalities, with by far the majority of the identifications generated in this event. The camp fire victims were on the extremes of degradation, and the Rapid DNA identifications were still the highest identification modality for the event. In comparison, the Conception Dive Boat Fire victims were all identified using Rapid DNA and in a much shorter time span of 10 days from time of the event, with the last victim found and identified on day 10. The victims also had succumbed to fire in the event like the camp fire victims, but they also had been submerged in salt water for an extended time prior to recovery.

Two factors contributed to a quicker turnaround time for this event. First, the agencies responding used Rapid DNA protocols and procedures from the beginning of the event when processing victims (instead of 4 days later as in the camp fire). Second, obtaining FRS was a high priority from the beginning of the event—in the camp fire, saving lives and controlling the fire understandably led to a lower prioritization for FRS collection. Establishing a, FAC right away and sending agencies out to obtain samples from families out of the area streamlined the entire process and ensured that the limitation of no reference sample to compare to victim profiles, as seen early in the camp fire, was not a roadblock to identification (Fig. 10.8).

9. Chapter summary

In summary, the inclusion of Rapid DNA into the identification process after a mass fatality event will lead to a much quicker turnaround time for DVI in the most horrendous of events and should be incorporated in any event where the highest likelihood of identification will fall in the realm of DNA. The major roadblock for DNA analysis is the same whether the user turns to Rapid DNA or chooses to use

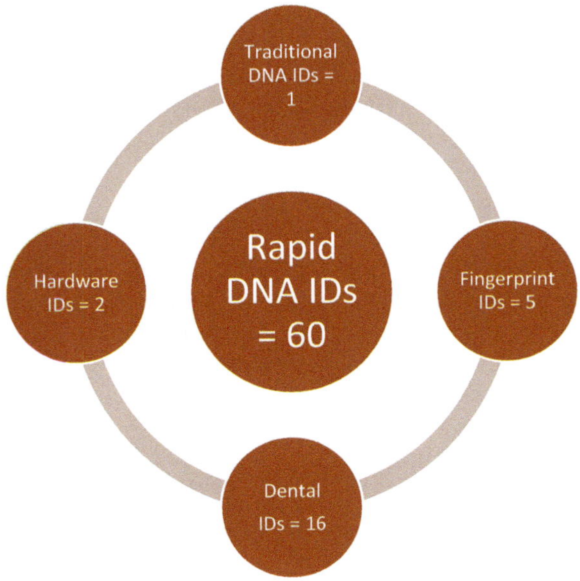

FIGURE 10.8

Breakdown of method of identification for camp fire victims by modality.

conventional DNA in DVI. That obstacle is obtaining the necessary reference samples from family. There are ways to mitigate this obstacle by setting up an FAC and making reference samples a priority from the beginning.

There are quite a few features of Rapid DNA technology that make it optimal for DVI. Rapid DNA equipment can be deployed near the disaster site, at an FAC, at a morgue, or at any combination of locations, and can be operated by nontechnical users. The only thing required at the site is electricity even if it is via a generator. The chips used in the instrument can be stored at room temperature, and each chip can hold up to five samples per run. For large disasters such as earthquakes, sets of 20 or more ANDE instruments can be used simultaneously—meaning that thousands of samples can be processed in a single day (note that set up of a run only requires 1–2 minutes).

Rapid DNA technology is orders of magnitude faster than traditional laboratory methods, eliminating lengthy laboratory processing time, the transportation time for samples to be sent to the laboratory, and for the availability of laboratory capacity. As a result, families had to wait, for years in many cases, to find out if their loved one was deceased after a mass fatality event. Rapid DNA technology can be used today by agencies tasked with identification and can bring closure to these family members much more quickly than ever before, making Rapid DNA an ideal method for identification in the most horrendous of mass fatality events.

References

Biesecker, L. G., Bailey-Wilson, J. E., Ballantyne, J., Baum, H., Bieber, F. R., Brenner, C., et al. (2005). DNA identifications after the 9/11 world trade center attack. *Science, 310*(5751), 1122–1123. https://doi.org/10.1126/science.1116608

Blau, S., & Briggs, C. A. (2011). The role of forensic anthropology in disaster victim identification (DVI). *Forensic Science International, 205*(1–3), 29–35. https://doi.org/10.1016/j.forsciint.2010.07.038

Boss, P., Beaulieu, L., Wieling, E., Turner, W., & LaCruz, S. (2003). Healing loss, ambiguity, and trauma: A community-based intervention with families of union workers missing after the 9/11 attack in New York city. *Journal of Marital and Family Therapy, 29*, 455–467.

Brenner, C. H., & Weir, B. (2003). Issues and strategies in the DNA identification of world trade center victims. *Theoretical Population Biology, 63*(3), 173–178. https://doi.org/10.1016/s0040-5809(03)00008-x

Buikstra, J. E., & Ubelaker, D. H. (1994). *Standards for data collection from human skeletal remains of Arkansas archaeological survey research series* (Vol. 44). Fayetteville, AR: Arkansas Archeological Survey.

CAL Fire. (2019). *Top 20 deadliest California wildfires*. https://fire.ca.gov/media/5512/top20_deadliest.pdf. (Accessed 5 April 2023).

CBS News 22. (2014). *10 years after tsunami, victims' relatives learn bodies weren't lost*. https://www.cbsnews.com/news/10-years-after-tsunami-victims-relatives-learn-bodies-werent-lost/. (Accessed 5 April 2023).

Deng, Y.-J., Li, Y.-Z., Yu, X.-G., Li, L., Wu, D.-Y., Zhou, J., et al. (2005). Preliminary DNA identification for the tsunami victims in Thailand. *Genomics, Proteomics & Bioinformatics, 3*(3), 143–157. https://doi.org/10.1016/s1672-0229(05)03020-2

Donkervoort, S., Dolan, S. M., Beckwith, M., Northrup, T. P., & Sozer, A. (2008). Enhancing accurate data collection in mass fatality kinship identifications: Lessons learned from hurricane Katrina. *Forensic Science International: Forest Genetics, 2*(4), 354–362. https://doi.org/10.1016/j.fsigen.2008.05.008

Green, R. E., Krause, J., Ptak, S. E., Briggs, A. W., Ronan, M. T., Simons, J. F., et al. (2006). Analysis of one million base pairs of Neanderthal DNA. *Nature, 444*(7117), 330–336. https://doi.org/10.1038/nature05336

Hartman, D., Drummer, O., Eckhoff, C., Scheffer, J. W., & Stringer, P. (2011). The contribution of DNA to the disaster victim identification (DVI) effort. *Forensic Science International, 205*(1), 52–58. https://doi.org/10.1016/j.forsciint.2010.09.024

Hsu, C., Huang, N., Tsai, L., Kao, L., Chao, C., Linacre, A., et al. (1999). Identification of victims of the 1998 Taoyuan Airbus crash accident using DNA analysis. *International Journal of Legal Medicine, 113*(1), 43–46. https://doi.org/10.1007/s004140050277

Latham, K. E., & Madonna, M. E. (2013). DNA survivability in skeletal remains. In J. Pokines, & S. A. Symes (Eds.), *Manual of forensic taphonomy* (pp. 385–407). Boca Raton, FL: Taylor & Francis Group.

Leclair, B., Frégeau, C. J., Bowen, K. L., & Fourney, R. M. (2001). Enhanced kinship analysis and STR-based DNA typing for human identification in mass fatality incidents: The Swissair flight 111 disaster. *Journal of Forensic Sciences, 49*(5), 939–953.

McEntire, D. A., Sadiq, A.-A., & Gupta, K. (2012). Unidentified bodies and mass-fatality management in Haiti: A case study of the January 2010 earthquake with a cross-cultural comparison. *International Journal of Mass Emergencies and Disasters, 30*(1), 301–327.

Moore-Jansen, P. H., Jantz, R. L., & Ousley, S. D. (1994). *Data collection procedures for forensic skeletal material* (3rd ed.). Knoxville, TN: Forensic Anthropology Center, Department of Anthropology, University of Tennessee.

Morgan, O. W., Sribanditmongkol, P., Perera, C., Sulasmi, Y., Van Alphen, D., & Sondorp, E. (2006). Mass fatality management following the South Asian tsunami disaster: Case studies in Thailand, Indonesia, and Sri Lanka. *PLoS Medicine, 3*(6), e195. https://doi.org/10.1371/journal.pmed.0030195

National Park Service (NPS). (2018). *2018 Woolsey fire*. https://www.nps.gov/samo/learn/management/2018-woolsey-fire.htm. (Accessed 18 July 2019).

Sudoyo, H., Widodo, P. T., Suryadi, H., Lie, Y. S., Safari, D., Widjajanto, A., et al. (2008). DNA analysis in perpetrator identification of terrorism-related disaster: Suicide bombing of the Australian Embassy in Jakarta 2004. *Forensic Science International: Forest Genetics, 2*(3), 231–237. https://doi.org/10.1016/j.fsigen.2007.12.007

Tan, E., et al. (2013). Fully integrated, fully automated generation of short tandem repeat profiles. *Investigative Genetics, 4*, 16.

The Washington Post. (2018). *Explosive and destructive 'Camp Fire' in Northern California is burning 80 acres per minute*. https://www.washingtonpost.com/weather/2018/11/08/explosive-destructive-camp-firenorthern-california-is-burning-acres-per-minute/?noredirect=on. (Accessed 5 April 2023).

Turingan, R. S., et al. (2019). Identification of human remains using rapid DNA analysis. *International Journal of Legal Medicine, 63*, 173.

Turingan, R. S., et al. (2020). Developmental validation of the ANDE 6C system for rapid DNA analysis of forensic casework and DVI samples. *Journal of Forensic Sciences, 65*, 1056–1071.

Turnigan, R. S., et al. (2016). Rapid DNA analysis for automated processing and interpretation of low DNA content samples. *Investigative Genetics, 7*, 41.

VC Star – Part of the USA Today Network. (2018). *Thousand oaks shooting: 13, including officer, killed at borderline bar & Grill*. https://www.vcstar.com/story/news/2018/11/07/multiple-victims-reported-shooting-t-o-bar/1927732002/. (Accessed 7 November 2018).

CHAPTER

Current standards in disaster victim identification

11

Jason H. Byrd[1] **and Ann H. Ross**[2]

[1]*University of Florida College of Medicine, Gainesville, FL, United States;* [2]*Department of Biological Sciences, North Carolina State University, Raleigh, NC, United States*

1. Introduction

Disasters, both natural and man-made, can occur unexpectedly and have devastating long-term consequences for both individuals and the communities in which they occur. Recent mass fatality responses have included earthquakes, tsunamis, hurricanes, transportation accidents, wildfires, and terrorist attacks. In the aftermath of such events, one of the most pressing concerns is the accurate and expeditious identification of victims. The Disaster Victim Identification (DVI) process is a complex and multidisciplinary effort that involves a wide range of forensic sciences, law enforcement, legal, and emergency management professionals to support the investigative and judicial process. The primary goal of DVI is to establish the identity of victims to provide closure for their families and loved ones and enable the release to the next of kin for burial or other arrangements. Accurate identification is also critical for preserving evidence and improving disaster response.

The DVI process involves multiple stages, including the recovery of bodies, documentation, and collection of physical evidence, collection of antemortem and postmortem information, comparison with existing law enforcement and missing persons databases, and notification of next-of-kin. DVI relies on various forensic sciences and investigative technologies and techniques, such as dental records, DNA analysis, fingerprinting, radiological comparisons, and forensic anthropology. Each step in the DVI process requires careful consideration of legal and ethical issues, including respect for the deceased, informed consent, privacy, and compliance with local laws and regulations. Given the importance of DVI in disaster response and recovery efforts, stakeholders must collaborate and coordinate their efforts to ensure a timely, accurate, and sensitive process. This includes emergency responders, forensic experts, healthcare providers, law enforcement agencies, NGOs, and victim identification coordinators. Their collective efforts can help provide closure to families, support disaster recovery efforts, and prevent similar incidents in the future.

Methodological and Technological Advances in Death Investigations. https://doi.org/10.1016/B978-0-12-819394-5.00008-0

2. The disaster victim identification process

The DVI process can be divided into four main stages.

2.1 Recovery

The recovery stage involves the search, retrieval, and transport of human remains from the disaster site to a forensic morgue or temporary disaster portable morgue unit. The goal of this stage is to ensure that all victims are located and removed from the disaster site as quickly and efficiently as possible, while also preserving the integrity of the remains and any physical evidence that may be present.

The recovery stage is typically carried out by emergency responders, such as search and rescue teams, firefighters, police officers, and military personnel. These teams work together to search the disaster site for any indications of human remains, using specialized equipment and techniques to locate and extract bodies. In some cases, the use of heavy machinery may be necessary to remove debris and access difficult-to-reach areas. Once human remains are located, it is examined for any visible signs of personal identification, such as associated clothing or personal belongings. Any such items are collected and preserved as potential sources of information for the identification process. The human remains are then removed from the disaster site and transported to the morgue or other designated location for further postmortem examination and analysis. This stage is a challenging and emotionally demanding process for all involved. Emergency responders must work quickly and carefully to locate and extract bodies while ensuring their own safety and well-being. They must also do so with respect for the deceased and their families, as well as any cultural or religious sensitivities that may exist.

In addition to the physical challenges, the recovery stage can present legal and ethical considerations. For example, authorities must ensure that the remains are handled in accordance with local laws and regulations, as well as international protocols for the management of mass fatalities. They must also respect the privacy and dignity of the deceased and ensure that legal next-of-kin are notified promptly of any developments in the identification process. Overall, the recovery stage is a critical component of the DVI process, as it lays the foundation for the subsequent stages of examination and analysis. It is essential that emergency responders and other stakeholders work together to ensure a thorough and respectful recovery stage, both for the benefit of next-of-kin and for the broader disaster response effort.

2.2 Postmortem examination

During this stage, experts in the forensic sciences and human identification use a range of forensic science and investigation techniques and technologies to collect postmortem information from human remains including the documentation of association physical evidence such as clothing, jewelry, indications of prior medical procedures, surgical implants, dentition, fingerprints, and any other identifying features or artifacts. The examination process begins with a preliminary assessment of the body (or triaged including both pathologists, anthropologists, and sometimes radiology), to determine its condition and the extent of any injuries or trauma. This process may include the following techniques.

1. Postmortem examination or autopsy. In the US, the medical examiner or coroner is the legal authority who determines if an autopsy will be conducted. In many cases, a full autopsy may not be possible due to the condition of the human remains, or the circumstances of the mass fatality event may not necessitate that a full autopsy be conducted.
2. Anthropological examination: Anthropologists examine the skeletal characteristics of the remains, such as age, sex, stature, and population affinity, to help establish the identity of the victim.
3. Dental examination: Dental records can be an important source of identification, as teeth are among the most durable parts of the body. Forensic odontologists compare the antemortem dental records of the victim with the teeth present to the recovered remains as a source of identification.
4. DNA analysis: DNA analysis is one of the most accurate and reliable methods of identification, particularly when other forms of identification are not available. Samples of tissue, bone, or blood are taken from the remains and compared to samples from the victim's biological relatives, or from items the victim may have been in contact with such as hairbrushes, toothbrushes, and recently worn and unwashed clothing.
5. Radiological examination: Radiographs and other imaging techniques can be used to examine the bones and other structures of the body, to identify any distinguishing features or trauma.
6. Toxicology analysis: Toxicology analysis is used to determine if any drugs or poisons were present in the body at the time of death. This information can be useful in determining the cause of death and may also help narrow down the list of potential victims.
7. Fingerprints: Once postmortem fingerprints have been obtained, they can be compared to fingerprints in a database or fingerprints obtained from family members of missing persons. If a match is found, the identity of the deceased can be confirmed.

The postmortem examination process requires careful handling of human remains and adherence to proper evidence documentation and collection protocols conducted under the jurisdictional authority of the medical examiner or coroner.

2.3 Antemortem and postmortem record comparison

This stage of the DVI process involves comparing the information gathered during the recovery and postmortem examination with known records obtained during the antemortem interview with families and others familiar with the victim. This antemortem and postmortem data comparison is conducted to establish the positive identity of the victim.

The antemortem and postmortem comparison process begins by compiling all available information about the victim, including physical characteristics, medical history, antemortem dental records, antemortem fingerprints, and any identifying artifacts or characteristics (e.g., orthopedic hardware, tattoos, breast implants, etc.). This information is then compared with known postmortem information such as items and associated evidence from the scene, postmortem dental records, postmortem fingerprints, forensic anthropology examination, and DNA samples to establish a positive identification.

The comparison process is a complex and often time-consuming stage of the DVI process, as it requires careful attention to detail and adherence to established protocols and procedures. Forensic experts must ensure that all available information is considered and that any discrepancies or anomalies are thoroughly investigated to ensure an accurate identification.

Often, the comparison process provides the first confirmation of the victim's identity, and this information is presented to the medical examiner or coroner for agreement and confirmation of the identity. Once confirmed by the medical examiner or coroner, the next-of-kin is notified. Forensic science experts and other stakeholders must work together to ensure a thorough and accurate comparison process while also adhering to legal and ethical considerations.

2.4 Notification of next-of-kin

Once a positive identification has been made, the families of the victims are notified, and the bodies are released for burial or other arrangements. This stage is often considered the most difficult and emotional part of the DVI process, as it involves delivering the news of a loved one's death in a compassionate and respectful manner. In many cases, this aspect is undertaken by law enforcement representatives and is not part of the medical examiner or coroner duties. However, there are situations in which this aspect of the DVI process is handled by funeral directors or mortuary officers, or representatives from victim assistance or DVI organizations, who are skilled in delivering the news of a loved one's death in a compassionate and sensitive manner.

During the notification process, the family members are informed about the fate of their next-of-kin, including the cause of death and any other relevant details about the disaster. They are also provided with support and guidance on how to deal with the emotional and practical issues that arise in the aftermath of a death. It is important to note that the notification process can be a complex and challenging process, particularly in cases where language or cultural barriers exist, or when families are dispersed across different locations. In such cases, special attention and sensitivity must be paid to ensure that the notification process is carried out effectively and with empathy, compassion, and sensitivity to cultural and religious beliefs.

3. Disaster victim identification standards and guidelines

International standards have been created for DVI. These standards are designed to ensure that human remains are identified accurately and efficiently and that families and loved ones are notified promptly. Some of the first guidelines were created by Technical Working Groups (TWGs) established by the Interpol DVI Steering Group in collaboration with various international organizations, including the International Committee of the Red Cross, the World Health Organization, and the United Nations Office for the Coordination of Humanitarian Affairs.

The TWGs are made up of experts from around the world with specialized knowledge and skills in various areas of DVI, such as forensic anthropology, odontology, and DNA analysis. They are responsible for developing and updating the guidelines and standards that govern DVI practices and procedures. The INTERPOL DVI[1] standards cover all aspects of the DVI process, including the collection and management of data, the use of forensic techniques, and the coordination of international efforts. They also establish guidelines for the training and certification of personnel involved in DVI and outline procedures for communicating with families and providing them with support.

Some of the guidelines produced by the TWGs include.

1. INTERPOL Disaster Victim Identification Guide—This guide provides an overview of the DVI process and covers topics such as the roles and responsibilities of DVI team members, the collection and management of data, and the use of forensic techniques.
2. Forensic Odontology Guidelines—These guidelines provide guidance on the use of dental records and other dental evidence in DVI, including the collection and comparison of dental records and the interpretation of dental evidence.
3. Forensic Anthropology Guidelines—these guidelines provide guidance on the use of skeletal remains in DVI, including the collection and analysis of skeletal evidence and the interpretation of postmortem changes in skeletal remains.
4. Forensic DNA Guidelines—these guidelines provide guidance on the use of DNA analysis in DVI, including the collection and preservation of DNA samples, the selection of appropriate DNA markers for analysis, and the interpretation of DNA profiles.

The National Institute of Standards and Technology (NIST) has produced several documents related to DVI to provide guidance and establish standards for the use of forensic methods in DVI. The NIST Forensic Science Standards program was established to develop and promote the use of voluntary consensus standards in the forensic science community. The program works with stakeholders from across the forensic science community, including practitioners, researchers, and standards development organizations, to develop and publish standards for a range of forensic

[1] https://www.interpol.int/en/How-we-work/Forensics/Disaster-Victim-Identification-DVI.

science disciplines. The standards developed by this program cover a range of topics, including quality management systems, forensic examination methods, and data analysis and reporting. They are designed to promote consistency and reliability in forensic science practices and improve the quality and reliability of forensic science evidence presented in legal proceedings.

The NIST publications include.

1. NIST Handbook 133: Guidelines for DVI Using DNA—This handbook provides guidelines for the use of DNA analysis in DVI. It covers topics such as sample collection, preservation, analysis, and interpretation in the context of DVI.
2. NIST Interagency Report 7928: Forensic DNA Analysis: A Primer for Courts—This report provides an overview of the scientific principles underlying forensic DNA analysis, including the accuracy, reliability, and limitations of DNA evidence. It is designed to assist judges, lawyers, and other legal professionals in understanding the scientific basis for DNA evidence and its potential role in legal proceedings.
3. NIST Special Publication 1158: Guidelines for Mass Fatality Management During Hazardous Materials Incidents—This publication provides guidelines for the management of mass fatalities resulting from hazardous materials incidents. It covers topics such as risk assessment, emergency response, fatality management operations, and recovery and restoration.
4. NIST Forensic Science Standards Special Publication 2000–02—This set of standards provides general principles and best practices for forensic analysis, including DVI. The standards cover topics such as quality management systems, testing and calibration methods, and validation and verification of results.

In addition to the NIST documents above, there are additional guidelines for DVI that have been established by the National Institute of Justice (NIJ) which include the "National Missing and Unidentified Persons System (NamUs) Standards for Missing Persons and Unidentified Human Remains Investigations." These standards outline the best practices for collecting and managing data, conducting forensic examinations, and collaborating with other agencies in DVI efforts.

NIST has also developed standards for forensic DNA analysis, which is a critical component of DVI. The NIST standards provide guidance on the use of DNA analysis in identifying human remains and help ensure that forensic laboratories produce reliable and accurate results.

Recently, the NIST Organization of Scientific Area Committees (OSAC), a collaborative forensic science initiative that aims to develop and promote forensic science standards and guidelines as published within the OSAC Registry, is a repository of high-quality, technically sound published and proposed standards for forensic science, has published several DVI Best Practice Recommendations:

(1) ANSI/ASB Best Practice Recommendation 008, *Mass Fatality Scene Processing: Best Practice Recommendations for the Medicolegal Authority*, First Edition,2021[2]
(2) ANSI/ASB Best Practice Recommendation 009, *Best Practice Recommendations for the Examination of Human Remains by Forensic Pathologists in the Disaster Victim Identification Context*, First Edition,2019[3]
(3) ANSI/ASB Best Practice Recommendation 010, *Forensic Anthropology in Disaster Victim Identification: Best Practice Recommendations for the Medicolegal Authority*, First Edition, 2018 | added September 5,2019[4]
(4) ANSI/ASB Standard 108, *Forensic Odontology in Disaster Victim Identification: Best Practice Recommendations for the Medicolegal Authority*, First Edition, 2021 | added October 4,2022[5]

Additionally, other organizations, such as the American Academy of Forensic Sciences (AAFS) and Academy Standards Board (ASB), provide guidelines and standards for DVI professionals in the United States. The guidance published by the ASB includes the NIST/OSAC documents listed above, plus the additional.

(1) ANSI/ASB Best Practice Recommendation 006 Best Practices Recommendations for DNA Analysis for Human Identification in Mass Fatality Incidents.[6]

A comprehensive set of standards and guidelines are available for DVI that are designed to ensure that the identification of disaster victims is conducted in a professional, thorough, and accurate manner. The NIST/OSAC and AAFS ASB best practices, guidelines, and standards provide a comprehensive framework for DNA analysis in DVI and help ensure that forensic laboratories produce reliable and accurate results that meet established scientific practices.

4. Conclusion

Disaster victim identification is a challenging and complex process that requires the use of various forensic science technologies and techniques. The process must be conducted with the utmost respect for the deceased and their families and must adhere to legal and ethical considerations. While the identification of victims is important for both closure and justice, it is also crucial for disaster response and recovery efforts. Accurate identification allows for the proper handling of bodies and the provision of support to families, while also enabling authorities to better understand the impact of the disaster and take measures to prevent future incidents. It is therefore essential that all involved parties work together to ensure a thorough, accurate, and culturally sensitive DVI process.

[2] https://www.aafs.org/sites/default/files/media/documents/008_BPR_e1.pdf.
[3] https://www.aafs.org/sites/default/files/media/documents/009_BPR_e1.pdf.
[4] https://www.aafs.org/sites/default/files/media/documents/010_BPR_e01.pdf.
[5] https://www.aafs.org/sites/default/files/media/documents/108_BPR_e1.pdf.
[6] https://www.aafs.org/sites/default/files/media/documents/006_BPR_e1.pdf.

CHAPTER

The applicability of bone mineral density for adult age estimation

12

Amanda R. Hale[1,2], Marin A. Pilloud[3] and Ann H. Ross[1]

[1]*Department of Biological Sciences, North Carolina State University, Raleigh, NC, United States;* [2]*SNA International for the Defense POW/MIA Accounting Agency, Joint Base Pearl Harbor-Hickam, Oahu, HI, United States;* [3]*Department of Anthropology, University of Nevada, Reno, NV, United States*

1. Introduction

Adult age estimation remains a challenging component of the biological profile (Campanacho & Alves-Cardoso, 2023; Cunha et al., 2009; Konigsberg et al., 2008; Ubelaker & Khosrowshahi, 2019). For juvenile remains, age estimation is largely straightforward and relies on known developmental rates (e.g., epiphyseal fusion (Cunningham et al., 2016) and dental development (Liversidge et al., 2015)). However, for adult remains, age estimation relies on gross morphological degradation (e.g., pubic symphyseal morphology (Brooks & Suchey, 1990; Katz & Suchey, 1986), patterned ossification of cartilage (e.g., sternal rib ends (Hartnett, 2010; Iscan et al., 1984)), or demineralization of dental tissues (e.g., dental root translucency (Lamendin et al., 1992)). Because these patterned changes in morphology can be influenced by extrinsic factors that can lower their correlation with chronological age, they often result in less precise age ranges that show increasing error as chronological age increases (Cappella et al., 2017; DiGangi et al., 2009; Hoppa & Vaupel, 2002). This is further complicated by the need to have sex-specific references for comparison, particularly when elements used for estimating sex are not available for analysis. One possible solution would be to identify age-correlated variables that are (1) intrinsic to hard tissue contributing to the patterned morphological degradation that we currently rely on, (2) quantitative with low interobserver error, and (3) do not require population or sex specific references.

Bone is a hierarchical, composite tissue with both organic and inorganic components organized into a collagen matrix and carbonated hydroxyapatite (Burr et al., 2014; Hall, 2015; Kranioti et al., 2019). The inorganic component, or bone mineral, is organized in a nanocrystalline structure that provides both stiffness and a framework for the organic portion (Hall, 2015). Proper mineralization is important because it protects against bone fragility and provides the structural framework for the organic matrix of bone (Burr et al., 2014). Therefore, bone mineral has

Methodological and Technological Advances in Death Investigations. https://doi.org/10.1016/B978-0-12-819394-5.00001-8

been identified as a useful measure for assessing bone health including both risks of osteoporosis and fracture (Binkovitz & Henwood, 2007; Marshall et al., 1996; Siris et al., 2001). Clinically, bone mineral is measured as a density, or the distribution of mineral across the mass and volume occupied (Lyman, 1984, 2013). Bone mineral density (BMD) is most commonly measured using dual X-ray absorptiometry (DXA) technology, which has been considered the gold standard for BMD scans since its introduction in 1987; specifically DXA scans of the lumbar spine (L1 to L4), hip, and distal forearm, as these are the easiest regions to capture volumetrically (Binkovitz & Henwood, 2007; Blake & Fogelman, 2007, 2010; Curate et al., 2013; Pezzuti et al., 2017). Further, BMD measured from DXA scans have demonstrated low interobserver error and do not rely on subjective experience for data collection (Binkovitz & Henwood, 2007; Blake & Fogelman, 2007, 2010; Patel et al., 2000).

Much of an individual's BMD throughout life is determined by their genetic makeup, with studies estimating 50–70% of an individual's BMD attributed to complex genetic factors with many traits controlling peak bone mass and any one gene explaining only a small proportion of the variation (Runyan et al., 2003; Seeman et al., 1996; Weaver et al., 2019). However, BMD has also shown correlations with intrinsic factors including age, sex, and population with varying results (Kranioti et al., 2019; Paschall & Ross, 2018; Warming et al., 2002).

Age has consistently demonstrated strong correlations with measured BMD in both juveniles (Hale & Ross, 2018; Ross & Abel, 2011) and adults (Botha et al., 2019; Warming et al., 2002) and is the result of age-related changes in bone metabolism that increase bone porosity resulting in increased bone fragility over the life course (Wang & Silva, 2013). To maintain healthy bone microstructure, constant bone remodeling must take place after an individual achieves peak bone mass typically occurring a few years after epiphyseal fusion, but as an individual ages, endosteal bone removal exceeds periosteal deposition rate, which leads to reductions in overall BMD (Kini et al., 2012; Seeman, 2008; Seeman & Delmas, 2006; Weaver et al., 2019). For example, one cross-sectional study documented an overall BMD reduction of 47% in the lumbar spine and a 39% reduction in the distal radius throughout life, particularly in older females (Riggs et al., 1981). They also noted a strong, linear relationship between age and BMD of the axial skeleton in young female adults but variable patterns in the appendicular skeleton (Riggs et al., 1981). Contrary to these results, Lee and colleagues (Lee et al., 2012) observed accelerated BMD loss in the hip during both early and late adulthood in a South Korean sample of males and females.

Studies investigating sex differences in BMD attainment indicate that males achieve peak bone mass at older ages relative to females related to general differences in growth and development between sexes (Macdonald et al., 2013; Weaver et al., 2014). Further, studies identifying sex differences in BMD loss throughout life have been variable across the skeletal sites studied. Warming and coworkers

(Warming et al., 2002) found that for ages 20–80 years, both males and females showed bone loss across all sites scanned: hip, spine, distal forearm, and whole body. Both males and females also showed a significantly accelerated loss in the 50 to 59 age cohort at all sites, but then loss begins to taper at later ages. Consistent bone loss in both males and females over the life course was only seen in the hip while the distal forearm and spine showed accelerated bone loss at different times throughout life, especially in females (Warming et al., 2002). Paschall and Ross (Paschall & Ross, 2018) found significant sex differences in BMD between weight- and non-weight-bearing bones in individuals over 55 years old. Specifically, females showed greater BMD loss than males in the non-weight-bearing cranium but not in the weight-bearing femur (Paschall & Ross, 2018). In general, studies demonstrate both males and females show BMD loss over the life course at all scanned sites after achieving peak bone mass after age 18, but BMD was the least variable between sexes for the hip (Alswat, 2017; Weaver et al., 2014).

Population differences in BMD loss have also been examined for clinical application. In a large Canadian sample, Morin and colleagues (Morin et al., 2022) compared BMD values among four reported groups: White, Black, East Asian, and South or Southeast Asian. They found that there were significant differences among the four groups for both total hip and femoral neck BMD values, but no significant sex differences within groups (Morin et al., 2022). However, this study grouped all ages examined for each population mean, and the mean age of each group investigated was different, which could influence the differences in the observed BMD. Wheatley (Wheatley, 2005) investigated population differences in femoral BMD and found statistically significant differences between black and white females in the femur. Other studies have found some population differences in BMD of the femoral neck, total hip, and lumbar spine when individuals have similar BMI (Kranioti et al., 2019; Nam et al., 2013). However, Meeusen et al. (Meeusen et al., 2015) found no differences in a sample of black, white, and Native American individuals. These results suggest that while population differences exist, they are likely negligible among individuals of comparable ages.

More recently, BMD has emerged in forensic anthropology with widespread application, including age-at-death estimation in juveniles (Manifold, 2014; Ross & Abel, 2011) and adults (Bethard et al., 2019; Castillo & López Ruiz, 2011; Curate et al., 2022; Navega et al., 2018; Paschall & Ross, 2018), an indicator of bone quality in fatal starvation and juvenile neglect cases (Hale & Ross, 2018; Ross & Abel, 2011; Ross & Juarez, 2014), for the identification of metabolic bone diseases (Curate, 2014; Hale & Ross, 2018), and to assess the survivability of skeletal elements in taphonomic research (Lyman, 1984, 2013). BMD's strong correlation with age and its inherent quantitative nature spurred research into its utility as a method of age estimation in forensic anthropology. Castillo and López Ruiz (Castillo & López Ruiz, 2011) investigated correlations between BMD and sex, age, and BMI in a sample of 70 individuals and found that age could be reliably estimated from Ward's triangle BMD—a 1 cm^2 area with the lowest bone density in the femoral neck—with relatively low standard errors when using sex-specific regression formulae. Curate and colleagues (Curate et al., 2013) tested the Castillo and López Ruiz (Castillo & López Ruiz, 2011) approach in a sample of individuals from two Portuguese skeletal collections and found that the mean absolute error was between 10 and 12 years, and the method tended to overestimate age in younger individuals and underestimate age in older individuals for this sample—a common problem for most aging methods when applied to cemetery populations (Bocquet-Appel & Masset, 1982; Hoppa & Vaupel, 2002).

Expanding from this study, Navega and colleagues (Navega et al., 2018) modeled femoral densitometry data from a sample of 100 female individuals aged 21–95 years selected from an identified skeletal collection. They found a moderate, negative linear correlation between BMD values and age-at-death with the greatest correlation between age and Ward's triangle areal BMD (Navega et al., 2018). Modeling this relationship, they used a computational approach to develop an online web application—DXAGE—to support age estimation based on the sample studied (Navega et al., 2018). However, when DXAGE was tested on a large American female sample, Bethard and colleagues (Bethard et al., 2019) found a weak correlation between predicted and actual age as well as an overall higher bias (−7.20 years) and inaccuracy (14.25 years) than expected. This finding is most likely because the reference sample for DXAGE is derived from a cemetery population that had been interred for at least 5 years; therefore, diagenetic changes could have altered bone mineral content through chemical interactions with the burial matrix (Galloway et al., 1997; Hale & Ross, 2018; Willey et al., 1997). Nevertheless, Curate and colleagues (Curate et al., 2022) recently published an updated version of DXAGE—DXAGE 2.0—that now contains predictive equations based on femoral bone densitometry data and radiogrammetry data from the second metacarpal for both males and females from the same cemetery sample previously tested. They found observed error ranges from 8 to 13 years for females and 11 to 16 years for males (Curate et al., 2022). Independent testing is still needed to validate the updated equations provided in DXAGE 2.0 on other samples, but considering the context of these reference samples caution is advised.

Approaches to adult age estimation using BMD are advantageous for multiple reasons that include: (1) BMD is an intrinsic factor that contributes to the morphological degradation relied on in other age estimation methods routinely employed in forensic anthropology and (2) interobserver error, subjectivity, and observer experience do not bias the results as in other anthropological methods (Bethard et al., 2019; Navega et al., 2018). Here we explore the applicability of BMD to adult age estimation in forensic anthropology using a large dataset of clinical BMD values from the femur: the National Health and Nutrition Examination Survey (NHANES) dataset.

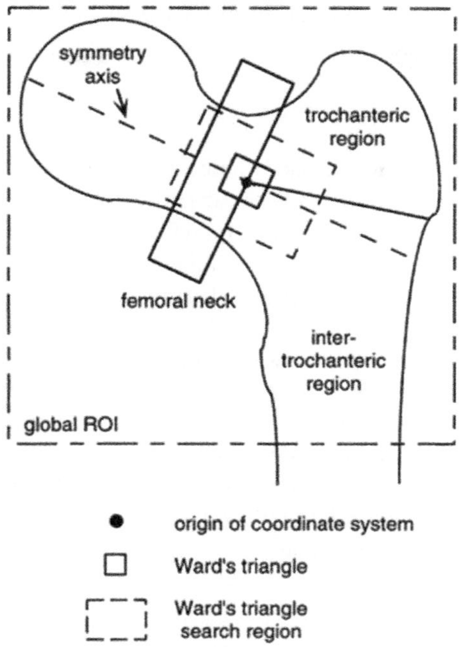

FIGURE 12.1

The figure presents the regions of interest in the proximal femur as given by the Hologic software. This study employs that rectangular area for the femoral neck and the smaller square region for Ward's triangle.

Credit: from Takada et al. (Takada et al., 1997) Fig. 12.1.

2. Materials and methods

2.1 Dataset

The NHANES femoral BMD and corresponding demographic data were collected in 2007–2008 and are freely available.[1] The data were collected for studies related to osteoporosis and other clinical conditions. All scans were collected with a Hologic® bone densitometer that employs DXA. The dataset includes BMD, bone mineral content, and areal data for the total femur, femoral neck, trochanter, intertrochanter, and Ward's triangle for male and female individuals aged eight to 85 years. For this study, BMD values from the femoral neck and Ward's triangle (Fig. 12.1) across ages 20–85 years (*n* = *8220*) were employed. This sample was chosen as the hip has demonstrated consistent, continuous bone loss throughout life in both males

[1] NHANES femoral BMD data available here: https://wwwn.cdc.gov/nchs/nhanes/2007-2008/DXXFEM_E.htm. Corresponding demographic data available here: https://wwwn.cdc.gov/nchs/nhanes/search/DataPage.aspx?Component=Demographics&CycleBeginYear=2007.

and females with the least influence from environmental factors (Kranioti et al., 2019; Warming et al., 2002).

2.2 Data analysis

The dataset was partitioned into decade cohorts (e.g., 20–29, 30–39, etc.). It should be noted that the dataset ends at 85 years, meaning the 80-year cohort would only have included individuals aged 80–85; therefore, they were included in the 70 and over cohort (i.e., 70–85) in this study. Tables 12.1 and 12.2 present the number of individuals in each decade cohort and descriptive statistics of the two femoral BMD variables in this study.

The data were partitioned into two cohort subsets (e.g., 20–29 and 30–39, 30–39 and 40–49, etc.), and each subset was subject to Bartlett's test to ensure equal variances across age cohorts for subsequent statistical analyses. A multivariate analysis of variance (MANOVA) was used to examine if sex differences significantly influenced the group cohort means and was found to be not significant for any of the age cohorts except the 70–85 cohort ($P = 0.0348$). Therefore, the data were not partitioned by sex for the following analyses.

Table 12.1 Descriptive statistics of the femoral neck BMD values by age cohort.

Age	N	Neck BMD mean	Neck BMD S.D.
20–29	1357	0.939	0.140
30–39	1375	0.892	0.133
40–49	1471	0.867	0.132
50–59	1265	0.816	0.137
60–69	1322	0.790	0.140
70–85	1430	0.720	0.138

Table 12.2 Descriptive statistics of the Ward's triangle BMD values by age cohort.

Age	N	Ward's BMD mean	Ward's BMD S.D.
20–29	1357	0.868	0.162
30–39	1375	0.779	0.156
40–49	1471	0.712	0.151
50–59	1265	0.631	0.157
60–69	1322	0.577	0.157
70–85	1430	0.487	0.144

Pearson's product-moment correlation coefficients were used to explore the relationship between both BMD parameters and age among the cohorts. Two-sample paired t-tests were used to test for significant differences between the sequential age cohort means. Then, a least squares regression was used to explore the linear relationship between age and both BMD variables while minimizing the variances across the groups compared.

Based on the results of the least squares regression, the relationship between age and the Ward's triangle BMD was examined using a Kernel smoother or Loess regression. This procedure is a nonparametric procedure that uses a local weighted regression to fit a smooth curve through points on a scatterplot to identify the best fit. To determine the best fit span parameter (0.5, 0.75, and 0.90), a k-fold cross-validation was performed, which evaluates the model performance by measuring the root mean squared error (RMSE) between the predicted values and the observed data (Cleveland & Devlin, 1988). The greater the span parameter, the smoother the regression line; therefore, the lower the span parameter the more the regression line will hug the data (Cleveland & Devlin, 1988). Loess regression was performed on all ages and separately on ages 50 and over based on results from Paschall and Ross (Paschall & Ross, 2018) where regression models performed better for ages 55 years and older. The RMSE was compared for both models to examine the error rate for both age groups. Prediction equations are provided for both age groups: all ages in the study and 50 years and older.

3. Results

Figs. 12.2 and 12.3 present the distribution of the two BMD parameters by age cohort. The Bartlett's tests for homogeneity of variance were not significant for all sequential age cohorts indicating that the variance across cohorts is approximately equal. Pearson's product-moment correlation coefficients indicate there is a stronger negative correlation between age and the Ward's triangle BMD measures ($cor = -0.647$, $t_{8218} = -76.901$, $P < 2.2e\text{-}16$) than between age and the femoral neck BMD measures ($cor = -0.474$, $t_{8218} = -48.798$, $P < 2.2e\text{-}16$). Table 12.3 presents the two-sample paired t-tests, which indicate that each of the sequential age cohort means are significantly different from each other suggesting they could be useful for estimating age from early to late adulthood.

The least squares regression indicates that for age cohorts 20–59 years, there is a significant relationship between age and both BMD variables (Table 12.4). However, for cohorts 60 to 85, only the Ward's triangle BMD showed a significant relationship with age (see Table 12.4).

Because the least squares regression results indicate that the Ward's triangle BMD is more reliable across all age groups, the Loess regression analysis focused only on this variable. The Loess regression of Ward's triangle BMD by age supports an approximately linear relationship between the two variables for all ages (Fig. 12.4) and for the 50 years and older group (Fig. 12.5). The Loess regression

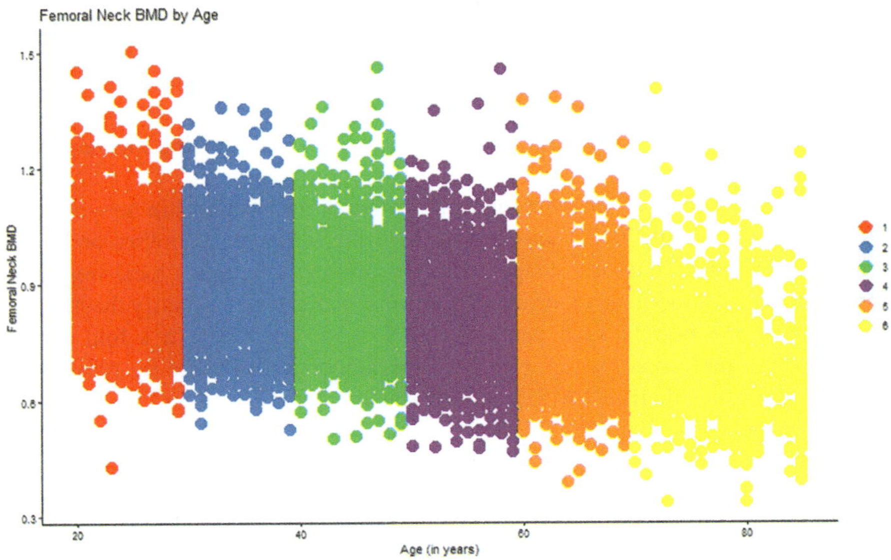

FIGURE 12.2

The figure presents the distribution of the femoral neck bone mineral density (BMD) values by age (in years). Color grouping is by age cohort divisions.

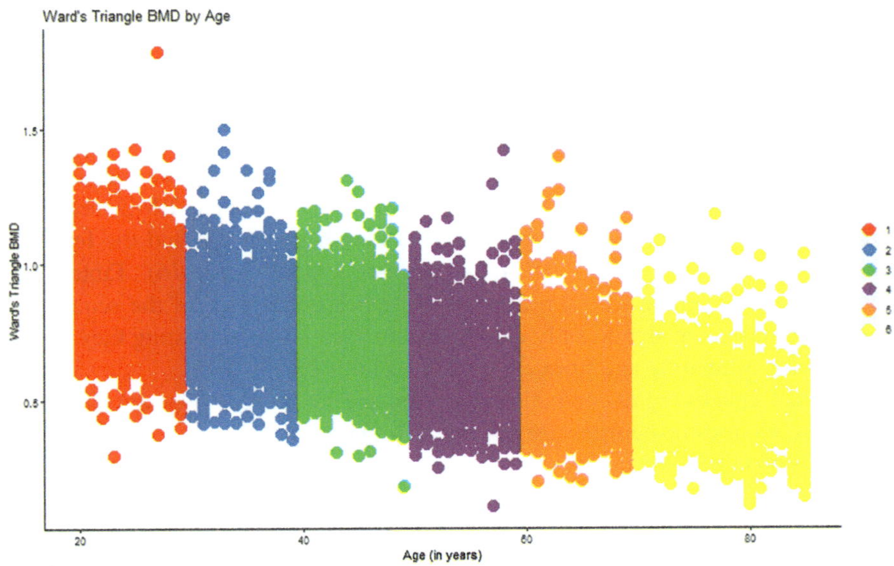

FIGURE 12.3

The figure presents the distribution of Ward's triangle bone mineral density (BMD) values by age (in years). Color grouping is by age cohort.

Table 12.3 Paired t-test results between all sequential cohorts.

Cohorts	df	t-statistic	*P*-value	Group 1 mean	Group 2 mean
20–29 and 30–39	2718	9.0534	<2.2e-16	0.939	0.892
30–39 and 40–49	2831	4.8951	1.038e-6	0.892	0.867
40–49 and 50–59	2643	9.8315	<2.2e-16	0.867	0.816
50–59 and 60–69	2583	4.9055	9.899e-7	0.816	0.789
60–69 and 70–85	2726	13.079	<2.2e-16	0.789	0.720

Table 12.4 Least squares regression results by age cohort for both the femoral neck and Ward's triangle BMD variables.

Age cohort	Variable	Estimate	Standard Error	t-statistic	*P*-value
20–29	Femoral neck BMD	5.9432	1.2079	4.92	**<0.0001**
	Ward's triangle BMD	−7.1334	1.0464	−6.85	**<0.0001**
30–39	Femoral neck BMD	3.9161	1.2146	3.22	**0.0013**
	Ward's triangle BMD	−5.2989	1.0331	−5.13	**<0.0001**
40–49	Femoral neck BMD	4.3726	1.0573	4.14	**<0.0001**
	Ward's triangle BMD	−6.4207	0.9323	−6.89	**<0.0001**
50–59	Femoral neck BMD	2.7184	1.1424	2.38	**0.0175**
	Ward's triangle BMD	−5.3713	0.9978	−5.38	**<0.0001**
60–69	Femoral neck BMD	2.1607	1.1506	1.88	0.0606
	Ward's triangle BMD	−3.3915	1.0234	−3.31	**0.0009**
70–85	Femoral neck BMD	−2.3673	1.5945	−1.48	0.1378
	Ward's triangle BMD	−5.0238	1.5331	−3.28	**0.0011**

model with the lowest RMSE had the lowest span parameter of 0.5 ($RMSE = 13.3$). For the over 50 years Loess regression model, the lowest span parameter was also 0.5 ($RMSE = 8.99$). Comparing the RMSE values for both models, the 50 years and older model has a lower overall RMSE of 9 years relative to the 13 years

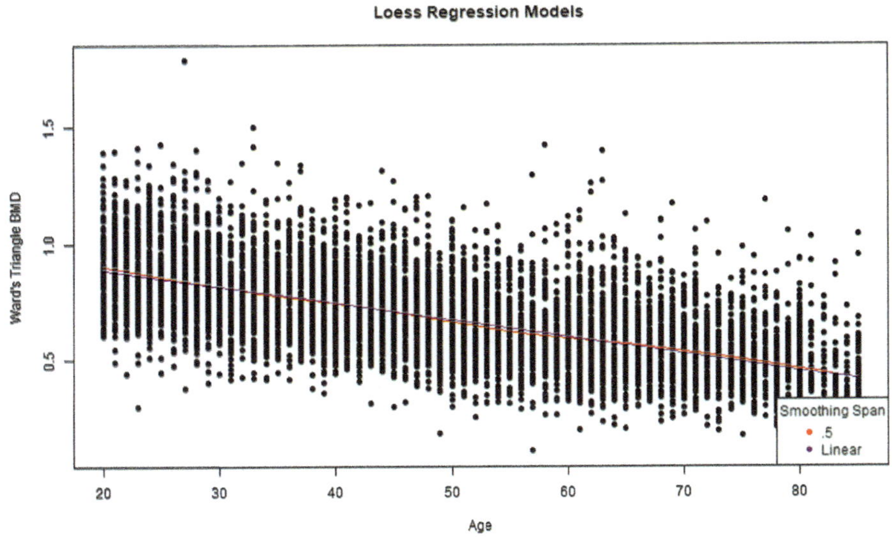

FIGURE 12.4

The figure presents the smoothing Loess regression lines with a 0.5 span parameter and the linear regression line on the Ward's triangle bone mineral density (BMD) data for all ages.

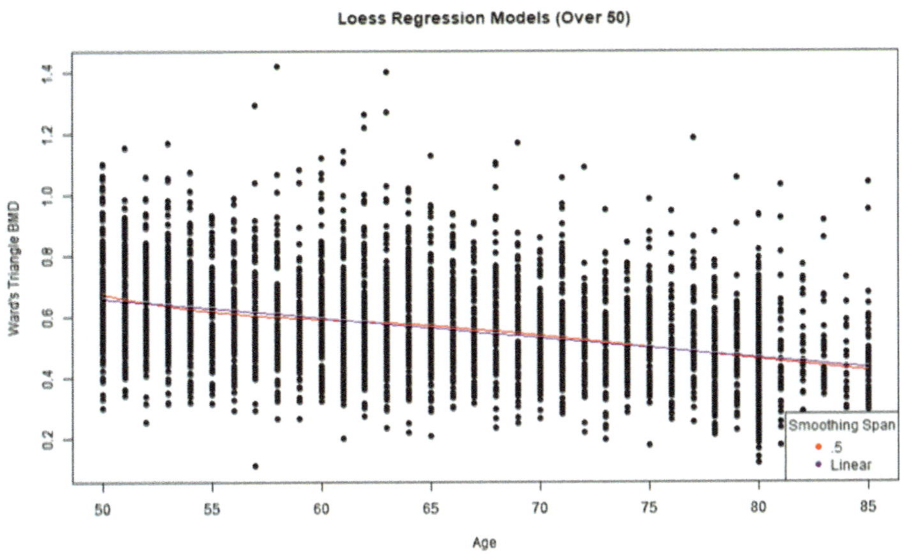

FIGURE 12.5

The figure presents the smoothing Loess regression lines with a 0.5 span parameter and the linear regression line on the Ward's triangle bone mineral density (BMD) data for ages 50 and older.

from the model of all adult ages. These results suggest that Ward's triangle BMD measures are more appropriate for estimating age in older individuals and provide a more precise range than most current methods. The prediction equation for all ages included in this study is:

$$Age\ (in\ years) = 84.92 - 47.37 * Ward's\ Triangle\ BMD$$

and the prediction equation for ages 50 years and older is:

$$Age\ (in\ years) = 78.94 - 24.15 * Ward's\ Triangle\ BMD$$

4. Discussion

Adult age estimation in biological anthropology still presents many challenges, particularly in the estimation of age in older individuals (Bocquet-Appel & Masset, 1982; Buikstra & Konigsberg, 1985; Campanacho & Alves-Cardoso, 2023; Hoppa & Vaupel, 2002). Conventional aging methods in adults that rely on age progressive skeletal changes continue to be problematic as causation remains largely unknown and are associated with intrinsic factors (such as sex and genetics) as well as extrinsic factors including activity, nutrition, and disease load (Boldsen et al., 2022). For modern skeletal remains, novel methods employing BMD as a variable are one potential solution.

After bone mass peaks in the third decade of life, bone loss begins with males losing approximately 30% of peak bone mass and females losing approximately 40% of peak bone mass between the age of 30 and 80 years (Weaver et al., 2019). However, for the hip (e.g., femoral neck and Ward's triangle), peak bone mass decreases by approximately 25% between ages 30 and 80 years in both males and females (Weaver et al., 2019), suggesting femoral neck BMD measures are better suited for age estimation for both males and females throughout the life course. While bone loss occurs in females at a greater rate than in males during menopause due to hormonal factors (e.g., estrogen deficiency), it has been shown that around 10 years, post-menopause hormonal-related bone loss ceases, and age-related bone loss continues (Weaver et al., 2019).

The purpose of the study presented here was to explore a large dataset and investigate its potential for estimating age in unidentified adult individuals from a forensic context that is not reliant on degenerative skeletal changes loosely associated with chronological age. The results presented here clearly demonstrate a negatively correlated, linear relationship between age and BMD that can be applied to skeletal remains recovered from some forensic contexts. Particularly those contexts where postmortem burial and taphonomic alterations are not likely to have impacted overall BMD.

Of note, the results of this study demonstrate that as BMD decreases with age the variance of the BMD values in each age cohort is approximately equal, which suggests a consistent rate of decrease in BMD across the life course. Of the two BMD measures explored here, the Ward's triangle BMD showed a stronger negative correlation with age (*−0.647*) across all age cohorts, which is consistent with previous studies (Castillo & López Ruiz, 2011; Curate et al., 2013, 2022; Navega et al., 2018). However, contrary to most of these studies (although see Paschall and Ross (Paschall & Ross, 2018)), we found that there were no significant sex differences for any of the age cohorts with consistent variance across the life course. In sum, these results indicate that sex-specific prediction formulae are not needed for femoral BMD, which could increase its utility in forensic casework.

While the NHANES dataset was collected from living individuals, this sample is derived from the same population as those relevant to contemporary forensic cases; thus, it is an appropriate reference sample for casework. Further, this dataset alleviates the shortcomings of relying solely on skeletal samples; addressing the issue of age mimicry or poor age distribution that plague most of the traditional methods based on skeletal degeneration (Hoppa & Vaupel, 2002). However, this would not be an appropriate method for remains recovered from prolonged burial contexts due to the high likelihood of diagenetic change that would produce artificial BMD measures as it has been shown that diagenetic alteration is microscopically visible as early as three months postmortem (Hale & Ross, 2023; Ross & Hale, 2018).

5. Conclusion

In conclusion, this study demonstrates the applicability of femoral BMD measures for estimating age in modern skeletal remains within a forensic context. Generally, these results indicate: (1) femoral areal BMD has the potential to provide narrower age ranges for older individuals than those currently available; (2) is not dependent on the ability to estimate sex in skeletal remains; and (3) is a less subjective approach to age estimation as it does not rely on the interpretation of gross morphological degradation. Finally, the approach taken here suggests there is a relative absence of population differences in BMD for the hip. As we continue to debate the significance of population variation in current methodology, this approach illustrates that large samples incorporating a range of variation can be used within forensic anthropology without comprising accuracy or precision.

References

Alswat, K. A. (2017). Gender disparities in osteoporosis. *Journal of Clinical Medicine Research, 9*, 382–387. https://doi.org/10.14740/jocmr2970w

Bethard, J. D., Berger, J. M., Maiers, J., & Ross, A. H. (2019). Bone mineral density adult age estimation in forensic anthropology: A test of the DXAGE application. *Journal of Forensic Sciences, 64*, 1125–1128. https://doi.org/10.1111/1556-4029.13987

Binkovitz, L. A., & Henwood, M. J. (2007). Pediatric DXA: Technique and interpretation. *Pediatric Radiology, 37*, 21–31. https://doi.org/10.1007/s00247-006-0153-y

Blake, G. M., & Fogelman, I. (2007). The role of DXA bone density scans in the diagnosis and treatment of osteoporosis. *Postgraduate Medical Journal, 83*, 509–517. https://doi.org/10.1136/pgmj.2007.057505

Blake, G. M., & Fogelman, I. (2010). An update on dual-energy X-ray absorptiometry. *Seminars in Nuclear Medicine, 40*, 62–73. https://doi.org/10.1053/j.semnuclmed.2009.08.001

Bocquet-Appel, J.-P., & Masset, C. (1982). Farewell to paleodemography. *Journal of Human Evolution, 11*, 321–333. https://doi.org/10.1016/S0047-2484(82)80023-7

Boldsen, J. L., Milner, G. R., & Ousley, S. D. (2022). Paleodemography: From archaeology and skeletal age estimation to life in the past. *American Journal of Biological Anthropology, 178*, 115–150.

Botha, D., Lynnerup, N., & Steyn, M. (2019). Age estimation using bone mineral density in South Africans. *Forensic Science International, 297*, 307–314. https://doi.org/10.1016/j.forsciint.2019.02.020

Brooks, S., & Suchey, J. M. (1990). Skeletal age determination based on the os pubis: A comparison of the Acsadi-Nemeskeri and Suchey-brooks methods. *Human Evolution, 5*, 227–238.

Buikstra, J. E., & Konigsberg, L. W. (1985). Paleodemography: Critiques and controversies. *American Anthropologist, 87*, 316–333.

Burr, D. B., & Akkus, O. (2014). Chapter 1 - bone morphology and organization. In D. B. Burr, & M. R. Allen (Eds.), *Basic and applied bone biology* (pp. 3–25). San Diego: Academic Press. https://doi.org/10.1016/B978-0-12-416015-6.00001-0

Campanacho, V., & Alves-Cardoso, F. (2023). Exploring adult age-at-death research in anthropology: Bibliometric mapping and content analysis. *Forensic Science, 3*, 125–148. https://doi.org/10.3390/forensicsci3010011

Cappella, A., Cummaudo, M., Arrigoni, E., Collini, F., & Cattaneo, C. (2017). The issue of age estimation in a modern skeletal population: Are even the more modern current aging methods satisfactory for the elderly? *Journal of Forensic Sciences, 62*, 12–17. https://doi.org/10.1111/1556-4029.13220

Castillo, R. F., & López Ruiz, M. del C. (2011). Assessment of age and sex by means of DXA bone densitometry: Application in forensic anthropology. *Forensic Science International, 209*, 53–58. https://doi.org/10.1016/j.forsciint.2010.12.008

Cleveland, W. S., & Devlin, S. J. (1988). Locally weighted regression: An approach to regression analysis by local fitting. *Journal of the American Statistical Association, 83*, 596–610. https://doi.org/10.2307/2289282

Cunha, E., Baccino, E., Martrille, L., Ramsthaler, F., Prieto, J., Schuliar, Y., Lynnerup, N., & Cattaneo, C. (2009). The problem of aging human remains and living individuals: A review. *Forensic Science International, 193*, 1–13. https://doi.org/10.1016/j.forsciint.2009.09.008

Cunningham, C., Scheuer, L., & Black, S. (Eds.). (2016). Front Matter, *Developmental juvenile osteology* (2nd ed., p. iii). San Diego: Academic Press. https://doi.org/10.1016/B978-0-12-382106-5.01001-X

Curate, F. (2014). Osteoporosis and paleopathology: A review. *Journal of Anthropological Sciences*, 1–28. https://doi.org/10.4436/jass.92003

Curate, F., Albuquerque, A., & Cunha, E. M. (2013). Age at death estimation using bone densitometry: Testing the Fernández Castillo and López Ruiz method in two documented skeletal samples from Portugal. *Forensic Science International, 226*, 296.e1–296.e6. https://doi.org/10.1016/j.forsciint.2012.12.002

Curate, F., Navega, D., Cunha, E., & d'Oliveira Coelho, J. (2022). Dxage 2.0 — adult age at death estimation using bone loss in the proximal femur and the second metacarpal. *International Journal of Legal Medicine, 136*, 1483–1494. https://doi.org/10.1007/s00414-022-02840-y

DiGangi, E. A., Bethard, J. D., Kimmerle, E. H., & Konigsberg, L. W. (2009). A new method for estimating age-at-death from the first rib. *American Journal of Physical Anthropology, 138*, 164–176. https://doi.org/10.1002/ajpa.20916

Galloway, A., Willey, P., & Snyder, L. (1997). Human bone mineral densities and survival of bone elements: A contemporary sample. In W. D. Haglund, & M. H. Sorg (Eds.), *Forensic taphonomy: The postmortem fate of human remains* (1st ed., pp. 295–317). Boca Raton, FL: CRC Press.

Hale, A. R., & Ross, A. H. (2018). Scanning skeletal remains for bone mineral density in forensic contexts. *Journal of Visualized Experiments: JoVE*, 56713. https://doi.org/10.3791/56713

Hale, A. R., & Ross, A. H. (2023). Investigating the timing and extent of juvenile and fetal bone diagenesis in a temperate environment. *Biology, 12*, 403–415.

Hall, B. K. (2015). *Bones and cartilage* (2nd ed.). London: Elsevier Academic Press.

Hartnett, K. M. (2010). Analysis of age-at-death estimation using data from a new, modern autopsy sample—Part II: Sternal end of the fourth rib*,†. *Journal of Forensic Sciences, 55*, 1152–1156. https://doi.org/10.1111/j.1556-4029.2010.01415.x

Hoppa, R. D., & Vaupel, J. W. (Eds.). (2002). *Paleodemography: Age distributions from skeletal samples*. Cambridge: Cambridge University Press. https://doi.org/10.1017/CBO9780511542428

Iscan, M. Y., Loth, S. R., & Wright, R. K. (1984). Age estimation from the rib by phase analysis: White males. *Journal of Forensic Sciences, 29*, 1094.

Katz, D., & Suchey, J. M. (1986). Age determination of the male Os pubis. *American Journal of Physical Anthropology, 69*, 427–435. https://doi.org/10.1002/ajpa.1330690402

Kini, U., & Nandeesh, B. N. (2012). Physiology of bone formation, remodeling, and metabolism. In I. Fogelman, G. Gnanasegaran, & H. van der Wall (Eds.), *Radionuclide and hybrid bone imaging* (pp. 29–57). Berlin, Heidelberg: Springer. https://doi.org/10.1007/978-3-642-02400-9_2

Konigsberg, L. W., Herrmann, N. P., Wescott, D. J., & Kimmerle, E. H. (2008). Estimation and evidence in forensic anthropology: Age-at-Death. *Journal of Forensic Sciences, 53*, 541–557. https://doi.org/10.1111/j.1556-4029.2008.00710.x

Kranioti, E. F., Bonicelli, A., & García-Donas, J. G. (2019). Bone-mineral density: Clinical significance, methods of quantification and forensic applications. *Research and Reports in Forensic Medical Science, 9*, 9–21. https://doi.org/10.2147/RRFMS.S164933

Lamendin, H., Baccino, E., Humbert, J. F., Tavernier, J. C., Nossintchouk, R. M., & Zerilli, A. (1992). A simple technique for age estimation in adults corpses: The two criteria dental method. *Journal of Forensic Sciences, 37*, 1373–1379.

Lee, E. Y., Kim, D., Kim, K. M., Kim, K. J., Choi, H. S., Rhee, Y., & Lim, S.-K. (2012). Age-related bone mineral density patterns in Koreans (KNHANES IV). *The Journal of Clinical Endocrinology & Metabolism, 97*, 3310–3318. https://doi.org/10.1210/jc.2012-1488

Liversidge, H. M. (2015). Tooth Eruption and timing. In J. D. Irish, & G. R. Scott (Eds.), *A companion to dental anthropology* (pp. 159–171). John Wiley & Sons, Ltd. https://doi.org/10.1002/9781118845486.ch12

Lyman, R. L. (1984). Bone density and differential survivorship of fossil classes. *Journal of Anthropological Archaeology, 3*, 259–299. https://doi.org/10.1016/0278-4165(84)90004-7

Lyman, R. L. (2013). Bone density and bone attrition. In *Manual of forensic taphonomy* (1st ed., pp. 51–72). Baton Rouge, United States: Taylor & Francis Group.

Macdonald, H. M., Hoy, C. L., & McKay, H. A. (2013). Chapter 42 - bone acquisition in adolescence. In R. Marcus, D. Feldman, D. W. Dempster, M. Luckey, & J. A. Cauley (Eds.), *Osteoporosis* (4th ed., pp. 1017–1036). San Diego: Academic Press. https://doi.org/10.1016/B978-0-12-415853-5.00042-X

Manifold, B. M. (2014). Bone mineral density in children from anthropological and clinical sciences: A review. *Anthropological Review, 77*, 111–135. https://doi.org/10.2478/anre-2014-0011

Marshall, D., Johnell, O., & Wedel, H. (1996). Meta-analysis of how well measures of bone mineral density predict occurrence of osteoporotic fractures. *BMJ, 312*, 1254–1259. https://doi.org/10.1136/bmj.312.7041.1254

Meeusen, R. A., Christensen, A. M., & Hefner, J. T. (2015). The use of femoral neck Axis length to estimate sex and ancestry. *Journal of Forensic Sciences, 60*, 1300–1304. https://doi.org/10.1111/1556-4029.12820

Morin, S. N., Berger, C., Papaioannou, A., Cheung, A. M., Rahme, E., Leslie, W. D., & Goltzman, D. (2022). Race/ethnic differences in the prevalence of osteoporosis, falls and fractures: A cross-sectional analysis of the Canadian longitudinal study on aging. *Osteoporosis International, 33*, 2637–2648. https://doi.org/10.1007/s00198-022-06539-z

Nam, H.-S., Kweon, S.-S., Choi, J.-S., Zmuda, J. M., Leung, P. C., Lui, L.-Y., Hill, D. D., Patrick, A. L., & Cauley, J. A. (2013). Racial/ethnic differences in bone mineral density among older women. *Journal of Bone and Mineral Metabolism, 31*, 190–198. https://doi.org/10.1007/s00774-012-0402-0

Navega, D., d'Oliveira Coelho, J., Cunha, E., & Curate, F. (2018). Dxage: A new method for age at death estimation based on femoral bone mineral density and artificial neural networks. *Journal of Forensic Sciences, 63*, 497–503. https://doi.org/10.1111/1556-4029.13582

Paschall, A., & Ross, A. H. (2018). Biological sex variation in bone mineral density in the cranium and femur. *Science & Justice, 58*, 287–291. https://doi.org/10.1016/j.scijus.2018.01.002

Patel, R., Blake, G. M., Rymer, J., & Fogelman, I. (2000). Long-term precision of DXA scanning assessed over seven years in forty postmenopausal women. *Osteoporosis International, 11*, 68–75. https://doi.org/10.1007/s001980050008

Pezzuti, I. L., Kakehasi, A. M., Filgueiras, M. T., de Guimarães, J. A., de Lacerda, I. A. C., & Silva, I. N. (2017). Imaging methods for bone mass evaluation during childhood and adolescence: An update. *Journal of Pediatric Endocrinology & Metabolism, 30*, 485–497. https://doi.org/10.1515/jpem-2016-0252

Riggs, B. L., Wahner, H. W., Dunn, W. L., Mazess, R. B., Offord, K. P., & Melton, L. J. (1981). Differential changes in bone mineral density of the appendicular and axial skeleton with aging: Relationship to spinal osteoporosis. *Journal of Clinical Investigation, 67*, 328–335.

Ross, A. H., & Abel, S. M. (Eds.). (2011). *The juvenile skeleton in forensic abuse investigations*. Totowa, NJ: Humana Press. https://doi.org/10.1007/978-1-61779-255-7

Ross, A. H., & Hale, A. R. (2018). Decomposition of juvenile-sized remains: A macro- and microscopic perspective. *Forensic Science Research, 3*, 294–303.

Ross, A. H., & Juarez, C. A. (2014). A brief history of fatal child maltreatment and neglect. *Forensic Science, Medicine and Pathology, 10*, 413–422. https://doi.org/10.1007/s12024-014-9531-1

Runyan, S. M., Stadler, D. D., Bainbridge, C. N., Miller, S. C., & Moyer-Mileur, L. J. (2003). Familial resemblance of bone mineralization, calcium intake, and physical activity in early-adolescent daughters, their mothers, and maternal grandmothers. *Journal of the American Dietetic Association, 103*, 1320–1325. https://doi.org/10.1016/S0002-8223(03)01075-7

Seeman, E. (2008). Bone quality: The material and structural basis of bone strength. *Journal of Bone and Mineral Metabolism, 26*, 1–8. https://doi.org/10.1007/s00774-007-0793-5

Seeman, E., & Delmas, P. D. (2006). Bone quality — the material and structural basis of bone strength and fragility. *New England Journal of Medicine, 354*, 2250–2261. https://doi.org/10.1056/NEJMra053077

Seeman, E., Hopper, J. L., Young, N. R., Formica, C., Goss, P., & Tsalamandris, C. (1996). Do genetic factors explain associations between muscle strength, lean mass, and bone density? A twin study. *American Journal of Physiology-Endocrinology and Metabolism, 270*, E320–E327. https://doi.org/10.1152/ajpendo.1996.270.2.E320

Siris, E. S., Miller, P. D., Barrett-Connor, E., Faulkner, K. G., Wehren, L. E., Abbott, T. A., Berger, M. L., Santora, A. C., & Sherwood, L. M. (2001). Identification and fracture outcomes of undiagnosed low bone mineral density in postmenopausal women results from the national osteoporosis risk assessment. *JAMA, 286*, 2815–2822. https://doi.org/10.1001/jama.286.22.2815

Takada, M., Grampp, S., Ouyang, X., Engelke, K., & Genant, H. K. (1997). A new trabecular region of interest for femoral dual x-ray absorptiometry: Short-term precision, age-related bone loss, and fracture discrimination compared with current femoral regions of interest. *Journal of Bone and Mineral Research, 12*, 832–838. https://doi.org/10.1359/jbmr.1997.12.5.832

Ubelaker, D. H., & Khosrowshahi, H. (2019). Estimation of age in forensic anthropology: Historical perspective and recent methodological advances. *Forensic Science Research, 4*, 1–9. https://doi.org/10.1080/20961790.2018.1549711

Wang, X. (2013). Cortical bone mechanics and composition: Effects of age and gender. In M. J. Silva (Ed.), *Skeletal aging and osteoporosis: Biomechanics and mechanobiology* (pp. 53–85). Berlin, Heidelberg: Springer. https://doi.org/10.1007/8415_2011_108

Warming, L., Hassager, C., & Christiansen, C. (2002). Changes in bone mineral density with age in men and women: A longitudinal study. *Osteoporosis International, 13*, 105–112. https://doi.org/10.1007/s001980200001

Weaver, C. M., & Fuchs, R. K. (2014). Chapter 12 - skeletal growth and development. In D. B. Burr, & M. R. Allen (Eds.), *Basic and applied bone biology* (pp. 245–260). San Diego: Academic Press. https://doi.org/10.1016/B978-0-12-416015-6.00012-5

Weaver, C., & Peacock, M. (2019). Skeletal changes across the lifespan. In D. B. Burr, & M. R. Allen (Eds.), *Basic and applied bone biology* (pp. 189–202). San Diego: Academic Press. https://doi.org/10.1016/B978-0-12-416015-6.00012-5, 2014.

Wheatley, B. P. (2005). An evaluation of sex and body weight determination from the proximal femur using DXA technology and its potential for forensic anthropology. *Forensic Science International, 147*, 141–145. https://doi.org/10.1016/j.forsciint.2004.09.076

Willey, P., Galloway, A., & Snyder, L. (1997). Bone mineral density and survival of elements and element portions in the bones of the Crow Creek massacre victims. *American Journal of Physical Anthropology, 104*, 513–528. https://doi.org/10.1002/(SICI)1096-8644(199712)104:4<513::AID-AJPA6>3.0.CO;2-S

Index

'*Note:* Page numbers followed by "f" indicate figures and "t" indicate tables.'

D

O

P

U

V

W

X

Y

Printed and bound by CPI Group (UK) Ltd, Croydon, CR0 4YY
11/06/2025
01899143-0012